# Dogging Steinbeck

How I went looking for John Steinbeck's America, found my own America, and exposed the truth about 'Travels With Charley'

Bill Steigerwald



True Nonfiction

Fourth River Press
Pittsburgh, Pa.



Words & photos

2n9
11.24

For Trudi,
my kids
and
my mom.

# Praise & Encouragement

*I compared Steinbeck's published letters with his travels and saw great discrepancies. These facts have been public for years, but no one cared to mention them. ... Steinbeck falsified his "Charley" trip. I am delighted that you went deep into this.*

– Paul Theroux
Author of "The Tao of Travel:
Enlightenments from Lives on the Road"

*I still believe John Steinbeck is one of America's greatest writers and I still love "Travels With Charley," be it fact or fiction or, as Bill Steigerwald doggedly proved, both. While I disagree with a number of Steigerwald's conclusions, I don't dispute his facts. He greatly broadened my understanding of Steinbeck the man and the author, particularly during his last years. And, whether Steigerwald intended it or not, in tracking down the original draft of "Travels With Charley" he made a significant contribution to Steinbeck's legacy. "Dogging Steinbeck" is a good honest book.*

– Curt Gentry
Author of "Helter Skelter: The True Story of
the Manson Murders" (with Vincent Bugliosi)

*I wanted ... first to express my personal admiration for the job you did. Second to tell you that you became a kind of a journalistic hero in my travel-story about Steinbeck, because you did such fantastic detailed research on the subject, and you did it alone, in sometimes-difficult circumstances.*

– Geert Mak
Dutch journalist/historian and author of
"Reizen zonder John op zoek naar Amerika"
("Traveling Without John in Search of America")

# Contents

*Down to Gehenna or up to the Throne,*
*He travels fastest who travels alone.*

– Rudyard Kipling

# Introduction

I discovered two important and surprising truths when I retraced the route John Steinbeck took around the country in 1960 and turned into "Travels With Charley in Search of America." I found out the great author's iconic "nonfiction" road book was a deceptive, dishonest and highly fictionalized account of his actual 10,000-mile road trip. And I found out that despite the Great Recession and national headlines dripping with gloom and doom, America was still a big, beautiful, empty, healthy, rich, safe, clean, prosperous and friendly country.

"Dogging Steinbeck" is the true story of my adventures on and off the road with John Steinbeck's ghost. It's about the dozens of good Americans I met and the great places I saw on my high-speed drive from Maine to Monterey along what's left of the Old Steinbeck Highway. And it tells how I stumbled onto a literary scoop that forced a major book publisher to finally confess the truth about "Travels With Charley" after 50 years. Part literary detective story, part travel book, part book review, part primer in drive-by journalism, part commentary on what a libertarian newspaperman thinks is right and wrong about America, my book is subjective as hell. But it's entirely nonfiction.

– Bill Steigerwald, April 1, 2013

# 1 – Taking the Trip

*So it was that I determined to look again, to try to rediscover this monster land. Otherwise, in writing, I could not tell the small diagnostic truths which are the foundations of the larger truth.*

– John Steinbeck, "Travels With Charley in Search of America"

## Laughing at Steinbeck's Ghost

No one could hear me talking to John Steinbeck's ghost. I was standing alone on a sunburned farm road in the earthly equivalent of outer space – the vast cornfields of eastern North Dakota. Fargo was 47 miles back. The closest "town" was Alice, a 51-person dot on the map of a state famous for its emptiness. The closest human was half a mile off, hidden in the brief cloud of brown dirt her combine raised as it tacked through a stiff wind across her family's 1,400-acre farm. It was Oct. 12, 2010. For three weeks and 12 states I had been retracing the 10,000-mile road trip Steinbeck made around America in the fall of 1960 and turned into his bestseller "Travels With Charley in Search of America." From Long Island to Maine to Chicago to Seattle to California to Texas and back, wherever Steinbeck and his poodle companion Charley went on their famed journey, I was going too – exactly 50 years later.

I wasn't following Steinbeck for any of the usual TV-docudrama reasons. He wasn't my real father. I wasn't hoping to find myself or lose anyone else. My old dog and I didn't each have prostate cancer and six months to live. I didn't even own a dog. The unromantic, un-cinematic truth was I thought it would make a good book if I followed Steinbeck's route and compared the country I found with the America he toured. It'd be a simple and easy way to show how much the country has changed along the Steinbeck Highway since Ike was president, Elvis was king and everything worth buying was still Made in America and sold at Sears, Roebuck & Co.

I wasn't a Steinbeck nut, a dog nut or a travel nut. I was a seasoned journalist – actually, a seasoned ex-journalist. For 30 years I had been a reporter/feature writer/ columnist/editor at the L.A. Times and two Pittsburgh daily newspapers. I had more than my share of fun and a little success working for an increasingly irrelevant 19th-century news-delivery system as it committed suicide by refusing to embrace the Internet. Then, in 2009, as I turned 62 and a minimal buyout came along at my paper, I dove from the deck of the Daily Titanic and swam off to look for books to write till I die.

Writing a book about America hooked around Steinbeck's trip would not be complicated or controversial. Or so I thought. I figured I'd simply retrace the trail he blazed as faithfully as possible, as a journalist, using "Travels With Charley" as my guide, map and timeline.

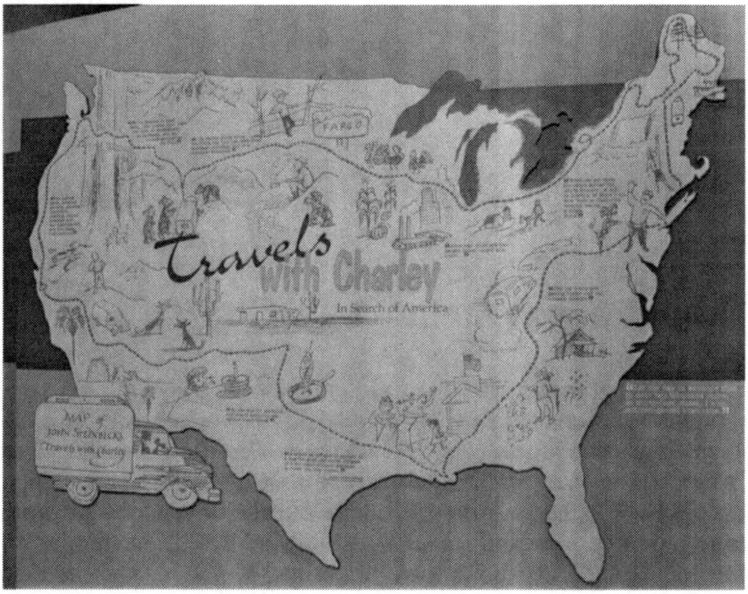


But when I reread the book I quickly learned "Charley" made a lousy map. Though it was a nonfiction book filled with real places, real people and real events, it was often vague and confusing about where Steinbeck really was on any given date. It was not a travelogue, not a serious work of journalism and, as I soon realized, it was not an accurate, full or reliable account of his actual road trip.

Since Steinbeck, who died in 1968, left no notes, no journal and no expense records from the road, I had a lot of work to do. I plotted every town and highway he mentioned in "Travels With Charley" on a 1962 road atlas. I read the major

Steinbeck biographies. I called up scholars and archivists from what I affectionately dubbed the West Coast Steinbeck Studies Industrial Complex.

In the spring of 2010 I traveled to central California's magnificent Monterey Peninsula – aka "Steinbeck Country" – to do research and scout old Steinbeck haunts like Cannery Row. I visited libraries at Stanford, San Jose State and in New York City, looking for clues of time and place in letters he wrote from the road and in old newspaper articles. By the time I arrived in the cornfields of Alice, I was – by default – the world expert on Steinbeck's actual trip. I was also a little road crazy. I was doing 300 miles of drive-by journalism every day on America's two-lane highways. I was waving my Professional Reporter's Notebook in the faces of strangers, interviewing and photographing them, blogging back to the Pittsburgh Post-Gazette.

I was traveling solo. Quickly. Cheaply. Doglessly. When I wasn't staying in a $60-a-night, 1960s-vintage mom & pop motel, I was sleeping in the back of my Toyota RAV4 along dark country roads in New England or in bright Wal-Mart parking lots. So far, despite the Great Recession, most of America was looking pretty good. I was moving fast, but there were few signs of real poverty. I had met no people who were seriously hurting.

I wasn't going out of my way to find poster children for America's rural poor or urban underclass. Ditto for 2010 America's nearly 10 percent unemployed, the 10 percent foreclosed upon, the freshly bankrupted, the deeply indebted and every other real or alleged victim of Crony Capitalism-gone-bad. Either they weren't living and working along the Steinbeck Highway or they were invisible in a down-and-out economy that was nevertheless overflowing with material wealth. Just the pickup trucks, boats and farm equipment I saw parked for sale along the highways exceeded the GDP of Greece.

Flying down the two-lane slivers of ordinary America that never seem to get covered when bicoastal journalists parachute into Flyover Country, I had already encountered scores of the everyday citizens who make America good and make it go. In 3,500 miles I hadn't bumped into a single soul who lived in a house made of highway signs or who'd wasted his life creating the world's greatest Museum of Mailboxes. But I wasn't seeking out new acts in the hackneyed sideshow of American weirdoes and eccentrics. After three decades of practicing on-the-road journalism from Hollywood to Key West to Cut Bank, Montana, I'd seen my share of cultural embarrassments and political and religious whack jobs. America itches with crazies. I had no desire to scratch around for fresh examples of the *reductio ad absurdums* of American individualism that populate great road works like William Least Heat-Moon's "Blue Highways" and Andrei Codrescu's "Road Scholar."

By the time I reached Alice, I was also a little Steinbeck crazy. He had been my invisible passenger on and off the road for 10 months. I had gotten to know the grumpy old New Dealer pretty well. We had some major political issues. But I was always thinking about him, trying to imagine what he had seen or thought as he droned through Maine's endless pine forests or pulled into a manure-carpeted truck stop for the night in Frazee, Minnesota.

Four decades after his death, Steinbeck was arguably the most widely read American writer in the world. Yet he wasn't as famous in his own country as I had thought. When I stopped for gas or snacks in unknown places like Milo, Maine, I'd ask clerks if they knew that the great John Steinbeck had passed down their main street exactly 50 years ago. The name Steinbeck might as well have been Solzhenitsyn. I usually had to remind dumfounded young and old people alike who the heck the Nobel Prize-winner was. "'The Grapes of Wrath'? 'Of Mice and Men'"? I'd prompt. "Oh yeah," they'd say. "I think I read them in high school."

I wasn't in the habit of speaking out loud to Steinbeck's ghost. But I couldn't help it. In "Travels With Charley" he says he camped overnight on the little Maple River somewhere near Alice and met a traveling Shakespearean actor who carried a letter from John Gielgud folded in his wallet. Long before I reached the boondocks of eastern North Dakota I knew Steinbeck's encounter with that actor never happened in the real world. It was pure fiction.

I already knew from my research he had invented the entire scene – and many others in "Travels With Charley." But when I actually stood in the middle of that absurd ocean of agriculture and looked around, I couldn't help but laugh out loud at the ballsy lie Steinbeck told his readers – and got away with for half a century. "Hah," I blurted, as a million dead cornstalks rattled in the hard chilly wind. "Who were you trying to kid, John? Who did you think would ever believe you met a Shakespearean actor out here?"

## Steinbeck's Mythic Journey

*In the fall—right after Labor Day—I'm going to learn about my own country. I've lost the flavor and taste and sound of it. It's been years since I have seen it. Sooo! I'm buying a pick-up truck with a small apartment on it, kind of like the cabin of a small boat, bed, stove, desk, ice-box, toilet—not a trailer—what's called a coach. I'm going alone, out toward the West by the northern way but zigzagging through the Middle West and the mountain states. I'll avoid cities, hit small towns and farms and ranches, sit in bars and hamburger stands and on Sunday go to church. I'll go down the coast from Washington and Oregon and then back through the Southwest and South and up the East Coast but always zigzagging. Elaine will join me occasionally but mostly I have to go alone, and I shall go unknown. I just want to look and listen. What I'll get I need badly—a re-knowledge of my own country, of its speeches, its views, its attitudes and its changes. It's long overdue—very long. New York is not America. I am very excited about doing this. It will be a kind of a rebirth.*

– John Steinbeck, letter to Mr. and Mrs. Frank
Loesser, Sag Harbor, May 25, 1960

John Steinbeck and Charley began their famous road adventure in Sag Harbor on the morning of Friday, Sept. 23, 1960. Sag Harbor was still cleaning up after a direct hit by Hurricane Donna, one of the 20th century's most potent storms. As Jack Kennedy and Dick Nixon were getting ready to debate who was tough enough to be the next boss of the embattled Free World, Steinbeck and Charley hopped three ferries to Connecticut and rode north into the heart of New England.

Steinbeck was 58 and a giant of world literature – the kind that aren't made in the USA anymore. He was also in lousy health. He had already experienced a series of "episodes" – small strokes – that betrayed the weakening heart that would slowly kill him over the next eight years. After living in New York City and traveling heavily in Europe for 20 years, he felt out of touch with his own country, which he was. He had decided he needed to reacquaint himself with America and its Flyover People and to do it alone and by highway.

In answer to the ribbing he got from friends and family who thought his ambitious quest to find America was not only dangerous but also quixotic, Steinbeck named his project "Operation Windmills" and christened his truck "Rocinante" after Don Quixote's heroic horse. The inside of the $750 camper shell on Rocinante's back was as efficient – and Spartan – as the cabin of a boat. It contained a propane stove, a refrigerator, a toilet and a table that could be turned into a platform bed. Overloading his truck with books, booze, spare parts and tools for every contingency he could imagine, Steinbeck also packed two rifles, a shotgun and plenty of ammo along with his fishing gear.

He wanted folks to think he was merely a vacationing subscriber to Outdoor Life from the state of New York, not John Steinbeck, world-famous novelist. Yet he wasn't exactly inconspicuous. He wore a hunting coat with corduroy cuffs and a big pocket for game, khaki pants, half-Wellington rubber boots and a blue serge British naval hat. Plus he had a beard, shaved cheeks, a moustache – and a standard French poodle born in France.

Dodging big cities and avoiding major highways, sleeping in his camper shell and in motels, Steinbeck's counterclockwise route around the USA is famously drawn on the inside covers of "Travels With Charley." He drove east to Bangor, touched the top of Maine, then dipped south and raced west through New Hampshire and Vermont. He hugged the southern shores of the Great Lakes, crossing northern New York and the tops of Pennsylvania, Ohio and Indiana to Illinois. As he noted in "Travels With Charley," he paused for about five days for a rendezvous with his wife Elaine in downtown Chicago. Then, alone again, he slanted across Wisconsin and Minnesota farm country and zoomed through the voids of North Dakota and Montana on old U.S. Highway 10 to the Pacific. Seven days and 2,100 miles after leaving Chicago, Steinbeck and Charley made Seattle, where his wife jetted out to rejoin them.

Elaine and John cruised like honeymooners for almost a week down the Pacific Coast to San Francisco, stopping at nearly empty resorts in the redwoods. In downtown San Francisco they stayed four or five days at the St. Francis Hotel, eating and drinking in the best North Beach cafes and bars with John's old friends. The Steinbecks then motored south about 120 miles to his native Monterey

Peninsula for a two-week stint at his family's small seaside cottage in Pacific Grove. There Steinbeck argued politics with his Republican sisters, viewed the changes of 20 years in his hometown with sadness and cast an absentee vote for John Kennedy on Nov. 8, 1960.

Steinbeck's month of leisure on the West Coast ended in mid-November. Without Elaine, he and Charley crossed the Mojave Desert to Route 66 at Barstow and raced to the Texas Panhandle. As he describes at length in the book, his wife met him again in Amarillo to attend a Thanksgiving "orgy" at a millionaire's cattle ranch. They visited her relatives in Austin and after about 10 days in Texas, Elaine flew on to New York and Steinbeck and Charley headed for home in the truck.

He made a point to stop in New Orleans for a few hours to witness the ugly racial demonstrations at a recently integrated public school that had become a daily national news story. Then, road weary and sickened by bigotry and hate, he sprinted almost nonstop across the Jim Crow South to New York City. Arriving in early December, he and Charley had seen more than 30 states, many only briefly through their windows at 50 mph. They had been gone for roughly 75 days and logged about 10,000 miles in Rocinante.

Knowing he had discovered no great insights or truths about America or its people, Steinbeck worked off and on, taking about 10 months to write "Travels With Charley in Search of America." Previewed in Holiday magazine in three installments under the title "In Quest of America," marketed as a work of nonfiction, the book quickly sold 250,000 hardback copies at $4.95 (about $35 in today's inflated money).

"Travels With Charley" was generally lauded by reviewers for its humor, its evocative nature writing and its insights into Steinbeck's little known personality. It became No. 1 on the New York Times nonfiction bestseller list on Oct. 21, 1962. It was replaced the next week by Rachel Carson's "Silent Spring" but stayed on the Times Top 10 nonfiction list for 57 weeks. It has since sold nearly 1.5 million copies around the world, earning its publisher Viking Press (now part of Penguin Group) tens of millions of dollars and never going out of print.

Though not a work of journalism or a travelogue, the book was accepted by scholars and critics as an accurate and honest account of Steinbeck's journey and his impressions of America and its people. Its commercial and critical success is thought to have helped him win the Nobel Prize for Literature on Oct. 25, 1962. Like Steinbeck's other greatest hits, "The Grapes of Wrath" and "Of Mice and Men," "Travels With Charley" has had a long commercial tail and has never lost its appeal to readers around the world. A fixture of book clubs and high school summer reading lists to this day, it's become a classic American travel book.

Its synopsis is embedded in our culture like a TV Guide movie listing: "Travels With Charley: Novelist John Steinbeck and his poodle spend three months alone on the American Highway, roughing it and camping out under the stars as the Nobel laureate carefully documents the soul of a changing nation and its people." For half a century "Travels With Charley" has been taught, reviewed and sold as a work of nonfiction. It was supposed to be the true story of Steinbeck's trip around the USA – or at least close enough for Oprah Winfrey's book club.

I wasn't the most gullible kid on the media block when it came to exposing the abuse done to reality by the creative sector. In the late '70s I had worked briefly in L.A. for CBS' docudrama unit, where my job was to make sure TV movies about real people and real events could be advertized as "The True Story of …." without incurring a slap from the FCC. After that, I spent half my newspaper career writing articles and columns aimed at separating fact from fiction in Hollywood's over-dramatized versions of history. I should have been warier about "Charley." But when I started my project to retrace Steinbeck's route in early 2010, I naturally assumed the "Travels With Charley" Myth was true. Why not? Two-and-a-half generations of Steinbeck scholars had never said otherwise.

# 2 – Stranger in Steinbeck Country

*Once a journey is designed, equipped, and put in process, a new factor enters and takes over. A trip, a safari, an exploration, is an entity, different from all other journeys. It has personality, temperament, individuality, uniqueness. A journey is a person in itself; no two are alike.*

– "Travels With Charley"

## Alone on Fremont Peak

My journey with John Steinbeck officially began seven months before I had my big laugh in the cornfields of Alice. I was sitting alone and shivering on top of Fremont Peak, a spectacular little spike of marble overlooking the entire Monterey Peninsula. I couldn't see Steinbeck's grave or his ghost, but both of them were out there somewhere under the glare of the dying California sun as it fell toward Monterey Bay.

Everything Steinbeck was down there somewhere – the house he grew up in, the statues, the things named after him, the museum/shrine that glorifies him and his works, the places and characters he made famous for eternity in "The Red Pony," "Of Mice and Men," "Cannery Row" and "East of Eden." It's why they called it "Steinbeck Country." Except for the pushy wind and the chirpings of a few invisible birds, I had Fremont Peak to myself. No tourists. No park rangers. No other ex-journalists with or without dogs doing books about "Travels With Charley." Just lucky me, my notebook, my cameras and a head full of conflicting thoughts about my famous new sidekick.

It was Day 4 of my extreme West Coast research tour. I had learned a ton of new stuff about the man, his last major book and his highway travels. I'd gone to Stanford's Green Library, where 300 letters from him to his agent Elizabeth Otis are kept. I'd been to San Jose State University's Steinbeck Center. I'd been to San Francisco to meet a writer who interviewed Steinbeck on his "Charley" trip. I'd checked out Cannery Row, downtown Monterey, Steinbeck's family cottage in Pacific Grove, plus his gravesite and the National Steinbeck Center in Salinas.

The only reason I was up on Fremont Peak was because Steinbeck said he climbed to that exact spot during his "Travels With Charley" trip. I was glad to be there. It was an awesome, rugged place, the star attraction of Fremont Peak State Park's collection of grassy round mountains and steep wooded canyons. The pile of gray boulders is only 3,169 feet above Monterey Bay, but its distinctive little tooth is visible from almost anywhere in the Salinas Valley. It was lonely, peaceful, beautiful, a little dangerous and a little scary. No wonder young Johnny,

who played on its slopes, hoped to be buried up there someday. It was the closest you could get to a heavenly view of Steinbeck Country without putting on wings. Though it was the end of a hazy day, I could see more than 20 miles in every direction. In the shadows behind me, dry valleys and barely green mountain ranges stretched eastward to the Sierra Nevada. The San Andreas Fault was down there somewhere too, which explains why Fremont Peak – not to mention the Monterey Peninsula, Los Angeles and the rest of the northbound Pacific Plate – had inched 8.33 feet closer to San Francisco since Steinbeck visited in 1960.

Twenty-five miles southwest across the valley floor, hugging chilly Monterey Bay, was the historic city of Monterey. To be honest, I couldn't see it, even with the zoom of my video camera. I only knew it was out there somewhere in the growing darkness, hidden by a strip of low coastal mountains, because that morning I had gone to Cannery Row to watch the sun come up over Monterey Bay. At my feet, sprawled on the valley floor, lay Salinas, the capital of Steinbeck Country and the barely fictionalized setting for "East of Eden." The city was an island in a shallow sea of strawberries, lettuce, tomatoes, spinach and other crops – the "green gold" that made Salinas rich 100 years ago and earned it the nickname "The Salad Bowl of the World." The valley's fertile black soil and sunny, ocean-cooled climate, combined with the labor of busloads of Latino farm workers, produced 80 percent of the lettuce Americans eat every year.

Salinas' population was 160,000. That was twice what it was in 1960 and 40 times larger than when Steinbeck was born there in 1902. The city was wracked by deadly Latino gang violence and, like most California governments in the spring of 2010, was in deep budgetary trouble. The Great Recession had slammed all of Steinbeck Country hard. The unemployment rate was 13 percent and going higher. Foreclosures were running twice as high as in 2006. Poverty rates were up, property tax revenues were down. But from atop Fremont Peak, California was as golden as ever and everything in the Salinas Valley looked fine and healthy.

Earlier that day in the old downtown of Salinas I had toured the main Steinbeck stops. I took a few photos of the restored Queen Anne-style Victorian house he grew up in. It was closed, so I didn't see the gift shop or gourmet restaurant that features local produce and $13 entrees like Asparagus & Ham Timbale with choice of Tomato Leek Soup or Green Salad. The corner house is on the National Register of Historic Places and Oprah Winfrey taped one of her shows in the front yard when her book club was touting "East of Eden."

Two blocks away was the National Steinbeck Center, one of the few reasons for tourists to divert from the sun and surf of the Pacific Coast to the scorched flats of Salinas. The largest museum in the country devoted to a single writer, it's smartly designed and visitor friendly. Steinbeck's life story and books co-star in a dozen well-staged exhibits that include loops of clips from movies like "East of Eden" and "Of Mice and Men." Recordings of his deep rough voice are never out of earshot.

The enduring popularity of "Travels With Charley" was evident at the center. The bookstore sold various editions of the entire Steinbeck canon – 16 novels, six non-fiction and five short-story collections. "Travels With Charley" had been the No. 1 seller since 2003 and the center's most popular attraction and holiest relic was the 1960 GMC pickup truck/camper combo Steinbeck rode on his search for America. You couldn't get inside the cab of the truck or the camper shell, or even touch them, because "Rocinante" was corralled behind a tall fence of Plexiglas. Squared-off and primitive, the cab's hard utilitarian interior was uncomfortable just to look at. It was proof of the punishment Steinbeck endured for 10,000 miles with only an old French dog, an AM radio and his imagination for company. Unfortunately, the $11 million Steinbeck Center was not doing well. Its annual attendance was running about 30,000, which doesn't sound so bad but works out to about 82 people a day. Chronically short of funds, it was dependent on subsidies from a city government that was in serious fiscal trouble.

Across the street from the Steinbeck Center, suckered in by the permanent sidewalk sign boasting that "Steinbeck Ate Here," I ate lunch at Sang's Café. Under my withering questioning the owner broke down and confessed the truth. The sign should more accurately say "Steinbeck Drank Here," because that's what young John did too much of there in the '20s and '30s when he was a struggling writer and the place was a bar. It wasn't the first or last time I'd bump up against a Steinbeck myth. A lot of what we know about him – good and bad – is either truer or less false than we think.

Until I began "investigating" him for my book idea, I didn't know much about him at all. "John Steinbeck" had been reduced to a famous literary name – a "Jeopardy!" question to the answer "This Californian was the sixth American to win the Nobel Prize for Literature in 1962." Whatever I had learned about him I'd forgotten. During high school in the 1960s I was forced to read the usual Steinbeck classics, but they had no more impact on my life than "Beowulf."

I liked "Of Mice and Men" then and appreciated it much more after re-reading it as an adult. But unlike Bruce Springsteen, my social conscience wasn't aroused by "The Grapes of Wrath's" expose of the cruelty of capitalism and the sufferings of the migrant working class. I was a Baby Boomer from another political planet, a red one. When I was 17, in 1964, I was watching William F. Buckley Jr.'s "Firing Line" and sneaking Barry Goldwater stickers on the bumper of my neighbor's Country Squire station wagon.

By today's definitions, Steinbeck was a ball of political contradictions. He was a highly partisan FDR big-government Democrat who went ape for Adlai Stevenson in the 1950s and became a White House-sleepover friend of LBJ and frequent weekend guest at Camp David. Like most of his New Deal generation, he had a naïve trust in the federal government to solve massive social and economic problems. But Steinbeck was never close to being the true-believing commie or socialist both his rightwing enemies and leftwing friends liked to claim he was. He was what we call today "a Cold War liberal." He supported labor unions, the civil rights movement and LBJ's war on poverty. He was also a staunch anti-communist who believed in containing the Soviet Union and what then was so impolitely called "Red China."

He was a sincere patriot, which, along with becoming too friendly with LBJ, may have blinded him to the folly of Vietnam and the fallacy of the Domino Theory. He was a loud public hawk on Vietnam in its early stages, but became a quiet dove when he realized the war was unwinnable. Intolerant of anti-war protestors, whom he thought were stupid and cowardly, he despised hippies and the '60s youth culture.

Steinbeck the man had personal issues that didn't appeal to me. He was a parochial New York City snob by the time he took his long road trip. He was an enthusiastic and daily boozer. And in the 1960s he forgot his earlier wise warning to artists to stay away from political power and cozied up to JFK and especially LBJ. His biographer Jackson Benson pointed out in his 1984 epic "The True Adventures of John Steinbeck, Writer" that Steinbeck's darker side included a quarrelsome nature and a "striking lack of charity and understanding." His sons John Steinbeck IV, who died from complications during surgery in 1991, and Thom, who is a California writer, felt their father neglected them after he divorced their mother and married Elaine, his third and final wife, in 1950. Yet whatever his faults as a father and husband, personally and politically Steinbeck was a living saint compared to many celebrities and famous writers of his era.

Despite our differences, I had grown to like the grouchy, contradictory guy. Underneath his New Yorker magazine limousine liberalism, he hid an admirable libertarian streak. He wrote fine paeans to individualism, understood the importance of private property rights and hated bureaucrats and government bullying. Plus he didn't moralize about things like prostitution. He treated prostitutes kindly in his books and thought they provided a service to the community, which of course they do.

If I wasn't captured by Steinbeck's New Deal politics or his social conscience, I sure was impressed by his writing skills. When I re-read "Of Mice and Men" and "Cannery Row," I was blown away by his spare style, beautiful descriptive powers, sense of place and storytelling. Just the first 500 words of "Cannery Row" should make any journalist envious or throw her laptop away and become a plumber. I didn't have the casual attitude about facts that Steinbeck did, which was why I'd ultimately get pissed at him. But I totally agreed with what he said about the impossibility of objectivity and the inherent and unavoidable subjectivity of journalism and all writing – fiction or nonfiction.

My last stop in Salinas that morning before climbing Fremont Peak had been his gravesite in Garden of Memories Memorial Park. Though a colorful "Steinbeck" sign pointed right at it, his small flat marker was hard to find among the weathered grey slabs and spiky old stone monuments. Seeking anonymity, simplicity and privacy even in death, Steinbeck's ashes are interred with his parents, wife Elaine and sister Mary in the Hamilton plot, the plot of his mother's family. A pot of bright yellow mums, wilted slightly and knocked over by the valley's unrelenting wind, gave away his final whereabouts: "John Steinbeck: 1902-1968." A 2-inch white ceramic poodle with a pink heart for its collar guarded the simple marker. I stood on Steinbeck's grave as respectfully as possible and took a few close-ups of the dog, which had been left by a "Travels With Charley" fan.

Was that chintzy totem of Charley a warning to let his master's reputation rest in peace? I had no clue. I was a journalist looking for facts, not symbols. Anyway, it didn't matter. In the spring of 2010 I was a guy with no job, a melting 401(k), a fat mortgage and too many leased cars. I had already invested too much of my life in Mr. Steinbeck, his travels around the USA and what I already suspected was his blatant fudging of the truth in "Travels With Charley." Chasing his ghost across America had become my destiny, my mission, my mad obsession, my brilliant act of entrepreneurial journalism, my big waste of money and time – I wasn't sure which. I only knew I was too many miles down the Steinbeck Highway to turn back.

# Crashing the Steinbeck Fest

Five months later, in August, I was back in Salinas attending the annual Steinbeck Festival. The National Steinbeck Center's theme for 2010 was the "Travels With Charley" trip and Steinbeck's many travels around the world. I was an outsider among the 150 Steinbeck experts, Steinbeck worshippers, Steinbeck collectors and "Travels With Charley" nuts in attendance, and I felt it.

That was not new or discomforting. I was used to trespassing in narrow, often alien subcultures populated by fans or insiders. As a newspaper reporter, I had spent three decades crashing other people's private parties, whether it was a roomful of federal transportation experts or a Saturday night KKK cross burning on a hilltop in the backwoods of southwestern Pennsylvania.

Compared to the amateur and professional Steinbeckies, I knew nothing about their hero or the literary nuances of his many important and famous works. But by then, just seven weeks before the start of my road trip, I knew a few things they didn't. In an attempt to accurately track Steinbeck's trail, I had put together a fairly detailed time-and-place line of his actual "Travels With Charley" route. For example, I knew where Steinbeck slept on Oct. 12, 1960. That piece of trivia wasn't exactly a reason to alert the Pulitzer Prize committee. But I also already knew there were some yawning discrepancies between what Steinbeck wrote in his nonfiction book and what he actually did or did not do on his trip.

At times during the festival it was hard to keep from screaming out that Emperor Steinbeck didn't have on all of his nonfiction clothes. I bit my tongue at what one headline speaker said. Ted Conover is a major-league journalist, a writer with a social conscience like Steinbeck's who's ridden the rails with hobos and crossed the U.S.-Mexican border with illegal farm workers for his nonfiction books. He told his rapt audience how much Steinbeck and "Travels With Charley" had inspired and influenced his participatory style of journalism. He loved Steinbeck's book because "it was nonfiction" and because it "let me see how a great writer in search of a story could meet people." It was what a journalist does, he said, and "Steinbeck showed me how to do it."

Conover should have known better. He should have smelled the fiction. But he wasn't the only one at the festival who assumed "Travels With Charley" told the true story of Steinbeck's trip and the people he really met. It was a given. One of the featured Steinbeck experts and speakers was Susan Shillinglaw, a San Jose State English professor and scholar in residence at the Steinbeck Center. She'd written introductions to new editions of Steinbeck books and was an expert on his journalism and nonfiction. In her talk about how Steinbeck's restlessness, curiosity and interest in the common man fueled his many world travels, Shillinglaw called "Travels With Charley" a quintessential road book and discussed how he carefully and holistically studied the America he found.

Shillinglaw or no one else questioned the book. No one mentioned its gaping holes in time and place. No one wondered how Steinbeck, known to be a shy man, could have been so lucky to have bumped into so many colorful Americans who spoke like actors in a bad movie. No one wondered – or cared – how he managed to capture all those pages of "great" dialogue without a tape recorder or even a notebook. No scholar explained the tricky academic bylaws governing the use of "creative nonfiction" in a true book.

No one cautioned that Steinbeck's book, though considered a work of nonfiction for half a century, was a lot like the Bible and shouldn't be taken literally. "Travels With Charley" was treated as it had always been – as true. When I asked Steinbeck biographer Jackson Benson if he thought "Charley" really deserved to be called the true story of Steinbeck's road trip, he said, "Yeah, it's a true story. It's abstracted and deleted and outlined, as all true stories are. I don't think there's anything in there that's made up.... The only thing fiction about it is that he left out a lot."

Midway through the festival, something strange happened. I was asking Shillinglaw and Benson trivia questions. I asked if they knew whether Steinbeck's wife Elaine rode with him in Rocinante from Seattle to San Francisco. Benson had said she did in his biography. But Shillinglaw was sure Elaine hadn't. She had gotten to know Elaine pretty well, she said, and was certain Steinbeck's refined wife would never have traveled in the cab of a pickup truck.

Shillinglaw and Benson were the reigning Steinbeck gurus. Yet they didn't seem to know much about how he actually traveled on his "Travels With Charley" journey and didn't seem particularly interested in finding out more. *Holy shit,* I suddenly realized. *I know much more about Steinbeck's road trip than they do.* It was a terrifying feeling. For the first time in my life, I was the expert in something – albeit a very minor, esoteric, inside-baseball something no one else cared about. In August of 2010, I had already become the global authority on John Steinbeck's iconic road trip – completely by accident. And I still hadn't read the first draft of "Travels With Charley" or driven a single mile down the Old Steinbeck Highway.

## 'Discovering' 'Charley's' First Draft

My pre-trip research ended with a bang three weeks later in New York City when I did something no one in the world had done in four years. I went to the Morgan Library & Museum in Manhattan and read the first draft of "Travels With Charley in Search of America." The handwritten manuscript – along with a typed and edited copy – had been stored at the Morgan like a holy relic for almost half a century. Few scholars or grad students had bothered to study it. If they had, the "Travels With Charley" Myth might have been debunked decades ago.

To be fair, the manuscript is not something anybody can just pop into the Morgan Library and paw over. John Pierpont Morgan's gift to posterity holds one of the world's greatest collections of art, books and music. Security is Pentagon-tight, inside and out. You've got to first establish that you are a legitimate researcher or writer and make an appointment. Once you make it past the security checkpoint, you're escorted to the reading room. You have to wash your hands, use pencils only and handle research material like it's sacred nitroglycerin. You can't take photos or make photocopies because of copyright restrictions.

For three days in late summer I sat in the Morgan's reading room like a monk. The "Charley" manuscript, kept there since Steinbeck donated it in 1962, is broken up into five or six handwritten chunks. Written entirely in his barely decipherable scribble, with hardly a word crossed out or changed, each page is filled from top-to-bottom and edge-to-edge. It's mostly in pencil on carefully numbered yellow or white legal pads.

Taking notes in longhand, I compared the first draft of what Steinbeck had given the working title "In Quest of America" with the copy of "Travels With Charley" stored on my smart-phone's Kindle app. According to Declan Kiely, the Morgan's curator of literary and historical manuscripts, fewer than six people had looked at the manuscript since 2000. I was the first since 2006. I learned important clues that helped me fill in some blank spots about Steinbeck's actual trip. I also saw how much the manuscript had been edited. There were dozens of minor and major edits. The most important ones entirely removed his wife Elaine's presence from the West Coast and stripped out 95 percent of his partisan political commentary.

Given what I was learning, the most ironic edit deleted Steinbeck's thoughts about what is really real and the writer's struggle/duty to straighten out the "chaos" of reality and make it understandable and "reasonably real" for a reader. The most justifiable edit removed a paragraph of filth and racial hatred that would have given "Travels With Charley" an X-rating, outraged the public and crippled its sales.

The manuscript was the big smoking gun – the smoking artillery piece. Reading it was shocking and exhilarating. I couldn't believe what I had found – or that it had been just sitting there in Manhattan for 50 years waiting to be discovered. It confirmed and reinforced my suspicions about the dubious veracity of much of "Travels With Charley." The first draft also explained the book's persistent vagueness about time and place. It was not due solely to Steinbeck's aversion to writing a travelogue or his lack of note taking. It was a result of wily editing by Viking's editors, which hid the frequently luxurious and leisurely nature of Steinbeck's road trip and made it seem like he spent most of his time alone.

After my last day of deciphering Steinbeck's handwriting, I left the cool quiet of the Morgan Library and popped back onto the baked streets of Manhattan. It was 4:05. I set out for Penn Station to catch a train back to Secaucus, where my car was parked and ready to take me home to western Pennsylvania. New York had so much pure city packed into a small space it was hard for someone from Pittsburgh to believe. I'd never want to live in NYC. It was 40 years too late for that adventure. But it was amazing to see the crazy energy and throbbing humanity of a real city at work and play. It was nothing like the open street markets and anarchic traffic of Lima or Guatemala City, the only teeming Third World madhouses I'd ever seen. But the sidewalks were thick with commerce and hurrying streams of people of every lifestyle and color.

Near the corner of Madison Avenue and East 33rd Street, two miles from the apartment Steinbeck died in, a prim matron with a plastic bag in one hand and a leash in the other waited for her toy poodle to take a dump at the base of a baby tree. On 34th Street a homeless man with a wild beard and dirty white shirt suddenly lunged out of the passing throng and rammed his bony shoulder hard into mine. It was no accident, it hurt, and it taught me a lesson to keep my eye out for trouble in the oncoming flow of humanity.

Closing in on Madison Square Garden and its basement of train tracks, I began tail-gaiting a hotshot in a blue blazer with a cell phone to his ear as he weaved through the crowd. He was young but had gray hair and carried a man bag swelling with paperwork. I didn't know it, but like me he was hustling to Track 11 to catch the 4:32 to Secaucus. On the un-crowded train I deliberately sat across the aisle from the hotshot so I could eavesdrop on his end of the conversation, which he made no effort to suppress. "At two billion dollars," he said, as if he were talking about the price of eggs, "we're going to make 800 k. I'm OK with one basis point…. We'd still be above two billion. Do me a favor. Check my math and fire me an email."

I had no idea what he was talking about, but it wasn't how tough it was to make a living on Wall Street in the Great Recession. During my brief ride to Secaucus I scrawled what I had learned from reading the Steinbeck manuscript in my Professional Reporter's Notebook: "Charley's a fraud. Steinbeck himself provided the details of his trip – the real ones – and betrays 'C' for the fraud it is." It was the first time I had used the f-word to describe his beloved travel book. It wouldn't be the last.

# 3 – On the Road

*On the long journey doubts were often my companions. I've always admired those reporters who can descend on an area, talk to key people, ask key questions, take samplings of opinions, and then set down an orderly report very like a road map. I envy this technique and at the same time do not trust it as a mirror of reality. I feel there are too many realities. What I set down here is true until someone else passes that way and rearranges the world in his own style.*

– "Travels With Charley"

## Cruising to Sag Harbor

In a last-ditch effort to attract national media attention, a few hours before I left my house I blasted a self-promotional email to nearly everyone I had ever known, worked for or pitched freelance articles to in journalism. It was as over-the-top as I could make it and as far as I can tell it did me and what was left of my career no good at all.

> Ex-newspaperman Bill Steigerwald to chase John Steinbeck's ghost for 10,000 miles.
>
> To go everywhere Steinbeck and dog Charley went in "Travels With Charley."
>
> Will follow great author's exact route half a century later.
>
> Desperate act of drive-by journalism by former Pittsburgh/ LA paperboy, columnist, editor.
>
> Will take no federal stimulus money.
>
> Will take no dog.
>
> Hello friends, former co-workers, fellow libertarians, people who have no idea why they're getting this email blast.
>
> On Thursday, Sept. 23, I'll leave John Steinbeck's former seaside home in Sag Harbor, New York, a place I could never afford to live or visit for more than two hours, and begin chasing his ghost around America's blue highways for 10,000 miles.
>
> I'm going to retrace the iconic road trip Steinbeck made in the fall of 1960 and turned into his 1962 nonfiction bestseller

"Travels With Charley." I'm not taking an iconic dog and I'm not driving an iconic pickup truck/camper. I do hope to write a book hooked around following the exact route Steinbeck took and telling the whole story of what he did or did not do on his journey exactly 50 years ago.

****

The hardest part of starting my road trip was just getting to Sag Harbor, which hides way out on the expensive, European end of Long Island, beyond the many Hamptons. Steinbeck, who lived in Manhattan starting in the early 1940s but loved the sea, bought a second home in the mid-1950s in Sag Harbor on a point of land poking out into Morris Cove.

I had never been to Sag Harbor. All I knew was that it was a historic old whaling port, thanks to its great harbor. Herman Melville and James Fenimore Cooper used to hang there. So did a fleet of whaling ships until Big Oil killed off Big Whaling, thereby saving the sperm whale from extinction and allowing Sag Harbor to evolve into a quaint working-class fishing village where rich & famous folks from Manhattan like Steinbeck could hide and live in peace.

From my old house in the woods 20 miles south of Pittsburgh to Steinbeck's summerhouse was 489 miles – straight east, right through the core of the Big Apple. My Tuesday night drive to a motel in Somerset, New Jersey, went the way it was drawn up in the playbook – quick and uneventful. All the way on the PA Turnpike to I-81 and into North Jersey the traffic was light to nonexistent. It was as if the country were in a Great Recession or something.

Smooth road, perfect weather, well-behaved trucks. No tailgaters. No construction zones. It was the way interstate travel was supposed to be – fast, safe and automatic. I had little to do, driving-wise, but put two fingers on the wheel, set the cruise control to 70, crank up the satellite radio and relax in the dark coziness of my personal earthbound space capsule. Steinbeck would have killed for such high-speed comfort. He also would have envied my peace of mind about the reliability of my new red Toyota RAV4. He carried tools and spare parts for his truck in case he broke down in the middle of Montana. I never worried for a second about repairs or breakdowns. There were Toyota dealers everywhere. I had the AAA for backup. Plus I knew from experience that unless you're the unluckiest man in North America, nothing bad happens to a Toyota for the first 60,000 miles.

I had checked out renting a small RV – too pricy. And I tried to get the CEO of Roadtrek Motorhomes to lend me a Sprint Agile, which would have been like steering a 20-foot cushy condo around America. He laughed off the promotional benefits to his company of my idea, which was just as well. The RAV4 turned out to be the perfect choice. At the Toyota showroom, the first thing I had the salesman do was put down the rear seats. After crawling in back and seeing I could stretch out with six inches to spare, I was sold. The back of the RAV4 was virtually flat. Six old This End Up foam sofa cushions fit tightly on the floor like pieces of a puzzle. Then came a mattress pad, a bottom sheet, my favorite blanket, my pillow, an open sleeping bag and blackout curtains with Velcro strips to attach above the windows. All I needed for a good night's sleep was nerve and a level place to park.

In 1960 Steinbeck covered some of the same interstate miles I was driving. After he left New Orleans he only wanted to get home fast. Hardly sleeping, he took U.S. 11 to Carlisle, Pennsylvania, and hopped on the PA Turnpike. He flew up the Jersey Turnpike and thought he was home free. But he had a last-minute glitch when he was turned away from the Holland Tunnel because of his potentially explosive propane tank.

Was that true, or a final metaphor from the great novelist? Were propane tanks really considered that dangerous in the bad old days? Steinbeck said in "Travels With Charley" he ended up having to take the ferry from Hoboken across the Hudson River to Manhattan, something you no longer can do with a car. Then, as he described in the ending pages, he got hopelessly lost in evening rush hour in his own backyard. He was forced to get directions to his townhouse on East 72nd Street from an "old-fashioned" cop who called Steinbeck "Mac" and thought the bearded, road-bedraggled and flustered old gent was drunk.

## Lost in New York, New York

Sag Harbor was 139 miles and almost three hours away from my motel in north Jersey. My plan was to outflank Manhattan to the south and reach Sag Harbor via Staten Island and the Verrazano Narrows Bridge. But I never got close to Staten Island. While answering a call on my cell phone from a Sag Harbor newspaper writer, I missed a key directive from my GPS Person. Before I knew it, I was sucked into the mouth of the Holland Tunnel and spit out into the madness of Lower Manhattan.

Gridlock at 9:42 a.m.

New York City has 8 million people. At least half of them were in the street pushing or pulling carts, surging along the crowded sidewalks like they were on speed or trying to walk while staring into the glare of their smart phones. The other half of the Big Apple's population was cops. NYPD traffic officers in light green vests stood in teams of four at every intersection and in the street, waving and pointing at cars and delivery trucks with nowhere to go. It didn't matter where the GPS Person wanted you to turn or what color the traffic lights were. It was the cops' call. They pointed. You drove.

For half an hour I drove around in squares trying to escape from New York. At one point it got surreal. I found myself inching along the same teeming stretch of West 34 Street I had walked down three weeks earlier when I went to the Morgan Library to read the manuscript of "Charley." Past Macy's. Past the Empire State Building. Past the FDNY ambulance being loaded with a gurney containing a strapped-down victim of assault, murder or second-hand smoke.

I thought I'd never see Long Island. A corner I shouldn't have turned took me to a NYPD precinct station where 30 uniformed cops were standing in gangs on the sidewalk taking a smoke break. "Help," I shouted over to them from the red light. "I'm trapped in New York. How do I get to Sag Harbor?" Half a dozen cops pointed behind a block of buildings. All I heard was laughter and "Midtown Tunnel." Thanks to the first of what would be hundreds of acts of distracted driving on my trip, I had eerily repeated the end of Steinbeck's "Travels With Charley" journey. Fifty years after he did – or said he did – I too was lost in Manhattan seeking help from cops. Eventually my GPS Person led me to the Queens Midtown Tunnel, which blew me like a poison dart under the East River and into daylight and the open road.

After five minutes of congestion I was permanently free, exploding east at hyper-interstate speed. The LIE – three smooth fast lanes plus an HOV – was better and wider than any road in Metro Pittsburgh. As I tunneled my way through the trees and concrete sound barriers separating me from millions of Long Islanders, I could see little of their flat, pizza-and-beer-based civilization. I couldn't even find Billy Joel on the radio.

While I was lunching at a Wendy's along the LIE, National Public Radio producer Peter Breslow called. For weeks I had tried to reach his boss at "Saturday Morning Edition with Scott Simon." I wanted to pitch my transcontinental Steinbeck-chasing expedition to her as a weekly feature for the show. It was a natural for radio and especially for NPR's small but literate audience. Though I had an inside-connection at NPR who touted my journalism skills like I was the ghost of Edward R. Murrow, I got no response to half a dozen emails and phone messages to Bridgette Kelley, the executive producer.

Finally, three days before I left home I caught Kelley at her desk on a Sunday morning. She apologized profusely for ignoring me, couldn't have been nicer, and said she was interested in the idea. She told me to expect a call from Breslow when I was on Long Island.

I was looking for national publicity from NPR for my "Travels Without Charley" road blog, which I was writing each day for the Pittsburgh Post-Gazette. But I was also hoping I could make a few hundred bucks as a freelance reporter. Breslow quickly disabused me of that pipedream. I was the story, not the reporter. But we agreed he should contact me in a week to arrange a time for Scott Simon to "join me" on the road in Vermont or New Hampshire.

## Town Without Chains

A hundred miles east of Manhattan on a narrow county road, I closed in on the village of Sag Harbor. The closer I got, the more I understood why the Hamptons are where the 1% of New York City go to play and hide. Old trees, old neighborhoods, old homes tucked into the old trees, pricy vacation homes, quaint country stores. Nothing out of place or shabby. Nothing modern or crass or commercial, just overly nautical.

The shine and smell of big money was everywhere. So was the conspicuous absence of affordable chain motels or cottages that would allow tourists, journalists and other members of the lower classes to sleep overnight in Zip Code

11963, where, not surprisingly, the 7,000 residents skew older, whiter and considerably richer than average. At 3:30 p.m. a bumper-to-bumper stream of vans poured at me from the direction of Sag Harbor. They were the contractors, plumbers and electricians who made their daily livings fixing and primping the shingled and over-mulched homesteads they could buy only if they hit the lottery.

The road to Sag Harbor's waterfront was like a string town for the Town & Country set. Everyone had at least one European car with a backyard on a bay. The harbor was a forest of sailboats and yachts, some more than a 100 feet long and owned by billionaires. Sag Harbor's downtown, humming with small-town commerce, exuded the well-preserved character, class and charm befitting a listee of the National Register of Historic Places.

Main Street was lined with flapping American flags, trees and handsome old red brick buildings with time-warped storefronts – a cramped stationery store, a hardware emporium, a five and dime, the Sag Harbor Movie Theater. Mixed in with the old and new Americana were art galleries, Bike Hampton, Book Hampton and Marty's Barber Shop, where Steinbeck got his haircuts. A real-estate office window looked like it was advertizing the homes of Third World despots. The Georgica Pondfront Estate in East Hampton was a steal at $39.5 million.

At 4 p.m. the sidewalks were busy and impressively age-diverse. Little old ladies, mothers and kids. A bald young father with his hot pregnant wife, 1.6 children, yellow Lab and $500 stroller. As two Latino day laborers with cell phones to their ears waited on a bench for the bus out of town, a scruffy high school kid weaved by on a skateboard without fear of complaint or arrest.

Unfortunately, the first Sag Harborite I picked at random to speak to was the Village Creep. The graying Baby Boomer was sitting on a folding chair in front of an antique store called Our Gig Too – "Whatever." He held a book on his lap but spent most of his time glowering at passing people. The front door of his store was propped open with a white ceramic lighthouse. After taking a quick spin of his nautical treasures, I said my usual friendly hello, identified myself and waved my Professional Reporter's Notebook around at the general streetscape.

"Has much changed in 50 years?"

"Have you?" he said, not looking up at me.

"I mean the town," I said, a little off balance.

"You can figure that out yourself."

Not a good start to taking the pulse of the American people. Maybe he was a cranky right-winger who thought I was a member of the stinking mainstream liberal media. I should have told him to screw himself, but I moved on. I'd met his miserable type before. I didn't know it then, but he would be the only certifiable asshole I'd encounter during the next 42 days.

Licking my wounds, I dashed across Main Street and ducked into the American Hotel and restaurant/bar. It smelled 168 years old, felt rich and had one of the scariest menus I had ever seen. I didn't actually see what the day's featured entree was because I averted my eyes when I saw that it cost $110. Maybe it was for 14 people. I didn't know yet where I was going to sleep that night, but it sure wasn't the American. A room went for something like $230, which was $170 over my budget.

Camera slung discreetly over my shoulder, notebook sticking out of my back pocket, I chose another random local to interrogate. Donnie – maybe he was 50 – was leaning against the brick front wall of Illusions, an artsy women's jewelry store. Donnie and his brother ran an auto repair shop for foreign cars whose customers once included Elaine Steinbeck, who died in 2003. Donnie was Australian. When he and his mother moved to Sag Harbor in the 1970s there were boarded up storefronts on Main Street. "It was a hard-drinking town," he said, claiming it had 30 bars including the Black Buoy, Steinbeck's old drinking hole.

Artists had always come to Sag Harbor for the light, the sea and the sunsets. But in 1960 Sag Harbor's residents were working-class Italians and Irish like the ones Steinbeck described in his 1961 novel "The Winter of Our Discontent." His book about the ethics of success and the decline of morality in America was set in New Baytown, a fictional rendering of Sag Harbor and its citizens. In 1960 black migrants from the South lived in rundown labor camps and worked the surrounding potato fields. Today most of the potato farms are gone, replaced by housing developments or vineyards, and Latinos are imported to do the agricultural grunt work. According to Donnie, because Sag Harbor was never a stop on the Long Island RR line, it was the last town in "the Hamptons scene" to be colonized by Manhattanites.

Donnie's friend Mike walked up. Mike, 54, earned his living building and renovating homes for rich people and getting their estates ready for sale. In the midst of the Great Recession, Sag Harbor was showing no outward signs of economic trouble. The unemployment rate was 3.5 percent, compared to the national rate of almost 10. Mike said it was the super-rich who were getting beat up by the bad economy. Estate values had been battered, he said, taking no noticeable proletarian pleasure in the fact. "Estates worth $12 million three years ago can't draw $8 million. There's been a big drop in the market. A lot of people have money here to buy, but they're holding it until the prices fall. Anyone who's bought in the last five years is probably underwater."

Mike happened to be from Pittsburgh's North Side, the downtown Allegheny Riverbank neighborhood where my dad grew up in the 1930s and where my last newspaper, the Pittsburgh Tribune-Review, had its offices in the old Clark Bar candy factory. He first came to Sag Harbor to renovate a vacation house for a Pittsburgh couple in 2000.

After 14 months he liked it so much he stayed, taking an apartment above a store on Main Street. Sag Harbor is bitter cold, wet and uncomfortable in the winter, but Mike said he didn't mind. "It's not as pretentious here. If you can make a living and stay here it's a great place to live because it's a nice quiet town." Except for summer, that is, when the Village of Sag Harbor's population of less than 3,000 swells to about 15,000 and a thousand pleasure boats spend their summers parked in the harbor.

Mike was full of local knowledge and his blunt socio-political commentary about Steinbeck's last hometown was more credible and a lot more interesting than any spinmeister from the chamber of commerce. He said Sag Harbor was leftwing. South Hampton was rightwing and WASPY. East Hampton was very Jewish. Jews had to buy their own golf club in Bridgehampton. "Sag Harbor is the 'un-Hampton,'" he explained. "It's not chain stores. It's boutiques and art galleries."

Mike was happy to report that Sag Harbor's frozen 1950s charm hadn't been ruined by invasive fast-food restaurants and national chains. But when Mike used the word "chain" he didn't mean the Unholy Trinity of Starbucks, McDonalds and Wal-Mart. The closest Starbucks was 5 miles away in Bridgehampton. The closest McDonald's was 11 miles away in Southampton. And the closest Wal-Mart in New York State was in Riverhead, 25 miles west. When Mike said "chain stores" he meant Saks, Tiffany and Gucci.

## Me and Steinbeck's Ghost

Before sunset I went out to Steinbeck's summer home on Bluff Point Lane. It was only a five-minute drive from downtown Sag Harbor. But because it was at the dead-end of a narrow private gravel road at the tip of a peninsula, the house was hard to find – exactly as the reclusive and publicity-shy author wanted.

I didn't use the driveway because John Stefanik's car was there. Stefanik has been taking care of the house since 1982, when Elaine Steinbeck hired him to do the job. The wood-sided house and its outer buildings, shallow swimming pool and shaggy lawn were looking pretty good beneath the heavy shade of tall oaks. The trees were much taller and fatter than when Steinbeck lived there, of course, especially the one that he playfully planted three feet from the front door and now nearly blocks it.

Stefanik usually required appointments for media pests like me. But when I explained why I was there he let me wander around the 2-acre lot. Stefanik couldn't have been friendlier. While he and his son did their buzzing yard work, I walked out on the dock where Steinbeck used to park his 22-foot cabin boat. I also checked out “Joyous Garde,” Steinbeck’s restored writing shack. Overlooking Morris Cove, and deliberately designed to dissuade visitors, it’s hardly bigger than the British phone box Dr. Who flies around in.

I didn’t ask for a peek inside the gray-painted house, which is still owned by Elaine Steinbeck’s heirs. But earlier in the week a New York Times reporter and photographer came to do a feature story about the place to commemorate the 50th anniversary of the start of Steinbeck’s "Travels With Charley" trip. Based on the Times’ pictures, the interior is homey, airy, simply decorated and hung with Steinbeck photos. Steinbeck was loaded, but frugal. It apparently still looked pretty much as it did when he lived in it.

By the time the Stefaniks drove off and left me standing in the driveway, the last sunset of summer was over and fall was arriving with a rare astronomical splash. The full moon was climbing through the trees like a gigantic yellow balloon. I thought its extra plumpness and brightness were due to my tired eyes. But according to NASA’s sky-watchers, for the first time since 1991 northern autumn was beginning on a night with a "Super Harvest Moon." Scientists don’t quite understand why, but somehow the light from the sun and the moon combine to create a 360-degree glow that makes the full moon look wider and brighter than usual. I knew none of this “moon illusion” stuff as I stood there alone with my notebook, cameras and, I guess, the ghosts of Steinbeck and Charley, who was buried somewhere in the yard.

# Steinbeck's 'Act of Courage'

John Steinbeck was especially brave to embark on his solo road trek in 1960 – and it had nothing to do with not having radial tires, GPS or air bags. Given his lousy health, his biographer Jackson Benson said the "Travels With Charley" trip could be best appreciated "as an act of courage." As Steinbeck's son Thom told the New York Times, "The book was his farewell. My dad knew he was dying, and he had been accused of having lost touch with the rest of the country. 'Travels With Charley' was his attempt to rediscover America."

Steinbeck's agent, doctor and everyone who loved him tried to talk him out of his trip, which he had been thinking about taking for at least six years. What if he had a heart attack and collapsed in the middle of nowhere? He'd die for sure and he might never be found. He refused to hear such cautionary crap. He was the contemporary rival and equal of Hemingway. He was the World War II correspondent who went on daring midnight raids in PT boats off the Italian coast with Douglas Fairbanks Jr. He was a future Nobel Prize-winner. He may have been born with a heart too small for his big body, as a European doctor once told him. But he was not a famous dead author yet, literally or figuratively. He was still a man – and not an old man. He still had balls. He still had stuff to say and write and prove.

Steinbeck wrote in letters to his agent and others that he was tired of being fussed over like a sick baby or an invalid who had to be "protected" and "hospitalized." He had to go on his great land-voyage of rediscovery – and go by himself, even though at the last minute he would ask his wife if he could take her 10-year-old standard French poodle Charley with him for company. Defending his solo project in a letter to his agent Elizabeth Otis, he said what he was proposing was not "a little trip of reporting, but a frantic last attempt to save my life and the integrity of my creative pulse."

The thing that came closest to thwarting Steinbeck's big trip was a random act of violence by Mother Nature. In early September 1960, Hurricane Donna, one of the 20th century's nastiest storms, hit Florida and wouldn't let go of the Eastern Seaboard until it got to the eastern tip of Long Island. Donna's oversized Category 3 eye passed directly over Steinbeck's summerhouse, wrecking his plans for leaving soon after Labor Day and almost killing him. As he described dramatically in the opening of "Travels With Charley," he braved Donna's 95-mph winds to save his boat after it became tangled with other boats anchored in the middle of Morris Cove and broke free of its anchor.

As "the trees plunged and bent like grasses" and the "whipped water raised a cream of foam," Steinbeck said he waded through chest-high water to his boat, which was pinned against a neighbor's pier. He started its 100 horsepower engine, moved it back to the middle of the cove, re-anchored it, jumped into the water and rode a wind-blown log to shore. If he really did all those heroics – and if he wasn't slyly creating a dramatic metaphor for the risky trip he was about to take around the USA – it was an impressive feat. Especially with a bum knee and a bad ticker.

Steinbeck also went in search of America and Americans for practical reasons. For 20 years he had been living on the Upper East Side of Manhattan and traveling around Western Europe like an archduke. As he explained in letters written before his trip, he constantly was expected to write and comment about America, to represent its values and culture. Yet he no longer knew his own country or people except from memory or by reading. He understood New York City was not really America. It was a political and cultural terrarium – an "island" he called it. The high-end celebrities and power people he loafed with – Elia Kazan, John Huston, Arthur Miller, Adlai Stevenson – were not representative of real Americans and he knew it.

Steinbeck hoped his road trip, undertaken discreetly, would put him back in touch with Real America. His plan was to get out into the sticks and meet regular people face-to-face. Anonymously. Alone. Not on tour buses or in motels, but where they lived and worked and drank and prayed. He wanted to see for himself what Americans were up to and what they were thinking and arguing about during a historic presidential election. It was Journalism 101 – a grassroots observing and reporting mission by one of the world's most popular writers. He and his agent, editor and publisher knew the great author's quest for America would make another successful Steinbeck book, which it did, in spades. It's just a shame that the ambitious trip he planned so carefully never really happened.

# 4 – Steinbeck's America

*Even while I protest the assembly-line production of our food, our songs, our language, and eventually our souls, I know that it was a rare home that baked good bread in the old days. Mother's cooking was with rare exceptions poor, that good unpasteurized milk touched only by flies and bits of manure crawled with bacteria, the healthy old-time life was riddled with aches, sudden death from unknown causes, and that sweet local speech I mourn was the child of illiteracy and ignorance. It is the nature of a man as he grows older, a small bridge in time, to protest against change, particularly change for the better.*

– "Travels With Charley"

Little remains of the country Steinbeck was determined to rediscover. In 1960 the USA was as simple as ABC, CBS and NBC, the only national networks its people were permitted by federal communications law to watch.

Stuck in a MAD nuke-rattling Cold War with the Soviet Union, the country had changed dramatically since the Depression and the end of World War II. But it was essentially still a collection of disparate regions with their own funny accents, strange foods, local laws, favorite kinds of music and distinct subcultures. About the only thing every region could agree on was the importance of preserving their own socioeconomic and cultural status quos.

To a lot of reality-challenged Americans today the America of 1960 was a kind of Golden Age. Everything that mattered was still "Made in America" by strong unions that were largely white and male and politically powerful. Society supposedly still made sense: Fathers worked, mothers stayed home, children were raised in packs of five. The family ate dinner together every night at 5:30. Laws and priests and teachers and parents were obeyed. Flags and politicians were saluted. Doctors came to your house. New immigrants were rare. Crime, taxes and prices were low and people paid with cash not credit cards. Baseball and college football were our simple and innocent co-national pastimes.

Of course 1960 America was not America the Beautiful. It had warts that took decades of bloody surgery to remove. Daily life and the 15-minute nightly network TV news programs were haunted by real and imaginary fears – thermonuclear war, juvenile delinquents, restless Negroes, communists, Playboy, Mad magazine, A&P supermarkets and so-called-life in the suburbs.

Despite the ideals of the Declaration of Independence and protections of the Constitution, about 18 million black Americans were humiliated, dehumanized or blatantly or subtly denied their civil rights by law or custom above and below the Mason Dixon Line. Almost all black women who worked were domestics. Only 20 percent of blacks graduated from high school, compared to 43 percent for whites. One in a thousand marriages was between a white and black, compared to 1 in 60 today. A higher percentage of white and black Americans were poor back then and far fewer members of either race were middle-class or rich or well educated. Latinos? They were called Mexicans and lived in the deserts of the Southwest or picked grapes in California. Women, who outnumber men in colleges today, were outnumbered by men on campus by 10-1.

In the economy, big numbers were much smaller and more sensible in 1960, but that's largely because the U.S. dollar was worth a little more than seven times what it is now. In other words, it took only one 1960 dollar to buy what it took seven 2010 dollars to buy and vice versa.

The federal budget in 1960 was a minuscule $91 billion, with a $300 million surplus. That did not include big-ticket items like Social Security or Medicare, which didn't exist yet. In 2010, the budget of the bankrupt state of California was $126 billion and the federal budget had ballooned to incomprehensibility – $3.5 trillion with a $1.3 trillion deficit. In 1960 the average manufacturing job paid $2.22 an hour and the minimum wage was $1. About 31 percent of the workforce was unionized compared to 12 percent in 2010. Gas cost 31 cents a gallon and Steinbeck's new GMC pickup-camper combo set him back less than $3,000. The median house in America was worth about $12,000 and the average family income was around $5,600.

Most people's lives resembled the stark working-class scarcity of "The Honeymooners," not the suburban perfection of "Ozzie and Harriet" or "Leave It to Beaver." Consumers had fewer choices in 1960 and everyone paid higher prices because of government policies that created or protected monopolies or oligopolies like the phone system, TV broadcasting and the airline industry. A long-distance phone call that's virtually free today cost $1 a minute in 1960 ($7 in today's money). A quarter of American households did not have telephones and a quarter of those that did shared party lines. It's a wonder anyone could communicate. The cutting-edge communication marvel of the day was the beeper.

Transportation was being democratized and radically transformed in 1960. Plane travel has become a form of mass torture today, thanks to the excesses of the security state and the economics of hauling humans like cattle, but it's a far cheaper and safer way to fly to grandma's house. Half a century ago only elites could afford a droning, bumpy plane flight from New York to L.A., which, because of federal regulations prohibiting price competition, could cost no less than about $210 each way – about $1,500 in today's money. In 1960, when 58 million Americans flew on U.S. airlines, more than 350 died in six major commercial plane crashes. In 2010, when 786 million Americans flew, both the number of crashes and people who died in crashes were the same in 2007, 2008 and 2009 – zero.

By 1960 cars had replaced trains as the country's mass mode of transportation. Interstates, truck stops and national motel and restaurant chains barely existed. Wal-Mart did not. About 75 percent of homes owned a car and 15 percent owned two. Automobiles were 4,000-pound death wagons with metal dashboards, crummy tires and lights and no safety gear; 1 percent of drivers used seat belts. America's highways were criminally lethal. About 36,000 of the country's 180 million people were killed in or by cars in 1960. In 2010, when there were three times as many autos and trucks on the road and 310 million Americans riding around in them, the annual death toll had fallen to 32,708.

Pockets of hipness existed in the pop culture of 1960 America. The Beat Poets and comedians like Mort Sahl and Nichols and May were headquartered in the North Beach neighborhood of downtown San Francisco. Jazz was the coolest sound on campus but folk music was rising. The hard-bop scene was happening in

New York City, electrified Delta bluesmen like Muddy Waters had migrated to Chicago and country & Western was still a regional taste. Barry Gordy's unknown record label was a year old and called Motown.

In the fall of 1960, a lot of things hadn't happened yet. The civil rights movement in the South hadn't earned its capital letters. The Berlin Wall hadn't been built. Hanoi was the answer to a "GE College Bowl" question no one could answer. But sweeping socio-political and cultural revolutions were quickening in the American womb. The Pill was okayed for sale by our puritanical federal government – but only to married women. Robert Allen Zimmerman, a college dropout, was a baby-faced folk singer in Minneapolis. The Beatles were reinventing rock 'n' roll in Hamburg. Elvis was an ex-G.I. who had not yet gone Vegas. Marilyn Monroe was about to divorce Arthur Miller.

Muhammad Ali was still Cassius Clay. Ronald Reagan was still a Democrat and Martin Luther King was a Republican. Jim Crow looked invincible. Billy Gates was four years old. Andy Warhol was earning $70,000 a year in New York drawing ads for ladies shoes, hats and handbags. And a crazy Harvard professor named Dr. Timothy Leary had just had his first breakfast of psilocybin mushrooms. When John Steinbeck and Charley took to the highway, America was a much different place. It was still mostly a square, well-behaved, soulless, church-going, booze-loving, white-Anglo-Saxon-Protestant-owned-and-operated country that wasn't living up to its founding ideals or its promises. But big changes were a-coming.

# 5 – The Dogging Begins

*"... my trip demanded that I leave my name and my identity at home. I had to be peripatetic eyes and ears, a kind of moving gelatin plate. I could not sign hotel registers, meet people I knew, interview others, or even ask searching questions. Furthermore, two or more people disturb the ecologic complex of an area. I had to go alone and I had to be self-contained, a kind of casual turtle carrying his house on his back.*

– "Travels With Charley"

## Steinbeck Timeline

Friday, Sept. 23, 1960 – Sag Harbor, New York

*Early in the morning John Steinbeck and his French poodle Charley leave his summer home in his overloaded pickup truck-camper combo Rocinante. He takes three ferries to New London, Connecticut, and drives north toward his son's boarding school in Deerfield, Massachusetts. His cargo includes spare parts for his truck, dozens of books, two rifles and a shotgun.*

## Sleeping With Yachts

The moon was almost down and the sun was almost up as the black sky turned pink and red above Sag Harbor's Long Wharf. My RAV4 had been one of three vehicles parked all night on the pier but the only one with a crazy person sleeping inside it. A local scofflaw in a coffee shop had tipped me off that the wharf was a safe place – i.e., I wouldn't be spotted by the cops and run out of town as a vagrant.

I cracked my sunroof so I wouldn't fog my windows and give myself away, but I still waited all night for the tap of the local gendarme on my window. I must have blended in well with the yachts. The blackout curtains my wife made worked perfectly. The inside of my car had been dark and comfortable – like a sleeping berth on a train. Pretending to myself that I got five hours of actual sleep, I drove out to Steinbeck's house again to see how many other nuts were there. I should have realized no real journalist would be crazy/brave/stupid enough to spend a month alone on the Steinbeck Highway, but I was worried about competition.

In Steinbeck's driveway I was afraid I'd find a scene from "Smokey and the Bandit, Part IV," starring Paul Theroux, William Least Heat-Moon, P.J. O'Rourke, Anderson Cooper and an international cast of travel writers, documentary crews and dozens of steinbeckians with dogs and 30-foot motor homes. But no humans were there, just noisy seagulls and tree frogs. It looked like I was going to have Steinbeck's ornery ghost and his old highway to myself for the next 10,000 miles.

I walked around the manicured yard like I had a constitutional right to trespass there, as journalists are wont to do. The little swimming pool shimmered and gurgled. Everything looked perfect for the 50th anniversary. I took a photo of my RAV4 idling in Steinbeck's gravel driveway, documented the mileage on my odometer (2,920) and headed for the first of three ferries that would deliver me to New London, Connecticut. Steinbeck had taken the same watery shortcut to the continent exactly 50 years before me, primarily to avoid driving through New York City. After my recent experience in Manhattan, I was extra glad he did.

## Island Hopping, Ferry Jumping

It was a smooth journey by land and sea from Sag Harbor to the ferry at Orient Point, where the Cross Sound Ferry departs for New London. Two 10-minute ferry crossings, sandwiched around an eight-mile drive, got me on and off Shelter Island, which is mostly a protected wetlands and nature preserve. Shelter Island has 2,200 lucky permanent residents and 6,000 summer invaders. A third of it is privately owned by the Nature Conservancy, which has promised to keep its property in its natural state forever. Not that Shelter Island is in any danger of becoming overdeveloped – or developed at all. Virtually every white shingled home, roadside store or berry farm I sped past was classy, picture-perfect and of pre-1960 vintage. Much of it was no doubt spiffier and pricier in 2010 than it was in 1960. But new development or sprawl of any kind simply didn't exist.

For a guy traveling on credit cards, ferry hopping was a pricy backdoor exit from Long Island. It was $12 and $9 for the two Shelter Island ferries and $49 for Cross Sound Ferry Service's 16.5-mile voyage to New London, which about 1,000 cars make each day. On Steinbeck's way to New London aboard "the clanking iron ferry boat," he says he saw U.S. Navy submarines surfacing nearby and met a sailor on leave – a nuclear submariner, to be exact. They talked about the nuclear subs that were home-ported at the U.S. naval base in New London on the Thames River, which in 1960 was the largest submarine base in the world. Like many Americans in those spooky Cold War days, Steinbeck was not fond of the U.S./Soviet strategy of mutual assured destruction (MAD), part of which involved building a fleet of Polaris-firing nuclear submarines. He didn't like subs, either. As he wrote in "Travels With Charley," despite their beauty they were "designed for destruction" and "armed with mass murder."

I didn't see any of New London's current school of 21 attack subs or meet any submariners on the boat ride from Orient Point. But as I waited to enter the gaping belly of the ferry Susan Anne, I met Blaize Zabel, a 20-year-old high school dropout. He looked tough with his big forearms, black T-shirt and shorts and cross tattoo. But he turned out to be an incredibly nice kid. He was on his way back to his home in Falmouth, Massachusetts, and said – without hinting for a handout – that he hoped he would have enough money for the Greyhound. His

immediate career plans were to get a GED and add his grandmother's name, Ruth Zabel, to his forearm.

On the ferry Susan Anne, I was jumped – in a friendly way – by a homeless Pulitzer Prize-winning crime reporter and his 130-pound companion Ace. John Woestendiek, 57, used to work for the Philly Inquirer and the Baltimore Sun. Houseless by choice, with all his possessions in storage, he was not sure where his next permanent address would be. He had taken a buyout at the Sun and was now the owner-operator of two dog-centric Web sites.

Ace, his Rotweiller/Akita/Chow/pitbull, was traveling around America with John – or vice versa. The duo had been living on the very cheap for several months, mostly down South. Finished with his book on dog cloning, "Dog, Inc.," John thought it would be cool for him and Ace to start following Steinbeck and Charley's trail exactly 50 years later. He was blogging, having dog-related adventures and surfing on the couches of friends and family as he went.

Since no affordable motels are allowed within 20 miles of Sag Harbor, he and Ace slept the previous night in one of the Hamptons behind a business called Sleepies. John's bed was the front seat of his red Jeep Liberty. Ace, 6, was so handsome, well mannered and friendly he made me wish I had a dog along too – for about four seconds. Though he provided John with security, somebody to talk to and unconditional love, Ace also ate like a 130-pound dog, had health and hygiene issues and consumed most of the interior of John's Jeep. Finding Ace-friendly motels was a daily issue on the road for John. Motel 6 was his fallback. It was a rare dog-friendly chain and his $40-a-night budget limit ruled out just about everything else.

John and Ace had also made a dawn pilgrimage to Steinbeck's summerhouse and found no one there. It was a tossup as to who was the most entrepreneurial ex-newspaperman: He was pretty much living with a pit bull so he could write another book and I was trying to faithfully retrace Steinbeck's trip like I was a Carl Bernstein or John Woestendiek. We rehashed the suicide of the American newspaper industry and I told him – off the record – some of what I had discovered about Steinbeck's actual road trip. When we reached New London, we parted in the hull of the Susan Anne with a handshake and a pat on the head. We both knew it made no sense to form a tag-team. Trips like ours had to be one-human affairs or they didn't work. Anyway, I'd be moving much faster without a massive you-know-what to care for. We hoped our paths might cross again either in Maine or Montana. But for the next two months, as John ate my dust and fell two or three states behind, it never happened. We emailed and shared inside-Steinbeck jokes as we followed Steinbeck's trail in our own nutty ways. We even slept in the same motel bed in Beach, North Dakota – two weeks apart. But I never met John or Ace again, on land or sea.

## Empty, Pretty and Rich

I used my GPS to escape New London and get to U.S. Highway 5. That's the path Steinbeck took to Deerfield, Massachusetts, home of the Eaglebrook School, which his son John IV was attending in 1960. As I was working my way out of New London on state Route 85, aka the Hartford-New London Turnpike, I passed a common sight in America that Steinbeck would have found both mysterious and depressing – a string of auto dealerships bearing names like Hyundai, Mazda and Subaru. Those Asian car dealerships were struggling with lower sales, along with the rest of the American car industry, but they were in no mortal danger from the Great Recession. Less than three miles away it was a different, crueler economic story. After four decades of doing business, Falvey's Chrysler was dead and closed. It had become one of 800 dealerships in the country to be dropped by Chrysler as part of its 2009 bankruptcy settlement.

Steinbeck would be shocked to learn how 50 years of foreign competition, poor management, greedy unions and second-rate cars teamed up to destroy the American auto industry. On the day he and Charley drove through New London in his new green 1960 GMC pickup, GM, Ford and Chrysler controlled more than 95 percent of new car sales in the USA. GM alone sold half. By 2010, the Big Three's market share had sunk to around 20 percent. Ford was hurt but alive and not taking corporate welfare. But hundreds of thousands of shareholders and workers had paid a heavy price for GM and Chrysler's failure to compete and change in a global marketplace. So had American taxpayers.

The Asian car lots of New London gave way quickly to undeveloped countryside and green woods of oak and pine. Some of the trees were too young to have been alive in 1960, when the land was probably still being farmed, but Steinbeck would have seen the same token bits of civilization I saw. The roadside along state routes 85 and 2 was loosely strung with old white houses, white barns, white roadhouse restaurants, weathered fruit stands and highway picnic areas that looked unchanged in 100 years. Somewhere in the sticks of Connecticut, Steinbeck said he stopped to lay in a stock of liquor at what he called "a little bottle store" but what Connecticut folk then and now call "package stores."

In "Charley" he says he ordered a frat party's worth of "bourbon, scotch, gin, vermouth, vodka, a medium good brandy, aged applejack, and a case of beer." One reason Steinbeck chose a camper shell was so he'd be able to invite people he met into his "home" for a drink. His defenders insist he wasn't an alcoholic, but on his trip sharing a shot of booze with someone was always on the guy's mind.

U.S. Route 5 pierces ancient towns like Enfield, Connecticut, before climbing into the underbelly of Massachusetts and becoming the main street of lively college towns like Springfield, Holyoke and Northampton. I don't know what Steinbeck would have thought of a Hooters, or if he would have wondered why there were so many Latinos riding bicycles in Springfield. But he'd have been impressed by Northampton's beautiful historic buildings and thriving downtown retail scene. On a Thursday night at 8 a diverse and thick mob of well-heeled college kids, professional counter-culture types and liberal political activists flowed along Northampton's sidewalks.

After so much unpopulated countryside, it was weird to suddenly come upon that bustling street scene. I wouldn't see that many young people and backpacks crammed into one place again until Missoula, Montana. The vitality of Northampton was testimony to the economic power of art, music, culture, tourism and the concentration of many millions of private and public dollars from the U. Mass-Smith-Amherst-Hampshire-Mt. Holyoke educational complex. They had combined to lift the region out of the decline it suffered when its manufacturing base rusted away in the 1970s. Leaving Northampton, I thought I could hear former Mayor Calvin Coolidge, my favorite do-nothing president of the 20th century, spinning in his local grave.

Mostly, U.S. Highway 5 was green, undeveloped and timeless. The drive from New London to Greenfield, Massachusetts, where I got a room for the night at a Day's Inn, reminded me yet again just how empty America is. I hadn't even seen North Dakota and Montana yet.

But the view from the "Purple Heart Memorial Highway" made Connecticut look as un-peopled and forested as central Pennsylvania or anywhere in West Virginia. When there were homes posted along the road – and there were hundreds – they were usually large, white, pre-Teddy Roosevelt House & Garden beauties with wide porches on big, perfectly landscaped lots. Steinbeck was a wealthy man and may not have been as impressed as I was by that gauntlet of mature American affluence. But as he drove up U.S. Route 5 to Deerfield in 1960 he would have gone by 99 percent of the same McMansions of yesteryear I did.

## Steinbeck Timeline

Friday, Sept. 23 to Sept. 24, 1960 – Deerfield, Mass.

*Steinbeck camps out Friday and Saturday nights in Rocinante in an apple orchard on a dairy farm on top of the mountain above his 14-year-old son John IV's exclusive boarding school, Eaglebrook. In "Charley" Steinbeck says almost nothing about his visit, but from a letter to his wife Elaine it's clear he stayed at the school until Sunday afternoon.*

# Ghost Farm

There can't be a more beautiful middle school in America than Eaglebrook. Its campus hangs on the side of an ancient round mountain overlooking the absurdly historic village of Deerfield on U.S. Highway 5, not 25 miles shy of Vermont. It's not your run-of-the-mill school for kids in grades 6 through 9. It's private, exclusive and all-boy. It's so pricy if you have to ask what a year's tuition and room and board cost, you're not rich enough to send your heir there.

Eaglebrook School was Steinbeck's first overnight stop. His youngest son John IV, who became a respected journalist in Vietnam and died from complications of back surgery in 1991, went to school there. So did many of the sons of corporate bigwigs at IBM and TWA and Michael Douglas, actor Kirk's son. Things have changed a great deal since 1960, Eaglebrook's former headmaster O. Stuart Chase told me when I met him in his office on campus.

Steinbeck would have found preppies outfitted in identical Navy blazers and thick-striped red and blue school ties. They also had a Sunday tie they wore when they walked to church in Deerfield village every Sunday morning. Today's 256 students, drawn from around the world, don't dress so formally. But Chase said they still aren't allowed to ruin the pre-prep-school milieu with blue jeans, torn pants or un-collared shirts.

Deerfield is about 160 road miles from Sag Harbor and Steinbeck arrived there Friday evening, Sept. 23, 1960. It was too late to see his son, he writes in "Travels With Charley," so he drove to the top of the mountain and "found a dairy, bought some milk, and asked permission to camp under an apple tree." Steinbeck writes that he preferred "to draw a curtain over my visit to Eaglebrook school" – the first of several places he stopped on his trip that he chose not to write about. But his first road-letter to his wife goes into detail about the visit, which included a school bonfire and a church service and lasted until Sunday afternoon.

Mr. Chase, whose father preceded him as Eaglebrook headmaster and whose son in turn succeeded him, gave me directions to the dairy farm. Climbing Pine Nook Road above Eaglebrook through the dense woods, I found the orchard right where Chase said it would be. He had called it a "skeleton" of an orchard and that's what it was. I parked under what could have been the same large apple tree

Steinbeck said he camped under. Strangled by wild rose bushes and vines, the trees were gnarly and heavy with red apples – apples that were no longer being sprayed, harvested and sold but allowed to fall into the weeds, where they provided a feast for the local fly and bee population. The rotting fruit made the whole orchard smell like apple juice.

Unlike Steinbeck, I found no dairyman with a Ph.D. in mathematics to shoot the breeze with. Humans had lost control of what had been a thriving dairy farm. The fields were uncut and the barns and silos were neglected and draped with wild grape vines, but the handsome big white farmhouse appeared to be in excellent shape. It was as if one afternoon someone just locked the front door and drove away to Boston, content to let Mother Nature slowly reclaim another 100-acre piece of her stolen property.

I left Deerfield in the late afternoon, pushing north on U.S. Highway 5 toward the Vermont line. At some point on the way I scribbled in the Professional Reporter's Notebook resting on my knee:

> Man. He must have been nuts to do this trip. I'm not that nuts because I'm following him. He was nuts first. The colors are just coming.... It's pure country. Very few homes and they are smaller. Old barns, old farmhouses, few new or modern homes. No development .... It must have been daunting to think he had 11 weeks and 10,000 miles ahead of him, yet instead of heading west he was driving north and east to Maine. Most of the places that exist now probably existed in 1960. Christ Church in Guilford, Vermont, for instance. A large white wooden church by itself with old cemetery attached. Its steeple looks like someone very big and important in the sky snapped or bit it off... Almost to Brattleboro. Welcome commerce. An outlet center – Bass shoes, Van Heusen... A Walgreen's. All the sudden a total traffic jam in Brattleboro. Six gas stations to choose from ... or a urologist. Lots of people on the sidewalks. Another great preserved little town that looks like it didn't get bulldozed by 1960s urban planning experts....

Except for the different names of the states and towns, I could have written that same note to myself at any time during my week in New England. Five decades had passed along the Steinbeck Highway, yet little had changed.

## Steinbeck Timeline

Sunday, Sept. 25, 1960 – White Mountains

*Steinbeck says in "Travels With Charley" that he left his son's school in Deerfield and drove north into Vermont, then east into the rugged White Mountains near Lancaster, New Hampshire. He describes camping on a farm that night and talking with the landowner about Nikita Khrushchev reportedly pounding his shoe on his desk that day at the United Nations. Khrushchev's tantrum at the U.N. actually happened nearly two weeks later. In 2010, a local writer searched hard for Steinbeck's farm and Yankee farmer near Lancaster and concluded both never existed.*

## Sleeping by the River

For almost two hours the Connecticut River, the black White Mountains of New Hampshire and a fat rising moon were on my right as I drove north along the ragged edge of Vermont toward St. Johnsbury. The GPS Person kept insisting I leave the valley and climb the ridge to Interstate 91, which parallels U.S. Route 5 to the west but didn't exist in Steinbeck's day.

I stuck religiously to the two-lane piece of the Steinbeck Highway with its small river valley towns and rural spaces. I stopped at a busy mom & pop motel somewhere but declined the opportunity to spend $70 for a tiny box with one locked window. It's always easier to stay awake on dangerous back roads, because they demand your constant attention or you'll hit something and die. But by 10 o'clock I was too tired to go on. On a dark curve on U.S. 5 I pulled into a shallow turnout lit only by the moon. After backing up so the trees would block my taillights, I locked myself in, climbed in back, hung my "blackout curtains" and crawled under the blankets. Once the spooks were put to rest and I got used to the whoosh of an occasional car, I slept straight through till dawn.

In the foggy morning light, I discovered I had slept barely 15 feet from the steep wooded bank of the wide Connecticut River, which was as flat and silent as a lake. If I had been the mythical John Steinbeck, I would have gotten out my fishing pole, caught my breakfast and cooked it over a fire. Instead I took a piss in the river and drove 23 miles north to St. Johnsbury, where I was hoping to stop at one of the dozens of hip Internet cafes I imagined would be open at 7 on a Saturday morning.

Things weren't quite poppin' yet in "St. Jay's" brick downtown, so I stuck to Steinbeck's trail and turned east on U.S. Highway 2. It quickly became a fast smooth ride in the country. With fall foliage at its peak, it was "Leaf Peeper" season, when motel room prices spike and locals complain about strangers from other states cluttering their underutilized highways. But the road was virtually empty. At one point I was doing 65 and being pushed from behind by a guy in a pickup pulling a racing car on a trailer. Otherwise, for about 20 miles almost nothing but gorgeous scenery existed beyond my windows and mirrors. A few snowmobiles and pickup trucks were seductively parked nose-first by the side of the road, hung with "For Sale" signs. But mostly I traveled alone through yellow and orange and red and green hills and woods broken by an occasional "Moose" warning sign.

Near the New Hampshire border was the first evidence that the upcoming off-year elections were important to some politically disturbed folks in the Obama-blue state of Vermont. The front yard of a small farm had a little roadside display of pumpkins for sale – just like half the places clinging to U.S. 5 and U.S. 2. It also had a dozen political signs for state and local candidates carefully staked along the curve. I would pass a thousand official red-white-and-blue political signs for both parties from Maine to Oregon to Los Banos, California. But this partisan's placards came with a special hand-lettered message that made his sympathies Tea Party-clear: "Take Back America Vote the Liberals Out."

## Town of White Churches

Steinbeck passed through the handsome Connecticut River town of Lancaster, New Hampshire, twice. Once when he was on his way east to the top of Maine and again five days later, when he was bound for Chicago. He made no mention of the town's surfeit of white churches. But I could see five steeples from the front door of the venerable Lancaster Motor Inn, where I squatted in their lobby and borrowed their Wi-Fi-after a fine $8 breakfast of steak and eggs.

A local man estimated 13 or 14 churches were doing their best to save Lancaster's 3,200 sinners. Lancaster's main drag – U.S. Highway 2 – was almost as busy as it must be on an Easter Sunday morning. A farmers market was setting up on the lawn next to the old brick courthouse. Among the sellers of maple syrup, organic vegetables and gluten-free breadstuff was photographer Gerry Gallick. He was putting his color photos and nature calendars on display in his booth.

Gallick, 52, was living in the state with the highest median income in the country, but he was a poster-victim for the national economic downturn. He had plenty of qualifications and experience. He was an ex-civil engineer, ex-cop, ex-truck driver, a musician, a poet. Now he was trying to support himself with photography, what used to be his hobby. He had lost his engineering gig in January of 2010 and could talk your ear off about all the jobs he had looked for since but didn't get. The father of four, he said he'd been rejected often because he was too old or over-qualified. Now he was scraping up $50 or $100 a week selling large color photos of the magnificent natural resources he said God made for everyone to enjoy – the surrounding mountains, woods and fauna.

Gallick wasn't bitter about his own fate, which he didn't blame on anyone or any party. "Everyone is suffering," he said. The top third of New Hampshire had less than 5 percent of the state's population and its tourist-and-ski economy couldn't overcome the long-term decline in the logging and paper industries. The state's unemployment rate was low at 5.8 percent, but Gallick said permanent jobs with benefits were scarce for 100 miles.

"It's economic, but it's also a mindset," he said. "If you go 50 miles south through Franconia Notch, you can get $10 more an hour and better benefits." He knew he could move to where the better jobs were, but he was living exactly where he said he wanted to be. "It's paradise here. It's God's country. I love to be here, but it's hard to make a living."

Gallick was only the second person I spoke to at the farmer's market. I stopped at his booth when I noticed his panoramic photos of downtown Pittsburgh and the confluence of its three rivers. It turned out that Gallick, like Mike from Sag Harbor, was an ex-Pittsburgher – 31 years removed. He was part of the Great Diaspora of young people who left during the Pittsburgh region's deindustrialization in the '70s and '80s. Hundreds of thousands of ex-Pittsburghers like Gallick who went looking for jobs after the mills closed are scattered around the USA. It was eerie how we found each other so easily, since neither of us was wearing a stitch of the city's holy colors, Steelers black and gold.

# 6 – Maine, the Big Empty

## Steinbeck Timeline

Monday, Sept. 26, 1960 – Deer Isle, Maine

*Steinbeck writes that he left New Hampshire and drove across the neck of Maine and stopped at a motel near Bangor. He says he was so put off by the sterile and plastic environment in his room that he went out and slept in the back of his truck. In fact, he drove 250 miles from New Hampshire to Deer Isle, Maine, an island south of Bangor, where he was expected at the seaside home of Eleanor Brace. On the night 70 million Americans watched the first Nixon-JFK debate from Chicago he slept at Brace's place in the back of Rocinante.*

## Bound for Bangor

Saturday afternoon I cruised east into and out of the White Mountains as New Hampshire's fall colors blended seamlessly into Maine's. In age and ruggedness the White Mountains fall somewhere between Pennsylvania's ancient dying Alleghenies and the jagged young ranges out West that are still growing. Steinbeck took the same route to Bangor, then dropped south to Deer Isle on the Maine coast. He would have recognized this part of his highway, too. Though a short stretch of U.S. 2 near the Maine border was under major reconstruction, little was new from 50 years ago. I passed the same farms, same houses, same white churches, same frozen-in-time intersections he did – at the same speed but in far greater comfort.

Not that I am especially sensitive to such things, but nothing I saw screamed "urban sprawl" or "development" or "over commercialization." In fact, a few of the drab Maine towns hanging on U.S. 2 – Rumford in particular – could use some national homogenization from a chain like Bob Evans. When I asked a young Maine state trooper washing his windshield at a gas station in Rumford where I could get something decent to eat for dinner, he thought hard. Being an honest cop, he pointed across the road and, with a mix of civic embarrassment and empathy, said, "There's the Subway."

Several hours and 170 miles later, after following a spooky dancing glow in the sky that I eventually realized was the Northern Lights, I reached the outskirts of Bangor. I thought I'd try doing what Steinbeck did fairly often on his trip – pull into a campground (what he called a "trailer court") and sleep there in my car. At about 10 p.m. I turned off the highway and followed the signs down a dark gravel road a mile into the pinewoods.

The campground was deathly quiet. The orderly rows of tents and RVs were dark and with my headlights off I couldn't see a soul. Where was the damn office? My RAV4 sounded like a Panzer tank. I was afraid if I turned on my lights I'd be shot. I knew nothing about the kamping kulture, which apparently goes to bed at 8 p.m. I decided then and there it was too late to learn. I managed to turn around and crunch slowly out of the campground to U.S. Highway 2, where I plugged the address of the nearest Wal-Mart into my GPS and aimed for the bright lights of Greater Bangor.

The Wal-Mart address in Bangor came from what turned out to be the secret weapon of my trip. Months before I knew I'd be chasing Steinbeck's ghost around America, I impulsively bought a 2010 Rand McNally Road Atlas for $5.97 at a Wal-Mart. Along with the usual state road maps with fonts too small to read if you're over 55, it contained a detailed directory of every Wal-Mart and Sam's Club in North America and Mexico – all 4,600 of them.

I had nothing against Wal-Mart and had defended it enthusiastically in op-ed columns for saving American consumers hundreds of billions of dollars over the years. But we were a Costco family. I never dreamed that someday I'd need to know the address of the Wal-Mart in Bangor or Bismarck, North Dakota. But unlike Steinbeck, who could and did travel like an archduke whenever he wanted, I had to travel cheap. I was sleeping in my car whenever it made sense. And thanks to founder Sam Walton, who long ago made it corporate policy at Wal-Mart to encourage RV-ers and truckers to park overnight in his company's parking lots, it made sense for me to become a frequent sleeper at Wal-Mart.

Finally spotting Wal-Mart's blue sign in a maze of malls at about 11, I joined a dozen RVs in a corner of an otherwise vacated parking lot. I was dead asleep in my berth within 10 minutes. Not that Bangor is known for its warring drug cartels, but I slept easy knowing that Wal-Mart's crack security detail was on patrol 24/7. The only catch to Sam Walton's hospitality is that Wal-Mart keeps its properties lit up all night like high school football stadiums. I woke at 3 a.m. and took a photo of my RAV4 bathed in what looked like sunlight. My joke – that you could have performed a heart transplant on my hood – was no joke. Only my blackout curtains saved me from the glare.

When I crawled barefooted out of my car shortly after dawn, Wal-Mart's lot was actually darker than it had been at 3 a.m. Overnight crisp sunny Indian summer had changed to cool gray fall. It was barely 50 degrees and the start of a damp and chilly Sunday in Maine. I changed out of my shorts into what would become my traveling uniform for the next 40 days and 20-plus states – blue jeans, golf shirt, old red crewneck sweater, baseball cap, Keen sandals and no socks. I had no interest in interviewing my Wal-Mart sleep-mates or exploring Bangor, even if it once was the lumber exporting capital of the world.

I wanted only to do what Steinbeck did in 1960 – cut through the city quickly on my way to the seacoast paradise of Deer Isle, where he spent two days at a gorgeous old house I hoped to find. Driving into the suburbs on state Route 15, the 55-mile trip to Deer Isle became a highlight reel of Maine's L.L. Bean culture. Boats and RVs of every size, truck caps, kayaks, logs, shingles and gigantic piles of firewood lined the roadside or adorned front lawns. Gas was $2.62 a gallon. The billboard "Guns, Ammo and Camo" pretty much said it all. The closer I got to Deer Isle, the farther back in time I went and the more upscale and artsy-crafty things got.

By the time I reached Caterpillar Hill and its panoramic view of Deer Isle and the rainbow-arched bridge that connects it to the mainland, I had passed dozens of pottery studios, antique shops, art galleries and ceramics shops. Plus Sow's Ear Winery and Sunrise Cottages. Not one sports bar or McDonald's. No doubt they were illegal. Neon apparently was outlawed too. But there were lots of U.S. flags flying from utility poles, plus roadside gardens of political campaign signs and 25-foot ships parked in nearly every third front yard. Roller-coasting Route 15 eventually delivered me to the ocean and the impossibly picturesque "Down East" fishing village of Stonington.

Seeing the harbor, the boats, the weathered piers and docks – not to mention the charming/funky mix of beautiful homes and old buildings holding on to the hillside or hanging over the water's edge – I understood why Steinbeck thought it was unlike any American town he'd ever seen.

## Steinbeck Timeline

Tuesday, Sept. 27, 1960 – Deer Isle, Maine

*Steinbeck says in a letter to his wife from Deer Isle that on Tuesday he "saw the island and talked to people." He visits the fishing port of Stonington, where he buys a kerosene lamp at a nautical hardware store on Main Street. He eats a lobster dinner at Eleanor Brace's house with Brace and her woman friend. He goes to bed early, sleeping another night in his camper Rocinante.*

# Where Cell Phones Can't Roam

Reachable from the mainland only by boat or the beautiful suspension bridge on Route 15, Deer Isle is about as far "Down East" Maine as you can get without sleeping with the lobsters in cold Penobscot Bay. Hikers, kayakers, birders, sailors, naturalists and artists swarm to the rural, spruce-covered island each summer, swamping its permanent population of 2,500.

Steinbeck reluctantly diverted to Deer Isle at the insistence of his long-time agent and friend, Elizabeth Otis. For 30 years she had been renting a small rustic cottage by the ocean owned by Eleanor Brace and Otis kiddingly told Steinbeck he'd better stop to see her favorite paradise or find another agent. Steinbeck wasn't sorry he took that side trip to Deer Isle. He flipped out over Stonington's architecture and timeless, "enchanting" feel, saying it reminded him of an English fishing village on the coast of Dorset. It still would. Its shingled houses with their oversized windows stare out at a harbor that buzzes with real work from May to September, when lobstermen go to sea before 5 a.m. to pull their traps and bring in their catches to the co-op's docks in the afternoon.

Stonington is the top lobster port by value of catch in Maine, I was told several times, and the creatures are so plentiful kids trap them in the harbor behind the shops on Main Street. The fishing port Steinbeck liked so much still has its character, but it had changed in important ways. In 1960 Stonington's granite quarries, which gave the town its name and would provide the stone for John F. Kennedy's memorial, were the major employer. In 2010 the granite industry was long gone. Today most young people have to leave to get good-paying jobs. The port's 1,200 citizens make their livings from the sea year-round and from the tourist invasion in the summer.

On Main Street, which is often too narrow for sidewalks, the businesses sprinkled among the houses include the Stonington Ice Cream Company, Island Fishing Gear & Auto Parts and Seasons of Stonington restaurant. There's also Boyces Motel, a friendly family-run place that cost me $60 for a small room with no view of the harbor. Chester Carter Jr. was the oldest of several Stonington natives I met. In a Maine accent with a hint of Georgia he told me he lived in Stonington in the summer and Savannah in the winter.

Carter was 78. In 1949, seeing little he wanted to do in Stonington, he left town. He made his fortune down South as an insurance salesman, but he always came back home for summer vacations. Now he owned two houses in Stonington, one to live in and one to rent. Carter said Stonington was still filled with good, hard-working people. And many of the summer people have been returning for so long they were like natives. But he remembered when Stonington had its own car dealership, its own high school. And Main Street had a grocery store, a fish market and a bowling alley. "Now it's galleries and photos for sale," he said with stereotypically dry Maine matter-of-factness.

Though the hotels and motels were full, on Sunday evening Stonington's drizzly waterfront was library quiet and post-card quaint. A "reduced" real estate sign on Main Street swung in the chilly wind. The Bangor Daily News in the newspaper box was four days old. A little old lady in a floppy fisherman's hat walked her dog below the historic Opera House, which now serves as a movie theater and performing arts center. A tourist couple in matching sweaters walked hand-in-hand past several antique shops and pricy seafood restaurants that once were homes.

I ate by the harbor's edge at the spacious Fisherman's Friend. Dozens of local families and tourists feasted on fresh lobster, halibut and $11 Stonington crabmeat rolls, which are nothing more than hunks of crab and a large gob of mayonnaise on a top-sliced hot dog bun. Nearby, in the little parking lot on Main Street that passes for Stonington's town square, two public pay phones stood side-by-side like relics from 1960. They had not been preserved by the local historical society. They were necessities. Cell phone signals still couldn't make it to the southern coast of Deer Isle, so landlines and public phones were as important to Stoningtonians in 2010 as they were in Steinbeck's day – especially to lobstermen coming off their boats.

Stonington was a rare place, an accidental theme park. But it was real, not artificial, and it wasn't prettified much for the sake of tourists. Its natural and man-made beauty was in constant collision with the tools and colorful junk of its lobstermen. Stacks of lobster traps and coils of rope sat in side yards. A fishing boat listed on a front lawn. A 1950s car rusted picturesquely in the weeds by the wharf. As long as hundreds of independent lobstermen lived and worked on Deer Isle, Stonington would never change or become too quaint to visit.

## Treasure House

My main job on Deer Isle wasn't to sightsee. It was to find the old Eleanor Brace house. I asked around Stonington, figuring everyone over 50 would know the famous story about the local woman who hosted the great author John Steinbeck for two nights. No dice. Eventually I learned Brace's place was on the west coast of Deer Isle, near Sunset, five miles away. On the way over something lucky happened. It was a lightly populated area, with the seaside estates and summer homes hidden in the pines at the end of dirt fire roads. The first human to show himself was a man unloading a John Deere lawn tractor from a trailer in the driveway of a big white house. I pulled over and asked him the Eleanor Brace question.

In a barely decipherable Maine accent that's no longer supposed to exist six decades into the Age of Television, Duke Shepard said he knew where the Brace house was and enthusiastically let loose a river of directions. They were precise down to the circular dirt driveway, the little garage on the right and the name of the current occupant, Brace's niece Brenda Gilchrist. Small island.

It turned out Shepard had taken care of the Brace place for about 10 years starting in 1968. He knew "Miss Brace" pretty well. She was an old maid, loved to sail and was alive well into the 1970s. Shepard, 59, was a Deer Isle native who lived in Stonington and had made his living as a professional caretaker for 45 years. His accent was so strong, I recorded part of his detailed directions – which he repeated at least three times – on my smart phone. When I told him I was retracing John Steinbeck's trail, Shepard said something like, "*Ahhh nev-ah ha-red* of Steinbeck. I don't *re-ad* many books." I read him what Steinbeck said about the Brace place from my desecrated copy of "Travels With Charley." He was thrilled. "*Ahhh* bet Miss Gilchrist would like to know her *a-unt* was in a book."

Miss Gilchrist, of course, knew all about her Aunt Eleanor being in Steinbeck's book. The retired art book editor from New York wasn't home when I politely crept through the pines to her house. But I was met by a young man and a woman being pulled up the driveway by two German Shepherds. I expected them to tell me to get the hell off their property. But they must have taken me for a prospective renter or a friend of Miss Gilchrist, not a trespassing ex-journalist. I'll never know who they thought I was, though, because they were French Canadians who spoke about 10 words of English and French is my 36$^{th}$ language.

Veronica and Dominick told me the owner was not home and they were renting the blue and yellow cottage in the pine trees that Steinbeck's agent Elizabeth Otis used to rent 50 years ago. Our mutual language and culture barrier worked to my snooping benefit. Next thing I knew Veronica and Dominick were showing me the inside of their tiny storybook love nest and simultaneously apologizing as they tidied up their bedroom and small kitchen. They had rented the seaside cottage over the Internet for $750 a week and were clearly pleased. By the time I took 20 photos and learned they had been living in French Polynesia and were moving back home to Quebec, a barking little dog showed up. "She is home," Veronique said. "She," as in owner Brenda Gilchrist.

I went across the lawn to the motherhouse and knocked and re-knocked on the front door. Brandishing my notebook as protection, I imagined Gilchrist was taking so long because she was looking for extra shells for her L.L. Bean shotgun. When the door finally opened I beheld a graceful gray-haired woman in blue jeans and a loose shirt exactly the color of my red sweater. Though I told her I was an ex-journalist, she invited me in. A sweet, smart, trusting woman in her late 70s, she fixed me coffee and gave me a tour of her green and gray shingled house, which was as spectacular inside as it was out.

Architect Alexander Wadsworth Longfellow, a nephew of the famous poet and Gilchrist's great uncle, designed the house in the early 1900s. Her maiden Aunt Eleanor willed it to her in 1977. It was a true prize, filled with old furniture and drawings and art. Sited close to the rocky shore, with a dozen big windows square to the sunset, it was as great a place to live as I'd ever seen. Gilchrist and I talked for an hour. She was truly disappointed to hear of Steinbeck's fictions and fibs in "Travels With Charley," but she took the news like an ex-book editor. She confirmed that he definitely slept in his camper during both nights of his stay at her aunt's house. She also explained a little "Travels With Charley" mystery.

Steinbeck wrote in the book that Eleanor Brace bought three 1½-pound lobsters in Stonington to cook for their dinner. But in the book there were just two people. The third lobster wasn't for Charley. Gilchrist said it was for a second woman, her aunt's friend Margaret. Steinbeck never mentioned it in the book, but her shy and very proper Aunt Eleanor – who was told that Steinbeck was coming at the last moment – was so terrified at the prospect of entertaining Steinbeck alone that she had hastily invited her friend to stay-over for a couple days.

Gilchrist spent many summers at her aunt's house and knew Steinbeck's agent Elizabeth Otis well. When Otis, who was tiny and elegant, rented the cottage in the pines each summer, she didn't spend her time sailing Aunt Eleanor's 16-footer around East Penobscot Bay. She arrived with a pile of books and manuscripts by authors like Steinbeck and Walker Percy and never changed out of her New York City clothes, including her high-heeled sandals.

Before I left, Gilchrist went upstairs and came back with a page from the memoir she was writing about her life on the island. "Steinbeck visits Eleanor in his camper Rocinante for a few days," she had written. "Theirs is an uneasy relationship: shocked by his profanity, she becomes increasingly proper. Charley drives Eleanor's cat, George, glowering into the woods, where Eleanor has to bring supper to her (George is actually a girl)."

Because Steinbeck described the strange gray cat in vivid detail in "Charley," and because he also thoughtlessly provided readers with directions to the Brace house, cat nuts from around the world began showing up at the door asking to see George. Serious "Travels With Charley" fans and crazy Steinbeck-trip-repeaters like me still occasionally appeared at Gilchrist's home, which wasn't as hard to find as I had thought.

Gilchrist let me photograph and video her place, but stupidly I forgot to ask her to pose for me. She was a lovely, warm and intelligent woman who treated me like a lost nephew and proved to me, for the zillionth time in my career, that the country is overpopulated with good people, not village creeps. I was sorry the only photo I took of her was when she was disappearing into the front door of her unforgettable home by the sea.

## Steinbeck Timeline

Wednesday, Sept. 28, 1960 – Deer Isle, Maine

*Steinbeck writes a letter to Adlai Stevenson, saying he "heard" part of the JFK-Nixon debate Monday, Sept. 26, and was distressed that both candidates were so courteous toward each other. He leaves Eleanor Brace's house in the afternoon and drives north along the coast on U.S. Highway 1 toward the top of Maine. He calls his wife from a grocery store, but where he stops for the night is not known.*

# Go North, Old Men

I was dead at the wheel. I had traveled only 130 miles from Deer Isle, picking up U.S. Highway 1 at Ellsworth and running up the coast. It was gloomy and rainy and then black and rainy. The ocean was there to my right, but un-seeable. Just long dark walls of pine trees and a string of depressing interchangeable small towns Steinbeck had passed through – Steuben, Machias, East Machias, Whiting.

Though a day ahead of Steinbeck's pace, I was not making good time. It was almost 10 p.m. I had left Brenda Gilchrist's home at 2:30, but stopped in Ellsworth for lunch and to buy a lightweight jacket at, where else, an L.L. Bean outlet. I lost more driving time blogging back to Pittsburgh after eating dinner somewhere on U.S. Highway 1. I would have stopped at a motel, if there had been one. I would have pulled off into a "wayside" or rest stop, if I had passed one. At Pleasant Point I drove into the center of town but turned back to U.S. 1 after seeing two cop cars and no motel. Less than a mile later a sign pointing toward the ocean said "Gleason Cove, 1.2 miles."

Following a hard dirt road down until it ended at a turnaround, I parked by some sea grass. It was pitch dark but I put up my blackout curtains so no one could see in. Discovering I had a Verizon cell phone signal, in the interest of Internet immediacy, I posted a blog to my Pittsburgh Post-Gazette site "Travels Without Charley":

> ## Sleeping by the Sea
>
> Gleason Cove, Me.
>
> Right now I am parked by the ocean not far from Pleasant Point, Me. It's not actually the ocean, it's the Bay of Fundy and the Canadian border, drawn somewhere in the water out there in the pitch dark, is not far. I'll not do any trick photography like I did in the Wal-Mart lot Saturday night, because I don't want to attract attention with a flash.
>
> I didn't see any signs that said I couldn't drive down here and sleep for a few hours – or the night – so I just did. I chose this road because I knew it led to a public access spot on the beach and because there is a Verizon phone signal, which means my Samsung phone's mobile hot spot will send this note all the way to Pittsburgh. … It's totally dark – except the glow from my laptop's screen – but I'm sure it's perfectly safe here.

It would have been very dramatic to have been robbed or murdered during the night, but I can't say that I was. The few local kids who visited my end of Gleason Cove Road turned around and left without setting my car on fire. I was parked all night where sand and grass met the sea in the extreme northeast corner of the Lower 48, not far from where the sun's morning rays first strike U.S. soil.

If the sun rose on Tuesday morning Sept. 28, 2010, it was news to me. Dawn didn't break, it oozed. At 6:15 there was no telling where the sun was. There was no horizon. The whole world was murky gray. The ocean could have been a pond. Sleeping on the "beach" turned out not to be so scary. It had been dark and lonely but safe as a Wal-Mart. And the Bay of Fundy's famous high tides didn't rise up and sweep me out to sea.

# Of Eggs & Books

We'll never know if Steinbeck stopped at the border town of Calais for a bed or a cup of bad coffee, but he had to pass down its main street as he drove north on U.S. 1 toward the top of Maine. Pronounced *callous* despite or perhaps in spite of its French origins, Calais is in Washington County, the state's poorest. Across the St. Croix River from New Brunswick, Calais was only 22 miles from my beach resort at Gleason Cove. Its economy was far healthier in 1960, according to one of the local "Down Easters"/"Up Easters" sitting with his wife at the counter in Karen's Main Street Diner.

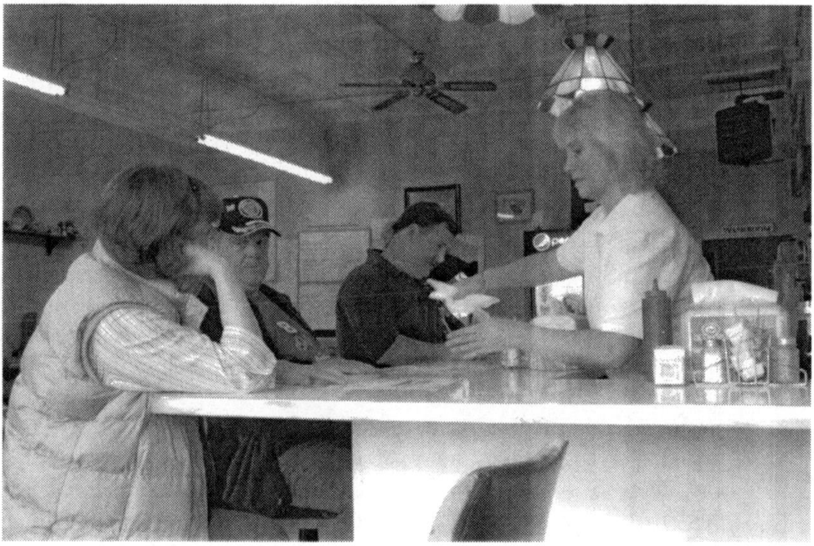

The 60-something man, wearing a pristine gold and black United States Army baseball cap, told a familiar story of change and decline. Hundreds of good-paying jobs had disappeared at the paper mills. Young people were leaving and would never come back. The town had lost 25 percent of its population since 1990 and was now about 3,100. Local unemployment was 11 percent compared to the state average of 7.9 percent. If it weren't for the fact that the department of homeland security beefed up the three border crossings with Canada after it learned one of the 9/11 hijackers entered the States at Calais, he said, there'd be even fewer jobs around.

Karen's had to be the best diner in a hundred miles – maybe the only one. A friendly pit stop for anyone following Steinbeck's trail into upper Maine, it's one of those priceless family-run eateries where getting a perfect breakfast is routine, not a matter of chance. I ordered what would become my signature breakfast for the rest of my trip. It was a #2 at Karen's – two eggs over medium, sausage, home fries, wheat toast and coffee. It cost $6.25 and became the standard against which I compared 25 others like it that followed. Steinbeck wrote that getting a bad breakfast on the road was almost impossible, and he was still right.

Waitress Traci Brown said the diner's owners, Karen and Lou Scribner, had been doing a steady business for five years. Their son Sean was the cook and daughter Caitlin the main waitress. Unless you went exotic and chose the fried fresh clams, you couldn't spend more than $9 on something sensible like a hot turkey sandwich.

Brown, a blonde in her thirties who'd soon be laid off, said her regulars included Ed, a man in his 80s. Ed came in every morning at 6:30, drank two cups of coffee at the counter and went out the door. Like other regulars, he kept his own coffee cup at the diner. "It's stuff like that that makes you feel so good," she said. "The diner's a part of his life. If he wasn't in here at 6:30 I'd worry about him." In "Charley" Steinbeck apparently didn't meet a single pleasant waitress like Brown on his trip worth mentioning. I met a dozen.

A few brick storefronts up the street from Karen's was something you'd never expect to find in Calais' corner of the world – the Calais Book Shop. Carole Heinlein, 59, was the owner/operator. She opened it around 2005 with the 8 tons of new and used books she trucked up from the toes of Florida. She grew up in Key West and worked for almost 20 years at various newspaper jobs in the South, including reporting. Unlike half the Maine folk around Calais who go south for winter or forever, Heinlein came north to start her own business. Unable to afford to hire any help, she said she was hanging on, running a semi-funky place awash with thousands of books of all genres. She originally intended to specialize in used books and Maine history, but quickly found she had to buy new titles too. A fresh copy of "Travels With Charley" sat two feet inside her front door.

It was "Banned Books Week," and Steinbeck would have cheered that annual fight by the American Library Association against censorship. Two of his greatest works, "Of Mice and Men" and "The Grapes of Wrath," were perennial victims of America's nuttier local school boards and professional bluenoses. The library association ranks him in the top 10 of most frequently banned authors. It's only a matter of time before his heavy use of the *n*-word in "Travels With Charley" attracts a modern wave of censors. Heinlein's friend Carol-Ann (below) pulled up to the curb.

A local newspaper reporter, she was either delivering or picking up a trunk-full of books, I wasn't sure which. I took her photo. But I didn't get her last name, her age, her address or her paper's name, which was pretty shameful for an ex-major league journalist. I think she may have actually lived in Canada. But she was a happy ambassador for what she called "Down East Mainers."

"We're very political," she said. "We're quirky. We talk politics. We talk hunting. Killing moose is a big thing. We go blueberry picking…." She didn't mention the regional traits I had noticed – that Mainers all wore hats, worshipped wood and had at least one exotic mode of transportation for sale parked on their front lawn. Carol-Ann said Washington County and the city of Calais voted for Obama, which was a surprise to everyone but maybe her: "We're independent. We change."

Part of the 2008 Obama electoral landslide, Maine was a Blue State. So was every state I'd been in so far. Though I was traveling through small towns and countryside that I assumed were populated by fairly conservative Yankee folk, I was deep in Democrat territory. I wouldn't see my first Red State on the Steinbeck Highway until I reached North Dakota and Montana. After that it'd be Obama blue again until Arizona, Texas and Louisiana.

Speaking of change and hope, Carole Heinlein knew she was going to have to build an Internet site and sell her books globally if she hoped to survive in her tiny market. Heinlein had chosen a tough path. She wouldn't call herself one, but she was a true entrepreneur, a risk-taker playing with her own money and life to make her living in hard economic times. Millions of women like her own and operate their own small businesses today, which is something that was not true in Steinbeck's time. Running a small business is never easy, especially solo. So far Heinlein hadn't made her initial investment back, but she was not about to give up. "I opened a bookstore in the poorest county in Maine – on April Fool's Day," she laughed. "The joke's on me. But I'd do the same thing again in the poorest county of any state."

# 7 – Touching the Top of Maine

*It isn't traveling to cross the country and talk to your pug instead of people along the way. Besides, being alone on the road makes you ready to meet someone when you stop. You get sociable traveling alone.*

– William Least Heat-Moon, "Blue Highways"

## Steinbeck Timeline

Thursday, Sept. 29, 1960 – To the top of Maine

*From wherever he stopped Wednesday night in northeast Maine after leaving Deer Isle, Steinbeck drives north into Aroostook County on U.S. 1 along the U.S.-Canadian border. He reaches the top of Maine, turns south on state Route 11 and plunges deep into the pine wilderness of Maine's interior. He parks alone for the night somewhere under a concrete bridge in the rain.*

## Fact Fudging 101

Aroostook County is famous for two things – potatoes and its enormous size. It's one fifth of Maine and bigger than Connecticut and Rhode Island combined. No one traveling north from Calais along the pretty St. Croix River would challenge those facts. I was 929 miles from Steinbeck's Sag Harbor driveway. Steinbeck drove the same stretch of U.S. Route 1 on Sept. 29, 1960, exactly 50 years ahead of me. He had a weird thing about wanting to touch the top of Maine before heading west, a weird thing he ultimately regretted as he realized how endless and empty the state was. Steinbeck also wanted to see the famed potato fields of Aroostook County, then the foremost spud-producing area of the country.

In 1960 families of Canucks were still crossing the border from Canada in large numbers to pick potatoes in the fall. Machines do most of the picking now, and, as with most backbreaking farm work humans once had to do, muscle and sweat have been replaced by brainpower and machines and technology. Aroostook's potatoes are still grown on about 400 farms and employ about 6,000 people in various ways. But the crop isn't what it used to be. Between 1928 and 1958, the county alone produced more potatoes than any other state. But when French fries became a major food group in America, Maine lost the national potato race to the Russet Burbanks of Idaho and the state is now in about seventh place.

Steinbeck noted in "Charley" that Maine's sparsely populated land already was being "abandoned to the creeping forest." Since 1960 Aroostook County has taken a big population hit, dropping from 106,000 to 72,000. To give an idea how big and empty Aroostook County is, its population density is 11 people per square mile, about the same as the Dakotas and 100 times less dense than New Jersey, the most people-packed state.

Though Aroostook is one of the most conservative counties in Maine, it too went for Obama in 2008. More pleasing to my radical political taste, the county keeps toying with the *s*-word – secession. Located at the very top of the state, far from the rest of what we know as Maine, Aroostookians feel a closer kinship to Canada. With a fifth of its population speaking French at home, some of its politicians have been proposing that the county join with New Brunswick or become the 51st state. The only dumb part of their commendable but hopeless plan is that they might call their new land Aroostook, which is unpronounceable to anyone not born north of Bangor.

Maine's size and desolation beat Steinbeck down. As he learned quickly, to his dismay, Maine's roads were long, lonely and rough. His ass already hurt. He had traveled nearly 1,000 miles yet he was still *east* of Sag Harbor. Though he had been gone a week and had actually been alone for only a few days, he was already feeling lonesome for his wife.

## Letters of Betrayal

Steinbeck's road letters to Elaine essentially served as the only notes he took on his trip. Many observations and opinions in them show up later in "Travels With Charley." But the letters, eight of which appear in the 1975 book "Steinbeck: A Life in Letters," betray that what Steinbeck actually did on his trip and what he said he did in "Travels With Charley" often were not the same.

What he did in Maine is an early good example. In the real world, after he left Eleanor Brace's front yard on Deer Isle Wednesday afternoon, Steinbeck spent only two more nights in the state – Wednesday and Thursday, Sept. 28 and 29, 1960. Nothing is known about where he stopped Wednesday night, just that it was on the way to Maine's rooftop. A logical guess is somewhere along U.S. Highway 1 around Calais, 150 miles north of Deer Isle. In the letter he wrote Thursday night, Steinbeck told his wife he had gone nearly to the top of Aroostook County that day and then turned south and went "in and way down" on what would have been state Route 11.

He told her "we are bedded down behind a bridge" in the rain, adding he thought he wasn't far from the New Hampshire border. The next day, Friday, he motored west on U.S. Route 2 to Lancaster, New Hampshire, which he had passed through going east earlier in the week. To build his storyline in "Charley," Steinbeck had to pull the fiction wrench out of his toolbox. In the book he switched around the two nights he spent in Maine. He wrote that he parked by a bridge in the rain on Wednesday night and then the next night threw a little after-dinner party in Rocinante for a family of Canuck potato pickers at a campground in Aroostook County.

The extended family of Canucks jamming into Rocinante is a favorite scene in "Charley." But like other favorite scenes in the book, it most likely never happened – certainly not in the protracted, theatrical way Steinbeck described. It's highly unlikely he could have made the 150-mile drive on Wednesday afternoon from Deer Isle to Aroostook County potato country in time to meet the Canucks and set up his little party. He obviously didn't entertain the Canucks with beer and brandy on Thursday night when he was parked under a bridge many miles south of potato country. So when did he entertain them? My guess is only in his novelist's imagination.

Switching two nights around or combining two nights into one, which Steinbeck also did later in "Charley," are petty literary crimes in a nonfiction book. So is inventing a character – or two. So is creating a composite character from two real people. Honest journalists never want to see facts fiddled with for any reason. But fudging reality for the sake of drama is not rare and it's not new. It's been done forever in movies and TV shows about real people and real places. And it's been done in nonfiction books since they were invented.

Most of the time these fictional tricks don't matter. But at some point they can squeeze reality and truth from a nonfiction book, leaving readers deceived or forced to guess which "facts" to believe and which to discount. And at some point "literary fraud" can escalate into charges of actual legal fraud. That's what happened with the "creative fabrications" in "Three Cups of Tea." The mega-seller by Greg Mortenson was touted by its publisher, Penguin Group, as the true story "of a real-life Indiana Jones and his humanitarian campaign to use education to combat terrorism in the Taliban's backyard." Mortenson sold nearly 5 million books, raised more than $60 million for his charity work in the remote mountains of Pakistan, passed himself off as a living saint, won nonfiction awards and became a Nobel Peace Prize nominee.

When "Three Cups of Tea" became a nonfiction bestseller in 2007, no one raised doubts about its veracity. It wasn't until 2011 when "60 Minutes" and other journalists fact-checked "Three Cups of Tea" – and traveled to remotest Pakistan –

that Mortenson and his self-serving lies were exposed. In "Three Cups of Deceit," author Jon Krakauer, a former supporter of Mortenson, did the most thorough job of discrediting the "nonfiction" book, charging that "Three Cups of Tea's" first eight chapters "are an intricately wrought work of fiction presented as fact." He also says "Mortenson has lied about the noble deeds he has done, the risks he has taken, the people he has met, the number of schools he has built." Otherwise, it was a true book.

Mortenson's fabrications did not only get him accused of literary fraud. Two class-action suits also were filed against him, co-author David Relin, Penguin Group and Mortenson's charity, Central Asia Institute. Some readers claimed they were bilked of $15 because they thought they were buying a nonfiction book and they weren't. And some donors who said they were duped by his book and his fund-raising speeches charged him and his charity with "fraud, deceit, breach of contract, RICO [racketeering and corrupt organization] violations, unjust enrichment and constructive trust."

Both lawsuits were dismissed, but Mortenson proved that "imaginative" nonfiction still pays big dividends for the authors that abuse it and the publishing houses that don't question it. It's also an indictment of the book-reviewing industry that no one questioned Mortenson's yarn. Or noticed, as Krakauer pointed out, that Mortenson described in detail how he went to a church in Calcutta in 2000 and knelt, alone, beside the body of his heroine Mother Teresa – who had actually died in 1997.

But exposing Mortenson didn't seem to matter to his publisher, the Penguin Group. A year after his story was discredited, Penguin – which conveniently argued that it was not its legal responsibility to check the veracity of its nonfiction books – was still hawking "Three Cups of Tea" on its web site as a work of nonfiction with words of high praise from Tom Brokaw, People magazine and the Washington Post. The introduction to Penguin's reading guide for book clubs still called Mortenson's fairytale "the true story of one of the most extraordinary humanitarian missions of our time."

## *Vive la* Potato Country

Cruising U.S. Route 1, taking for granted the beautiful bright morning and the fall colors of Aroostook County, I wasn't thinking about fact-checking Steinbeck. I was hoping to see a big potato farm – or big potato factory – or big whatever it is that potatoes come from these days. I never did. I did notice something else. Nothing I had passed since Deer Isle was in the process of being built or was obviously newish. No new houses. No new malls or crossroads or new chain restaurants that didn't start with "Mc" or "Sub." But then came the river town of Madawaska.

A metropolis by upper Maine standards, with 4,035 people, and proud to be the northernmost town in New England, Madawaska sits on U.S. Highway 1 on the American side of the St. John River. Leaving its business district I saw something I hadn't seen in 1,000 miles – a serious construction site with heavy construction equipment. Steinbeck noted a similar lack of newness on his loop through New England. He passed through villages he said hadn't changed in 100 years except for the paved roads and traffic. Half a century later, that was still true.

The previous night I had decided to behave like an adult and get myself a motel room. Since the alleged homogenization of America by national chains isn't happening in Maine north of Bangor, finding lodging was like it was in 1960. It was either risk a Bates Motel or spend another night in the Red RAV4 Inn. I threw the dice and used my cell phone and Hotwire.com to find the Aroostook Hospitality Inn in Van Buren, aka "Gateway to the St. John Valley and Canada."

The town of 2,171 is stretched along the St. John River across from Canada and was named after President Martin Van Buren. According to Wikipedia, 76.6 per cent of its citizens "are habitual speakers of French." I would have never suspected that disturbing fact from my overnight stay, but I trust homeland security forces in Washington are aware French Canadians are quietly colonizing the top edge of Maine. Lower America will know it's too late when Van Buren votes to change its name to De Gaulle.

The motel in Van Buren, pricy at $69, was a mom & pop of 1960s vintage with lots of un-corporate character. But it came with all the important amenities the modern Steinbeck ghost-chaser needs – strong Wi-Fi, plenty of 3-pronged wall plugs and an endless hot shower. After 2,400 miles tracing the edge of the East Coast all the way from Key West, U.S. Highway 1 evaporates without fanfare in the town of Fort Kent. As Steinbeck did, when Route 1 vanished I turned south on state Route 11 for the long haul back to New Hampshire and the way West.

Before I left Fort Kent, I suffered a shock that made me realize what a strange, atypical part of America I had been traveling through. It happened when I saw a black college student on the street. She was the first non-white person I could remember seeing since a pizza shop in downtown Northampton.

The 2010 Census tells the statistical tale. The previous three states I had been in – Vermont, New Hampshire and Maine – might be full of color in the fall, but year round their lilywhite populations don't look like much of the rest of the country. Each had black populations of about 1 percent. The national percentage was 12.6 percent. The same lack of color would be true for other long stretches of the Steinbeck Highway, especially from Chicago to Seattle.

## Route Without End

For some reason – maybe because Steinbeck said little about the road itself – I dreaded Route 11. On the map it goes straight through the middle of nowhere to nowhere. I had imagined running all day long through solid pine trees over a marshy flatland, crashing into a moose or two or being crushed like a fly on the grill of a logging truck. In reality Maine's longest highway was prettier, far more interesting and more enjoyable than foggy, flat U.S. 1 was on the Atlantic coast – until the sun set anyway. Route 11's two lanes raced over, around, up, down and through the hills and low mountains in deepest, darkest, woodsiest, least-populated Maine. There was virtually no traffic. No reason to go slower than 65.

Taking photos through my windshield of the green-red-orange-yellow forests and oncoming logging trucks, I began to suspect the wide, pristine highway was built either just to prove how unbelievably empty the middle of Maine was or to give logging trucks their private speedway. Other cars were rare as houses, farms and towns. Wallagrass, Eagle Lake and Winterville were towns. So was Portage, which along with 390 humans had its own lake in the middle of town, a municipal seaplane base and, if I did the math right, 1 resident who was not a Caucasian.

Steinbeck apparently saw more moose along state Route 11 than I saw people. The only moose I saw were silhouetted on warning signs. But I flew past things for sale that Steinbeck didn't see and probably would have decried as evidence of the materialism of spoiled Americans if he had. Snowmobiles, including four Arctic Cats still in shipping crates, were the most common outdoor toys for sale along the highway. But I could have bought a shed, a boat, a motorcycle or a refrigerator and had my pick of several pickups, farm tractors and riding mowers.

No one guarded these items, just as no one guarded the roadside pumpkin and firewood stands of Vermont and New Hampshire. Theft was deterred by the basic honesty of rural folks and the heavy weaponry they all owned, plus the self-policing logic of low-population density and geography. Tourists zipping by were too spooked by the wilderness to slow down and shop, much less steal. And if any locals swiped something of their neighbors' from the roadside, they'd have to go to another time zone to use it or sell to avoid being caught.

Route 11 took me longer than it should have. The weather and scenery were too fine to ignore. I pulled over a dozen times to take photos of sagging abandoned farm houses, long stretches of lonesome highway or the cute little rest stops that MaineDOT has cut into the pine and hardwood jungle. The rustic "waysides" provide more than quiet places for picnics or nature calls. When it dawned on me that I might not find a restaurant for a day or two, I pulled into a rest area to scarf down some peanut butter and crackers.

Greeting me were three empty parked vehicles and one person smoking a cigarette at a picnic table. After 10 minutes the mystery of the missing two drivers was solved when a middle-aged man and woman emerged from the flaming woods, went directly to their respective pickup trucks and drove off in different directions. Further proof of central Maine's chronic motel shortage.

On I drove. Peter Breslow, the NPR producer, called and we set up a time for Scott Simon to interview me the next day when I'd be in Lancaster, New Hampshire. I had my first face-to-face encounter with a human on state Route 11 when I drove through the sad little burg of Patten. I had doubled back to photograph a bush-choked old house on Main Street that was obviously inhabited when Steinbeck hurried by 50 years ago. As I got out of my car, a young woman stopped, rolled her passenger window down and asked if I needed any help. She thought I was lost, which it looked like I was. But I was just driving as if traffic laws didn't apply to journalists. When I told her I was chasing Steinbeck, she gave me a quick history of her town of 1,200 mid-Mainers.

The future didn't sound too promising for Patten. It owed its existence to the lumber boom of the 1800s and still relied on forestry, hunting, fishing and the wood products industries for a disproportionate share of its jobs. Before the woman drove off she suggested I take a picture of the Patten General Store down the road. "Why?" I asked. "Because it's going to be torn down tomorrow."

She wasn't the first woman in timeless/spaceless/changeless Maine to think I was a helpless man in distress. She was the fourth in less than 24 hours. The first time was in Calais. After I left Karen's Main Street diner and the Calais Book Shop, I stopped by the side of the road on my way out of town to write what I thought would be a quick blog item.

It was a pleasant spot by the St. Croix River, but mainly I wanted to take advantage of the sudden surge in Verizon's cell phone signal. (Three weeks later, when my wife got our bill, I'd learn the strong signal had been coming from across the river in Canada. Two days of cross-border roaming charges in upper Maine would cost $900. In Billings, Montana, I'd waste an afternoon at a Verizon store getting the charges reduced to zero.) I wrote a blog entry about Calais and its people while sitting in the driver's position, but because my laptop was on my "bed" in the back I had to twist around between the front seats to type. Because I am journalism's slowest writer, the blog, which was really more like a long newspaper feature story, took almost two hours to write.

The first visitor was a U.S. Customs and Border Control officer, who pulled up behind me in her patrol car. She had passed me three times and seen me in the same strange position, so she naturally thought I had a heart attack or had been the victim of a Canadian mob hit. Apologizing as abjectly as possible, I assured her I was fine and explained what I was doing. She was as sweet as any police person could legally be and with a smile left me to my pathetic, contorted typing.

Ten minutes later, I looked up from my keyboard to see two cars parked behind my RAV4 and a pair of women with worried faces hurrying toward me. They too thought I was dead or dying and were genuinely relieved, and not the least bit annoyed, to be told I was physically fine, just mentally challenged. I finally drove across the road to a parking lot, feeling like a jerk.

Maine people – Mainers? Manians? Mainsters? – of both sexes couldn't have been more pleasant and they obviously had been brought up to be kind to strangers. But it was comforting to know the good women of The Pine/Potato State were looking out for me. I'd meet dozens of other women on my trip who were unnecessarily sweet or went out of their way to help me – waitresses, motel managers, county government officials, mothers at home. Whether they were just doing their job or answering my fool questions when I appeared unannounced at their front door, not a one was sour or unfriendly or even wary. When you are old and scraggly and alone, as I was, you're an object of pity and a threat to no one.

## Destination Milo

The Aroostook County line finally appeared, but Route 11 refused to end. I watched a protracted sunset from a hilltop and small-talked to two overly serious photographers from Montreal who had set up their tripods in the tall grass to capture the glorious panorama. The middle of Maine feels even emptier when the sun is gone. It was dark when I pulled into Millinocket, the lumber mill town where the Pelletier family of "American Loggers" fame lived. After a surprisingly good spinach salad and a beer at Pelletier's crowded family restaurant/bar, I drove into the black night for the next significant town, Milo.

In the dark I covered a distance of 39 miles to Milo, but the road I traveled could have been a high-speed treadmill in a tunnel. As far I could tell, except for Brownville Junction, it was deep forest all the way. I took photos of the twisting road ahead as I chased its white lines at 60 mph, straddling the centerline through a narrow channel of trees. A few mailboxes flashed by, a house with no lights, maybe a river. My Sirius XM radio, cranked up extra-loud with jazz, cut in and out because of the terrain or overhanging trees, I didn't know which. I met my third car after 17 miles. In 45 minutes I counted 12. Steinbeck, who slept overnight in his camper shell by a bridge somewhere along Route 11, traveled the same lonely desolate way, but probably in daylight, when the local moose population would have been awake. Maine has 30,000 moose but I didn't run into one.

I passed through downtown Milo, a town of 2,400 in the dead center of Maine. Once a thriving railroad repair facility for all of New England, Milo earned its Wiki-immortality in 1923 when 75 members of the Ku Klux Klan sullied the town's Labor Day parade by holding its first daylight march in the United States. South of town I stopped for gas at the C&J Variety store. A true variety store, it carried booze, paperback books, pizza, live bait and Milo hoodies. Out front it even had a public pay phone, something Steinbeck would have appreciated if C&J Variety hadn't been a Studebaker dealership or whatever it was in 1960.

"Did you ever hear of John Steinbeck?" I asked the 20-something girl behind the counter when she came outside for a smoke.

"I don't think he lives around here," she said.

Too tired to laugh, I held my smart-ass tongue. I provided her with some context.

"He's the author of 'The Grapes of Wrath' and 'Of Mice and Men.' Did you ever have to read them in high school?"

Her face brightened. "Now that you say it, I've heard the name. I thought you were asking me if he lived around here." She wasn't the last person, young and old, who would not recognize John Steinbeck's name until I also mentioned his two most famous books, which most high school kids in America still read – or at least are still assigned.

I'll never know how close I was to a motel when I gave up. I drove another 70 or 80 miles south of Milo, trusting my GPS Person to figure out the best way to get from endless state Route 11 to U.S. Highway 2. My notebook from that night faded into scribbles and went blank. "Dover has a McDonald's .... Guilford, no business district...." For an hour I looked for a decent turnout or rest stop. On a long grade on U.S. Route 2, somewhere east of Farmington, Maine, I flew past a poorly lighted used car dealership sitting by itself. I hit the brakes hard, backed onto the grassy lot and parked at the end of a row of vehicles. With the nose of my RAV4 pointed at the road, I locked myself in, cracked my sunroof, installed my blackout curtains and instantly fell asleep.

Impersonating a used car worked flawlessly. Even with its cargo carrier, my RAV4 blended in with the 30 or 40 other vehicles parked on the lot. Trucks and cars and the local law hurrying by in the night took no notice. Up at 4:50, by 5:15 I was in the Farmington McDonald's sipping coffee, reading my email, writing a blog item and eavesdropping on four Republican geezers saying kind things about Sarah Palin that would offend and frighten most of my ex-colleagues in journalism. It was there that I discovered two reliable things about McDonald's that benefitted me for the next 10,000 miles: You can count on every McDonald's to have strong, free Wi-Fi that you can use for as long as you want any time of day. And you can count on finding a gang of 4 to 6 wise old guys in bad hats who will be thrilled to answer a stranger's questions about what their local world was like in 1960.

## Steinbeck Timeline

Friday, Sept. 30, 1960 – Return to Lancaster

*After sleeping in his truck, Steinbeck says in the book that he drives "long and furiously" all day Friday to get back to Lancaster, New Hampshire. He sleeps in his camper at a "ghost" motel/lunch counter by the Connecticut River because, though the office is open, no one is around to rent him a cabin.*

# Where Steinbeck Really Slept

It poured most of the 100 miles to Lancaster, which along with northern Vermont was about to be flooded with 4 inches of rain over the next two days. My missions of the day were to be interviewed by Scott Simon and to find out as much as I could about the mysterious "ghost" motel Steinbeck described in "Travels With Charley."

Steinbeck left behind some good clues about where he stayed in Lancaster and, as I would soon learn through the serendipitous ways of drive-by journalism, a mystery. He says in "Charley" that after a hard day of driving he arrived before sundown at a group of white cabins by an iron bridge over the Connecticut River. It was Friday, Sept. 30, 1960, the day after he spent his lonely rainy night by the concrete bridge in Maine. Steinbeck wrote a long, informative letter to his wife that evening. Sadly reporting that no one was around to share a drink with him, he summed up Maine as "a big empty place where people have been – and gone." He took two cheap swipes at Richard Nixon, who had been campaigning in Maine earlier that day. Then he wrote, "Tomorrow night I will probably put up at a motel for the sake of a bath and if I find one with a phone I will call you."

In Lancaster he also whipped off a postcard to his agent Elizabeth Otis. Maine was a "big, big place," he wrote in his pinched scrawl, "and lots of those lumber roads are lonely." As for what he'd learned on his trip, he said, "So far I have no ideas – none whatsoever. But I do get very tired. Perhaps it's from trying to take in too much." He closed with "I'm down on the N.H. Vt. line now and headed west tomorrow." The postcard was postmarked the next day, Oct. 1, in Concord, Vermont, 20 miles west of Lancaster on U.S. 2.

A woman I had met on my first pass through Lancaster had insisted that Steinbeck's ghost motel was part of a long-gone place on the Connecticut River near Concord. In a heavy downpour, I drove for Concord to check out her theory. It was almost time for my phone date at 2:30 with Scott Simon of "Weekend Edition Saturday." In the Smart Phone Age you'd think doing a radio interview would be simple and could be done anywhere. But NPR producer Peter Breslow had said cell phones were too iffy and I'd need a landline to ensure sound quality. On U.S. 2 in Lunenburg, Vermont, I stopped at the Lunenburg Variety Store to use a pay phone to call Breslow, who'd then tell Scott Simon where to call me.

Unfortunately, the only public phone in town stood wet and naked in the middle of the variety store's parking lot. It was more like a public shower, plus it had no phone number I could give Breslow. With only minor begging and explaining, I persuaded storeowner Mary Lou Ingalls to let me use her private phone – the one over by the meat slicer. I called Breslow and gave him the store's number. Scott Simon phoned me – and the call dropped. Twice. Simon and I eventually talked for 15 minutes. In a nutshell, I told him that 95 percent of what I had seen along U.S. Highways 5, 2 and 1 Steinbeck would have seen as well. Simon was as personable in person as he is on your kitchen radio. Two days later, when the interview would publicize my adventure on NPR from coast to coast, I should have been very pleased. But when I would hear it, I'd be disappointed and very annoyed.

After hanging up with my new friend Scott, I told storeowner Ingalls why I was headed to Concord. No way, she said. Steinbeck's ghost motel wasn't there. It was in Lancaster along U.S. 2, near the iron bridge over the Connecticut River. Where a sprawling RV park, gas station and truck stop were now. Back I went through the monsoon to Lancaster. The owner/operator of the Beaver Trails RV Park and Munce's Convenience store did not remember what her place looked like in 1960, mainly because she didn't exist then. She sent me across U.S. 2 to talk to Mike and Sally Beattie, who once owned the property. In her busy basement home-office I handed Sally Beattie my copy of "Travels With Charley" and asked her to read the passages describing the ghost motel.

That's the Whip o' Will Cabins, Sally confidently proclaimed. It had six small cabins, a little office, a larger house and a barn. Everything was long gone except one cabin, which was out in the swamp that was becoming a pond in the back of the Beatties' house/farm/business complex. The cabin had been moved across the road from the Whip o' Will site decades ago and was being used as a storage shed. I asked if I could check it out. Sally said sure, so into the deluge I splashed to take photos of a cabin just like the one Steinbeck said he didn't sleep in.

Sally Beattie wasn't done helping me. While I was outside she grabbed a phone book and looked up the numbers of three locals who could tell me more about the motel's history. The only person who answered his phone was Jeff Woodburn. He was a local freelancer, ex-politician, sometime social-studies teacher and rental property owner.

For months he had been working on a New Hampshire Magazine article about what John Steinbeck really did in the fall of 1960 when he came through the Lancaster area. I was afraid Woodburn might not want to share his scoops with a pushy out-of-town big-city journalist. But he couldn't have been more generous. Plus he dropped what to an amateur Steinbeck-hunter like me was a bombshell.

## You'll Need a Tie, Mr. Steinbeck

On one of his stops in Lancaster, Jeff Woodburn said, Steinbeck stayed nearby at the Spalding Inn, then a super-exclusive mountaintop hotel/retreat. Not only that, but remember the Adlai Stevenson-like Yankee farmer/political scientist in "Charley" that Steinbeck said he met in the White Mountains? Woodburn said he didn't exist. Neither did his farm.

Woodburn learned about Steinbeck's clandestine stay at the Spalding Inn by accident. Assuming that what was in "Charley" was actually true, he had set out to find the wise local Yankee farmer who discussed the geopolitical news of the day with Steinbeck. "I searched and searched and talked to a lot of people," Woodburn said. "I grew up here and have a lot of contacts. I should have been able to find him, but I couldn't find that White Mountains farmer." Woodburn was disappointed – and felt a little betrayed. "He built up this farmer on all bullshit. To me, it was a composite of several people." When he realized the local farmer did not exist, he asked on a local Facebook page if anyone remembered John Steinbeck passing through the area in 1960.

Several people told him the same story: Steinbeck had a room at the Spalding Inn. He didn't socialize and kept busy with some writing. When he tried to enter the dining room for dinner he was refused entrance. He lacked the proper attire, as they used to say at such stuffy old-fashioned inns. When he told them who he was, they quickly rounded up a coat and tie for him. Woodburn offered to meet me at the inn, which was owned by the producers of the TV show "Ghost Hunters," and in 1960 catered to the rich and privileged of New York and Europe. Over a beer in the dank basement bar of the otherwise empty and strange inn we shared our esoteric Steinbeck knowledge.

The Spalding Inn is high in the woods of the White Mountains about 7 miles south of Lancaster in Whitefield. It describes itself – without doing its gloriously old-fashioned character enough justice – on its Web site: "Surrounded by manicured lawns, orchards, perennial gardens and a 360-degree view of the Presidential Mountain range, it offers you the perfect escape from city life."

Despite its many un-modern charms and reasonable $140 per-night price, the Spalding Inn had only ghosts eating in its spacious and formal dining room. With leaf-peeping season over, there were more friendly employees than overnight guests. When Woodburn and I were led down a hall and shown a room the inn might have given Steinbeck, "The Shining" came to mind.

Months afterwards, back in Pittsburgh, I called Iris Glidden, 87. She was the Spalding Inn's owner's secretary in the fall of 1960. She didn't see Steinbeck herself, but said he showed up in a plaid shirt and expected to be able to eat dinner in the dining room. "The story is," Iris said, "he was told he had to dress properly if he wanted to eat. It's probably true. It was a very exclusive place for the wealthy in those days." She said Steinbeck had a dog with him and that it probably had to stay in Steinbeck's car (camper) overnight. Did Steinbeck definitely sleep overnight at the Spalding Inn? "Oh yes, he did," Iris said. "I'm sure of that. Only one night. He probably stayed through breakfast and cleared out."

Donald Spalding, the son of the original owners and operators of the inn, confirmed Glidden's account. He said there is no doubt Steinbeck ate dinner and slept at the inn during "foliage season" 1960. It's a 50-year-old story, part of the inn's rich lore, he told me over the phone. "I heard the story from my parents. He was traveling with his dog Charley and didn't socialize. He checked in, ate and kept to himself. He stayed the night."

Case closed. It's safe to conclude Steinbeck slept at the Spalding Inn during his "Charley" trip. Given that he made up his evening with the Yankee farmer, the best guess is he stayed at the inn Sunday, Sept. 25, 1960, on his way east to Bangor. Steinbeck wrote a letter to his wife from St. Johnsbury, Vermont, that evening but provided no clues about his lodging. He easily, and logically, could have driven another 30 miles east and checked into the Spalding Inn.

Furthermore, there's little doubt Steinbeck was at the Whip 'o Will Cabins by the Connecticut River on Friday, Sept. 30, 1960. He all but says he's there in his letter to his wife that night. In a road letter the next night – Saturday, Oct. 1 – he told her he was staying at a trailer park but didn't say where it was. He was probably somewhere to the west in Upstate New York, so he didn't spend that night at the Spalding Inn, either.

But it doesn't really matter what night it was. Jeff Woodburn had discovered proof of Steinbeck making up people and places and leaving out the truth. By the time I left the New Hampshire-Vermont border, I was operating under the assumption that everything in "Travels With Charley" was fiction until proved otherwise.

# 8 – Escape From New England

*... I cannot commend this account as an America that you will find. So much there is to see, but our morning eyes describe a different world than do our afternoon eyes, and surely our wearied evening eyes can report only a weary evening world.*

– "Travels With Charley"

## Steinbeck Timeline

Saturday, Oct. 1, 1960 – Upstate New York

*In the morning Steinbeck crosses the iron bridge over the Connecticut River on U.S. Highway 2 west, bound for the northwest corner of Vermont, Upstate New York, Niagara Falls and ultimately Chicago and his wife Elaine. In a letter written late that Saturday night, he tells his wife he had pulled into "this trailer park." He doesn't say what state he is in, but unless he drove only 160 miles that entire day and stopped for the night before he left Vermont soil, it had to be somewhere along U.S. 11 in Upstate New York.*

## Eating in the Dark

My prayers for a sign of neon were answered by a humble family diner in Nowheresville, New York. Actually, it wasn't neon that lit up my dark world. And actually it was not Nowheresville. It was Churubusco, which is on U.S. Highway 11 in the middle of Clinton County in rural Upstate New York.

I was hot on Steinbeck's cold trail. He left New Hampshire Saturday, Oct. 1, 1960, for points west. I did the same on Friday, Oct. 1, 2010, riding down U.S. 2 in heavy rain as it twisted through soggy green Vermont. Montpelier and the rest of the state had been pounded with 36 hours of rain. As I followed the gorged Winooski River I did a 60-minute phone interview with talk-show guy Bob Smith of NPR station WRUR in Rochester, New York. An angry churning brown snake, the Winooski scoured the bottom of every bridge and turned the lowlands into shallow lakes as it rushed to Lake Champlain.

In Vermont I had originally planned to swing down to Middlebury to interview Middlebury College professor Jay Parini. The author of the 1995 Steinbeck bio "John Steinbeck: A Biography" was up for it. But despite our emails and phone messages, when I was within striking distance of Middlebury he was out of town and I was hurrying west. Too bad I didn't meet biographer Parini. In 1997 he also wrote an introduction for a paperback edition of "Travels With

Charley." Though he pointed out its fictional elements, he treated "Charley" in the introduction the same way he did in his biography – as if was a true account. Actually, Parini tried to have it both ways. First he writes in the introduction that "the fictional aspects of 'Travels With Charley' are noticeable on most pages, the chief of these being the use of dialogue." Ten paragraphs later he quotes the cab driver Steinbeck supposedly talked to in New Orleans as if the cabbie's bigoted talk about New York Jews causing all the trouble and stirring "the niggers up" was a true and factual event indicative of the racist South.

Parini and other academics argue that Steinbeck's fictionalizing – i.e., lying – in a nonfiction book doesn't matter because he was telling greater truths – in this case portraying the extent of bigotry in the South. Of course, that "truth-telling" begs some questions. At what point do all the fictions discredit his book's value as an accurate and honest account of reality? And at what point do all those phony quotes from dozens of made-up characters in a nonfiction book add up to literary fraud? I wanted to ask Parini what he thought about what I was learning about Steinbeck's fictions and fibs, but it didn't happen. Six months later Parini became one of the Steinbeck scholars who told the New York Times my discovery of Steinbeck's serial fictionalizing and fibbing in "Travels With Charley" was no big literary deal.

Not seeing Middlebury College's campus was also a disappointment. My dad went there during World War II as part of the Navy's V-12 training program for commissioned officers. It would have changed his life and probably precluded mine from being conceived, but he flunked out after a year because he couldn't handle the calculus. Being a star second baseman on the college team didn't save him. He raved often to me about Middlebury's beautiful campus, which he never saw again after 1944. Since my dad died in 2008, I had been carrying his Navy dog tags on my key ring. When I got to the Middlebury campus I was going to take a photo of his tags somewhere really important – maybe at the baseball field on second base.

In Burlington, the sun returned from its vacation. I experienced my first serious traffic jam since Manhattan near the airport and whatever university all the kids in the bike lanes were attending. Bike lanes: That's something else Steinbeck didn't see in 1960. It took me a while to realize it was Friday evening rush hour. I faithfully followed the U.S. Route 2 signs through pre-1960 working-class neighborhoods in Burlington and through the squared-off rotary of downtown Winooski, where the enraged and throttled Winooski River looked like it was going to take out the bridge. Vermont was the same old story. Except for some new malls and offices on U.S. 2 on the way into Burlington, the Steinbeck Highway was as empty, rural and pretty as when its namesake saw it.

I crossed Lake Champlain on skimpily populated and barely developed South and North Hero islands. Under a cloud-filtered sunset I zipped past the islands' parks, marinas, farms, handsome/shabby old houses and pricy vacation homes facing the water. Just before the Canadian border, I hung a hard left and took the bridge to Rouses Point, New York, which was where Steinbeck crossed into Upstate New York and met the northern terminus of U.S. Highway 11.

Steinbeck plotted a beautiful if eccentric route for his circumnavigation of America. He stayed close to rivers, lakes and oceans and as far away from big industrial cities as he could. And he deliberately avoided the nascent interstate system, choosing instead what we and William Least Heat-Moon today romantically call "Blue Highways." The roads on the Old Steinbeck Highway – U.S. Routes 5, 2, 1, 11, 20, 12, 10, 101 and 66 – were the two-lane interstates of their day. They were what tourists followed, trucks ran on and the early commerce of travel clung to. The highways cut straight through the downtown hearts of cities like Rochester and Buffalo and became the main streets of small towns from Calais to Amarillo.

Except maybe in the boondocks and deserts, in 1960 there was nothing lonely or quiet or safe about the Blue Highways. They were often worn, bumpy, high-traffic death traps – narrow, shoulder-free, poorly painted and lighted. And they didn't have 24-hour rest stops every 13 miles where you knew you could fill up on gas, coffee and humanity when you ran low. Today the Blue Highways are much safer and smoother because most of their traffic has shifted to the interstates.

****

In the failing light, the land west of Rouses Point on U.S. 11 looked more like a hilly Iowa than New York. By the time I made Churubusco, it was pitch black in every direction. I was getting pretty hungry but I wasn't seduced by the garish light show pointing to the Pizza Barn. Minutes later my willpower was rewarded by a roadside apparition named Filion's Diner. Half of Clinton County must have stormed in and out of there for the Friday night specials – fish and chips ($5.75) and the hot pork sandwich ($5.95). A dozen unoccupied tables groaned under the inedible debris the diners left behind. At the counter, Nikole Patnode, 20, became my guide to her local universe, a universe she intends to stay in and raise her kids in, just like her parents did.

Nikole was in college, taking human services. Her high school graduating class numbered about 60 and half of them were leaving her land of dairy farms close to the Canadian border. She liked where she was because life was quiet and without the hassles of big cities. She said she knew all about the hassles of big cities because she had seen New York and Washington, D.C., on high school field trips.

After consulting with Nikole, I chose the pork dinner – real pork roast, real mashed potatoes and fresh green beans. Everything, including the pies, was homemade, basic and good. The meat was so tender and juicy, my Filion's meal instantly shot to Number 2 on my best-meal-of-the-trip list. The spinach and chicken salad at the Pelletier family's restaurant/bar in Millinocket, Maine, still held the top spot even though Scott Simon had ridiculed it. When he interviewed me, which seemed like a week earlier but had only been the day before, he asked what my best road meal was so far. I was stumped. I hadn't been chasing 5-star restaurants, I'd been chasing Steinbeck's ghost and eating pretzels and power bars for lunch.

Simon laughed in disbelief when I told him a simple spinach salad in Maine was my top meal. I couldn't remember how to pronounce Millinocket, so I knew my garbled and stumbling answer was never going to make it onto NPR's airwaves. But I wished I had said something cogent like, "Scott, it's all relative. When you're in the empty gut of Maine and you're desperate to eat something that doesn't have a wrapper on it or begins with 'Mc-,' a good spinach salad made by a family of TV lumberjacks is tough to beat." It was even better than finding a homemade pork dinner in the dark of upstate Upstate New York.

## Steinbeck Timeline

Sunday, Oct. 2, 1960 – Upstate New York to Chicago

*Steinbeck says that on his last day in New England he attended Sunday services at a white wooden "John Knox" church in Vermont. He can't remember the name of the town or church and gives no useful clues. It's highly improbable Steinbeck was still in Vermont on Sunday morning Oct. 2. More likely, he woke up in a trailer court in Upstate New York. Whether his mystery church was actually in New York or existed at all, only Steinbeck knows. Between the trailer park in Upstate New York and his arrival in Chicago about three days later, the only clues to Steinbeck's travels are in "Charley." He went south on U.S. Highway 11 to state Route 104, where he turned west, went through Rochester and shadowed the southern shore of Lake Ontario to Niagara Falls.*

# Midnight Suntans

I slept alone in Potsdam, New York. No other travelers or truckers shared the bright asphalt with me at Wal-Mart's Sunspot Inn. Up with the hunters on Saturday, I was flying down the road in the crisp pre-dawn. The flat land on both sides of U.S. Highway 11 was lined with prosperous dairy farms offering pumpkins and tomatoes for sale on the honor system. Occasionally I passed a collapsing barn or overgrown dead motel. The main streets of the slow-down-to-30-mph villages – Canton, Gouverneur, Philadelphia – were sleepy, unmemorable but healthy, despite the presence of nearby Wal-Marts.

U.S. 11 also cuts through the classic American town of Watertown. Like many New England towns I had seen, it was an important manufacturing center until the cruel deindustrialization of the mid-20th century. Birthplace of the safety pin and the Dulles Brothers of Cold War fame, it still has 27,000 people and a city park designed by landscape architect Frederick Law Olmsted. I didn't see the park. But an alternate branch of U.S. 11 led me through the kind of old-fashioned neighborhood they don't make anymore. Broad streets, sidewalks, handsome old brick and wood houses, mature oak trees. When Steinbeck plied those quiet, friendly streets, the neighborhood was already old.

Somewhere along Route 11, I stopped to listen to my interview with Scott Simon on "Morning Edition Saturday." Our 15-minute chat had been artfully boiled down to 3 minutes, which was a minute longer than I thought I'd get. It sounded NPR-good. I seemed rational and appeared to know what I was talking about. They had edited out all my "ums" and "ahs." I was pleased – how could I not be? A million NPR listeners would hear about my adventure and become future buyers of my book. But then I listened to the segment again on the recording I had made with my smart phone. Nowhere were the words "Pittsburgh," "Pittsburgh Post-Gazette" or "TravelsWithoutCharley2010.com." My hard-earned NPR publicity coup was largely wasted. I was just "a former newspaperman" from nowhere.

The whole point of getting myself on NPR's airwaves was to drive its listeners to my road blog. When I whined in an email to producer Peter Breslow, he said the missing information was my fault. It had been up to me to tell him beforehand I wanted to plug my website, he said, or I should have mentioned the site during my interview with Simon. I knew that was bullshit. Breslow was aware of my Post-Gazette blog. I had urged him to read it for background, though I had the feeling he didn't. NPR should have mentioned my blog at the end of the interview with me – not for my sake but so its listeners would be able to follow my journey if they wanted to. It was Radio 101 and NPR failed me.

But NPR's sloppiness/laziness didn't stop there. When it posted the transcript and audio on its web site NPR.org, there was no link to my Post-Gazette blog. I asked Breslow in an email to have NPR's web wizards add a link, which they did. When I finally got around to checking the link, a week after my road trip was over, I found it was broken. It was a link to nowhere. It's not that NPR's listeners actually would have scrambled en masse to my web site, but if anyone tried they were rewarded with incompetence.

For the rest of Saturday I glumly rode the sunny Steinbeck Highway through northern New York. Turning west onto state Route 104 at Mexico, I passed by Oswego and almost touched Lake Ontario before taking a spin down the central business district of what's left of poor Rochester. In 1960 it was a wealthy industrial powerhouse and the home of Eastman Kodak. Now it was a victim of globalization and the digital camera.

Like the previous 1,700 miles, the 90 miles of countryside under Lake Ontario from Rochester to Niagara Falls had changed little over the last 50 years – or last 100. Route 104 was rural, barely populated, shabby in spots but generally prosperous. The few eyesores only added to its character. Bait shops, antique stores, auto repair, welding services.... It was a super-thin strip mall/flea market – a long supermarket aisle for anyone who wanted to buy a pumpkin, a snowplow or an 1800-something farmhouse made of pink cobblestone, the road's locally "grown" building material.

## Steinbeck Timeline

Sunday, Oct. 2, 1960 – Niagara Falls

*Steinbeck writes says in the book that he planned to cross into Canada at Niagara Falls and cut across southern Ontario to Detroit. But a Canadian border guard warns him U.S. officials might not allow him back in at Detroit because Charley didn't have the proper inoculations. Steinbeck says he changed his mind and decided to go to Chicago by way of Erie and Toledo. First, he says, he checked into "the grandest auto court" he could find in Buffalo.*

# Your Papers, Please

Route 104 led Steinbeck and me to Niagara Falls, where he planned to save time by crossing into Canada at the Whirlpool Rapids Bridge and angling across southern Ontario from Hamilton to Detroit. Steinbeck was a world traveler and, though he didn't need it in those innocent days, he says in "Travels With Charley" that he had his passport with him. However, as he describes, he didn't have written proof from a veterinarian that Charley had his rabies shots. Canadian customs officers were OK with Charley's lack of paperwork and were happy to let him into their country. But they warned Steinbeck that when he tried to re-enter the U.S. at Detroit, American customs would make him first get fresh shots for Charley.

Steinbeck opted to skip his stretch in Canada and take the Buffalo-Erie-Toledo route to Chicago. When he returned to the U.S. end of Whirlpool Rapids Bridge, however, he says he was greeted by U.S. customs like he'd been out of the country 10 years, not 10 minutes. The border scene in "Charley" – whether true or, more likely, an embellished composite drawn from Steinbeck's many experiences at international border crossings – is an entertaining and accurate snapshot of the U.S.-Canada border reality then and now. Because my family has vacationed in southern Ontario for 63 years, I've crossed back and forth into Canada a hundred times on the Peace Bridge at Buffalo. I once faced the same annoying choice Steinbeck did and had to take our family dog to a vet before we entered Canada.

As he also showed, Canadian border cops were more welcoming and less officious than their hard-guy American counterparts. Canadian guards have always been more human and still were in 2010. They don't manage to make you feel like you're a smuggler, a terrorist or a welfare tourist who's sneaking into their country. Steinbeck milked the border scene for all its irony and humor. It also gave the New Deal Democrat a chance to impersonate a libertarian for a few paragraphs – to arouse what he called his "natural anarchism."

His annoyance at what happened at the border is more of a complaint about government bureaucracy and "the fine-print men" who enforce the rules than a resounding defense of the natural rights of man or a cry for limited government. But his experience caused him to write libertarian applause lines like "this is why I hate governments, all governments" and "I find out of long experience that I admire all nations and hate all governments."

My border crossing at Niagara Falls on a quiet Saturday evening was not nearly as exciting or humorous as Steinbeck's version of his. I had to use the Rainbow Bridge because these days the Whirlpool Rapids Bridge is reserved for people who commute to jobs on both sides of the border. Thanks to the hysteria of 9/11, passports are required to cross the U.S.-Canadian border. But I had no trouble talking my way into Canada without one. I told the Canadian border guard I didn't have it and explained what I was doing and why. I suspect she let me in out of pity. Or perhaps she sensed I was half-Canadian, since my mother was born there in 1917.

The border guard also cheerfully gave me directions to the Canadian end of Whirlpool Rapids Bridge. There a second equally charming Canadian border guard told me that if Steinbeck showed up with an un-vaccinated Charley in 2010 he would be confronted with the same dilemma. Dogless, I was immune to this requirement. After working my way through drizzly Niagara Falls I slept cheaply and well that night at my family's cottage on the shore of Lake Erie in Port Colborne, Ontario. I had wrung up about 2,000 miles since Sag Harbor. My trip was nearly one-fifth complete. The next day's job was to break into my own country without a passport.

## Home Free

On Sunday morning, hundreds of feet above the broad and deceivingly friendly Niagara River, the long line of traffic crept across the Peace Bridge until I had my one-on-one with an American border guard. "This is all I've got," I said, handing my fellow countryman my Pennsylvania driver's license. I expected to find myself hustled into a cold little room to explain what kind of un-American crap I was trying to pull.

"They let you in, huh?" the cool guard said, betraying how little respect he had for his counterparts protecting Canada. He looked me up on his computer and found I wasn't wanted for murder or felony plagiarism. Handing back my license, he said, "There you go, guy." That was it. No trick questions about where I had been or how much duty-free booze or smokes I was smuggling. It was one of my quickest and least irritating re-entries into my own country in years. It was not the heavy-handed response I was expecting – and secretly hoping for. I was hoping for a hint of post-9/11 totalitarianism – a search of my car, a search of at least one body cavity. I was hoping for some border excitement, like the time in 1987 at Checkpoint Charlie in East Berlin when I had to empty my pockets, take off half my clothes and watch a punk commie border guard rummage through my wallet.

Lucky me. It was Oct. 3. Steinbeck spent five days rendezvousing with his wife in Chicago and didn't get back on the road until Oct. 10, 1960. That meant there was time for me to kill a few days in Pittsburgh. I planned to continue matching Steinbeck's pace across the country as closely as possible until San Francisco and Monterey, where he relaxed for three weeks. Because Erie was only two interstate hours north of my house, I went home for some R&R. It was only a brief pit stop. I needed to adjust some things with my car bed and get the Bluetooth hooked up in my RAV4. Otherwise I was going to wreck while trying to unlock my smart phone every time someone called me. Hands-free calling also made it easier to take notes, check maps, drink coffee, eat pretzels, shoot photos and video and talk on the phone at the same time while doing 70 on the interstate.

Interstates may have taken the curves and joys out of driving. And I've laughed at Charles Kuralt's clever but untrue quip about interstates making it so you can cross America without seeing anything or meeting anyone. It's a quip he cribbed from Steinbeck's line in "Travels With Charley": "When we get these thruways across the whole country, as we will and must, it will be possible to drive from New York to California without seeing a single thing." But interstates get a bum rap, usually from people in Manhattan or DC who don't use them every day to save time and money. Interstates are blindly accused of causing suburban sprawl by car-haters, the smart-growth crowd and Big Transit interests who want everyone to ride a government bus or a bike to work and pack themselves into cities denser than Calcutta.

Our high-speed rivers of concrete aren't without sin. They shouldn't have been sent ripping through the downtowns of cities like Pittsburgh or Cincinnati or used as slum-clearance tools by local governments. They're also supremely hideous, which is what you get in America when government civil engineers are commissioned to build big public things with concrete. But since 1956 our boring, safer interstates have easily saved a million American lives and too much time and money to count. And anyone who's driven out West knows it's absurd to say you can't see anything from them.

On his way to Chicago, Steinbeck describes using interstates for the first time on his trip, or possibly his life. Sounding like an old lady stuck in the Indianapolis 500, he was tortured by the speed and flow of the intense truck traffic on "this wide, eventless way called U.S. 90," aka the New York Thruway, which he took from Buffalo to where it ended at Madison, Ohio. The thruway and the Indiana Toll Road, which he also used, were some of the earliest pieces of the Interstate Highway System, which in 1960 was 16 percent complete and barely existed outside major population centers. Steinbeck also had a practical reason for wanting to avoid interstates. His journey was "designed for observation," he said, not self-reflection or daydreaming. He wanted to stay "as much as possible on secondary roads where there was much to see and hear and smell."

Steinbeck preferred two-lane highways to interstates. He said he missed being able to stop at fruit stands or local diners. He didn't mention the small towns, traffic lights, deadly intersections, stop signs, blind turns, business districts, schools, farm tractors, stray dogs and 1,001 other hazards to life and obstacles to efficient car travel. Interstates eliminated 99 percent of them. Steinbeck didn't realize it, but statistically he was much safer dueling with "trucks as long as freighters" on those four-lane "gashes of concrete and tar" than he had been when he was touring the two-lane roads of New England. But he understood that the quickest way to his wife's embrace in Chicago was via the Indiana Toll Road, which he was happy to use.

Growing up in Pittsburgh in the late 1950s, we prayed for the interstate system to get done. Before the New York Thruway and I-79 existed, the 240-mile trip from Pittsburgh to our rented cottage in Canada 20 miles west of Buffalo could take 8 hours. How long it'd take the seven of us to get to the Peace Bridge was a crapshoot. It depended on how many trucks, farmers and pile-ups my dad encountered on clogged U.S. Route 19, which was the main street of a dozen small Pennsylvania towns between Pittsburgh and Erie, or whether we hit Buffalo just as 10,000 Bethlehem Steel workers were changing shifts.

My non-stop cruise from the Peace Bridge to my home in Pittsburgh, entirely via interstates, took 3½ hours. I saw many things Steinbeck didn't in 1960. I saw more woods and less open farmland. Ironically, the new growth of tall trees crowding the road often blocked any view of Lake Erie or the flat countryside of farms and vineyards. There was infinitely more development clinging to exits, where dozens of chain motels and 24/7/365 restaurants Steinbeck never heard of exist only to serve the nation of pampered travelers we've become.

I passed cell towers every few miles and counted a dozen McDonald's signs sticking in the air. In 1960 there were fewer than 100 McDonald's in the country, not 13,000 like in 2010, so I doubt if Steinbeck ever passed one. He probably would have griped about the visual pollution from the "new" stuff I saw, especially the commercialization. But as a tinkerer and amateur inventor, I'm sure he'd have appreciated the simple genius of rumble strips, which every day save the lives of countless Americans who fall asleep on interstates because they're so damn boring and safe.

# 9 – Pit-stopping in Pittsburgh

## Steinbeck Timeline

Monday, Oct. 3, 1960 – Somewhere west of Ohio

*Leaving Buffalo, Steinbeck takes his maiden interstate trip, driving 150 miles on I-90 to Erie and into Ohio, where the highway then ended at Madison. In "Travels With Charley" he says he picked up "the equally wide fast U.S. 20" at Madison and it carried him across northern Ohio "past Cleveland and Toledo, and so into Michigan." He describes camping overnight somewhere between Toledo and South Bend, Indiana. U.S. 20 almost touches the southern border of Michigan, where there are some lakes that might have attracted Steinbeck. No one knows where he really stopped, or if. It's a mystery night. But he was definitely not "sitting alone beside a lake in northern Michigan," as he writes. "Northern Michigan" was clearly a geographic mistake Viking's copyeditors missed.*

## My 1960

When John Steinbeck and Charley hurried past Erie, 120 miles to my north, I was 13 and living in a new housing plan on the edge of Pittsburgh's exploding suburban frontier. At that time Pittsburgh, aka the "Arsenal of Democracy," was still an industrial powerhouse, a clanging, crowded, productive city of smoke and fire and money that employed armies of unionized workingmen.

In the fall of 1960 you couldn't see the corrosion that would soon turn "The Steel City" into the honorary capital of the Rust Belt and cut its metropolitan population by 400,000 in 50 years. Miles of steel mills and manufacturing plants and railroad tracks lined the dead Monongahela, Allegheny and Ohio rivers. Deepened and tamed by locks and dams to serve as canals for fleets of barges heaped with coal and coke and slag, the three rivers were industrial sewers laced with dozens of bridges and squeezed by healthy blue-collar steel towns like McKeesport and Clairton.

The city of Pittsburgh, population 604,000, was the hub of a vibrant metropolis of 2.7 million people. It was a big league town in every way. Wealthy and important, a national leader in cleaning up its infamously smoky air, it was the 12th biggest TV market in the country. It had been built on the brains of capitalist titans like Carnegie, Westinghouse and Mellon and the muscles of waves of Eastern European immigrants. In 1960 it was the corporate home of industrial giants like U.S. Steel, Alcoa, Gulf Oil and Westinghouse. Its ex-mayor David L. Lawrence, who had just been elected Pennsylvania's first Catholic governor, was known as "the maker of presidents" for the way he used his clout within the national Democratic Party to help FDR, Truman and JFK secure their presidential nominations.

I was the oldest of five Catholic baby-boomers – Bill, John, Paul and Dan sandwiched around my poor sister Mary. We lived on Raven Drive in a dangerously dense Catholic-Democrat housing plan packed with kids and dogs that everyone called "Birdland." I was a B student who loved sports and devoured World War II books and news magazines.

I didn't know it then, but I was genetically and environmentally predestined to grow up and become an op-ed columnist. I was already a working member of the mainstream media, making $7 a week as an afternoon paperboy for the Pittsburgh Press, the second biggest paper in the state. I had 55 of its unluckiest customers.

My family wasn't rich or poor, it was ordinary and normal. We had just about what everyone else had in the homogenized confines of Birdland. Besides five kids, we had a working dad, a stay-at-home mom, a dog, a five-year-old $20,000 brick house on a quarter-acre lot, four bedrooms, a dishwasher, a station wagon and a power mower.

As a bonus, we had my Aunt Weeze, my mom's sister, who lived with us and worked as a secretary at Gulf Oil, one of a dozen major corporations then headquartered in Pittsburgh. Plus we had Elizabeth Taylor – aka Lizzie. She was our maid who arrived by bus from Pittsburgh's Hill District once a week and was paid $12 a day. Except for Nat King Cole and Sammy Davis Jr. on TV, Lizzie and the garbage men were the only black persons we regularly saw who weren't on a local sports team. The civil rights movement was of no importance to our lives and the N-word was heard often among my friends.

It was a great time to grow up. There were too many kids per family for parents to over-parent, so we were always outside, adult-less and free. We played ball of some kind every day after school in the crowded streets. We built our own baseball fields after the bulldozers graded farmland for more new homes. We rode our bikes as far from home as we could go and still make it back for dinner. We became professionals in petty vandalism. We shot cows in the ass with BB guns. We threw snowballs at the milkman's truck from Don Nelson's rooftop. We bought copper tubing bean shooters at the hardware store every year for Devil's Night, a secular holy day we faithfully honored.

My sainted mother Kathryn, or "Red" as my father called her, was a Canadian from Welland, Ontario. In 1960 she was helping me write 8th grade English compositions. She had gone to the University of Pittsburgh in the late 1930s. She was an English major on a journalism track but quit in her senior year during World War II to go to business school. She never learned to drive. After the five of us were grown, she got her first job in an insurance office in her early 50s and worked as a secretary until she was in her early 70s.

In the fall of 1960, while my mother was preparing to vote with enthusiasm for John F. Kennedy, my father Bill was preparing to vote with enthusiasm for Richard Nixon. A sarcastic, witty, likable World War II Navy vet who never had a bullet fired at him, my dad was a sports nut and politically incorrect long before the term was invented. At 40 he was a moderately successful stockbroker who worked downtown in Pittsburgh's bustling Golden Triangle. His income peaked at about $14,000 a year in the mid-1960s – about $95,000 in current dollars. That was pretty good money when newspapers were a nickel and a pair of low-cut Converse All Stars for one of his boys cost $5.

Unfortunately, my dad never earned that much in a year again because the owner of his small firm got caught charging discounted commissions for stock trades. Until the brokerage industry was deregulated in 1975, commissions were fixed at a high rate by the industry itself and charging consumers anything less was against federal security laws. A sweet government-protected racket for the broker community, it was similar to federal regulations that in 1960 prohibited airlines from competing for customers by offering cheaper plane fares. When my dad lost his broker's license and therefore his job, I got an early lesson in how existing businesses use government regulators to prevent competition, pad their profits and rob consumers.

In our universe of middle-class Germans, Italians and Irish, where diversity of any kind was noticeably absent, my dad stood out as an odd nonconformist. He was a well-read conservative Republican – the only open Republican I knew growing up. He loved Sinatra, Count Basie and Steve Allen and taught us all to revere Lester Young and Billie Holiday. He wore Bermuda shorts, played his jazz LPs full blast whenever he could and subscribed to an exotic biweekly political magazine called National Review put out by his superhero William F. Buckley Jr.

My dad never went to Mass but he sent us to Catholic schools. He never drank beer or booze of any kind but smoked a pack a day of Camel straights. He was a scratch golfer and excellent baseball player. He had season tickets to the Pirates, Steelers and Pitt football. He had hard, black-or-white opinions about everything. He hated Elvis, loved Mort Sahl despite his liberal politics. He thought "I Love Lucy" and everything else on primetime TV except news, sports and Buckley's conservative talk show "Firing Line" was so moronic he'd tell us we'd be better off staring at a blank wall.

A Brooks Brothers man, he'd wear only button-down dress shirts, three-button suit coats, khakis, black socks and brown penny loafers or cordovans – and so did his four sons. Our brains were shaped/distorted by my dad and humanized by my mother and aunt. Being a media junkie was his most important long-term influence on us. In 1960 he was bringing home three papers from work every day – the afternoon Pittsburgh Press, the Wall Street Journal and the New York Daily News. The Pittsburgh Post-Gazette, where I would work 30 years later, arrived before dawn.

He subscribed to the Sporting News. We had the latest issues of Time, Life, Newsweek, Look, the Saturday Evening Post and U.S. News & World Report in the house at all times. Every night, as we ate together as a family, Douglas Edwards and 15 minutes of the CBS nightly news blared from the black-and-white TV in the other room. My father provided the criticism and running political commentary. It's no surprise that every one of his kids ended up working in some kind of print or electronic media. In 1960 our house was noisy with his music, his radio stations, his newspapers and his opinions. It was also filled with hundreds of books. If there were any written by John Steinbeck, I didn't know it.

# First Impressions

Back home in Pittsburgh on my pit stop, I waited for Steinbeck to get to Chicago. I had retraced the New England leg of his trip in 10 days. That was almost exactly how long it took him. I saw part of the country that on average was whiter, less obese, more Democrat, richer and more likely to be employed than the rest of America was in the fall of 2010. I had already learned some generalities about America and Americans, at least the America and Americans along the Old Steinbeck Highway.

Speeding somewhere in Upstate New York I wrote in the notebook that was always on my knee that "America looks pretty good on U.S. 5, 2, 1 and 11. Richness and wealth predominate. People have tons of stuff – much of it for sale on the roadside. People take care of their houses – most of them. People cling to the water, like Steinbeck did, in their RVs, mobile homes, tiny cottages and mansions. ... People drive safely and sanely. People don't like to throw things away or tear down old houses or barns, no matter how slumped and sagging they are. People are inside their houses. People are friendly, clean and don't seem to litter much."

Those were my early drive-by impressions of the USA, but I could have written them at any time on my trip. What was true of the Eastern Time Zone would be true for the rest of the country. So far, I had driven virtually the exact highways Steinbeck did. But even with the help of dates and locations provided by his letters from the road, I often couldn't sort out what he actually did from the account he gave us in "Charley."

Much of his New England trip remained a mystery. We know he drove fast and furiously. We know he never really camped on a farm in the White Mountains. We'll never know if he really stayed at an over-sanitized motel, really entertained a family of Canuck potato pickers in Aroostook County or really had a run in with border guards in Niagara Falls. We have only his nonfiction book to rely on and it was unreliable, to say the least. The more I learned about Steinbeck's journey, the more obvious it was becoming that nothing in "Charley" could be believed.

## Steinbeck's Mystery Church

My sprint through changeless beautiful New England left me with a religious mystery – where was that "blindingly" white wood church Steinbeck said he attended in Vermont? In the book he describes getting dolled up and going to a church service on his last day in New England. He called it a "John Knox church" and enthused about the minister's fire-and-brimstone, God-is-going-to-kick-your-ass sermon. The scolding made Steinbeck feel bad and guilty inside, like a first-rate sinner whose sins were his own fault, not, as the "psychiatric priesthood" of the day would have it, "accidents that are set in motion by forces beyond our control." He was so "revived in spirit" by this booster shot of God-fearing guilt, he said, that he put $5 in the plate ($35 in 2010 money) and shook hands with the minister warmly at the church door.

Until I woke up and smelled the fiction in "Travels With Charley," I thought it'd be a breeze finding that white church. I even hoped to dig up the scary sermon Steinbeck heard. Because I was a 100-percent-pure product of a Catholic education, first grade through Villanova, I was taught little about Protestants except that I'd go to Hell if I attended their Sunday services or dated one.

I assumed "John Knox" was Steinbeck's indirect way of saying it was a Presbyterian church. So before I ever set tire in New England, and long before I realized every other one of its 1.3 million lovely old churches was white and made of wood, I called Presbyterian presbyteries in Vermont and northern New York to ask if they could help. The good Presbyterians of New England tried like hell but failed me.

After my tour of New England, his mystery church remained a mystery. I still didn't have any idea where it was – or if it ever was. That sly dog Steinbeck, I had come to realize, could have heard that sermon in a church anywhere and at anytime in his life. The only Sunday he could have attended a church service in Vermont was Oct. 2, 1960. But on that day he was already in Upstate New York motoring toward Niagara Falls and Chicago.

Initially, when I was being too soft on his fictionalizing, I wrote in my road blog that the "true" facts about the church didn't matter because the scene reveals something important about his religious psyche. But that was a rookie literary detective's mistake. What the scene actually reveals is how hard he was working to pad his nonfiction book.

There's another religious issue. In "Charley" Steinbeck wrote, "All across the country I went to church on Sundays, a different denomination every week, but nowhere did I find the quality of that Vermont preacher." If he really attended church every Sunday – and there's no evidence he did – he never wrote another word about it in "Travels With Charley" or in his letters. Was that statement about going to church each week another innocent bit of creative nonfiction or another white lie?

# 10 – Westward, Ho

*In my quixotic travels with Charley about America I paused five times, in Chicago, in Seattle, in California and twice in Texas. Then I saw and felt beloved people who knew me as I knew them. It would be quite easy to recount every moment of these steps but it would be out of drawing with the rest. A book has to be one thing, just as a poem does – or a chair or a table.*

– Cut from first draft of "Travels With Charley"

## Steinbeck Timeline

Tuesday, Oct. 4 to Oct. 9, 1960 – Chicago

*Steinbeck writes in the book that the morning after camping on private land by a lake along U.S. 20 in northern Ohio or southern Michigan he went fishing with the young man who had let him stay there. Steinbeck writes that at noon, "growing increasingly anxious" to meet his wife in Chicago, he climbs on the Indiana Toll Road and drives almost all night, arriving at the Ambassador East Hotel early the next morning. No one will ever know what he really did between Buffalo and Chicago or what he made up. He could have driven the entire 550 miles in one hellish day/night, or rented a motel room or, least likely of all, really camped by a private lake. Monday, Oct. 3, remains one of four mystery nights of his trip. In Chicago, Steinbeck's wife jets out from New York. Together until Oct. 10, they stay at the Ambassador East Hotel and spend at least one night visiting Adlai Stevenson at his farm in nearby Libertyville, Illinois.*

## Going to Chicago

I could tell the Ambassador East Hotel was in a really good city neighborhood because there was nowhere to park. Actually, there were plenty of parking spaces along the curbs of Chicago's Gold Coast. But you had to be a constitutional law professor from the University of Chicago to figure out if you could park for five minutes without being towed to some foreign country.

I had left Pittsburgh 24 hours earlier, picking up Steinbeck's trail on U.S. Highway 20 in Madison, Ohio. I originally intended to follow U.S. 20 through Cleveland, where it became Euclid Avenue. But the "fast wide" four-lane road that Steinbeck took through the city in 1960 was "fast wide" no more. I wanted to ride through the heart of downtown Cleveland to witness the damage inflicted by 50 years of bad federal urban and social policy. But the suburban traffic quickly became too thick and annoying. Though it was nothing any American alive today hasn't seen a thousand times, the malls and Target stores and Jeep dealerships on U.S. 20 would have appalled Steinbeck, whose sprawl early-warning system was famously sensitive.

When I pulled into a local Verizon Wireless store to get someone to unclog the email on my smart phone, I asked a businessman shopping for a new Blackberry if U.S. 20's traffic was just as hideous all the way through Cleveland. Worse, he said. Not only that, he added, they've got cameras at some red lights and U.S. 20/Euclid Avenue goes through "many atmospheric changes." Now that was a great euphemism for describing what I assumed was a sketchy black part of town. Based on that unintentionally frank local scouting report, I decided I had more important things to do than waste two hours crawling though the sad/mean streets of a city rustier than Pittsburgh. I jumped back on I-90, aka the John Glenn Highway, and did an end run around poor battered Cleveland.

When it was safe, I dropped south to U.S. 20 and went back to 1960 again. Large farms separated towns like Bellevue, Clyde and Fremont, which still had the highway as their main streets. Beyond Toledo, northwestern Ohio continued its spot-on impression of rural Indiana until it actually became rural Indiana.

I never figured out where Steinbeck might have turned off U.S. 20 and camped overnight along the Ohio-Michigan border. The book is a geographic garble about where he was and when. It could have been anywhere there was a lake, and there were plenty of them. As he said he did, I abandoned the rural desolation of U.S. 20 for the fast and busy Indiana Toll Road. In his day it cost 2 cents a mile in tolls and was not a private investment owned and operated by a Spanish-Australian consortium. Well after dark I ended a long day of driving at a unchained motel in South Bend, Indiana, narrowly missing the exorbitant $300-per-room rates charged for the Pitt-Notre Dame football game over the coming weekend.

The next morning, Friday, Oct. 8, I traveled 90 miles on private toll roads past Gary and into downtown Chicago – a rare thrill for a libertarian. Steinbeck says he drove the same route late at night. If that were true, he would have seen Gary at the peak of its fiery glory. The Gary I saw was, shall we say, looking kind of deceased. The elevated highway presented an amazing view of the shore of Lake Michigan, a vast petrified forest of cranes, smokestacks, monstrous electricity towers, furnaces, mills, oil tanks and esoteric industrial hardware that once produced steel in pittsburghian proportions. A wisp of white smoke rose from somewhere in the gigantic corpse. Somewhere out there was the Gary Works, which no longer employed 30,000 but was still USX's largest operating U.S. manufacturing plant.

It was an awesome industrial landscape, especially for someone who'd spent the previous 20 years watching thousands of acres of Pittsburgh's riverbank steel mills being scrapped and redeveloped into offices and shopping malls. Yet Gary was nothing like the hell-with-the-lid-off scene Steinbeck must have witnessed in 1960, when the city had 100,000 more highly paid citizens to tax and was world famous for turning out steel not Jacksons.

# The Chicago Way

I had cruised into the Ambassador East Hotel's dense neighborhood of brownstones and apartments with little trouble or traffic. I came via I-90 and the privatized Chicago Skyway, plus whatever other expressway the GPS Person said I needed. My E-ZPass handled the tolls. I felt no shame in using GPS. I wasn't on a serendipitous road trip, ready to wander off on a 100-mile tangent because I liked the looks of a river valley or saw a billboard for the Rutherford B. Hayes Presidential Center.

I had a route to follow – Steinbeck's. Most of the time that meant just following U.S. Highway signs from town to town, from Main Street to Main Street. For that I didn't even need a map. My Tom-Tom GPS Person and the GPS Robot on my smart-phone were invaluable guides through the tangled freeways of mega-cities like Chicago. I didn't have time to get lost, literally or figuratively, like poor Steinbeck so often did with only his state maps.

My parking problem at the Ambassador East was solved the Chicago way – with a bribe. Actually, it was a perfectly legitimate market transaction of the type that has made America the richest country in the history of Earth. When I asked the Ambassador's doorman where I could park for an hour without going broke or to jail, he looked across the street at my RAV4 and said, "Park where you are, I will take care of you." I can't spell out the sounds of his accent, the way Steinbeck and other great writers can, but it wasn't from Pittsburgh. Since I was parked in a spot at the curb under a sign that said it was reserved for taxis, I quickly figured out the unspoken business deal I had just made with the street-smart doorman.

Handing him my car keys without fear, I went inside the hotel while he continued doing his doorman's job – which meant loading and unloading luggage for guests, helping people open doors, helping scofflaws park illegally and pretty much doing the work of five men who were born in the USA. No specifics were discussed, no handshake or nod-nod, wink-wink was traded. But we both knew what would ultimately go down.

The Ambassador East was John Steinbeck's kind of place. Like the St. Francis Hotel in downtown San Francisco, where he would stay a few weeks later, in 1960 it was already the kind of full-service hotel they were never going to make anymore. Glass, mirrors, chrome, heavy dark wood, marble floors, marble walls, marble steps, marble elevators, a lobby with expensive furniture too heavy to be moved – it had character carved, soaked and burnt into its old soul. It was where the biggest celebrities, movie stars and cool guys of the era like Sinatra stayed when they came to Chi-town to party or pay respect to their mob patrons.

In "Travels With Charley," Steinbeck reveals little about his pleasant rest stop in Chicago. He spins a yarn about how he drove all night and arrived at the hotel looking like a bum before his room was ready. Rather than have him sit in the main lobby and offend their guests, management let Steinbeck wait in a room that had been occupied by a traveling salesman but had not been cleaned yet. Playing detective, looking in the wastebasket and under the bed for clues, Steinbeck does a CIS routine to recreate the salesman's evening of drink and sex with a call girl or girlfriend. Like so many other scenes in "Charley," it's too good to be true. In the book, the cheating salesman's name is "Lonesome Harry." In the first draft Steinbeck called him "Lonesome George" and provided some more specific information about him. He also said he considered sending the salesman's wife a note ratting him out.

Otherwise, Steinbeck drew a blackout curtain over his stay in Chicago. "Chicago was a break in my journey, a resumption of my name, identity, and happy marital status," he writes in "Charley." He left out details of his time there, he explains, because it posed a literary difficulty for him: "It is off the line, out of drawing. In my travels, it was pleasant and good; in writing it would contribute only a disunity." It was more than a "disunity," of course. Detailing his luxurious layover in Chicago, which also included a sleepover at Adlai Stevenson's nearby farm estate, didn't fit with the author's heroic quest to rediscover America, and he had to know it. In the first draft of "Charley" he also confessed that he "paused" five times on his trip – in Chicago, Seattle, California and twice in Texas. Viking's editors quickly deleted that incriminating line.

Steinbeck, who became lonely a few days after leaving Sag Harbor, writes in "Charley" that he was "delighted" by his four- or five-day rendezvous with his wife Elaine in Chicago. It brought him back to his "known and trusted life." Later, hitting the highway for Seattle with just Charley, he mentions how he had to get used to being lonely again. What he doesn't tell the reader (because it was cut from his first draft) was that in seven hard-driving days he would be ensconced in a gleaming modern motel in Seattle, waiting for Elaine to join him again and cure his loneliness for the next month.

When Steinbeck and Elaine stayed at the hotel, it still had an annex called the Ambassador West. The two buildings were connected under the street by a "secret" tunnel, which was commonly used by celebrities to duck the public, the paparazzi and the private detectives hired by their wives. The tunnel was closed, now that the Ambassador West had been converted into a condo. But the likes of JFK, who stayed at the Ambassador East when he debated Nixon in Chicago a week before the Steinbecks arrived, and Michael Jackson used it to their advantage. The night before I showed up President Obama had shacked up at the Ambassador West with enough security to take over Chicago. I was assured by an unnamed hotel source they didn't reopen the tunnel so the president could dodge the media and meet secretly with his old homeboys Bill Ayers or The Rev. Wright.

While I was talking to the desk clerk in the lobby a young woman with a big smile appeared next to me. "Are you Bill Steigerwald?" she asked. I was afraid I knew her from somewhere. But she quickly explained she had been reading my blog "Travels Without Charley" online for several weeks and had spotted me getting out of my red RAV4 with my big camera and Professional Reporter's Notebook.

Rachel Dry was a serious Steinbeck fan. She was also retracing his highway, or a portion of it. She and her mother were in the middle of driving a 1,500-mile stretch of his route that had started in her native upstate Vermont and would end in North Dakota. She was a friendly, smart, inquisitive Harvard grad, but a tad evasive. When I asked her if she was staying at the Ambassador, she lied and said she was staying nearby with friends. She also waited a little too long into our conversation before revealing that she worked in the opinion section of the Washington Post. Dry asked me to keep her name and her trip off the record and off my road blog, which I did. My discreetness paid off.

Six months later, in response to an article I wrote in Reason magazine, she wrote a defense of Steinbeck's fabrications in "Travels With Charley" for the Post. It was a nicely styled op-ed feature story. Her Ivy League education may have made her too forgiving of Steinbeck's factual misdeeds, but she fabricated no facts herself. She described our encounter exactly as it happened, confessing she had lied to me about where she was staying. She even called me "charming," for which she should have won a Pulitzer for nonfiction.

The Ambassador East was once culturally famous for its Pump Room, where big stars of every variety sat in booths in order to see each other and to be seen. The walls of the bar/restaurant/cathedral were still neatly plastered 20-feet high with 8x10 black-and-white glossies of hundreds of celebrities and power people dating back to 1938. The rugs were thick and the tablecloths white. The wood was dark and heavy and everywhere.

A relic of an age long gone, the Pump Room was closed for lunch. But the hotel general manager said the magic word and the heavy gate was unlocked so I could poke around by myself in the semi-darkness of a priceless time capsule that had only months to live. For 20 minutes I searched the walls for Steinbeck. He may or may not have had his mug posted there. But among the familiar faces beaming from the VIP booths were Reagan, Nixon, Sinatra, Steve Martin, Richard Pryor and Bozo the Clown. One of the few stars born after the Korean War was comedian Dennis Miller.

After I finished scouting the Ambassador East from marble lobby to marble 17th floor exercise room, I found the doorman out front at his marble post. As he handed me my car keys I slipped a tightly folded $10 bill in his palm. We both said thank you and goodbye. No harm, no foul. Rachel Dry and her progressive colleagues on the Washington Post editorial page would not have countenanced what we did. We probably broke 13 federal, state and city laws, but two consenting adults had engaged in a mutually pleasurable capitalist act. A voluntary free-market transaction – black-market-style, maybe – had occurred on the sidewalks of Chicago. As I drove off for my personal tour of Adlai Stevenson's former farmhouse, I felt the American economy perk up a tick.

Not long after I visited, the Ambassador East was closed, remodeled into an "urban-contemporary" hotel and renamed the Public Chicago Hotel. When the Pump Room reopened, all that was left from its golden days was its name and some old celebrity photos, which were moved to the walls of a tiny vestibule inside its street entrance. The old-fashioned hotel Steinbeck knew and loved had disappeared forever.

## Steinbeck's political superhero

Libertyville, Illinois, sounds like it should be the national headquarters of the Libertarian Party. It's not. It's where Steinbeck's political hero and pen pal Adlai Stevenson had his 70-acre farm. It's also where John, Elaine and Charley Steinbeck stopped for a sleepover in the fall of 1960. On a perfect sunny day, as the temperature neared 80, I went straight from the Ambassador East Hotel to

Stevenson's "gentleman's" farm in the horsey part of Libertyville. I had arranged to meet Nicole Stocker of the Lake County Forest Preserve, which owns the farm's current 40 acres, for a personal tour of the modern/Art Deco house Stevenson lived in from the late 1930s until he died in 1965.

Steinbeck and Stevenson were more than contemporaries and pen pals. They had several interests in common – liberal/New Deal politics, agriculture, dogs and the legend of King Arthur and the Round Table. Politically, Steinbeck was a Stevenson Man, 110 percent. He helped the former Illinois governor during the 1950s with some speeches and desperately wanted him to become the president in '52 and '56 and to win the Democrat nomination again in 1960. He was still pulling for Stevenson long after it was clear that his days as the Democrats' standard-bearer were over.

Stevenson's white, squared-off house at "The Farm" was simple, practical and smartly designed, with airy rooms, huge windows, a wild Art Deco bathroom and a long back deck looking out at the lawn and blazing oak trees that stretched to the Des Plaines River. The house had been restored for tours in 2008 and was used for meetings but still needed several rooms of furniture. Only Stevenson's study – the most important room in the house, Nicole said – was completely furnished. It had his old desk, his books and his address book – which happened to be opened to "S." Steinbeck's name and Sag Harbor phone number were there.

In 1960 Stevenson's place was still a working farm. He grew corn and soybeans, and had horses, sheep and a pack of Dalmatians, all named after characters from King Arthur's Court. He, like Steinbeck, lived relatively frugally for a wealthy man, but Nicole said a housekeeper and a caretaker were on the premises. One of Stevenson's near neighbors was Marshall Field, who owned a little department store in Chicago.

Many historic figures of the era came to talk politics with Adlai in his ample living room – from Senator Robert "Mr. Republican" Taft of Ohio to a young, ambitious rogue with the initials JFK. Nicole said the three Steinbecks probably slept in the guest suite, where Eleanor Roosevelt would crash whenever she dropped by.

Steinbeck says nothing in "Travels With Charley" or his road letters about his visit to Stevenson's farm, which is 35 miles north of downtown Chicago. Biographer Jackson Benson mentions Steinbeck's visit in his book. And a Steinbeck letter to Stevenson that I read at Princeton alludes to their walk in Stevenson's "blazing" woods in the fall of 1960. Exactly when the Steinbeck family stayed in Libertyville is not known and doesn't matter.

What is certain is that on the morning of Monday, Oct. 10, 1960, Steinbeck and Charley were back on the road together, heading north on U.S. Highway 12 into Wisconsin while Elaine was jetting back to New York. We know these facts because Steinbeck wrote to Elaine that night from a truck stop in Mauston, Wisconsin. It was the first of four detail-rich road letters Steinbeck wrote that week as he raced west to Seattle. It was their contents – ironically, made public in 1975 when Elaine chose them to be included in "Steinbeck: A Life in Letters" – that would betray Steinbeck's most egregious fictions.

## Steinbeck Timeline

Monday, Oct. 10, 1960 – Mauston, Wisconsin

*As Elaine flies back to New York, Steinbeck and Charley set out from Chicago in Rocinante for Seattle. He drives about 220 miles north and sleeps in his camper at a truck stop on busy U.S. Highway 12 in Mauston, Wisconsin.*

## An MRI of America

Driving, eating, blogging, driving, eating, I didn't make it too far north into Wisconsin on Friday evening. After leaving Adlai's Stevenson's house in Libertyville in late afternoon, I cut over to the village of Volo and hooked up with U.S. Highway 12, an official leg of the Steinbeck Highway System. Rush hour traffic finally disappeared, evaporating along with the suburban developments and malls. I entered a prosperous land of farms, lakes, YMCA camps and antique malls, sullied – some would say – by the occasional mini-mall, cheesy vacation place and new housing tract with a name like Remington Pointe. Richmond, Illinois, a healthy upper-middle class town of 1,000 near the state line, was closer to Milwaukee than Chicago.

Crossing into Wisconsin didn't change a thing outside my windows, except that U.S. 12 became four lanes. It was still mostly single houses spaced randomly among cornfields and woods and smallvilles like Cambridge. I noticed few motels, not that I cared. I was aiming at Wal-Mart store No. 2335 in Madison, where I arrived at 10:30 on Friday night. It was no Ambassador East Hotel. But my blacked-out berth was comfortable and warm and I didn't have to bribe anyone to watch my car.

It had been a big, long day of driving – South Bend to Chicago to Madison. Urban, suburban, exurban, rural, small town and college town – in just 250 miles I'd taken a pretty decent MRI of 2010 Middle America. Indiana, Illinois and Wisconsin, like every state I had been in and every state I was headed for, were noticeably much more empty than full, much more rich and white than poor or black, much more clean and green than dirty. The Chicago I saw was bustling. Even the highways were fast and smooth. Signs of the Great Recession I was traveling through were nowhere.

A few cars and a bus kept me company overnight in Wal-Mart's parking lot, which was lighted more humanely than the Wal-Marts of Bangor and Potsdam. I woke at 5:15. It was 62 degrees and sunny, the start of another fine Midwestern day. My smart phone informed me coffee and Wi-Fi were .8 miles away at a McDonald's, then told me how to get there.

My destination for the day was Mauston, Wisconsin. I hoped to find the truck stop on U.S. 12 where Steinbeck made his first overnight stop on his 7-day, 2,100-mile dash from Chicago to Seattle. Mauston was only 75 miles north of Madison. But because of a charming small town in the Wisconsin Dells and scary encounters with two political extremists I wouldn't get there until dinnertime. After escaping the streets of Madison and Middleton on U.S. 12, it was back to Wisconsin-as-usual – rolling farmland to the max. Nearly every inch of flat dirt was fenced for dairy farms or contoured for corn. Every perfect farm had a house, a barn, metal outbuildings and two or three tall shiny silos that could have been hiding ICBMs.

As the Saturday sun was coming up, I came upon an eye-catching photo-op. Two very aerodynamic roller-bladers in black were gliding in synch along a bike trail paralleling the highway. I passed the two women, then pulled over and ambushed them with my video camera as they pumped by me in their skin-tight suits. It was a cruel and sexist thing to do, and if I had committed it inside liberal Madison's city limits it probably would have been a capital hate crime. But the muscled duo was all smiles. Good thing, because they probably could have beaten me up for breakfast.

## A Scary American

Just north of Sauk City, as U.S. 12's traffic was becoming noticeably thicker, partisan Tea Party politics reared its ugly head. It started at 8:30 when I flew past a large homemade billboard in front of a John Deere equipment rental place. In all caps it presciently screamed "OUR PRESIDENT WILL PUT US IN DEBT BEYOND OUR WILDEST NIGHTMARE."

I doubled back to take the billboard's picture, but as I made my illegal U-turn at a rural intersection I was distracted by another photo-op and potential interview victim. By the road an older man in sunglasses was sitting on an ATV by a little shed with a sign that said "Campfire Wood." He wore a camo hat, a camo shirt and rode a camo ATV. If he hadn't been wearing those shades, I joked to myself, I might not have noticed him.

I parked, grabbed my camera and snapped off a quick shot as I walked toward him.

"You didn't take my picture without my permission did you?" he asked in a way that troubled me enough to make sure he didn't have a camo shotgun in his lap.

"No sir," I lied. "I just want to get a picture of your little shed."

For the next 20 minutes I asked questions and Camo Man answered them. Let's just say his name was Jim, so he doesn't come looking for me. Jim lived 200 feet off U.S. Highway 12 in a house he built in 1962 on 40 acres of flat farmland, which 48 years later was covered by neat rows of mature pine trees. From Google's satellite camera his personal square of Middle America looks like a green wool area rug surrounded by 40-acre squares of corn.

He had been a carpenter since 1953. He was the youngest of 13 kids. His dad was a farmer – not a big rich farmer, but "a regular farmer" who grew grain and corn and raised hogs and beef. An avid duck and goose hunter, Jim was uncomfortably believable when he said he used to be a tough guy who wasn't afraid to use his fists. His shed – no bigger than a freezer chest – was the only retail establishment for miles. He sold split and seasoned firewood on the honor system to campers and Sauk City city folk for $3.50 or $6 a bundle all year round.

"Most people are honest," he said, accurately summing up the human race, as far as I was concerned. "Ninety-nine percent are good. Some are losers. There always will be losers."

The extra money he made from selling wood Jim put aside for the education of three granddaughters who lived with him. Health-wise, he was a wreck. He had a heart attack and two days later had a stroke. Now, he said, "I've got a pacemaker and two artificial knees."

He spoke so slowly and coherently I had no trouble taking perfect notes.

"I've had my knees for 16 years. If not for them, I'd be in a wheelchair. I had five kids to raise. It's not like you could go on welfare right away, the way you do now. I've never had a credit card in my life and never will. We were brought up if you didn't have the money, you didn't buy it."

"How old are you?"

"Too damn old – 77."

I asked Jim if there was as much traffic on U.S. 12 half a century ago as there was that morning.

"In 1962, 12 cars a day came by on Route 12. There was no traffic on the road – none. This is Saturday. Weekdays are worse. Some days if you want to cross the highway you have to wait 10 minutes because of the commuters and people going to school from the countryside."

"Was it lonely out here in 1962?"

"It wasn't lonely then. It was just right."

Jim looked and sounded like a pretty conservative Midwestern guy – until I asked what he thought about the big anti-Obama billboard I had seen up the road. Then he started channeling an MSNBC talk show host on fast-forward.

"They're all money men. They're all Republicans. I was born a Democrat and I'll die a Democrat. If you're a workingman, you don't want to vote Republican. I belonged to Carpenters Local 314 in Madison for 55 years. Every time we had a Republican administration, we were out of work and starving. Once the Democrats got in, we had feasts. When the Republicans were in, we had famines. If they want to vote for those damn people again and put them back in, let them pay the price. It's the working people, the children – they're the people that will suffer. John McCain was a sensible guy. When he got tangled up with 'Motor-mouth,' I call her, and chose her as his running mate, that took all the credibility out of him. I said, 'You've got to be a fool to pick someone like her. She's dumber than a stump.' McCain proved one thing else to me. He's also stupid. How could he expect to win with a running mate not much smarter than that stop sign?"

Wow.

What a great American.

Steinbeck would have fallen in love with Jim's angry brand of workingman's politics. I didn't argue, I didn't agree. I scribbled and let him rant. Jim wasn't finished with Republicans.

"They've been fighting Obama since day one. Everything he tries to accomplish, they shut it down. John Boehner. He's nuts. They call him the 'Tan Man' on TV. He doesn't have too much between the ears. He's a typical Republican. We've got Republican politicians right now. Once they get a little power they'll try to abolish Social Security and Medicare. That's their main goal. Social Security has been a thorn in the Republicans' side since day one. I call them like I see them. If they don't like it, tough."

For a guy in camo with a box of shotgun shells in his pocket, it was a MacArthur Award-winning monologue. I had told him roughly why I was driving around the country, but he didn't seem interested and never warmed up to me. He didn't ask me a thing about myself or what I thought about Obama or the Tea Party or anything else until I was about to leave.

"Who's financing you?"

"I wish," I said.

He probably suspected I was being bankrolled by rightwing moneymen Rupert Murdoch or Roger Ailes. I told him I was paying my own way – with credit cards. He clearly didn't think that was too wise, but he held his tired tongue. I didn't dare ask to take his portrait, but wish I had.

Several hours later I would do something very stupid with my camera's digital memory card and wipe out the entire day's photos. When I had to retrace my steps 90 miles to retake the most important shots, I stopped and took a replacement picture of Jim's firewood shed. Not for a second did I consider knocking on his front door. A year and a half later I dropped the little yellow man from Google Maps onto Jim's corner of North America for a 360-degree look-see. Jim's shed was there, but not him – unless he was really well camouflaged.

Jim was a lucky random encounter – and the first angry Democrat I'd bumped into on my trip. He was politically intense and deeply grouchy, but he wasn't nuts. The guy I met wearing the "Obama '08" T-shirt two hours later in downtown Baraboo was nuts. Proudly. Defiantly. Publicly. Professionally.

## A Scarier American

Bob Oehner was sitting two empty stools away from me at the counter in Jen's Alpine Café and Soup Kitchen. I was innocently eating my usual breakfast of two eggs over medium. Outside, Fourth Street was already curb-to-curb with local farm folk who were pouring into downtown for the annual Baraboo Arts Fair. Bob was finishing breakfast, reading the paper and indiscreetly trying to make a date with Anna, the cute 30-something waitress who had recently cut her dreadlocks and quit her local realtor's job because the housing market was so bad. I don't remember how we started talking, but suddenly Bob was sitting next to me and we were loudly and seriously discussing national politics.

One of the few people I would meet on my trip who knew all about "Travels With Charley," and who had even read it, he introduced himself as "a poster child for all the good things the Democrats have done to save the economy." Democrat social programs – extended unemployment benefits and Cobra health insurance subsidies, mainly – had saved his life, he said, after he lost his job as a computer consultant 18 months before. He also proclaimed himself as "the meanest damn liberal in the United States."

Bob lived in South Chicago, where he was born and raised. He was 54, in good shape and full of life, big laughs and himself. He was in Baraboo to rock-climb at Devil's Lake and to play golf. I was relieved to be able to tell him I hadn't thought to bring my clubs on my trip. Bob, who said that on his first Halloween as a boy he dressed up like JFK, had been a political activist *in extremis* since 1968.

Five months earlier he had posted a live grenade on Daily Kos, the leftwing web site. "I have declared war on all Righties, Neo-cons, Tea-baggers and Libertarians," he wrote. After bashing Nixon and Cheney he dared his enemies to engage in either a "legit, in-the-ring" boxing match or a "Non-Contact Shouting Match," which he would have been a 10-1 favorite to win.

Bob hated Big Business and CEOs, who he said were really "Hell's Angels in suits" and/or psychotics who wanted "cheap labor, low taxes and no regulations." But what he hated most of all were Republicans. He hated them so much he currently was starring in several self-produced YouTube videos in which he ranted into the camera about Tea Baggers and challenged anyone to the right of Barack Obama's favorite college professor to a fight. He provided his phone number and email address.

In one video Bob – whose father was an entertainer who worked in resorts and was known as "Angry Al" – called himself "the craziest SOB you've ever seen." It was a boast Bob repeatedly proved to me in person. Though I had told him I was a libertarian who didn't like war-mongering Big Government Republicans any more than wealth-stealing Big Government Democrats, it didn't let me off the hook. He pretty much used me as a Tea Party/GOP punching bag for an hour.

He happily posed for photos on a bench out front of the Alpine Café, then tagged along as I made a quick tour of the street festival. Echoing several others in Baraboo, Bob insisted that I see Devil's Lake. He offered to take me there and even sketched a map of its best hiking trail in my notebook. "You can't go through here without going through Devil's Lake," he said, suddenly becoming serious. "It's very spiritual."

Tragically, the photos I took of Chicago Bob were among the victims of my camera-card disaster, so I had go to his YouTube channel to refresh my memory of him. His provocative videos do justice to his volatile persona, but he was a much scarier American when he was right in my face.

## Baraboo

Baraboo, the biggest city in the county with 12,048 people, was an interesting All-American town, albeit embarrassingly monochromatic. With a population that was 97 percent white, and with more Native Americans and Asians than blacks, it'll never win any diversity prizes from the NAACP. Its downtown blocks looked healthy and patriotic and its side streets were lined with trees and lovely homes.

Teams of wholesome high school kids were decorating its storefronts with cornstalks and autumn-themed stencils. It was creepily idyllic in a Rockwellian way. Of course, for all I knew, Baraboo was riddled with meth labs and brothels and as bankrupt as California.

The arts and crafts fair on Fourth Street had stalls hawking the usual handmade crap no one needs or wants, but it was fairly classy fare, not tacky. As a decent blues band provided the soundtrack, at least half of the county's populace sat in the sun on benches, checked out the artistic rocks, stained-glass windows and quilts on display or dined on bad food being grilled to death by overweight guys wearing Packers jerseys.

Baraboo used to be the home base and wintering headquarters of the Ringling Brothers circus, which became one of the largest circuses in the world when it merged with Barnum & Bailey in the early 1900s. Baraboo's Circus World Museum was closed but is said to contain circus wagons and other artifacts, plus the planet's largest library of circus information.

The other big tourist draw was the Al Ringling Theatre. A beautifully restored movie house built downtown in 1915 by Ringling brother Albert, it was designed like a grand French opera house with fancy drapes, plasterwork and a ceiling fresco. Like small-town movie palaces I'd seen in Trinidad, Colorado, and Lewistown, Montana, it had been faithfully restored to its original grandeur and showed Corn Belt-friendly movies like "The Wizard of Oz" on Saturday afternoons.

Half the town told me I had to see Devil's Lake, the most popular state park in Wisconsin. Ordinarily, I would have avoided a popular destination for the sole reason that it was massively popular. But I was writing a travel piece from the road each week for the Sunday Pittsburgh Post-Gazette, and I already had decided lovely Baraboo and Devil's Lake would make a good article. Created by glaciers and surrounded by cliffs as high as 500 feet, Devil's Lake is enmeshed in miles of hiking/biking/skiing trails and home to hundreds of campsites and two small sandy beaches. An old forest of red, orange and yellow oak, ash and maple trees hid a horde of people and the cars they had come in. If you wanted to be alone in that human swarm you had two choices – launch a kayak or other non-carbon-spewing boat or scale a cliff made out of some of the hardest rock on the planet.

I don't know what John Steinbeck saw in the Wisconsin Dells that was so "enchanting," but I sure didn't see it. It's a pretty place. But he saw less of the "Wis Dells," as the highway signs say, through his windshield than I did. The casino and the new massive developments on U.S. 12 weren't there in 1960. And he had no time to linger in Baraboo, visit Devil's Lake or ride the Wisconsin River's "dells" – from the French word "dalles," which means "a fast-moving stretch of water."

I didn't have the time or interest to do any of the hardcore tourist stuff, either. After my token tour of Devil's Lake, I headed north on U.S. 12, hitting a serious Saturday traffic jam and passing through a Vegas-like strip of garish theme motels, amusement parks and water parks that Steinbeck would still be bitching about if he had seen it. The Hotel Rome, a huge Trojan Horse, the Pink Flamingo, a fake ruin of the Coliseum. Everything was closed until next season, thank God.

The gauntlet of tackiness on U.S. 12 wasn't entirely new. Steinbeck said in a letter that the Wisconsin Dells in 1960 were "lousy with tourist places." In "Charley," with his usual contempt for the vulgar pleasures of the proletariat, he said the Dells' "dreamlike waterways" were lined by "the litter of our times, the motels, the hot-dog stands, the merchants of the cheap and mediocre and tawdry so loved by summer tourists." I'm no fan of cheap tourist hells like Niagara Falls, Atlantic City or Hollywood Boulevard, but I appreciate neon and outdoor advertising in all its forms. No doubt the Dells' strip looked better at night, but I got out of there as fast as I could.

# 11 – Into the Corn Belt

*"There are certain limitations inherent in our method, you understand that. Whole segments of American life are cut off from us. The life of business, the life of cities, of the well to do middle class.... In our contacts are we seeing anything but a fringe? Fringe people, fringe associations."*

– Conversation with Charley,
cut from first draft of "Travels With Charley"

## Steinbeck's Truck Stop

"This is what we called a 'skinny road,' " my new friend Bob Rose said. Bob was referring to U.S. Highway 12, the "skinny" two-lane road outside American Legion Post 81's front door in south Mauston, Wisconsin. Whatever Bob said about highways, trucks and what life was like in 1960 in Mauston, I believed. He had credibility. Not only had he been a truck driver for 47 years, he said he racked up enough career miles – 5 million – to go around the earth 232 times. I didn't check his math, but he had a commemorative pen to prove it.

Bob worked for Consolidated Freightways from the time he got out of the Korean War in 1951 until 1998. He was 81 but he could still tell me what it was like to drive every mile of just about every U.S. and state highway in the USA. He took aluminum from Oswego to St. Paul, cattle from Billings to Minneapolis and cast-iron woodstoves from Wisconsin to Pittsburgh. In the early years, he wore a collared shirt and a tie while he drove.

If Bob Rose said the truck stop/coffee shop where Steinbeck slept in his camper on the night of Oct. 10, 1960, was probably Ernie's Truck Stop, then it was. Ernie's is long gone now, along with the other truck-servicing businesses that flourished on U.S. 12. Until I-94 sucked the trucks off it in the '60s, U.S. 12 with its 45 mph speed limit was the main freight route from Chicago to the Twin Cities. Now all the truck stops are clustered at Mauston's interstate exits.

Mauston, a town of about 4,400 compared to 2,100 in 1960, was Steinbeck's first stop after leaving Chicago. He wrote a letter that night to his wife, saying, "I am camped in a cornfield behind a truckers service area and coffee shop." In "Charley" he mentions Charley's delight in finding piles of manure that had been cleaned out of cattle trucks. And he also says he walked to a valley and looked down at a sea of turkeys being raised for America's thanksgiving dinners.

I had found Bob and his wife Dona at the legion hall, where they had come to dance to the music of a country band called Shitz & Giggles. They both were born and raised in Mauston and had lived in places like Chicago and Minneapolis. Bob was retired and they wintered in Yuma, Arizona. After hearing what Steinbeck said in his letter and weighing their local knowledge, Bob and Dona agreed the place he stopped had to be Ernie's Truck Stop. Ernie Schmoker and his wife Anne ran it. "On Sundays we'd go there from church for lunch and pie," Dona remembered. "Anne made the best pies – all homemade."

The part about the turkeys didn't make sense to the Roses, though. A turkey farm was in the area in 1960. And cattle trucks would occasionally have to be hosed out at one of Mauston's several truck stops. But Ernie's didn't have manure piles and provided no view of the turkey farm. It soon would become clear to me that Steinbeck, employing his dramatic license, created a composite truck stop based on Monday night in Mauston and his stop the next night near Detroit Lakes, Minnesota. It was another harmless rearrangement of reality.

As the sun went down, and after the longhaired veteran leader of Shitz & Giggles sprinkled salt on the dance floor so the Roses and their gang could start their Saturday night fun-making, I drove over to the former site of Ernie's Truck Stop. It was about a mile south of town – where the busy and prosperous Brenner Tank Services operation was and where two-dozen tanker trucks were haphazardly parked. Behind Brenner's garages and offices was the stubble of a cornfield. It all fit. I took a few photos, drove through downtown Mauston on U.S. 12 and headed into the black wooded hills of central Wisconsin, where I was destined to find my fourth great American character in a long, long day.

## A Good American-German

At first I flew right past the Target Bluff German Haus. But realizing it might be my last chance to eat in a while, I turned around. A crazy mixed-up place on U.S. 12, it was an Old World German restaurant and gift shop that also rented bicycles for the Omaha Bicycle Trail. The dining area was busy, dimly lighted and loud with the voices of an office party that was starting to break up.

I sat down by myself near the buffet table, rubbed my eyes and ordered something embarrassing for someone with my last name in an old-style German supper club – a ham and cheese salad and coffee. While I waited, a large man in a long white dirty apron staggered out of the kitchen and sort of fell down by himself at a table. I studied him for a while. He was beat but still alert. “You must be the owner of this place,” I yelled over to him. He nodded. Before I could finish my next question, Rolf Kurandt waved me over with his big thick hand.

For the next hour, as we ate dinner together, he told me war stories. Rolf was born in 1934 in a small German town east of Frankfurt. “I saw Hitler at age 8,” he said in a strong German accent. “I sat on the top of a stepladder as he drove by. I remember it vividly. It’s funny how some things stand out in my mind.”

In the early 1940s Rolf’s father was drafted into the German Air Force. When the government seized his dad’s restaurant, Rolf and his mother and brother had to move out of the city to a village of 300. It may have saved his life. Though he could watch the sky light up from the Allied bombing attacks that pulverized and set Frankfurt afire, the war never touched his village. During the war Rolf lived in a nice three-story house. His mother rented a room to an elderly professor who taught Rolf and a friend how to make a phone from components dug out of the rubble of Frankfurt. Rolf and his friend spent a whole year building two phones. The other boy lived over the hill, so they needed phone cable, which only the army had.

"One day," Rolf said, "we saw German soldiers running wire into our village. We all knew the war was over. We found an empty spool, followed the soldiers and wound the phone wire on the spool. If we had been caught we would have been shot on the spot. Then we had to run the wire three-quarters of a mile through the oak trees. We got it into my friend's house and into his bedroom without his parents finding out. We hooked it up and it worked! It soon became known we had the only phone in town other than the grocer."

In 1944, Rolf's father, a food service officer, was captured by the Russians in Romania and listed as dead. "My mother told us, 'Don't worry. I know. I feel it in my heart. He will come home again.' Others in town said he was gone." When the war ended Rolf lucked out again. His village was occupied by U.S. forces, not the Soviet army. "I was scared shitless when the biggest black man stuck a rifle in my ribs and told me to go inside. I was 11." The U.S. soldiers were allowed to loot and trash the village, Rolf said. They threw beautiful furniture out of windows and made a big bonfire in the town square. But he lucked out yet again. Because the U.S. commanding officer chose his mother's house as his headquarters, its contents were spared, even the wine cellar.

A year after the war ended, Rolf's mother was still telling him his father was coming home. Everyone in the village thought she was nuts. "One day in the summer of 1946, my mother said, 'Kids, get up. I had a dream. Dad's coming home. I know it's true. We have to make the house clean before dad comes home.' All the neighbors got together and said, 'Oh, my God. The poor woman has finally lost it. She has grieved so hard and so much."

The next day Rolf's homemade illegal phone rang in his bedroom. It was not his friend, it was his friend's mother. "She wanted to speak to my mother. She said, 'Your husband will be at the bus stop in an hour.'"

Rolf's mother hadn't been crazy after all. His father had been released early from a Russian POW camp. Rolf's father looked like a skeleton. The Russians worked POWs until they were almost dead and then sometimes released them to show how humane they were.

"Talk about mental telepathy," Rolf said. "I believe in it until this day. That strong bond between husband and wife. That signal connected them." Nursed back to health, his father died in 1970 at 69.

In the 1950s, after one year of high school in Germany, Rolf took an apprenticeship to be a chef and immigrated to Chicago. He was about to return to Germany when he met a woman from central Wisconsin. In 1959 he married Lynnette Rawhouser and the same week they opened the Target Bluff Café and Esso gas station on U.S. Highway 12 in Camp Douglas, in what was then the poorest part of Wisconsin. A year later, when Steinbeck drove by – or perhaps stopped for a coffee break or a tank of gas – Rolf's café was selling only hamburgers, French fries and beer. He had no place for big trucks to park, but he pumped 27-cent-a-gallon gas, changed oil and cleaned windows for the heavy car traffic on U.S. 12. The coming of I-94 didn't hurt him, because luckily the Camp Douglas exit was built at his doorstep.

It took Rolf a while to drop the burgers and introduce real German food like *Wiener Schnitzel* and *schweins haxen*. His "Restaurant, Bicycle, Snack & Gift Shop" looked pretty busy and healthy to me. The bike rental business, which began when the Chicago & Northwestern Railroad line nearby was abandoned and turned into a bike trail, wasn't doing as well as he'd like. But he had done all right for an immigrant who never learned to write English.

As Rolf talked and I took notes, several regular customers came over to say hello on their way out. One guy handed him an old plaque written in German and asked him to translate it. Rolf was obviously well liked by locals and especially by his staff. They seemed to be taking special care of him. Maybe it was because his wife Lynnette had died a few months earlier.

Rolf had lost 100 pounds and was down to 210, but at 76 he still looked as solid as one of his restaurant's heavy wood doors. Before I left him, he guided me over to the pictures of his German village and his old house hanging on a wall. He had recently gone back to Germany to visit his parents' graves. Much had changed in his village during almost 60 years. His house had been converted into a small community center. But the stolen phone wire he and his friend had run through the woods when he was 11 was still strung through the oak trees.

## Steinbeck Timeline

Tuesday, Oct. 11, 1960 – near Detroit Lakes, Minnesota

*Steinbeck and Charley leave Mauston, Wisconsin, and drive northwest to Minnesota. They crawl slowly through the traffic of Minneapolis-St. Paul, cross the Mississippi River and pass through Sinclair Lewis' hometown of Sauk Centre, Minnesota. After about 430 miles, they stop for the night at a truck stop Steinbeck says was "not far" from Detroit Lakes, Minnesota, on U.S. Highway 10 about 60 miles east of Fargo.*

# A Digital Disaster

I woke up in the dark on the wrong side of the car. I had good reason to be a little cranky. I had spent Saturday night in another Wal-Mart parking lot, this time in a place called Sparta. I was moving at the same pace Steinbeck did but didn't seem to be getting anywhere. I was still in fricking central Wisconsin. By 6 a.m. I was back on the road, blowing through thin ground fog in total darkness. No one else was on the narrow state highway or living beside it. Cruising uphill on smooth fresh blacktop at 60 or 70 mph, wondering how many deer there were in Wisconsin, I had nothing to look at but three bright lines as they tried to converge into a vanishing point on a horizon I couldn't see and never reached.

My spirits returned to their normal teen-age levels near Black River Falls, when it began getting light and U.S. 12 appeared again. I whizzed through the village of Merrillan and out into a rolling land of corn and Christmas trees on my way north to Detroit Lakes, Minnesota, my next scheduled stop on the Steinbeck Highway. A few minutes past a "Fight Terrorism, Vote Republican" sign, I pulled over to take a picture of an ancient grey horse with his nose hanging over a fence.

Ooops. Major problem. Every photo I had taken the day before had disappeared from my digital camera. I had learned the tragic way that you have to format a new memory card before you use it or all your photos can dematerialize, which 134 of mine did. Devout Democrats Jim and Chicago Bob, the Good German Rolf, Bob the Ex-Trucker – their images and every shot of Mauston and Baraboo were lost to history. I had to turn around. I had to go back to Mauston, 90 miles south, and retake as many photos as I could.

When I came back through Merrillan again, I stopped for Sunday breakfast at the Merrillan Café. It didn't look like much from the road, but it was one of those priceless local treasures everyone says they don't make anymore in America but they do. Kathleen Sullivan opened at 5 a.m., every day, year round. Farmers, hunters, ATV-ers and the stray trucker were her customer base in a town of 585 – another 266 if you counted nearby Humbird. When I walked into Sullivan's bright and tidy eatery, her only customers were five burly, bordering-on-fat older farmers who were spread out over three booths. They were nursing coffees and arguing about football, moaning about taxes, discussing land prices and kidding each other the way only old friends can.

"If you paid your fair share of taxes, they wouldn't need to borrow money for a new school." ... "You're a better negotiator than I am." ... "You're all right. You know all the angles."

A guy they all knew – but obviously not a farmer – strolled in and sat down. He had seriously white long hair bunched at his shoulders. A white fu Manchu moustache. Tattoos on both biceps and forearms. A floppy hat. His black T-shirt – cut to the armpits – read "Born a genius. Slacker by choice." You would have thought the least-stereotypical guy in the Corn Belt had come in to discuss the latest news about Harley Davidson, Led Zeppelin or hemp deregulation, but he wanted to talk about something truly important – Wisconsin Badger football.

In the time it took to eat my perfect breakfast of two eggs over medium, sausage and home fries, four young studs came in, plus two duck hunters in camo and a middle-aged couple in church clothes. The Merrillan Café was a two-woman operation, but Beverly the waitress handled the rush with ease. She ran from table to table taking orders, delivering plates, refilling coffee cups and praising her boss Kathleen's work ethic. "She pulls off miracles on that grill every day. She does it all." Before leaving I invaded Kathleen's cramped kitchen and found the miracle worker in a do-rag, apron and Chicago Bears shirt. I explained myself, asked the usual nosy questions and took pictures. I had no fear Kathleen might do what she had every right to do – tell me to get the hell out of her kitchen or hit me with something sharp. She was too busy feeding Merrillan.

****

I spent much of my Sunday backtracking to Devil's Lake, Baraboo and Mauston. Using the interstate helped. Devil's Lake was just as nuts with people as it had been Saturday, but the arts fair had disappeared without a trace from downtown Baraboo. It was already 5 p.m. by the time I returned to the German Haus to take a better photo of my old friend Rolf standing in his parking lot. In time I hit U.S. 10. It was still a major highway in Steinbeck's day, stretching from Detroit to Seattle, but now it vanishes at Fargo. For several hours I squinted into the setting sun as I passed scores of large farms that have separated U.S. 10 towns like Strum and Durand and Plum City for a hundred years. Chasing a spectacular sun fall, I crossed the Mississippi River in the dark and checked in to a Super 8 motel in St. Paul, Minnesota. Only a 300-mile day, it seemed like 3,000.

After two peaceful, lonely nights in a row in bright, vacant, secure Wal-Mart parking lots, I was terrified by all the human activity at the Super 8. Its commercial neighborhood had too many shadows. So did its jammed parking lot. I was afraid my RAV4 would be stolen or molested before I fell asleep. The motel's younger customer base and a few shifty characters lurking outside also made me nervous. So did, paradoxically, the visit of a St. Paul Police Department cop. He sat in the parking lot for half an hour with his front door open, patiently questioning an unhappy young pregnant black woman. It turned out I had nothing to fear. My car was fine in the morning. I had been silly and paranoid. Spending too much time in the white-Anglo-Saxon-Protestant-Republican sticks of Wisconsin will do that.

# Clean Republican Politics

Tooling along U.S. 10 the next morning, I looked over and saw a steep grassy knoll covered from top to bottom with campaign signs aimed at the freeway traffic. You'd think I would have had my fill of partisan politics after my encounters in Greater Baraboo. But this was the congressional domain of Michele Bachmann, future failed presidential aspirant, bane of Rachel Maddow and Keith Olbermann, Tea Party heroine of Sean Hannity and the entire Fox News Network.

Pulling off at the next exit, I found two men on the hill repairing campaign signs that had been knocked down the night before. Andy Anderson was attaching signs to the rebar that once held them up. As a newsman, I immediately suspected dirty politics. But Anderson, a veteran of election wars, had no doubt it was just the work of rowdy kids, not party operatives. "It's seldom the other party," he assured me. "Everyone respects each other's signs." Anderson was 68. He owned an auto-repair place nearby, cleverly named Andy's Service. Though he was a conservative Republican, he was re-assembling every fallen sign irrespective of political party "because it was the right thing to do."

No question about it, I was in the Corn Belt.

The other Republican, Pat Walker, was on the scene for a less communitarian reason. Some of the signs lying flat on the grass had his name on them. "I'm the Blimp Man,' " he said, standing up his "Elect Pat Walker" for council sign, which had a blimp on it and the slogan "A Common Man With Common Sense." A contractor, Walker was running for a council seat in Anoka, a city of 18,000 that was designated "The Halloween Capital of the World" by Congress in 1937 because it held one of the world's first Halloween parades in 1920.

It wasn't long before Walker introduced himself to Anderson. Walker quickly established that their ideological Venn diagrams overlapped very well. He declared to Anderson and the visiting out-of-town media (me) that, "I'm a conservative. I'm pro-life and pro-Second Amendment. I love my gun rights." True to his individualistic principles, Walker fixed his own team's signs first. But then he too began setting up downed Democrat signs. His spirit of bipartisan fair play made me want to cry or call Keith Olbermann.

A long time Republican activist making his first try for office, Walker confidently predicted victory in three weeks, but he would be disappointed. When I asked him where a good local diner was, he made sure I would find Sparky's Cafe by leading me across town in his brown contractor's truck. If I lived in Anoka, and if I believed in Republicans, and if I believed in voting, I'd have given Walker mine.

In "Travels With Charley" Steinbeck said he had carefully planned his route through the Twin Cities so that he'd cross the Mississippi River three times. He also wanted to drive through Golden Valley, a city west of Minneapolis, which he said had drawn his attention with its name. Instead he got swept up in "a river of trucks." He never saw the Twin Cities, the Mississippi or Golden Valley, where General Mills' world headquarters were located.

Steinbeck eventually found himself again on U.S. 10 north. In "Charley," when he asks a waitress for directions to Sauk Centre, the hometown of Sinclair Lewis, she ridicules him for getting lost in a place she knew so well. Steinbeck paints the waitress and the cook in the restaurant to be seriously grammar-challenged, stupid and not nice or likable. Maybe Steinbeck had a natural knack for pissing off common people. Or he may have created or embellished the scene to generate some laughs or tension or to show off his dialogue skills. All I know is, his series of unpleasant encounters with everyday people resembled nothing like mine. After my unpleasant brush with the Village Creep of Sag Harbor, no one, repeat, no one, showed me anything but kindness and helpfulness.

## Sauk Centre's Favorite Dead Son

Steinbeck ultimately made it to Sauk Centre the same way I did – by turning off U.S. 10 and running up U.S. Route 52. He was making a side trip because he was curious to see how his old pal Sinclair Lewis had been treated by his hometown after he died. Lewis' big early books, "Main Street" and "Babbitt," were uncomplimentary fictionalizations of the folks of Sauk Centre, especially businessmen. Though he turned out so many hits in the 1920s that he became the first American to win the Nobel Prize in Literature in 1930, Lewis was not declared a local hero until he was safely dead, as Steinbeck wryly noted. Then Sauk Centre's city fathers started naming streets after Lewis and using his name to draw tourists.

By 1960 Steinbeck already knew his own fame was going to be exploited in the same way by his hometown Salinas. "Cannery Row" and "East of Eden" were works of fiction clearly written about real people and places in Monterey County. They didn't exactly flatter the local folks or the power brokers, who were conservative Republican businessmen and not at all appreciative of Steinbeck's sympathies for the New Deal, unions and migrants from Mexico or the Dust Bowl. "The Grapes of Wrath," though set 200 miles south in Kern County at the bottom of the Great Central Valley, was publicly burned in Salinas only months after it came out in 1939.

No matter how world-famous Steinbeck had become, by 1960 he had not been honored as a homegrown hero. He knew after he died he'd be rehabilitated as a "good" writer by his hometown, like Lewis did. In fact, the process that would lead to the creation of "Steinbeck Country" had already started in Monterey, where the city had renamed Ocean View Avenue "Cannery Row."

Based on my quick spin around Sauk Centre, Sinclair Lewis didn't seem to have much to complain about. It well may have had some slimy civic boosters in Lewis' day, but the town of 4,300 Middle Americans looked ideal to me. Sleeping in the sun, the business district had broad streets, old brick storefronts, a restored movie theater and a visible pulse but few humans. The tallest buildings in town were churches.

The tiny homes on Original Main Street were priced way under $100,000, a guy living in one told me. Even two-story beauties were in the $150,000 range. Residential streets like the one where Lewis' home is preserved were lined with tidy wood-frame homes on tree-shaded lots and laid out in a grid of square blocks bordered with sidewalks. You could buy one for $120,000. Sauk Centre was another of those livable, lovable, walkable, affordable late-1800s dream-towns that today's New Urbanists try to recreate from scratch but never can.

I've forgotten what local crimes and hypocrisies Lewis was all worked up about in his anti-capitalist books. But decrying them made him a very rich and world-famous writer and gave Sauk Centre something to be known for besides being a model of Midwestern town planning. Steinbeck ended up blowing right through Sauk Centre. I was in a hurry too. I didn't have time to visit the Sinclair Lewis Boyhood Home on Sinclair Lewis Avenue, the Sinclair Lewis Interpretive Center or the Sinclair Lewis Campground. I followed state Route 71 toward Wadena and a welcome reunion with U.S. Highway 10.

Minnesota dairy country is no doubt special in many ways, but to a non-farm boy like me it had the same look and feel of rural Wisconsin, rural New England and rural everywhere else. Almost nothing was new – almost nothing was there at all, in fact, except the usual meager allotment of farms, harvested cornfields, woods, little lakes and a few small towns like Long Prairie and Eagle Bend. The two-lane state road was smoother, wider, faster and safer than in Steinbeck's time. He would have seen more trucks on Route 71, because there were no interstates nearby. But they couldn't have been as intimidating as the 18-wheel hay wagons that thundered by my left shoulder every 5 minutes.

I cruised over strangely sculpted terrain at 70 mph through nearly invisible clouds of fat, suicidal bugs. Humans were nowhere to be seen off-road. Even the GreyStone Golf Club, a nationally known public course with a high pedigree, had no one hacking around it on a beautiful autumn day. Evidence of human economic life littered the roadside. A turkey farm. Pumpkins and corn for sale on the honor system. A cord of split firewood already on a trailer and ready to go. An auction tent near Clarissa. An Amish co-op. A Christmas tree farm. A live person on a palomino horse!

Steinbeck would have seen most everything I saw on Route 71, including what looked like a combination car museum and junkyard trying to hide behind some trees outside Eagle Bend. Zooming by, I counted a dozen cars from the 1940s and '50s, their hoods neatly pointed at the highway like they were sitting on a used car lot time forgot. Auto junkyards ringing cities offended Steinbeck's tender eyes, but seeing one was so rare, so out of date and so strangely out of place, I regretted not stopping.

Speaking of shocking juxtapositions, one sight Steinbeck definitely never saw was the graceful monster standing on the horizon as I approached Hewlitt. It was a lone wind turbine. Its three wings slowly swept a huge patch of the sky, supplying all the energy needs of Metropolitan Hewitt's 267 people and still having plenty of juice left over to sell to the power grid owned by Minnesota

Power. I stopped to take its picture and listen to its hum, but wind turbines, like redwoods, are too huge to photograph up close. How and why that towering boondoggle of subsidies and energy credits ended up in the middle of nowhere would probably make a good "60 Minutes" horror story, if "60 Minutes" cared about exposing such green horror stories. But no matter how uneconomic wind turbines are, or how much noise they make, or how many birds and bats they kill, they sure look pretty when they're standing alone in a place they shouldn't be.

At Wadena I rejoined U.S. 10, which from then on would be my main street all the way to Seattle. I saw the glow of Detroit Lakes' motels, malls and billboards long before I saw the vacation playground's empty resorts. It was too late to poke around much, but it was easy to see that the City of Detroit Lakes was more popular and more electrified than it was in 1960. It had 5,600 residents then instead of 8,300. And in 1960 Detroit Lakes didn't have quite so many fishing, boating, sailing, jet-skiing, swimming, scuba diving, river tubing and, for landlubbers, horse riding and golfing opportunities. Not to mention an amusement park, a paintball arena and a mile-long beach on Lake Detroit that drew tourists and desperate water-sport enthusiasts from the surrounding dry plains.

An old-timer told me Detroit Lakes ain't what it once was. A lot of the old resorts were closed. The Canadians didn't come down to spend their money anymore. And rich people from North Dakota had grabbed up all the lakefront property. "It used to be cheap to live on the lake," he said. "Not now." After a quick spin through Detroit Lakes' dark original downtown, I opted for another quiet night under the lights at Wal-Mart.

# Trucks, Cattle & 22-foot Turkeys

In "Travels With Charley" Steinbeck mentions Detroit Lakes, but only says "I stopped near there late at night and so did Charley, and I don't know any more about it than he does." He went into greater detail in his nightly road letter to his wife. On Oct. 11, 1960, he told her he had pulled into a truck stop for the night "not far from Detroit Lakes" and was "camped in a row of great cattle trailers" in "turkey country."

The next morning, without even peeking at the beach, I went looking for Steinbeck's truck stop. It only took two hours to find and my quest was a textbook lesson in the how-to's of drive-by journalism. First I went to the nearest McDonald's, ordered a coffee and sat in a booth next to the six old-timers I knew would be there. After waiting for a lull in a heated conversation about the deficiencies of the Minnesota Vikings, I gently butted into their world.

Excusing myself as a traveling journalist, I explained I was chasing the ghost of John Steinbeck. After explaining who John Steinbeck was, I told the old coots I was looking for a truck stop near Detroit Lakes that in 1960 handled cattle trucks and was near a turkey farm. In a chorus, three of them agreed I was looking for Daggett Truck Line in Frazee, Minnesota. Thanking them profusely, I headed eight miles back down U.S. 10 to Frazee, famous to motorists across all of western Minnesota as the "Home of the World's Largest Turkey." I found Daggett's operations right where they had been in 1960. The company stopped hauling local cattle to Fargo a long time ago and its 95 refrigerated trucks now carried frozen food, pet food and junk food all over the country.

In the first secretary's office I saw I asked if there was a Daggett I could talk to. Soon I was reading Chris Daggett the part in "Travels With Charley" where Steinbeck describes his overnight at a truck stop. Then I read him the letter Steinbeck wrote to his wife where he mentions a truck stop with cattle trailers and a small valley carpeted with thousands of turkeys.

I stipulated to Daggett that Steinbeck's letter to his wife was credible, but what he described so beautifully in "Travels With Charley" was not. It was a fictionalized composite of his stays at a truck stop in Mauston, Wisconsin, and one near Detroit Lakes, I said. I wrote down exactly what Chris Daggett told me: "This was the place he's talking about. Absolutely, it was. It was the only place around Detroit Lakes that handled cattle." I thanked Daggett, took my photos and got out of town. I never saw where Frazee kept the world's largest turkey, but the town's big sign on U.S. 10 was a felony case of false advertising. "Big Tom" the town turkey was large all right – 5,000 pounds and 20 feet tall. But he was made out of steel and fiberglass, not white meat and dark meat.

The story of Frazee's attempts to use a huge piece of hideous public art to publicize its local turkey industry is so pathetic it sounds like a lost episode of "Parks and Recreation." The original "Big Tom" was born in 1986. Made from the finest fiberglass, cardboard and insulation $20,000 could buy, "Big Tom" quickly justified his price tag by getting covered by ABC's "Good Morning America." By the mid-1990s, however, "Big Tom" was in serious trouble. Not only did he need to have his shabby exterior painted white all the time, local turkey interests were complaining he wasn't proportioned like a real turkey.

A new bird – the current properly proportioned one – was commissioned. But while the original "Big Tom" was being dismantled in 1998, a misdirected welding torch turned him into a 22-foot flaming butterball. The news report and photo of "Big Tom" engulfed by fire made the embarrassing kind of news Frazee's booster community never intended.

"Big Toms I and II" have put Frazee and its 1,377 people on the national map of dumb roadside tourist attractions. Somehow I missed meeting "Big Tom II," I'm not sorry to say. But I did see some of his little brothers and sisters. Their faces were staring out through the screened windows of a dozen massive turkey barns, including one next door to Daggett's trucking operations on old U.S. 10. The barns, stuffed with tens of thousands of doomed birds, were up to 1,000 feet long. They were impressive sights, but not the kind tourist families would want to stop and see.

# 12 – Making Time in North Dakota

## Steinbeck Timeline

Wednesday, Oct. 12, 1960 – Beach, North Dakota

*Sticking to U.S. 10, Steinbeck moves from Frazee, Minnesota, through Fargo and Bismarck to Beach, North Dakota, a small agricultural town near the Montana border. He drives about 425 miles, almost straight west. In Beach he checks into a small motel, the Westgate, and has a bath.*

## Town Without People

Steinbeck had romantic ideas about the city of Fargo and he was looking forward to seeing it for the first time. But when he drove through its downtown on Wednesday morning Oct. 12, 1960, he apparently got swept along in the traffic and didn't stop. I had a similar experience in Fargo when crossing over the Red River of the North into North Dakota from Detroit Lakes. The "West 10" signs I was following vanished and I ended up on North Broadway Drive. In the lunch-hour rush I inched bumper-to-bumper past the Fargo Theater, the city's signature downtown landmark, and the stone-faced Fargo National Bank.

Steinbeck's description of Fargo in "Travels With Charley" shows how much information a great writer can pack into half a sentence: "... it was a golden autumn day, the town as traffic-troubled, as neon-plastered, as cluttered and milling with activity as any other up-and-coming town of forty-six thousand souls." Except that there were more than twice as many Fargonians alive in 2010, that sounded like the town we both briefly met. Fargo and its "broken-metal-and-glass outer-ring," as Steinbeck called its trashy outskirts, extended farther west into the void of eastern North Dakota than when he complained about it. I didn't see any auto graveyards or landfills. But soon the malls, pawnshops, car dealers, tank farms and fairgrounds evaporated. U.S. 10 West and its signs vanished, too, buried forever under Interstate 94.

The land west of Fargo on I-94 was flat and wide, un-peopled and plowed to the max – like it'd been since about 1900, I'd bet. Turning off the interstate at County Road 38, which went nowhere in two directions, I went south toward the town of Alice, where Steinbeck says in "Charley" he camped out overnight. North Dakota is the fourth least densely populated state and most of it is farmland, facts that would surprise no one driving across it. The combines I saw from Route 38 looked like ants, and there were more combines on the horizons than houses. Traffic simply did not exist.

From outer space, Alice is a little splash of civilization spilled on a gigantic grid of farmland and perfectly straight roads. Everything around Alice is disturbingly parallel and perpendicular, except one thing – the drunken Maple River. Starting northwest of Alice and flowing south, it wriggles and wanders for miles, doubling back on itself, forming little pools, disappearing into wetlands and almost encircling Alice before trickling northeast to join larger rivers and lakes that ultimately empty into Hudson Bay.

I was looking forward to Alice. I had Google Mapped it before my trip and it wasn't really a town or even a village. From its satellite photo, it looked more like an unfinished, poorly zoned suburban development – a random scattering of a few dozen homes, buildings, a church or two, with a lot of empty space tied together with what looked like gravel roads.

When I arrived in Alice at 3:30 in the afternoon, no one was there to greet me. That was because hardly a soul is left in Alice. When Steinbeck wrote about it, it had only about 160 inhabitants, but it still had all the proper parts of a town. By 2010 Alice was down to 50 humans. The post office was closed. So was the town grain silo, the town school and the town Catholic Church, St. Henry's. It still had a mayor. And the town cemetery was still alive and well, though it was going to run out of dead people long before it ran out of space.

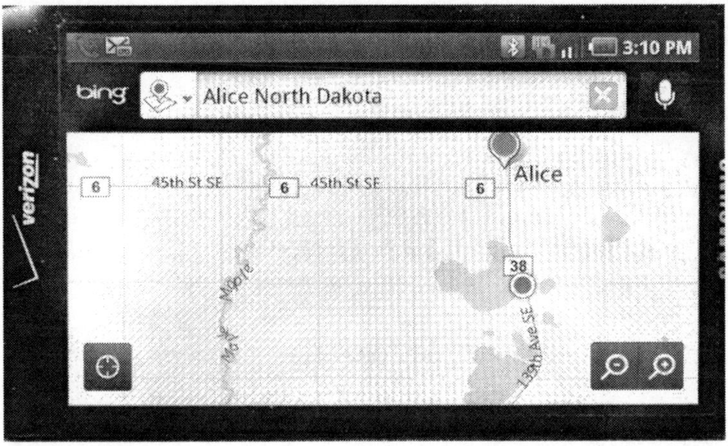


Steinbeck says in the first draft of "Travels With Charley" that he "found a pleasant place to stop on the Maple River just north of Alice." While there alone, away from the road, he says an itinerant Shakespearean actor pulled in and parked his trailer not far from him. Steinbeck describes the actor in minute detail. He had a classic profile and wore a leather jacket, olive-drab trousers and a cowboy hat with "the brim curled and held to a peak by the chin strap." Eventually the two men share coffee and whisky and discourse for five boring pages about the joys and sorrows of the acting profession. The tedious scene could have been worse. Steinbeck originally had the actor deliver 20 lines of Hamlet's "To be or not to be" rap. Wisely, that overt hunk of page filler was cut from the first draft.

The actor says when he performed Shakespeare on the road he respectfully borrowed the "words, tones and inflections" of John Gielgud. Then he pulls out a treasured letter he kept folded in his wallet. It was from Sir John himself. Steinbeck quotes the brief note in full. His lucky encounter with the actor, long on dialogue, is rich in specifics and detail. But it never happened.

## A Farmer Gets the Joke

Two miles west of Alice, near the vacant intersection of 45th and 137th streets, I stood next to an impenetrable dry cornfield on an elevated farm road. It was the highest ground for miles. It was sunny and warm, but the chilly wind whipped up whitecaps on the small lake nearby and slapped little high-frequency waves against its grassy shore. I was looking for signs of the Maple River – what in Pennsylvania we'd more accurately call Maple Creek.

It was there that the absurdity of what Steinbeck tried to pull on his readers really hit me. I already knew from a letter he sent to his wife that he lied in "Charley" about camping overnight in Alice. I also knew he didn't bump into his quotable thespian soul mate. Not anywhere near Alice, anyway, and not in the theatrical, stilted way he described.

But standing in the middle of that middle of nowhere, trying to imagine anyone meeting anyone else there at all – I really did laugh out loud. You had to be there with all that corn and farmland to appreciate the joke. I was still laughing when I found a farmer, or he found me. He was running a big blue Ford tractor, pulling a disk plough that magically turned a wide swath of his soft green field to black. Looking as pathetic as possible, I hailed him.

He climbed down from his cab to see what was wrong with my car or my head. We were both wearing blue jeans, T-shirts and baseball caps, but he was wearing work boots and, presumably, socks. After I explained what I was doing, he trusted me with the basic facts of his life as long as I promised not to tell the whole World Wide Web his name.

He was 50, the son of a farmer and a farmer himself for 23 years. He had what he called a "smallish" farm – 1,400 acres, a little over 2 square miles. He grew half wheat and half soybeans, not just corn like most of his neighbors, because he said wheat doesn't take as many people or trucks to produce. I didn't pry into his finances. But an Internet business directory listed his company as having $95,000 in annual revenue and a staff of 1, which I assumed was him. The only help the farmer had was his wife, two daughters and a good credit line. His wife – he pointed to a dust cloud half a mile away – was running the family combine. His older daughter ran it when she wasn't away at college.

I told the farmer what Steinbeck said he did near Alice. Then I asked if he knew a spot nearby where Steinbeck might have camped overnight by the Maple River and met a traveling Shakespearean actor with a John Gielgud letter in his wallet. He looked around, got the joke and laughed.

In "Travels With Charley" Steinbeck states without equivocation that he camped overnight near Alice. He didn't. In the real world, the nonfiction world, he passed by Alice on Wednesday, Oct. 12, 1960. It was Day 3 of his 2,100-mile, seven-day sprint from Chicago to Seattle and he spent it crossing the entire state of North Dakota. In the morning he may have paused for several hours along the Maple River somewhere near Alice. It's even possible he met an itinerant Shakespearean actor – or a man from Mars.

But in a day that started in Frazee, Minnesota, Steinbeck logged about 425 miles before stopping for the night in Beach, North Dakota, an agricultural town in the Badlands near the Montana border. By sundown Wednesday he was already 321 miles past Alice, about to take a hot bath in a motel. We know all this is true because it's what he told his wife in a letter he wrote that night from Beach.

Alice wasn't the only overnight campout in North Dakota that Steinbeck invented. The next night he didn't sleep under the stars in the spooky Badlands, either. In "Charley" Steinbeck beautifully describes how the slanting evening sunlight warmed the strange and harsh landscape of the Badlands, how he built a fire, how the starry night was filled with sounds of hunting screech owls and barking coyotes, and how the "night was so cold that I put on my insulated underwear for pajamas."

It was total fiction. On Thursday night, Oct. 13 – Day 4 of his Chicago-Seattle sprint – he was actually already 400 miles west of Beach and the Badlands. He was in Livingston, Montana, watching the third Nixon-Kennedy TV debate at a trailer court. Because he was moving so quickly from Chicago to Seattle, Steinbeck was forced to make up two overnight camping adventures in North Dakota and stick them in between his actual stays in Frazee and Beach.

Steinbeck's two flights of "creative nonfiction" under the stars in North Dakota are important, but not just because they are such bald-faced fabrications. Along with his non-meeting with the Yankee farmer in New Hampshire, they are the scenes in the book that created the myth that he was traveling slowly, camping out and roughing it alone in the American outback.

After snapping a corncob in half and telling me it was fit only for ethanol, the friendly farmer went back to his disking. For half an hour I drove to several places where farm roads intersected with the tiny Maple River as it squirmed through the tall grass. I didn't know it then, but there were a dozen possible places west, south or east of Alice where the river meets a road. Bumping into a sophisticated thespian anywhere near Alice – or anywhere else – would have been a fantastic bit of good luck for any traveling writer. It wasn't impossible. It's just that it doesn't happen like that in the real world.

I left the cornfields near Alice and aimed for Bismarck, 165 miles west on I-94. Somewhere in the hilly terrain I crossed the Continental Divide. The elevation was only 1,490 feet because, though North Dakota is rich in oil and gas and energy jobs, it's poor in mountain ranges. In Bismarck, where the supply of motels was not keeping pace with the demand from the energy boom, I couldn't find a room under $125, but I was more than happy to check in at the nearest Wal-Mart.

## A Day at Beach

It was a gorgeous morning to be cruising the Old Steinbeck Highway. The sun was behind me. The sky was big and blue with only the thinnest gauze of high white clouds. It was 54 outside but 68 in my personal space capsule. The North Dakota headwind, which Steinbeck complained about, had not yet risen to its usual afternoon car-shoving intensity.

Beach was my target *du jour*. Twenty minutes out of Bismarck, I was cruising at 70 mph on I-94, five miles below the speed limit. My Professional Reporter's Notebook was on my right knee. My laptop, cell phone and camcorder were sipping their morning juice from the cigarette lighter and the RAV4's 110-volt plug, a bonus I never thought I'd come to depend on so much.

Gobbling up mileage, I was alone and free and in total control of my life. I had nothing to fear and nothing to do but listen to CNBC on my blessed satellite radio and steer with one finger. As the local universe scrolled by like an abstract painting on a video loop, the emptiness of North Dakota became manifestly ridiculous. I could see two miles of four-lane superhighway ahead of me and a mile behind. I counted five cars and trucks. In every direction were desolate zip codes of smooth green-brown grassland and low hills. I counted one farm. One tree taller than a house, but no house. A few plump rolls of hay near a stray fence line. Power lines and the occasional cell tower were my only reliable companions. The black dots on the horizon were probably cows – OK, cattle.

North Dakota's excess of space and shortage of humankind became more glaring at noon when I exited I-94 at what I thought at first was my personal interstate rest stop. One vehicle was parked there, but it was leaving. It belonged to a hunched-over North Dakota grandma with a cane and a friendly attitude toward strange men with no socks who asked her questions. When grandma drove away, the place was all mine. Made of reddish sandstone, unattended by anyone, the "wayside" was pretty and architecturally in synch with the vacant windswept landscape. It looked more like an art museum or a modern church than a place to answer nature's call or grab a brochure about where to picnic in the Badlands.

The grounds – teen-age pine trees, country-club thick grass and picnic tables – were as spotless as the bathrooms and chapel-like lobby. I thanked the good taxpayers of North Dakota for their generous hospitality and taste, though of course as a libertarian I questioned their government's extravagant expenditure of state funds for something so underused.

I don't know how Cranky John Steinbeck would have reacted to the place. He was repulsed by the primitive interstate rest stops of his day, which he discovered laying in wait for him on the New York Thruway and Indiana Toll Road. He didn't like the lunch counters, steam-table food or deodorized bathrooms. Vending machines dispensing coffee and soup were high tech then, and the stuff that came out of them was god-awful. He was entranced by their mechanics and seemed to appreciate their convenience. Over all, however, he thought the flower-bedecked and sanitized rest stop represented "life at a peak of some kind of civilization" – a kind he didn't like.

Sitting in the sun writing a blog item on my laptop, I became annoyed when other people began invading my personal wayside. At least a dozen cars stopped in an hour. And a long truck. Half of the cars contained dogs like Sam Iversen, 12, and Jack Graff, 5. Sam the gentle black Lab and Jack the wired-up pointer belonged to a pair of Minnesota hunters, Eric Iversen and Jason Graff. It was pheasant slaughtering season and they were making their annual pilgrimage to their secret hunting grounds in Scranton, North Dakota. They stopped their overloaded Suburban at my wayside so their bird dogs could make a pit stop. Keeping with the Steinbeck-Charley subtext of my trip, I took portraits of each man-dog combination and again silently gave thanks that I was traveling doglessly.

Crossing North Dakota made me realize how fast Steinbeck moved west – without the aid of interstates. Steinbeck drove from Fargo to Beach on old U.S. Highway 10, which in its glory days stretched to Seattle and served as the Main Avenue of every North Dakota town hanging onto it. The towns were later bypassed by I-94 and most of U.S. 10's old route is buried now beneath four lanes of concrete.

Though U.S. 10 no longer officially exists west of Fargo, I found an old two-lane piece of it paralleling I-94 and followed it through dry farmland toward the town of Hebron. In spots I could fly along at 60 or 70, then it'd get too bumpy and rough. No shoulder to speak of, sometimes no painted lines. It couldn't have been that bad in 1960, could it? No wonder the auto death rate was so high then.

Most of Hebron's 747 humans must have been feeding their cattle or working down at the 106-year-old Hebron Brick Company factory, because I didn't see many people when I stopped for gas. Anyone looking to join North Dakota's energy boom, which has kept the state's unemployment rate well under 4 percent despite the Great Recession, might consider relocating to rural, dusty Hebron.

Its municipal web site almost blew a disk touting the community's awesome amenities. "We have a hard working Post Office, a movie theater with a modern projection system, two restaurants, two banks, two gas stations, three auto repair places, and a RS Jack and Jill Market that will deliver groceries to you every Friday during Winter." Not only did Hebron have a swimming pool and fiber optic cable service, it was "just 30 minutes to Wal-Mart."

After another 25 miles of time-travel through pastureland on a stretch of deserted old U.S. 10 that Steinbeck and Charley drove on, I resumed my pleasant cruise on I-94. A few minutes later I turned a big bend and found myself in the dead, grey, brown, craggy, eroded, hilly, unfriendly but not unattractive moonscape of the Badlands. At the Medora exit I drove in and out of "town" as fast as possible. North Dakota's No. 1 tourist trap – the gateway to Theodore Roosevelt National Park's rough outdoor recreations – was closed for the season. Medora's 112 citizens, like most of North Dakota's populace, were in hiding.

# Where Steinbeck Took His Bath

Steinbeck arrived in Beach, North Dakota, on the evening of Oct. 12, 1960. It was the end of Day 3 of his Chicago-Seattle leg. He never mentions his stay in Beach in "Charley," obviously, because that was the night he was pretending to be sleeping under the stars near Alice. But he betrayed where he was in a letter to his wife Elaine. Telling her he had stopped at a place that had the only public phone for 40 miles, he joked that he was staying "in a motel called the Dairy Queen."

He told Elaine that when he went into a bar, all the talk was about deer hunting, not Game 6 of the Yankees-Pirates World Series, which he had listened to that day on his truck's AM radio. He could have walked over to the Bijou Theater a few blocks away and seen Alec Guinness in "Our Man in Havana." But Steinbeck probably didn't take in a movie for the same reason I didn't go to the Bijou to see Angelina Jolie star in "Salt." We had both spent our days driving across North Dakota and were both pretty beat.

As part of my pre-trip research, I had called the only motel I could find online in Beach, the Westgate Motel on Old Highway 10. The manager, Sandy, told me there was never a Dairy Queen Motel in town but there had been a Dairy Queen franchise. It used to be right across the street.

By the time I arrived in Beach, 50 years and one night after Steinbeck did, I had come to realize he had been kidding his wife Elaine about staying in a motel called the Dairy Queen. But what motel was it? Was it the "modern" Westgate, the obvious choice, where Sandy had kindly saved me one of her 11 rooms without my asking? Or did Steinbeck stay in one of the old-style motel cabins that once stood on the vacant lot across from the Westgate?

I spent the next early morning sleuthing around Beach. Based on a random drive-around, Beach was a mix of good homes and a few shabby ones in mostly older neighborhoods. It still seemed to have everything it needed for a town that had shrunk from 1,460 people in 1960 to 1,019 in 2010. No Wal-Mart was closer than 60 miles. But there were several churches, a couple of banks, a county courthouse, a hardware store, a pharmacy, a supermarket, a few shaky restaurants. Beach had a busy railroad line through its heart and one of those cool old water towers that looks like a fat rocket taking off. It even had some history. General Custer and his doomed column came through Beach on their way to immortality at Little Big Horn.

Beach was a real town. In no way was it quaint or charming or hip or artificially polished to appeal to tourists. To a parachuting journalist it looked exactly like what it was – working-class. Susan Davidson, the Golden Valley County Recorder, preferred the term "blue-collar" town. I had stopped in her office at the courthouse shortly after 8 and read her the description of Beach that I was going to put on the World Wide Web for the entire planet to read. I explained what I was doing, begged forgiveness for my superficial 25-mph assumptions about her fine town and got the names of several local historians who never answered or returned my phone calls. Recorder Davidson clued me in on a few things I never could have learned from driving around Beach: Its economy, like the rest of North Dakota's, was doing better and still improving, thanks to the regional oil and gas boom. Unemployment was down. A local entrepreneur was starting up a vineyard east of town on Old Highway 10.

By noon, I had stopped by the office of the Golden Valley News newspaper, which had 1,000 subscribers and seemed to be located in a fabric store. Editor Richard Volesky interviewed me briefly after I told him why I was in town, then let me look through his newspaper's archives. I read the Oct. 13, 1960, edition of the News. I was hoping to find a front-page story about famous John Steinbeck being spotted the night before at the Bijou with a French dog or getting punched out by a cowboy in a bar fight. No such luck. Just dozens of 2-inch long local items on Page 1 bearing headlines like "Mrs. J. Ballard Succumbs Oct. 5" and "Feeding Calves Becoming Big Business in County."

Inside its 12 old-fashioned pages, the News held an array of large display ads that would make a starving big-city newspaper publisher of today weep. Ads for political candidates. Quarter-page ads for $15.95 Goodyear winter tires. The new 1961 Ford was coming. So was the compact 1961 Rambler American with its infamous reclining front seats, which the Hammond Implement & Mt. Co. of Beach was offering for as little as $1,845.

At the paper I met Harold Lassell. Wearing pressed jeans, a pressed shirt and the shiniest cowboy boots in town, he introduced himself as "the oldest mechanic left in Beach." Lassell, 86 and a lifelong Beach resident, instantly became the last word on what the intersection of U.S. 10 and 1st Avenue NW looked like in 1960. He knew the names of the original owners of the Westgate Motel, the owners of the Dairy Queen that sat diagonally across from it and the owners of the long-gone tourist cabins. He even knew whether they were dead or alive.

He listened patiently to the evidence I presented: John Steinbeck came into town from the east on U.S. 10. The Westgate was the only modern motel near enough to the Dairy Queen to become a Steinbeck joke. Steinbeck called it a "motel" in his letter, not a "cabin," and he raved about a bathtub in his room. Lassell agreed with my logic and my conclusion – Steinbeck slept at the Westgate.

But final confirmation, at least as far as I was concerned, didn't come until two months later. Back in Pittsburgh, I got a call from Doug Davis of Bozeman. He was only 8 in 1960, but his father built and owned the Westgate Motel, his uncle designed it and he grew up helping his mother run it. Davis, who called because he heard I was looking for information, said it was too bad he hadn't heard about me sooner. His mother had died a few weeks earlier and he and his older brother found all the motel's registration books, including those from the fall of 1960, stored at her house – and immediately pitched them in the trash.

Davis said there was no Davis-family lore about John Steinbeck visiting their place, but he believes the Westgate was the "Dairy Queen." It was the only modern hotel in Beach at the time. Across the street were some rustic "It Happened One Night"-style cabins. But they didn't have what Steinbeck lusted after and what Davis said the Westgate Motel definitely had in each of its rooms in 1960 – a bathtub.

# 13 – Loving Montana

*I am in love with Montana. For other states I have admiration, respect, recognition, even some affection, but with Montana it is love...*

– "Travels With Charley"

## Steinbeck Timeline

Thursday, Oct. 13, 1960 – Livingston, Montana

*Steinbeck rides U.S. 10 from Beach into Montana. He passes through Miles City, drops down to the Custer Battlefield site briefly and continues on old U.S. 10 West through Billings to Livingston. At the end of his fourth long day of driving since he left Chicago, he says in a letter to his wife he's parked in a trailer court.*

## Sleeping with Snakes

"Rattlesnakes have been observed. Please stay on sidewalks." When you wake up and see a sign like that on the way to the bathroom, you know you're out West. The Buffalo Country rest stop on I-94 had been as quiet as a Wal-Mart parking lot, except for the sound of trains rumbling by somewhere in the dark. The five RVs and cars I bunked with had already cleared out by dawn.

Overnight parking wasn't expressly forbidden, which to a libertarian meant it was therefore permitted. The official signs at the rest stop only cared about the important things – rattlesnakes and where you let your pet poop. I wasn't far from the exit to the Custer Battlefield, which was about 50 miles south. Steinbeck went there – he said so in a letter to his wife – but he barely mentions it in "Travels With Charley." I was going there too, then on to Billings and Livingston by about dinnertime.

Steinbeck was a hard ghost to keep up with. He traveled from Beach to Livingston on old, skinny U.S. Highway 10, yet managed to pack a lot into Day 4 of his dash to Seattle. He told his wife he genuflected at the Custer memorial at the Little Big Horn and stopped at about six bars in towns along U.S. 10 – not to drink, necessarily, but to gather information. He arrived at a motel or a trailer court near Livingston in time to watch the third Nixon-Kennedy debate. Though Steinbeck almost certainly listened to Game 7 of the World Series on his truck's radio, there was no reaction from him in the book or in his letters about the amazing finish, which ended – as every Pittsburgher knows – with Bill Mazeroski slaying the mighty Yankees with a homer in the bottom of the ninth.

# Brave Ghosts

The Little Bighorn Battlefield National Monument, as the site of Custer's Last Stand is officially called, was a lovely place for a massacre. In every direction the rolling brown land was big and the blue sky even bigger. The only sound was the hard steady wind that rippled the dry grass and starched the American flag flying high above the Custer Memorial Cemetery.

Everything – the parking lot, the visitors center and the cemetery and its ring of protective trees – looked up at Last Stand Hill, where a stone monument, a low black iron fence and 41 white gravestones stuck out of the thin grass. Talk about ghosts. If they exist anywhere, they exist on the silent windswept hilltop where Gen. Armstrong Custer and 40 of his men died on June 25, 1876.

Getting myself to the site of Custer's Last Stand had been a pleasant cruise through tall cornfields and short hayfields, but for the local wildlife one stretch of State Route 47 was a killing field. In a minute I saw a dead coyote, a dead skunk, two dead raccoons, a dead something else. Whatever hit them – including one of the trucks overloaded with lumpy sugar beets like the ones they left sprinkled on the road – was probably doing 75 like me. Not far from Hardin I passed one of the best ambiguous road signs of my trip – "Slow Down When Dusty."

On a bright sunny Friday morning only 10 cars were in the Custer Battlefield parking lot. Steinbeck would have been annoyed to see the "No dogs off leash" sign. When he and Charley took their side trip to "pay our respects to General Custer and Sitting Bull," as he put it, they both were able to wander indiscriminately over the battlefield. Park ranger/historian Gerald Jasmer told me that except for some landscaping and the stone or gravel pathways laid out through the grassy slopes, no dramatic changes had been made to the site since Steinbeck's time. The most significant difference since 1960 is how much more we know about what really went on during the battle itself.

Fifty years ago most of what Steinbeck and everyone else in the country knew about Custer's Last Stand came from Hollywood, where history and facts go to be tortured on the bloody altar of bad drama. But Jasmer said a lucky break occurred in 1983 when a wildfire burned off the battlefield's grass and gave forensic archeologists access to thousands of artifacts – spent cartridges and human remains – strewn over the slopes during the fighting. The legend of a heroic last stand by Custer and his soldiers, built up first by 19$^{th}$ century newspapers Back East and then Hollywood, was spoiled by facts and cold science. A more realistic, more likely, scenario is that in the face of certain death the horse soldiers scattered and died in a state of panic and fear.

Steinbeck would have heard the white-man's politically incorrect version of what happened at the Little Big Horn. Visitors today get a more fair-and-balanced account of a military "engagement" – now there's a great euphemism – in which 260 men from the U.S. Army's 7th Calvary and 100 Lakota-Cheyenne warriors slaughtered each other in an unnecessary battle in an unimportant place. There's also an Indian Memorial in memory of the tribes who died "defending their way of life at the Battle of the Little Big Horn." In a letter to his wife Steinbeck called Custer a "dumb bastard," which he was. But in "Travels With Charley" he writes that when he went to the battlefield site he "removed my hat in memory of brave men." If that's what he did, it was a classy thing to do at a beautiful, almost spiritual monument to unimaginable human bravery, savagery and stupidity.

# To Livingston, I Presumed

He had never visited Montana before, but Steinbeck chose the right place for the first of his two sleepovers in the state. After leaving the Custer battlefield site, he worked his way west to Livingston, which is stretched along Old Highway 10 on the bank of the Yellowstone River. He had covered about 400 miles on Day 4 of his Seattle Sprint. Crossing the sweeping plains of eastern Montana and slowly climbing into the shadow of the Rockies, he fell in love with Montana at first sight, as most normal people can't help but do. Montana's spectacular natural beauty put a spell on him. As he would famously write in "Charley," "Of all the states it is my favorite and my love."

Steinbeck confessed his new love to his wife Elaine in a letter from Livingston that night. Though he told her he was at a trailer park "outside of Bozeman," he was almost certainly in Livingston. It's only 27 miles east of Bozeman and the towns are separated by the desolate and motel-less Bozeman Pass, which nears 6,000 feet as it cuts through the Gallatin and Bridger mountains. Adding the long day's events to the letter he had written the night before but had not mailed yet, Steinbeck gushed over Montana's "grandeur."

He described "the little square burnt-up men" he saw in the bars, mentioned his Little Big Horn side trip and told his wife about the old-fashioned stockman's hat he bought in Billings to replace his naval cap, which he said was attracting too much attention so far from the sea. It was very cold and Steinbeck said there was snow in the Rockies and on the "great snowy mountain beside me." He was heading toward Idaho in the morning, he said, but didn't think he'd make it. Montana was not only huge; it was so beautiful he drove slower than usual so he could gawk at it.

As Steinbeck did 50 years earlier, I got a stunning dose of what Montana was most famous for on my relaxed drive from Billings to Livingston on I-90: Gigantic sky, gigantic land, jagged mountain ranges running every which way, an endless sunset and not enough humans to form a Wednesday night basketball league. With a population of almost 1 million, Montana has 300,000 more people today than when Steinbeck blew through it. Huge and rural and wild, it's still 99 percent empty. Like so many of the states on the Steinbeck Highway, it's not even close to being a microcosm of America. In 2010 it was 90 percent Caucasian with twice as many Native Americans as Latinos and more Asians than blacks. It had so few blacks – 4,000 in the whole state – that Butte, a city of 34,000, had fewer African-Americans than registered sex offenders.

Montana's economy is powered by minerals, cattle, wheat and millions of visitors who are lured by a magnificent outdoor rec room that is inhumanely cold in winter and catches fire every summer. Despite its newfound oil and gas riches, the presence of mega-landlord Ted Turner and a trickle of celebrity immigrants from Hollywood, Montana is shockingly poor – the 6$^{th}$ poorest state in terms of median family income. In the fall of 2010 its unemployment rate was about 2 percentage points lower than the national average of 9.5. Oil and gas development was nothing like North Dakota's bonanza. And there were no six-figure corporate jobs open in Round Up or Big Timber. Still, Montana was a cheap place to live and housing could be laughably affordable if you didn't want to own a mountain.

When I pulled into Livingston's Yellowstone Inn it was almost dark. I knew my way around the artsy tourist town, which is on the (relative) doorstep of Yellowstone Park and is a popular base camp for fishing and hunting expeditions. I'd been to Livingston half a dozen times before. I'm not a hunter, hiker, kayaker or fly-fisherman. But I've seen a fair amount of the state's "grandeur" and its neighborly people on vacations at my wife's family's log cabin in the Lewis & Clark National Forest north of Bozeman.

I had also seen most of Montana's collection of livable small cities. Missoula was a hip college town. Great Falls, where my wife grew up, and Billings, the biggest city in the state with 104,000 people, were dustier and working class. Bozeman was part Missoula/part outdoor-recreation Mecca. Butte was an ex-copper boomtown that belonged Back East in the Rust Belt. Lewistown was a small jewel set among several mountain ranges in the dead center of the state.

Helena, the capital, I had only seen once, but I imagined it had too many politicians, bureaucrats and lawyers per square mile than was healthy. But as far as I knew, all of Montana's mini-cities had old residential neighborhoods and solid, healthy, original downtowns with cool old buildings that had made it through the 20$^{th}$ century without being bulldozed, wrecking-balled, gentrified, redeveloped or otherwise "improved" by their local politicians.

# Drinking with Batman

On the drive from Billings I had set up a quick meeting with actor Michael Keaton, who was from Pittsburgh but lived on a ranch east of Livingston. I knew Keaton a little bit through my sportscaster brother John and from my time in Los Angeles during the 1980s. Thanks to the magic of cell phones and Keaton's personal assistant in L.A., we met for a beer at the 2nd Street Bistro in Livingston's historic downtown.

The bistro is on the ground floor of the Murray Hotel, a creaky, uniquely time-warped treasure right on old U.S. 10. The hotel is the most famous of Livingston's old buildings, thanks to its flamboyant neon sign, crazy Western decor and rowdy 106-year-old history. Calamity Jane and Buffalo Bill stayed there – not as a couple, mind you. And there are not-so-tall tales of a grizzly bear in the bar, cowboys riding horses up the stairs and movie director Sam Peckinpah, a permanent resident from 1979-1984, shooting holes in the ceiling of his room.

The bistro, more civilized, was prized for its fine grub and good wine. It had become a safe hangout for Livingston's colony of artists, writers and actors, who included landscape painter Russell Chatham, author Tom McGuane, Margot Kidder and Keaton, who's well-liked in Pittsburgh as a regular guy who got to play Batman in a movie and make out with Michelle Pfeiffer but never went Hollywood.

Keaton lived up to his good-guy rep. Though we hadn't seen each other in 15 years, we were like old friends who'd gone elk hunting together the previous weekend. We sat at a mini-bar in the bistro with just the bartender and an actor from New York. Unbelievably, he used to live in the same 1927-vintage French-style apartment building I once lived in on Franklin Avenue in Hollywood in the late 1970s. It has a major role in the 1977 Art Carney/Lily Tomlin detective movie "The Late Show."

Keaton had been out bird shooting and had an SUV full of dogs at the curb. But before he left we went around to the proletarian Murray Bar to check the score of the Yankees-Rangers playoff game. Dozens of lonely young Montana homeboys were sipping beer, playing pool and praying a bored starlet would walk through the door and ask for a lift back to Hollywood. The Fossils, who did not choose that name by accident, were tuning their guitars.

No one bothered or seemed to recognize Keaton, whose only disguise was a baseball cap. The Murray Bar was the kind of under-illuminated neighborhood man-cave Steinbeck might have slipped into for a dozen beers when he was 25 or 30. The 2nd Street Bistro was more like the upscale places he frequented on his "Travels With Charley" trip. But like the celebrity colonists from Tinseltown, the bistro wasn't there in 1960.

## Steinbeck Timeline

Friday, Oct. 14, 1960 – Somewhere west of Missoula

*Before heading west from Livingston, Steinbeck says in the book he abruptly decides to drive about 55 miles south on U.S. 89 to Yellowstone Park. When Charley goes nuts every time he sees a grizzly bear, Steinbeck quickly leaves and retraces his path to Livingston. He turns west on U.S. 10, buys a rifle in Butte and drives past Missoula before stopping. In an undated letter to his wife Friday night he mentions his Yellowstone detour that morning and says he was camped on the property of an old woman west of Missoula about 60 miles from the Idaho line. That would have been near Tarkio, but local old-timers there could not provide any further clues.*

# Where John Got His Jacket

In "Travels With Charley" Steinbeck doesn't mention his night in Livingston. He merely jumps from the Little Big Horn to his snap decision to veer south to see Yellowstone National Park. He had no interest in seeing the park. As he writes in the book, he thought national parks enclosed and celebrated the freaks of nature. Yellowstone was "no more representative of America than is Disneyland."

It's a cynical, environmentally incorrect, interesting and semi-defendable point of view. But Steinbeck knew his friends and neighbors would never let him forget it if he was so close to the park and didn't go, so he drove about 90 minutes south on U.S. 89 to its north entrance. His day-trip was a disaster. Charley apparently went nuts every time he saw a bear – which was every 30 seconds in the era when grizzlies loafed by the side of the roads waiting for handouts. Today if a bear is sighted in the woods half a mile away, it instantly creates near hysteria and a 100-car traffic jam.

I skipped Yellowstone, not needing to see it for the sixth time. I had been there before and after the 1988 fire burned nearly a third of it. It was tremendous, spectacular. But it also was an overcrowded, over-regulated theme park best visited in winter on a snowmobile. I opted to poke around Livingston. Its official tourist attractions include a fly-fishing museum, a cool train station and some old whorehouses from the early 1900s. But its best feature is the town itself.

Its priceless turn-of-the-19$^{th}$-century downtown buildings testify to Livingston's early wealth as a 1880s railroad hub and original gateway to Yellowstone. Behind the handsome storefronts were art galleries, boutiques, coffee shops, hotels, sports bars and real estate offices. Sax & Fryer, which sold office supplies, stationery, books and newspapers, has been in business 127 years and looked it. It still uses mechanical adding machines and cash registers. The woman running the store was the daughter of a silver miner and, amazingly, she was born in infinitesimal Neihart, Montana, where my wife's family has had their log cabin since the late 1950s.

She asked me not to tell anyone that Tom Brokaw and Carl Hiaasen, the star Florida writer who had a place nearby, were among Sax & Fryer's regular happy customers. She wasn't a summer resident and held no grudge against them. She and 7,000 others lived year round in Livingston, which she warned was not as idyllic as it seemed in summer or on a 50-degree fall day. "It's a neat place to live until January, when the winds are blowing at 60 miles an hour and there's horizontal snow."

Since Steinbeck said in his book that he bought a jacket in Livingston, I walked into another old building to see if it might have been at Bob's Outdoor. Bob's has been selling Western clothes since 1946. I asked owner Shelly Chapel if she had an old family story to tell me about the day the great John Steinbeck bought a hunting jacket at Bob's. She didn't. I had just as little luck trying to figure out which "pretty auto court" or trailer court Steinbeck might have stayed at exactly 50 years before. Inquiring at four or five older motels and two RV parks, I came up empty and took the highway to Butte, where Steinbeck bought his gun.

## What's Left of Butte

After another 120 miles of I-90's all-natural beauty pageant, I wasn't ready for the sight of post-industrial Butte. I'd been through Butte once years before. It was a mile-high city built on a mountain of copper – literally and figuratively. Old Highway 10 zigzagged me through parts of town that looked semi-abandoned, then led me to the city's amazing historic downtown, which, because it is halfway up a mountain, is called Uptown.

I'd seen my share of de-industrialized cities. I grew up, lived and worked in one. But Butte's ghost downtown was an unbelievable amalgamation of hundreds of 19th century brick buildings, benign urban blight and glaring signs of lost wealth and missing people. Uptown was built to serve Butte's peak population of 100,000 in 1910, when it was one of the country's wealthiest cities and the Copper Capital of the World. But a hundred years later the city-county population was stuck at 34,000. Painted on the walls of larger buildings were the "ghost signs," some 70 years old, of once successful hotels and businesses that had died and disappeared.

Butte's copper industry is now all but nonexistent, but vestiges of it weren't hard to find. The skyline was broken by a dozen steel "headframes" – derricks, really – that once stood over the mouths of mineshafts and lowered workers thousands of feet underground and also brought the copper to the surface. A gigantic open-pit copper mine filled with acidic water had become an unlikely but symbolically apt tourist attraction for Butte. It's also a substantial part of the enormous ongoing environmental cleanup that was trying to repair the damage from a hundred years of copper extraction and smelting.

Butte is best known today for its colorful past and Knievel Days. Each summer its empty streets attract 50,000 bikers and daredevils from around the world who come to honor hometown hero Evel Knievel and his kin. But on Saturday afternoon, the Uptown streets and sidewalks were deserted. Most of the buildings had retail businesses on the ground floor. But most of their upper stories were vacant, with fake curtains or tarps hanging in place of windows.

I parked along East Park Street, which used to be U.S. Highway 10. On Friday, Oct. 14, 1960, John Steinbeck is said to have stopped near there and popped into Phil Judd's Sporting Goods and Hardware to buy a used Remington bolt-action .222 rifle and scope. I was looking for Phil Judd's old store – or, more likely, the building it used to be in. Barging into Rudolph Furniture's showroom, I interrupted the lives of the innocent people working there with my standard drive-by journalism routine.

As had become the pattern, the local folk were more than happy to help me. Mike Rudolph ran the store. His family had been operating it since 1919, when Butte was a rich, crowded, busy, violent, sinful, corrupt city famous for its red-light district, saloons, plutocratic copper kings and tough union mineworkers. Mike told me the bad but not surprising news – Phil Judd and his store were history. The good news was that Judd's building was only five doors away, where Rediscoveries Vintage Clothing was.

Next thing I knew I was on the phone with Mike's father, Lou Rudolph. He was 88 and sharper than a day trader. Lou was also Phil Judd's brother-in-law, so I couldn't have found a better source. No, Lou answered, there was no Judd family lore about the great John Steinbeck buying a rifle and a scope in their store and hanging around for an hour. And no, he knew of no autograph, no photos, no receipt and no framed canceled check for $73.50 signed "John Steinbeck."

## A Tall Tale Debunked?

I asked Lou about the cancelled check because of a newspaper article written by a writer/artist from Butte named Bill Baltezar. In a lengthy 1993 first-person piece in the Salinas Californian newspaper, Baltezar claimed he was in Phil Judd's store the day Steinbeck walked in. He said Steinbeck paid for a secondhand Remington rifle and Weaver scope with a personal check for $73.50. Baltezar said he and Judd both saw the check and were surprised as all get out when they saw Steinbeck's signature.

Judd was dead. Unfortunately, so was Baltezar, who eventually moved to Salinas, California, and died there in 2009. He wasn't around to defend his too-tidy tale. He made about a dozen mistakes that erode his credibility. Most are minor factual flubs or could be chalked up to what looked like a steinbeckian effort to squeeze every drop of fictional drama from a brief real-world encounter with a famous American.

Baltezar said it was a "sweltering summer day," when it was actually Oct. 14 and the day's high temperature in Butte that day was 42 degrees. He described Rocinante, a new GMC pickup with about 4,500 miles on it, "as a beat-up old truck." And he said Steinbeck was going to follow his advice and go trout fishing in the mountains near the town of Dillon. But Steinbeck was hurrying west to Seattle to meet the missus. There was no way he'd consider wasting half a day by diverting to Dillon, which was 60 miles south of Butte.

In addition to its factual errors, Baltezar's elaborate story fails the basic smell test. Phil Judd was shocked to see John Steinbeck's name on the check, yet we should believe he never told his family that the author of "The Grapes of Wrath" bought a gun at his corner store? Not likely. In "Charley," Steinbeck says he bought a rifle and a scope in Butte, but doesn't say where or how he paid for it. Baltezar said he was at Phil Judd's the day Steinbeck came in and had a long chat with him. Maybe so. But until that canceled Steinbeck check turns up, Baltezar's tall tale belongs on the fiction shelf with "Travels With Charley."

I asked Lou Rudolph – who said he knew Baltezar – how Butte had changed in the last 50 years. Like Pittsburgh and other fallen industrial powerhouses Back East like Cleveland and Buffalo, Butte's population in 2010 was half what it was in 1960. Lots of miners were still working underground then, Lou said. Uptown had many more bars and restaurants. When Steinbeck drove through Butte, Park Street (U.S. 10) would have been congested with local traffic and cars and trucks working their way to Seattle or Fargo.

I-90 put a merciful end to that traffic nightmare, but things had gone to the other extreme. At 4 p.m. on a Saturday I stood in the middle of Old Highway 10 at the corner of East Park and North Wyoming, taking all the photos I needed without fear of being hit by anything larger than a raindrop.

I wanted to go to the top of the mountain, high above Uptown, to see the panoramic view of Butte. But first I had to check Rediscoveries Vintage Clothing for Steinbeck ghosts. Heather Meeks was in there looking for Halloween costumes for her two kids. She was 44 and not originally from Butte. But since she arrived she had learned a lot about the city's boom-bust history, its current environmental debacle and its clashing natural and manmade charms.

"Butte is a gritty, grimy, hardworking, take-no-prisoners city," she said. "Butte is what America claims to be – a true melting pot. English, Cornish, Welsh, Chinese, Eastern Europeans – they all crossed the country to come here to make their fortunes. Three dollars a day were top wages for miners for decades."

Though Meeks referred to herself as "an old hippie," she and Steinbeck would have got on well politically. She didn't hide her working-class sympathies when she described how the Anaconda copper mining company and its executives got filthy rich for decades while the miners just got filthy.

I disagreed with most of Meeks' progressive politics, of course. But like so many of my fellow Americans I met from Maine to Wisconsin to Montana, she was smart, friendly and quick to reveal her passions and opinions to a stranger armed with a Professional Reporter's Notebook.

To my discredit, I never found out the names of her kids or what Meeks did for a living, just that she was born in Hawaii, was well-traveled and somehow ended up in Butte. She clearly loved her adopted city and knew it well. Summing up its gloried past and troubled present, she sounded like a native when she quipped, "Butte used to export copper, now it exports people."

## Steinbeck's Two-Night Stand

Steinbeck fell hard for Montana. As he mooned in "Travels With Charley," "Montana has a spell on me. It is grandeur and warmth. If Montana had a seacoast, or if I could live away from the sea, I would instantly move there and petition for admission. Of all the states it is my favorite and my love." He can't be blamed for being smitten. But his relationship was more like a two-night stand than a serious love affair. He drove down the main streets of Billings, Bozeman, Butte and Missoula and other smaller U.S. 10 towns. He stopped in bars, a clothing shop and a gun store. He stayed one night in a trailer court near Livingston and a second on private land west of Missoula along the Clark Fork River.

Other than gawking out his windshield for hours at the state's natural grandeur, that was pretty much it for Steinbeck's fling with lovely Montana: Two days, two nights, two sunsets. Fifty total hours and about 850 miles of driving. All packed into 2.5 pages of "Travels With Charley." Steinbeck obviously missed a lot of Montana. Curving from southeast to northwest on old U.S. Highway 10, he saw just a sliver of the country's fourth biggest state.

He didn't see Glacier National Park, Flathead Lake or the Missouri Breaks. He didn't have time to do signature outdoor Montana things — fly fishing in the Yellowstone River, hiking up creeks to the toxic but cool ruins of silver mines, driving 10 miles into a pine forest on a dirt road for a picnic in a meadow at 7,000 feet or conquering your own nameless mountain. Yet after only 50 hours in Montana, Steinbeck got it. He nailed her and its people.

In "Travels With Charley," he writes "... It seemed to me that the frantic bustle of America was not in Montana. Its people did not seem afraid of shadows in a John Birch Society sense. The calm of the mountains and the rolling grassland had got into the inhabitants.... Again my attitude may be informed by love, but it seems to me that the towns were places to live in rather than nervous hives. People had time to pause in their occupations to undertake the passing art of neighborliness."

How he figured out Montana so quickly testifies to Steinbeck's superior powers of observation. I'm just a Montanan by marriage. My wife Trudi grew up in Great Falls in a family that was part working class and part bohemian. Her dad James Logan, who dropped dead of a heart attack at age 54, was a foreman at the Anaconda copper smelter by day and a prominent Montana artist and Paris Review subscriber the rest of the time. Her mother Ele was a Northwestern grad and drama major who after the death of her husband taught at the Goodman Institute in Chicago and did acting in New York with young bucks like Danny DeVito.

Trudi's family lived on Smelter Hill, a storybook company-owned neighborhood at the foot of the copper smelter's colossal smoke stack along the Missouri River. They spent their summers at a log cabin on federal forestland in Lewis and Clark National Forest near Neihart, a gas station/variety store "town" of 51 on U.S. 89 about 150 miles north of Bozeman.

Near their cabin, scattered about the beautiful wide and winding canyons of the Little Belt Mountains, were rectangles of fenced-in concrete. Located at the end of conspicuously well-maintained gravel roads, they looked like vacant parking lots that someone had perversely carved out in the middle of the vast forest of spruce, fir and lodge pole pine. The only clues that you had come upon an armed-and-ready Minuteman ICBM silo were a strong razor-topped cyclone fence and a small, serious sign that warned that lethal force would be used against trespassers, KGB agents or Washington Post editorial writers like Rachel Dry.

For decades, thanks to the Cold War's doctrine of Mutual Assured Destruction and those Minutemen silos, the empty beauty of North Dakota, Wyoming and Montana was a prime target for Soviet ICBMs. Steinbeck worried about "The Bomb" and complained about the absurdity of the nuclear arms race. But local Montana folks – what few there were scattered around Neihart – didn't seem to notice the nukes in their backyards. They had learned long ago to live with the fact that if World War III broke out they would be among the first conservative Republicans to die.

From what I know of the state and its lucky inhabitants, what Steinbeck wrote about Montana was still true. Since the early 1980s I had spent a total of about three months of my life there. I liked the natives as well as the land. My favorite Montanan was my sister-in-law's boyfriend Bud. He had a big place on a hill where he could see four different mountain ranges and the lights of downtown Lewistown, population 8,000 in a spacious county of 15,000.

Bud's apparently a fairly common Montana type, but to an effete Easterner like me he looked, thought, talked and acted like an old-time Western movie hero. In his 70s when I met him, his hair and sideburns were gray, his skin thick and suntanned. As solid as a Marine recruit, with powerful forearms and hands, on a family picnic he carried my six-year-old daughter Lucy on his back across a swift icy creek that was hip deep and wide as an interstate.

Bud was an archetypal American success story. He migrated to Montana in the late '30s from Missouri, when he was 17. A farm boy, he arrived with an eighth grade education, $15 in his blue jeans and a yearning to get his own place some day. His first job was as a ranch hand. By the time Steinbeck and Charley sped by, Bud was well on his way to owning 2,500 acres and 350 head of cattle. He also would get his very own Minuteman silo. One day in the mid-1980s Bud decided to run for county commissioner as an independent and was elected in a landslide. He didn't say much at the public meetings. But when he did, it was exactly what he thought. He kept his own tax return on public display at the courthouse and spent most of his time helping troubled local kids, fixing fences and remodeling the county jail.

Bud was my kind of politician – a throwback from the 19th century. His inherent common sense and simple ideas about government and its duties would terrify anyone living east of the Hudson River, but they sprang up from inside his "own self," as he might say. They were pure Jeffersonian – keep government limited, local and out of people's hair. He thought people should own up for what they do, pay their own way and be left alone if they weren't hurting anybody. Sounded pretty progressive to me, but I was a radical.

# 14 – Sprinting to Seattle

## Steinbeck Timeline

Saturday, Oct. 15, 1960 – On the road to Seattle

*Steinbeck left his overnight camping spot midway between Missoula and the Idaho border and rode U.S. 10 into the top of Idaho. It is here where things again get vague and confusing. In "Charley," Steinbeck says he stopped overnight at an isolated, rundown motel/gas station in the mountains near the Idaho-Washington border and rushed sick Charley to a vet in Spokane the following morning. If Steinbeck did stop in northwest Idaho Saturday night, however, it means he drove only 136 miles that entire day. It's possible Charley's sickness really did slow Steinbeck's pace, as he says in the book. Maybe Charley really did have to see a vet. But given his haste to meet his wife in Seattle, Steinbeck probably spent the night somewhere farther into Washington or drove to Seattle in one 400-mile gulp. Whatever he did on this date, it's a mystery with no clues.*

## Metropolitan Saltese

Leaving Butte behind, zooming toward Missoula on I-90/Old Highway 10, I got another overdose of what captured Steinbeck's heart. Even at 80 mph the broad valleys and mountains ranges just rolled on and on. The sinking sun and wispy rain clouds played tricks with the light. Gray-brown mountainsides and valleys were spotted or smeared with dark pine and spruce trees. The flatlands by the shallow rivers were yellow with what? Oaks? Cottonwoods? Steinbeck would have known.

About 25 miles east of Missoula, the mountains squeezed the road as it threaded through the Sapphire Mountains. Arriving in downtown Missoula, I joined the mobs on the streets. The Saturday night scene was a stark contrast to Butte's dead Uptown. Every one of the University of Montana's 15,000 students apparently was out looking for a beer. At 63, I was the oldest man on campus – and the only one without a backpack or a bike. I ate at the crowded bar of a crowded restaurant and slept at the crowded Holiday Inn for a Hotwire.com price of $63. By noon Sunday I was halfway to Idaho. I was on the wet, warm, Pacific side of the Rockies. It was sunny, 50 degrees and still only token traffic. I was 4,630 Steinbeck Highway miles from Sag Harbor and had yet to wear socks.

As I twisted west down a long mountain valley, crossing and re-crossing the Clark Fork River as it fell toward the Columbia River, I made a rookie mistake. For some unknown reason, I completely forgot to look for where Steinbeck spent his second night in Montana. In a letter to his wife, part of which is in Jackson Benson's biography, Steinbeck said he was camped on private land west of Missoula, 60 miles from Idaho. I should have stopped at Tarkio, or near there, to perform my drive-by journalism act, but I mindlessly cruised by the Tarkio exit on U.S. Highway 10.

I lucked out, though. Tarkio was probably not the place after all. Months after my trip ended, I called a seventh of the population of the Tarkio Valley – four people – to seek their help. One person said it was possible Steinbeck parked by the Clark Fork River at the old Forest Grove Campgrounds. But some of Tarkio's oldest and most helpful citizens were stumped. Exactly where Steinbeck slept on his second night in Montana remains another trivial "Travels With Charley" mystery.

In the thick forests of northwest Montana I pulled off at the Saltese exit to inspect a well-preserved stretch of Old Highway 10. About half a mile long between its two dead ends, the main street of "The Recreational Capital of the Northwest" was a compact 1960s time warp with about 20 buildings. Steinbeck drove down Saltese's main street on Saturday morning, Oct. 15, 1960. Mangold's General Store & Motel had a different name then. But the grocery, six pine-paneled motel rooms and the big "M-o-t-e-l" sign were all there by the edge of the road when Steinbeck and Charley motored past. So were the decommissioned state highway maintenance shed, most of the homes and the building housing the Old Montana Bar & Grill.

Terri Mangold has owned and operated the grocery store/motel complex on the bank of the Clark Fork River since 1995. She played local historian for me. When I-90 was poured on top of U.S. 10's right-of-way in the early 1960s, Saltese's only street – U.S. 10 – was frozen in time and the town got its own interstate exit. Saltese, which Mangold said was in the middle of "a winter play land," had about 60 permanent residents. It gets 20 feet of snow a year and sits under a steep, rugged forest at the foot of the Lookout Run ski resort. Mangold's all-pine motel rooms were absurdly reasonable – $30 a day and up depending on the size. She said they were usually full year round, thanks to the hunters, fishermen and snowmobilers who stay for a week at a time and spend their days killing big things in the woods.

# A Modern Man of the Mountains

At the other end of Main Street was the Greater Saltese region's one-stop entertainment complex, the Old Montana Bar & Grill. Part slots casino, part restaurant, part bar, part gallery of local historical photos, it had a wild kingdom of dead game animals mounted on its walls and on its menu.

Bryan Teeters, 48, was the mountain man personally responsible for many of the elk heads, bear skins and the stuffed mountain lion. He said except for the moose, the animals were locally grown and shot. Teeters, who lived across the street, bagged his trophies the old-fashioned way – with a bow and arrow. Pointing to the mountain lion high above the pool table, he said, "I got that one with a bow out back." By "out back," he meant the infinite forest and looming mountainside that was his backyard. He said he tracked the mountain lion in the snow and when it climbed a tree, it was all over for the big cat. "I shot it from 30 yards," he said, as if the magnificent beast was an ordinary gray squirrel.

Teeters came to Montana from California with his parents when he was 12 and basically grew up and became Jim Bridger with a snowmobile. The wilds of Montana were a paradise for him and his restaurant was full nearly every night. But Teeters was miffed that Montana's he-man government was turning soft – and kicking him in the pocketbook.

The state had recently banned smoking in all public buildings, which he said hurt his casino business. And state wildlife experts were talking about reintroducing wolves into the area. Teeters didn't like wolves for both sensible and selfish reasons. He said wolves kill for the fun of it and kill a lot more game than they can eat, unaware that he was also describing what human hunters do. But that was not a fair thought. It was a city-boy's cheap shot. Teeters was a smart guy. He was worried that the wolves would wipe out the elk. Then there'd be no hunters to come to his backyard to hunt elk by day and eat them at his place by night.

As I left he recommended that I take in some of the local attractions, including the 8,300-foot long Taft Tunnel and the unlucky ghost town of Taft. Taft was a rollicking but nameless young railroad town in 1907 when William Howard Taft visited and, according to Teeters, declared it "the most wicked town in the country." The civic fathers forgave Taft and named their city after him in 1908 when he became America's heftiest president. It didn't matter much, though, because Taft the town was soon destroyed in "the Big Burn," the 1910 wildfire that scoured the valley of its pines and log houses. Only the trees grew back, which they always do.

I thanked Teeters for his suggestion, but I had no time for side-trips. Steinbeck's ghost was moving too fast. As I was getting into my car on Main Street, I told Teeters that the great John Steinbeck drove down the exact road we were standing on 50 years and one day earlier. He thought that was pretty cool. I didn't have to explain who the great John Steinbeck was to Teeters. He knew a lot more about him than the average Montana mountain man because he and Steinbeck had something pretty important in common. They were both born in Salinas, California.

# Steinbeck's Ratty Cabins

Between Saltese and Seattle Steinbeck's trail disappears for a few days into the fog of time and fiction. There are no letters to his wife or editor or agent to consult, no newspaper articles to believe or disbelieve. Because he said it in a letter to his wife, it's certain that Steinbeck and Charley spent Friday night encamped somewhere along U.S. 10 about 40 miles west of Missoula.

On Saturday morning, Oct. 15, 1960, they would have started out on Day 6 of their Sprint to Seattle. Steinbeck would have come through downtown Saltese on Highway 10, then up and over the pine-green mountains at Lookout Pass into Idaho, down the long and swerving hill to the quiet streets of Wallace, across the top of Idaho through Kellogg to Cataldo near the Washington border.

In "Travels With Charley" Steinbeck says he stopped for the night in the mountains "under the ridge of a pass" near the Idaho-Washington border at a ratty motel/gas station combo. He described the place in his usual fine detail, saying it was "a little put-together, do-it-yourself group of cabins, square boxes, each with a stoop, a door, and one window, and no vestige of a garden or gravel paths." He says that "The small combined store, repair shop, and lunch room behind the gas pumps was as unprepossessing as any I have ever seen."

For several pages of mostly dialogue, Steinbeck mediates an argument between a burly, he-man father and his fey 20-year-old son. The mother was gone. The son had a light voice, dressed flamboyantly (he wore an ascot) and was interested in theater, fashion and in becoming a hairdresser. His father was interested only in hunting, fishing, drinking and not seeing his son become a hairdresser. If this caricature of a young gay man trying to escape the mountain-man culture of Idaho sounds like something Steinbeck-the-great-novelist made up, it's because he almost certainly did. Steinbeck said the young man even subscribed to The New Yorker, which to me was the most unbelievable thing of all.

By this time in my trip I had little doubt that the father and son were dramatic inventions – just like the itinerant actor in Alice, the Canucks, the Yankee farmer, et al. But just in case Steinbeck really did stop near the Idaho-Washington border, I left the interstate and looked for Steinbeck's crummy cabins. Not far from Cataldo, within earshot of where I-90's traffic arced through a mountain pass toward Spokane, I searched for several miles along a piece of old U.S. 10. In the Mission Inn restaurant I read some locals the description of the cabins from

"Travels With Charley." I followed up a tip from a long-time resident. I knocked on the doors of several older houses. I peered into heavy underbrush looking for the ruins of a gas station or a collapsed tourist cabin. No luck. Steinbeck had to stop somewhere the night of Oct. 15, 1960, on his way to Seattle, which was about 400 miles from his last known campout. East Canyon Road, the two-lane remnant of U.S. 10 north of Cataldo, fit Steinbeck's description pretty well. But if the cabins had really existed, they shouldn't have been so hard to find. Then again, maybe the cabins existed but the father and son didn't.

As I crossed into Washington I wasn't too happy with my man Steinbeck. His creative-nonfictions in "Charley" had caused me to go driving in circles and knocking on people's doors in an under-populated, over-armed part of country I'd never been to before and would never see again. Thank God the natives were so friendly. Pushing hard until midnight, I made it to all the way to Moses Lake, Washington. After a 300-mile Sunday I slept eagerly, happily, in my seventh Wal-Mart parking lot. I had gotten to be a fan of Wal-Mart's hassle-free lodging: Just pull in, park with your windshield pointed away from the nearest light standard, kick off your sandals and climb in back.

## Steinbeck Timeline

Sunday, Oct. 16, 1960 – Seattle

*While there's no way of knowing for sure where or if Steinbeck stayed in eastern Washington Saturday night, he almost certainly made it to Seattle by Sunday evening, Oct. 16, since he was hurrying and the drive from Spokane to Seattle on U.S. Highway 10 was only 300 miles.*

# Sprawling in Seattle

The temperature in Moses Lake bottomed at 33 degrees, but I barely noticed in my cozy berth. Only my nose and my indispensible Apple MacBook Pro were icy when I woke at 5:50 and aimed at Seattle, only 180 miles west. The previous night I had crossed most of Eastern Washington's dry agricultural tundra, but I was still in the rain shadow of the Cascades. The tree-less land, scrubby with green sage, was almost desert-like. At dawn I swooped down one long hill to the wide Columbia River and up to the top of the other side, where an orderly line of wind turbines twirled in the orange light. It became dry and dead again. No people. Nothing green. Nothing alive taller than a four-year-old.

I-90/Old Highway 10 climbed gently for miles. For a little while I was aiming straight at a large snow-capped mountain that was pinking up nicely in the sun. Mt. Rainier? No idea. The mountaintop disappeared as I entered semi-green valleys and began passing thirsty, untidy farms with cows, horses and pigs. Gigantic open sheds stuffed with bales of hay waited for winter. I even spotted a few stray humans who were not behind a wheel.

Steinbeck came the same way on old U.S. 10 to get to Seattle – and he traveled just as fast. In the first draft of his book, in a paragraph that would be deleted, he wrote, "As before reaching Chicago, I found myself packing on the mileage and for the same reason. My lady wife was to fly out to meet me in Seattle and to travel with me down the West Coast for she had never seen the great real woods. I drove farther and faster than I intended. Increasingly I chose the wider and faster roads." This was one of several instances where Steinbeck admits he was rushing almost blindly to meet his wife Elaine – and where he betrays how little time he actually spent studying the country or meeting its people. When he was alone on the road – whether he was on his Chicago-Seattle sprint, his California-Amarillo dash or his New Orleans-New York City final kick – he was busting ass, not searching for the heart and soul of America.

In Seattle I was going to be staying at a Holiday Inn near the Seattle-Tacoma airport for $65, thanks to Hotwire.com. It would take great luck to find Steinbeck's motel. According to his original manuscript, he cooled his heels at the airport in a modern motor court for three days while he waited for Elaine to jet out from Manhattan.

The Cascade Mountains and their thick evergreen coats finally showed up in my windshield at 10:30, when I was 90 miles east of Seattle. It began to look like Montana again, with a smaller sky. The surface of I-90 got worse by the mile. Spokane had already won the prize for worst roads of the trip, but Seattle's grooved pavement was trying hard to compete. As he approached Seattle on U.S. Highway 10, Steinbeck barely recognized the "little city of space and trees and gardens" he knew as a skirt-chasing young man. He had read about the West Coast's post-war population explosion, but he couldn't believe the changes.

More with sadness than anger, he wrote, "Everywhere frantic growth, a carcinomatous growth. Bulldozers rolled up the green forests and heaped the resulting trash for burning. The torn white lumber from concrete forms was piled beside gray walls. I wonder why progress looks so much like destruction." That out-the-car-window observation of suburban sprawl on the march forever endeared Steinbeck to future generations of the no-growth crowd as a Nostradamus. But it only proved how out of touch he was with 1960 America and the needs of middle-class Americans. With his extra house and two acres by the sea, he didn't need an affordable new home with a little yard in the suburbs. But millions of ordinary urban American families did – and in 1960 they were getting them.

In the 20 years since he'd last seen the city, Seattle's population had jumped from 368,000 to 557,000. Those extra 189,000 humans had to live somewhere. And suburbs, which Steinbeck rarely if ever saw on his trip, were being built where farmers' fields and wooded hilltops used to be. I was growing up in one of them six miles south of downtown Pittsburgh.

Steinbeck wasn't automatically against change – an attitude that he wisely knew was "the currency of the rich and stupid." He knew change was inevitable and unstoppable. But he would be amazed and possibly appalled to see how much more Seattle has spread and changed since he saw it in 1960. In step with the population boom of the West, its metro area has exploded from about 1 million people in 1960 to 3.4 million in 2010.

As far as I could tell, as I hurtled down the steep grades and curves of the Cascades to the valley floor, nothing of significance had changed in Seattle since the last ice age. Steinbeck and I dodged the same ancient monoliths covered with trees, just as we had both passed 95 percent of the same farms, little towns and scenic wonders since Sag Harbor. In spite of Steinbeck's worries about overpopulation and rapid growth, in more than 5,000 highway miles I had seen little evidence that America had added 130 million citizens since 1960. I have a pretty good idea where all those new Americans are living their happy lives, and it's definitely not between Chicago and Seattle.

## Steinbeck Timeline

Monday, Oct. 17 to Oct. 20, 1960 – Seattle

*Steinbeck stayed in Seattle longer than he intended. Based on a handful of detailed scenes he wrote in the first draft of his book but were cut entirely, he checked into a modern motel near the Seattle-Tacoma Airport. He waited three days for Elaine to fly out from New York. He then showed her his old haunts in downtown Seattle before heading south. There's no way to tell when he left Seattle, but based on when he arrived in San Francisco and what he wrote in the first draft, a good guess is that it was Thursday, Oct. 20.*

## Steinbeck's Old Seattle

When Steinbeck took Elaine downtown to show her Old Seattle, they went to Pike Place Market, a busy waterfront marketplace on the brink of a steep hill where locals bought seafood, farm produce and flowers. Seattle's waterfront then was nothing like the official tourist attraction it has become since. I arrived in time for the evening light show. As the red and blue sky slowly dimmed over the harbor, a ferry full of commuters headed out to sea and the moon rose between two skyscrapers.

Though it was Monday night, thousands of people were milling around on cobblestone streets warmly lit by dozens of classic neon signs. Pike Place Market's disorderly maze of fish stalls, flower shops, veggie stands, restaurants, bars and specialty shops is the city's Number 1 destination, attracting as many as 40,000 residents and tourists on a summer's day.

Pike Place Market has its artificial, touristy spots, but overall it's an organic, real marketplace oozing with character. Miraculously, in 1963 an alliance of preservationists and private groups prevented the mayor, members of city council and their chosen developers from replacing it with a redevelopment project that included a hotel, apartments, office buildings and a parking lot. Since then a public-private group has run it with a mission to preserve its unique historic charm.

Packs of raggedy older men occupy the market. Many were residents of the neighborhood who took advantage of low-cost housing and a free medical clinic. They squatted on benches and patrolled the sidewalks. Many were homeless and some clearly crazy. Like thousands of their brothers and sisters who are permanently encamped in the public spaces of downtown San Francisco, they were unsightly but no more dangerous than pigeons.

Before I left Seattle for Oregon, I made a brief attempt to find the motel Steinbeck stayed in at SeaTac, the Seattle-Tacoma airport. I went around to several older motels. But there had been too many changes in 50 years and he provided no helpful clues in the West Coast scenes cut from the first draft of "Travels With Charley." There were interesting details in those lost scenes, however.

For example, Steinbeck said he waited for three days in a "modern" glass and Plexiglas motel room while wife Elaine struggled to book a direct jet flight from

New York to Seattle. He rattled on about luxuriating in its bathtub and soft bed. He played with modern push-button gizmos. He listed – and mocked – the TV shows he watched. "The beauty and culture of our time," he wrote sarcastically: "Gunsmoke. Have Gun Will Travel. I Love Lucy. I love Dinah Shore. I love Barbara Stanwick. The greatest engineering minds in the history of the world had made these marvels available to me. Just looking at all those buttons brought home to me what a primitive life I had been leading."

Steinbeck went on way too long about how horribly his poor "lady wife" suffered from the stress and disappointments of jet travel. When she tried to get a direct flight, he wrote, she found that first-class seats on jets to Seattle were sold out for two weeks. She had to fly a prop plane to San Francisco and switch to a jet there. Then came a luggage snafu. No wonder Elaine was distressed and cranky upon her arrival. Steinbeck made it sound like the poor woman had walked from Manhattan. It was lame and dull stuff, and deserved to be cut. It's hard to believe Steinbeck thought anyone but his own famous friends would want to read about the travails and minor agonies of the jet-setter class.

# 15 – Cruising the Coast

*A writer must so rearrange reality so that it will seem reasonably real to the reader.*

– Cut from first draft of "Travels With Charley"

## Steinbeck Timeline

Friday, Oct. 21 to Oct. 26, 1960 – The Pacific Coast Highway

*There are virtually no hard clues to determine where the Steinbecks stopped as they came down the Pacific Coast through redwood country to San Francisco. Based on scenes deleted from the book's original manuscript, in California they stayed for at least two days at a large, nearly empty resort in the shade of redwoods. The only reliable clue is a postcard Steinbeck mailed on Monday, Oct. 24, 1960, to his editor Pascal Covici from Trinidad, California, where he said he and Elaine stopped for the night at a motel by a redwood grove on U.S. 101, about 300 miles north of San Francisco.*

## America's Prettiest Drive

Following the coastal route Steinbeck took, I drove south on Interstate 5 / U.S. 12 from the Seattle-Tacoma airport to Aberdeen, Washington, and got on U.S. 101, which stays close to the Pacific beaches most of the way to San Francisco. A third of the traffic seemed to be logging trucks, which roared up and over the fir-and-spruce-plastered coastal mountains as fast as their cousins in central Maine. Except for small towns like Cosmopolis and Raymond, western Washington was the usual story – nothing but nature, a smooth two-lane road and token traffic.

After crossing the big mouth of the Columbia River at Astoria, Oregon, U.S. 101 picked up the same theme but added a few more cars and enormous beaches to the mix. The road ran close to the ocean except when it was cutting over, around and through the forests and tree farms of the Oregon Coast Range. People not in cars or trucks were rare. U.S. 101 in Oregon could be the most spectacular drive in the USA. Its biggest downside – besides hundreds of scary Tsunami Hazard Zone road signs – was that it was too beautiful and took so long.

I must have stopped a dozen times to catch views of the Pacific surf, walk along deserted beaches, or take photos of cathedral-sized stacks of basalt rising from the sea. There were places where you could hear the surf or the barking of California sea lions from the highway. The ocean was accessible at dozens of small turnouts. All you had to do was park, lock your car and walk a few hundred

yards to the water's edge. At Arcadia Beach, where a 747 could land if it weren't for the basalt spikes, I counted eight cars, 15 people and four dogs. I passed scores of vintage mom & pop motels, few if any chains and little of anything that screamed new. There were resorts, campgrounds, B&Bs, rental cottages and the lucky few permanent residents with a Highway 101 address who watched the sun fall into the Pacific every day from their living rooms.

At Tillamook, the monstrous Tillamook Air Museum suddenly appeared dead ahead. A manmade mountain 1,000 feet long, it was almost 200 feet high with "Air Museum" stamped on its roof in letters 50-feet tall. It had to be what it looked like it once was – a hangar used for Navy blimps. Under its roof were 30 airplanes and aviation artifacts, but there was no time to visit them. By nightfall I made Neskowin, Oregon, where, 283 miles south of Seattle, I stopped at an almost vacant motel. From the parking lot you can hear the surf crashing, but in the morning I didn't even bother to check out the beach. To adapt a line from Ronald Reagan, if you've seen a dozen spectacular beaches in the last 24 hours, you've seen them all.

## Bikers in the Bush

Sunny, 62 and no chance of tsunamis. Day 24 of my trip was another high-speed nature show: Hours of beauty interrupted by a few coastal towns and the hibernating infrastructure of commerce needed to serve the mobs of summer. U.S. 101 flew me by the beaches, cliffs and massive sand dunes of Oregon's hilly coastline and straight toward the heart of California redwood country. Traffic felt heavy for mid-October, but what did I know? Occasionally I'd blow by a long-distance bicyclist grinding up a steep hill. I didn't feel the least bit guilty.

After I made it through the hippie-flavored downtown of Coos Bay, the highway was suddenly straighter and lonelier. Even at 70 mph, there was no one left to pass. In Coos County Forest, in a tight channel of tall spruce and fir trees, I was starting to worry that everyone in Oregon had overdosed on raw beauty or been carried away by a tsunami.

Then, as I slowed down for a few buildings known only to cartographers as the unincorporated town of Langlois, I passed the Greasy Spoon Café and came upon a young man on a bicycle who was from, where else, France. To tell the nonfictional truth, Boris Skrobek was only living in France. He was really a Pole. Boris was with two other equally colorful and totally mad long-distance bikers, Scotty from Denver and Don from Alaska. They were greedily carbing and hydrating their fat-free bodies in front of the Langlois Market & Deli, the only retail pit-stop on U.S. 101 for dozens of miles.

Boris, who spoke at least Polish, French and English, was 24 and well hidden behind a full beard and glasses. He had worked for a year in Normandy, France, to get up enough money to spend a few months biking across North America by himself. His bike, like the others, was draped with saddlebags holding all his camping gear and clothes.

So far Boris had pedaled his way from Montreal to Vancouver. On a budget of $30 a day, he was sleeping mostly in campgrounds in the USA. But in Canada he slept "a lot in the bush." His final destination was San Francisco, 450 miles south. I asked him for his total distance traveled so far. He said he didn't know it for sure, but in Quebec alone he rode 3,000 kilometers, which was European for 1,800 miles.

Scotty of Denver, 32, was scarfing down a whole tube of Pringles when I pulled up. He and Boris had each started out alone, but they met on the road somewhere, liked each other and paired up. They weren't really traveling with Don, who was on a short 1,500-mile cruise from Bellingham, Washington, to San Diego.

Almost two months earlier Scotty quit his job at a bike shop in Denver and biked through Yellowstone Park and Missoula to Seattle and Vancouver, British Columbia. Rarely riding in the dark, averaging 60 miles a day, he was a few short of 3,000 – miles, not kilometers. His final target was either San Diego or New Mexico. He had been sleeping mostly at campgrounds and RV parks, where he paid a hiker/biker rate, or, when it was permitted, sleeping in city parks. Sometimes he slept off the side of the road "in the bush."

Scotty's trip down the Pacific Coast was part of the Adventure Cycling Association's network of bike routes. The Pacific Coast trail starts in Vancouver and runs 1,853 miles to San Diego. It's not all downhill. The association's description of the 415-mile Oregon leg gives you an idea what a bicyclist – or a motorist – has to suffer to partake of the coastline's stupendous beauty.

"During the peak tourist season," the association says, "there is heavy recreational vehicle traffic along U.S. Highway 101 along the coast, so cyclists must ride cautiously and defensively. This route can be ridden from early spring to late fall. Heavy winter rains can cause flooding and mud slides and may close roads, especially along the coast in the spring. Fog can also be a problem during any season. Due to changing local conditions, it is difficult to predict any major wind patterns."

I thought I was roughing it until I met Boris, Scotty and Don. I took photos of them and their bikes in front of the market and ambushed them again a little bit down the road. In the next hour, I drove farther than they could go in a day. I stopped to eat in the working fishing village of Port Oroford, which boasts that it is the oldest town on the Oregon Coast and the most westerly town in the Lower 48. The shingles, boats, dock, sea air and fresh seafood at The Crazy Norwegian's Fish & Chips shack reminded me of Deer Isle and Stonington, Maine. But the prices and homes in Port Oroford were cheaper and plainer. And the 1,100 inhabitants – wherever they were – were too busy sweating for a living to fully enjoy the ocean views or stand around looking quaint.

Not long after the sun went down I parked to rest my eyes somewhere along the seacoast near some low sand dunes and high grass. I accidentally hit "home" on my Tom-Tom GPS. I was 2,893 miles, 43 hours and 48 minutes due west of my house in the southern exurbs of Pittsburgh. By dark I had breezed past Brookings-Harbor, the only spot in the continental U.S. to be bombed by a foreign power, thanks to a Japanese World War II seaplane launched from a submarine. And then I crossed into beautiful bankrupt California, where more than a fifth of all the country's foreclosed homes were located.

# No Space at the Wal-Mart Inn

In the fishing port of Crescent City I was deeply disappointed to learn – in defiance of Sam Walton's wishes – that the Wal-Mart did not allow bums of any class to park in its lot overnight. The store manager, after apologizing twice for my pain, explained that a local ordinance outlawed sleeping in cars, even on private property. The law, a special affront to property rights worshippers like myself, was designed to thwart the indigenous homeless population, she said. Of course most homeless folk weren't affected because they were carless and were sleeping in the bush with the long-distance bicyclists.

My sleeping crisis ended in a pleasing and memorable way when I lucked upon a room at California's least politically correct mom & pop motel, the fabulous Curly Redwood Lodge. The Curly Redwood sits directly across U.S. 101 from the Crescent City harbor, which regularly gets battered by tsunamis like the one caused by the earthquake off Japan in March of 2011, which created 8-foot waves and destroyed 35 boats.

The Curly Redwood wasn't the place you'd want to spend your first honeymoon, or third. But what it lacked in contrived charm was more than made up for by its character, low price ($55) and what it was built from – a single redwood tree. Redwood paneling, redwood roof posts, redwood siding, solid redwood closet doors. Redwood was the 1950s-vintage motel one and only motif – 57,000 board feet of it.

It was no accident the Curley Redwood was made of redwood. It sits on the front door of Redwood National and State Parks on U.S. 101, aka "The Redwood Highway." Taking a side trip down Old U.S. Highway 101 to the ocean, I did what Steinbeck, trucks and everyone had to do in 1960 before the bypass was constructed.

I drove at 40 mph for almost 15 minutes through a forest of giants 10 and 15 feet wide at their base. Not a redwood grove, but a redwood forest. I don't know how many *Sequoia sempervirens* there are growing in California, but half an hour after leaving the Curly Redwood I was no longer worried about their survival as a species.

Sixty miles south of Crescent City I passed Trinidad, where a Steinbeck postcard to his editor Pascal Covici was postmarked on Oct. 24, 1960. Steinbeck said he and Elaine had stopped the night near the grove of redwoods illustrated on the card. It was the only proof I had that pinpointed where they were at any given time between Seattle and San Francisco. Steinbeck never wrote a word I could find about the magnificent Oregon Coast, which is kind of surprising if he and Elaine had seen it but doesn't prove they didn't.

## Travels With the Duchess

It was on the West Coast that "Travels With Charley" reached its height of deception. In the real world, John, Elaine and Charley made their slow trip down to San Francisco in their overloaded pickup truck. But in the book Elaine is not there. It is only the author and his faithful poodle who visit Seattle, fix a flat tire on a rainy Sunday in Oregon and commune with the great bodies of the redwoods.

It wasn't that way at all in the original manuscript, which co-stars Elaine and reads like the travel log of the Duke and Duchess of Sag Harbor. As soon as she made it to Seattle, Elaine – aka "my wife" – is in about six straight scenes at the waterfront and on the road. Some of those scenes were dropped completely and some were retained, but her presence was stripped out.

One scene completely dropped from the first draft mentions "the several days" Mr. and Mrs. Steinbeck stayed "at a partially closed resort in a big redwood grove." Holed up in "a cottage at the base of a cluster of monster trees," he wrote that he was sore and scraped up after having to flounder in "thick yellow muck" while fixing Rocinante's flat tire, which he said he did as Elaine sat in the cab reading a book.

Steinbeck wrote that the cottage in the redwoods seemed like "the perfect place to rest and refurbish our souls." Apparently, he was halfway to heaven. As he soaked in "a tub of near boiling water," he wrote, "My lady wife slipped in and set a scotch and soda on the edge of the tub. And the world and the people there of, the grasses and the trees became very beautiful."

Another totally dropped scene does not reflect well on Steinbeck's vaunted love for the common man. After he and Elaine hear about a good restaurant nearby, they decide to get dolled up and do the "town." They were disappointed to find that the eatery in the sticks of Northern California was not a Trader Vic's franchise but a neon hellhole. Sounding like an old fogey, Steinbeck wrote that the restaurant possessed "every damnable feature of our civilization – cold glaring light, despondent roaring music from a cathedral juke box, batteries of coin machines, Formica counters and tables. One wall was a cemetery of ugly … pies."

Great descriptive writing, as usual. But when Steinbeck – who rarely let a commoner he meets on his journey escape without uttering a "he don't" or a "them people" – made fun of the waitress for saying "fried tatters" and "We ain't got no (liquor) license," he doesn't sound like a friend of the working class. Later he was happy to report that while he and Elaine slept close to the redwoods, there were "no trippers, no chattering troupes with cameras" to spoil their stay. The entire restaurant tragedy was easily snipped from the final version of "Charley." But excising Elaine from the other scenes posed a larger editorial problem. On the West Coast, whenever he writes "we" in the book he was originally referring to himself and Elaine, not himself and Charley.

He handwrote a short chapter – obviously never published – answering the criticism that Charley was being ignored and assuring everyone he was feeling fine. He explained that with the missus onboard, the standard Steinbeck family pecking order had reasserted itself: "When Charley and I traveled alone together, the dog was indeed man's best friend. But Charley knows better than anyone when the wife is present, he is man's second best friend, and he finds this a normal relationship and perhaps a better one."

In the end, Charley was restored to top billing and Elaine's presence on the West Coast for four weeks was completely eliminated. It was editorially smart – and necessary – to dump the duchess. First of all, the scenes focusing on her were boring as hell. But most important, she seriously undermined the book's romantic conceit. With her by his side every night, Steinbeck was no longer the man alone. He was a love-struck honeymooner. Whoever made or ordered the changes in "Charley" saved the day. They ensured that the book would become a classic story about a famous writer, his beloved dog and the lonely road they traveled, not a book about a wealthy New Yorker, his spoiled "lady wife" and their quest for the perfect cocktail in Northern California.

"Travels With Charley" wasn't the first time one of Steinbeck's wives was dropped from one of his nonfiction books. It also happened in "The Log of the Sea of Cortez," his journal about the six-week scientific expedition to the Gulf of California he took in 1940 with marine biologist friend Doc Ricketts. Steinbeck's first wife Carol was never mentioned yet she was aboard the whole time. It's up to Steinbeck scholars, if they care, to find out who made the editorial decision at Viking Press to remove Elaine from "Travels With Charley." For extra credit, they can explain why pretending Steinbeck was alone on the West Coast wasn't, by itself, an act of deceit that broke faith with readers and disqualifies "Travels With Charley" as a work of nonfiction.

## So many redwoods ...

After passing among so many redwoods, I was afraid I'd be bored with them by the time I got to the Avenue of the Giants. I wasn't. The narrow highway – also once a part of old U.S. 101 – snaked for 33 miles through 51,000 acres of redwood groves. Often impenetrable to sunlight and the signals of cell phones and satellite radio, and connecting a chain of small communities like Pepperwood and Miranda, the avenue was surrounded by a state park that contained the largest stand of virgin redwoods on the planet.

The curvy two-lane highway was often so narrow the monstrous tree trunks touched the edge of the pavement. It didn't seem possible that until the mid-1960s, when the bypass was put in, the avenue was a main route for truckers and the only road to the outside world for Humboldt County marijuana growers. With plenty of small places to pull over, you could shut off your engine and just listen to the silence or walk a hundred yards into the darkness. A million people visit the Avenue of the Giants every year. Yet on Thursday afternoon in October I was able to stand in the middle of the road for five minutes and take all the photos I wanted.

Running out of daylight, I searched for the old Hartsook Inn at the southern end of the avenue. The inn, closed and now owned by the Save-the-Redwoods League, was a real getaway in its day with 62 rustic cabins in the woods and no phones. It was once the place to go for the Hollywood crowd and celebrities like Steinbeck. Several local people at an organic fruit and veggie stand near Pepperwood told me the Hartsook was most likely the resort the Steinbecks stayed at when they were consorting with the redwoods. Maybe so. The Save-the-Redwoods League had no old guest records. And in the failing light I never did see the inn, though everyone told me it was impossible to miss.

Emerging from the dark redwood forest, I stopped for dinner in a grocery store/cafe in downtown Garberville, the prosperous capital of Marijuana County. I swear everyone was stoned. Demographically, everyone on the sidewalk was either old and homeless looking or young and homeless looking (they were the ones with the overstuffed backpacks).

As I was getting back into my RAV4, a stereotypically solid citizen of Garberville was squatting with his back against a storefront.

"Is that a 2010?"

"Yeah."

"I've got an '09."

*Sure you do, pal.*

He asked where I was from and I told him Pittsburgh.

"I've got an uncle in Pittsburgh and I went to a football game at Three Rivers Stadium in the '80s, when I was a teen-ager."

Then he hit me with the closer that I should have seen coming.

"I've got some good weed if you're interested."

Good old California. It was bankrupt in myriad ways, but it still had some of its old ‘60s spirit. I declined the sidewalk weed vendor’s kind offer, which was 20 years too late for my lifestyle, and missed the chance to contribute to the GDP of Humboldt County.

That night I tried to make it all the way to my daughter Michelle's house in Mill Valley, but I couldn't stay awake. After sleeping in my car for three hours in a big open patch in the hills somewhere lonely along U.S. 101 near Willits, I polished off the remaining 100 miles. Pulling into my daughter's driveway at 2 a.m., I slept in the back of my car until 6, no doubt breaking several dozen zoning laws in her upstanding community.

Because I didn't dawdle in Seattle or relax for days in the redwoods, I was a week ahead of Steinbeck's pokey pace. Like a poor migrant journalist, I crashed on my daughter's couch. She lived on a street lined with small, highly polished, late-1940s California ranch houses – wood, stucco, no basements, no second floors and .17-acre lots. Their average price was about $900,000. Or used to be, until the housing bubble burst and values fell 20 or 30 or 40 percent.

I couldn't tell which, if any, houses in her neighborhood were in foreclosure or had mortgages that were underwater, but everything seemed Marin County normal. The driveways still had their Audis, BMWs and hybrid SUVs. Handsome dogs were being walked. Handsome children were being swung in the community park-let. As long as no homeowner lost his/her six-figure job or needed to quickly move out of paradise, no one needed to panic. The Northern California real-estate roller coaster was always going up and down. You just have to be careful, and lucky, about when you decide to jump on and off the thrill ride.

# 16 – Fun in San Francisco

*San Francisco put on a show for me. I saw her across the bay, from the great road that bypasses Sausalito and enters the Golden Gate Bridge. The afternoon sun painted her white and gold – rising on her hills like a noble city in a happy dream. A city on hills has it over flat-land places. New York makes its own hills with craning buildings, but this golden white acropolis rising wave on wave against the blue of the Pacific sky was a stunning thing, a painted thing like a picture of a medieval Italian city which could never have existed.*

– "Travels With Charley"

## Steinbeck Timeline

Wednesday, Oct. 26 to Oct. 30, 1960 – San Francisco

*According to city columnist Herb Caen, the Steinbecks arrived in San Francisco on Wednesday evening, Oct. 26, 1960. They socialized with John's friends and stayed at the posh St. Francis Hotel downtown through Sunday. He was interviewed in his suite on Oct. 28 by Curt Gentry, a freelancer for the San Francisco Chronicle's book section.*

## Steinbeck Hearts 'The City'

San Francisco did nothing special to seduce John Steinbeck. She has put on the same lovely show he described so well in "Travels With Charley" for millions of people who were not already in love with her, as Steinbeck was. Thousands of tourists, day-trippers, photographers, hikers and bicyclists from around the world enjoy the sight of San Francisco from the hills above the north end of the Golden Gate Bridge every day.

While I killed a week in the Bay Area revisiting Steinbeck sites and watching the Giants play the Rangers in the World Series, I went to the top of the Marin Headlands. I had been there at least 20 times since 1974. It was always a treat and never the same. Details of light and color differ wildly from season to season, day to day, even hour to hour, depending on the whims of clouds, fog, wind and rain. Sometimes you can hear the hum of the bridge traffic far below, sometimes you can't even see the bridge. It's an absurd panorama, a superior example of man and nature showing off their greatest engineering works and collaborating at their best – at least until the same tectonic violence that created all that natural beauty destroys it.

The wide-angled view of the city and the bay and the islands and the mountains and the towering bridges that tie them together has not changed since Steinbeck took his stunning verbal snapshot. From afar San Francisco still looks like the same place. It has the same tourist attractions that made it world famous as a place where it's simply great to be – fabulous views in every direction, the Golden Gate, Alcatraz, cable cars, terrifyingly steep streets, Coit Tower, Chinatown, Fisherman's Wharf, fog, beaches, parks, good food and restaurants.

But 50 years have brought dramatic changes, and they've not all been for the better. Republican bitching notwithstanding, it's not because it's become America's most politically liberal city. Or that its percentage of gays, immigrants, Asians and Latinos is much higher than in 1960. Or even that it's overrun with computer geeks. It's that San Francisco exacts such a cripplingly high price on anyone who wants to live there. America's most beautiful and visitable city is much more crowded with people and especially cars than in 1960. Its home prices and rents are obscene, beyond the reach of not only the working class but also the middle class. Its parking shortage is chronic, its parking enforcement sadistic.

The city's infamous Skid Row, where in Steinbeck's day squalid flophouses provided cheap rooms for the city's indigent and street drunks, is history, wiped out in the 1970s by urban renewal. But slum clearance, as usual, only moved the problem elsewhere. By 2010 almost 10,000 homeless and/or crazy people lived on downtown sidewalks and in shelters, an intractable civic embarrassment and tourist turnoff that cost city taxpayers $200 million a year.

From his description, Steinbeck didn't drive to the top of the Marin Headlands, where you can wander around the ruins of coastal defense forts, look down on container ships squeezing under the Gold Gate or risk your life peering over the grassy cliff to see the surf foaming against the shore 800 feet below your feet. Most likely, he cast his loving gaze from Vista Point, the popular scenic lookout at the north end of the Golden Gate Bridge. Essentially level with the bridge deck's six lanes, 200 feet above the icy bay, Vista Point was already open in 1960. Its parking lot/viewing area was like an international block party the afternoon I was there. Half my time was spent taking pictures of couples from Australia, Florida, France, Japan and Berkeley – with their own cameras – so they could prove they were together in San Francisco.

But it didn't really matter where Steinbeck stood. He could have described the sparkling skyline of San Francisco from memory. As he wrote in "Charley," it's where he spent his "attic days" struggling to become a writer. During the 1920s, while Hemingway and the other literary supernovas of his generation were losing themselves and becoming rich and famous in Paris, Steinbeck, who didn't have the money, the desire or the Ivy League pedigree to move to France, said he "fledged in San Francisco, climbed its hills, slept in its parks, worked on its docks, marched and shouted in its revolts."

Despite his fondness for San Francisco, Steinbeck had little to say about it in his book. After describing the city from the other side of the Golden Gate Bridge, he wrote, "Then I crossed the great arch hung from filaments and I was in the city I knew so well. It remained the City I remembered, so confident of its greatness that it can afford to be kind. It had been kind to me in the days of my poverty and it did not resent my temporary solvency. I might have stayed indefinitely, but I had to go to Monterey to send off my absentee ballot."

That's it for San Francisco. Steinbeck's next paragraph is about the politics of Monterey County, "where everyone was a Republican" including his family. But in the nonfiction world, Steinbeck had no intention of zipping past his favorite city without partaking of its pleasures. He spent four busy days downtown, staying at the handsome St. Francis Hotel in Union Square.

Apparently, booking a room in San Francisco had been difficult even for him because of conventions. If scenes cut from the book's first draft can be believed, Elaine made several fruitless calls ahead to hotels from roadside pay phones before they landed a suite at the St. Francis, where Caruso, Fatty Arbuckle and Hemingway had once been regulars and Steinbeck was a familiar face. In the deleted scenes, Steinbeck described arriving with Elaine via U.S. Route 101 and the Golden Gate Bridge. After getting lost for a while, he found his way to the St. Francis downtown.

Now the Westin St. Francis, it has undergone many cosmetic changes since 1960. But in 2010, when I prowled its halls and stairways, it still had dark wood, heavy rugs, mirrored ceilings, monstrous chandeliers and a two-ton oak shoeshine stand. Everything else – the floors, the back steps, walls – was made of marble. Steinbeck wrote that he parked Rocinante at the luxury hotel's entrance – and just left it there, where it was in the way and attracting the wrong class of attention. He went straight to his hotel room and jumped in the bathtub with a whisky and soda at his side. He really enjoyed sitting in bathtubs with whiskies and sodas.

In the cut scenes Steinbeck purred that the spacious suite was "pure grandeur." He was pleased to find no Formica, no plastic, no cheap ashtrays in the St. Francis, which in 1960 was already old, prestigious and, as he admitted, "outmoded" and "trapped in an ancient and primitive way of doing things." He wasn't complaining about the hotel's old ways. Eating in the living room on white linen, he was pleased in his first draft to report being attacked by an army of servants – "valet, waiters, maids, pressers, housekeeper." Apparently, after her punishing ride in Rocinante and a week's worth of rustic resorts, Elaine was back in her idea of lodging heaven. She preferred well-staffed English country inns to the "do-it-yourself" style of the modern American motel, where you had to fetch your own ice at the end of the hall and lug your own luggage. "My lady wife was very pleased," Steinbeck wrote.

As he sat in his bathtub "like a sunburned Buddha," Steinbeck wrote, the phone rang. It was the doorman. Rocinante was blocking traffic and it didn't fit in the underground parking garage across the street under Union Square. What should be done with it? The unsightly pickup truck was moved to a parking lot and the hotel scenes end with Elaine calling the hairdresser. It's not hard to understand why this glimpse of the Steinbecks indulging themselves on the road was purged from the book. And where was faithful Charley in these dropped scenes? His presence at the St. Francis was never mentioned. Apparently he'd already been checked into a kennel.

## Steinbeck meets the press

Headquartered at the St. Francis, Steinbeck hung out with old friends at some of the city's top bars and restaurants. The local print media instantly discovered his arrival. Herb Caen, the famed city columnist of the San Francisco Chronicle and "the uncrowned prince" of the city, reported in his daily column on Friday, Oct. 28 that his friend John Steinbeck had "chugged" into town "from New York" on the evening of Oct. 26.

The next day local writer Curt Gentry got a tip from a Chronicle staffer. Doing what any hustling freelancer would do, Gentry called the famous visiting author in his hotel room and begged for an interview. Steinbeck was notoriously publicity shy, but he told Gentry to come to the St. Francis the next morning. Gentry, then 29, would go on to write more than a dozen books, including his biggest one with Vincent Bugliosi, "Helter Skelter: The True Story of the Manson Murders." But in 1960 he was a struggling writer, ex-newspaper reporter and bookstore manager. He lived in North Beach, the super-hip Italian neighborhood in downtown San Francisco. He mixed with jazz musicians, young writers and the Beats, who were headquartered at Lawrence Ferlinghetti's City Lights Bookstore at the corner of Broadway and Columbus. He knew Jack Kerouac and Allen Ginsburg in passing and novelist/poet Richard Brautigan well, but Gentry was also a serious Steinbeck fan.

On my research trip in the spring of 2010 Gentry met me at the Washington Square Bar & Grill. In its heyday the dim, aging, wood-lined North Beach landmark was a hangout for writers, politicos, musicians and the city's in-crowd. But the WashBaG, as Herb Caen had nicknamed it, was almost empty when I was there and in a few months would close forever. Gentry, as well known to the staff as the owner, was easy to spot at the bar, looking dapper in his brown cap. He was the real deal. “Helter Skelter” made him rich. His 1991 New York Times bestseller “J. Edgar Hoover” exposed Hoover’s paranoia, his serial abuses of power and how he created the myth of the FBI as invincible and incorruptible.

At 79 Gentry was still writing tough books like the one he was working on about the Las Vegas mob. He couldn’t have been nicer, more helpful or more supportive of my “Charley”-retracing project. Not only did he buy me lunch and ignore our wide political divide. But he told me stories about the 1960 North Beach scene, repeated his favorite Steinbeck gossip and, when I expressed doubt about pulling off a book deal, kindly said, “I have faith in you.” On top of that moral support, Gentry gave me something else that was priceless – 10 pages of notes he had typed up after his meeting with Steinbeck. An observant record of what Steinbeck was doing and thinking in mid-“Charley” trip, Gentry’s account depicts a politically partisan 58-year-old at the top of his game, not lonely, not depressed, but full of piss and vinegar.

When Gentry went to the St. Francis for his 11 a.m. interview on Friday, Oct. 28, he said, Elaine was still in bed, Charley was in a kennel and John was hung over. “It looked like they both had quite a night," Gentry told me. A longtime admirer of Steinbeck, Gentry showed up at Steinbeck’s hotel suite with two shopping bags filled with every Steinbeck title he could carry – 21 books. He asked Steinbeck to sign the books, which he cheerfully did. Steinbeck had just finished sending Adlai Stevenson a telegram containing some silly anti-Nixon jokes and was sewing together the clasp for his walking stick. Later, after Steinbeck finished a rant about what he called the immorality of Americans, Gentry wrote that “he tossed the stick across the room in anger.”

In his notes, Gentry described Steinbeck as friendly, talkative and animated. They discussed, among many subjects, the presidential election, what was wrong with America, why his friend and neighbor Dag Hammarskjold would make a great president and why Hemingway should write about people not bullfighting. Steinbeck told Gentry he was driving across the country in an attempt to find out what the American people thought about politics. "Everywhere he has traveled," Gentry wrote in his notes, "there is fantastic interest. People are not indifferent, or undecided. They just won't say."

Telling Gentry he had lately been seeing signs of a close Kennedy victory, Steinbeck made fun of Eisenhower and bemoaned the fact that for the previous eight years the Republicans had "made it fashionable to be stupid." Gentry also noted that Steinbeck "had much to say on Richard Nixon, a great part of it unprintable." According to Gentry, Steinbeck was down on Americans for becoming soft and what he called “immoral.” Previewing what he would express in his recently completed but not yet published novel “The Winter of Our Discontent,” Steinbeck defined “immorality as ‘taking out more than you are willing to put back.’”

Steinbeck, wrote Gentry, “went on to note emphatically that ‘a nation or a group or an individual cannot survive immorality. The individual can’t survive being soft, comforted, content. He only survives well when the press is on him. In Rome when they began taking more out than they put in they began to decay.’ And then his voice grew louder, his gestures became more emphatic as he added

'If a fuse blew out in the Empire State Building today a million people would trample themselves to death ... No one can do anything anymore. Who could slaughter and cut up a cow if they had to? No it has to be carefully cut for them, cellophane wrapped. They have lost the ability to be versatile. When either people or animals lose their versatility they become extinct.'"

John Steinbeck: 'America's King Arthur Is Coming'

JOHN STEINBECK

When Gentry asked if he'd ever come back to live in California, Steinbeck said what he would later write in "Travels With Charley" after visiting his old haunts in Monterey. Steinbeck, according to Gentry, "said, sadly, 'The truest words ever written were Thomas Wolfe's "You Can't Go Home Again." I wish it weren't so but when I come back to California to stay it will be in a box.' "

Gentry had another gift for me. He gave me a copy of his original Steinbeck article, before it was edited. The piece ran in the San Francisco Chronicle on Sunday, Nov. 6, 1960, under the headline "John Steinbeck: 'America's King Arthur is Coming.'" (In an eerie presaging of Jackie Kennedy's post-assassination comment that her husband's presidency had been "an American Camelot," Steinbeck had said, apparently in reference to JFK, that all countries have legendary King Arthur-types who show up during times of trouble.)

In his article Gentry described Steinbeck as "big in body, mind, and heart" and "full of humor, vitriol, compassion and strong feeling." What Gentry had written was printed verbatim until it came to his attempts to share some of Steinbeck's stronger political opinions with the Chronicle's readers. A 500-word chunk at the end of his article containing all the mean things Steinbeck had said about Nixon and Eisenhower had been simply lopped off. The newspaper, which along with the San Francisco Examiner gave its editorial support to Nixon, wasn't going to let a famous author trash its Republican hero two days before the election.

The edits didn't surprise Gentry. He was very involved in politics in 1960. Like Steinbeck, he was a devout Adlai Stevenson Democrat. During the 1956 presidential year, when he was active in the Young Californians for Stevenson, Gentry was called upon to drive Stevenson around town a couple times. In 1956 he also was a driver for JFK, who apparently was on his best behavior because Gentry had no sexy story to share.

Gentry and Steinbeck kept in touch, exchanging several letters over the next few years. After Steinbeck's death Gentry wanted to write a book about him and his relationship with his close friend Ed Ricketts, the marine biologist and real-life model for Doc in "Cannery Row." Steinbeck's agent, Elizabeth Otis, liked the idea, Gentry said. But widow Elaine – who controlled Steinbeck's estate with a firm hand – nixed it. Elaine was, to put it kindly, not Gentry's favorite Steinbeck. One thing that bothered him, he said, was the closeness of Elaine to Steinbeck's biographers, Jackson Benson and Jay Parini.

"They automatically accepted anything she said about his first two wives, Carol or Gwen," he said. "Everything I've read and heard is that Elaine was a real ball-buster and a terrible person, with her ex-husband, Zachary Scott (the movie actor), manipulating her in the background." That was a new bit of inside-Steinbeck World gossip/dirt for me. I had no idea if it was true and didn't care one way or the other, but it sounded like something a guy who wrote an expose of J.E. Hoover might know.

Since Gentry had lived almost exclusively in North Beach since the mid-1950s, he was a good person to ask about how the neighborhood had changed. The biggest difference, he said, was the proliferation of striptease joints. That was pretty much all the "entertainment" there was in 2010. But in 1960, the clubs and bars spinning around the intersection of Columbus and Broadway were booking stars of the present and incubating stars of the future.

Miles Davis, John Coltrane and Art Tatum played in clubs. Johnny Mathis got his start in North Beach in the mid '50s right after high school. The famous North Beach nightclub the Hungry i, by itself, is said to have launched the careers of Lenny Bruce, Mort Sahl, Bill Cosby, Jonathan Winters and Barbra Streisand.

The Hungry i was owned by mad impresario Enrico Banducci, who also opened up Enrico's Coffee House on Broadway. Upstairs was Finochio's, the famous nightclub featuring a vaudevillian floorshow of female impersonators. Gentry knew and liked Banducci. As soon as he made enough money, Gentry said, he basically lived in Enrico's sidewalk cafe, which by day was a Herb Caen watering hole and by night a de facto after-hours club for cops, prostitutes and scuffling writers like him.

Enrico's Café still exists. But its glory days, like North Beach's, are ancient history. The afternoon I went to check it out it was closed for lunch. Basically unchanged since 1960, its sidewalk tables were jammed inside behind big glass doors. The sidewalk patio was showing its age, its concrete cracked and its booths worn at the corners. The three-story building needed a paint job. The top floor where Finochio's raunchy floorshow once shocked or entertained the straight world looked vacant.

Enrico's Café's near neighbors in 2010 were strip clubs like the Hungry I Club ("The Best Girls in Town") and Big Al's adult bookstore. But still on the corner of Columbus and Broadway was City Lights Books, which became world famous in 1956 after its owner Lawrence Ferlinghetti published Allen Ginsberg's poem "Howl." The precedent-setting First Amendment test-case that followed ultimately overturned the country's obscenity laws and allowed banned books like "Lady Chatterley's Lover" to be published in the Land of the Free.

For several days in the fall of 1960 Steinbeck loafed only a few hundred feet from City Lights, yet he had nothing to do with the Beats and their revolutionary scene, and vice versa. Ferlinghetti's assistant told me Ferlinghetti and Steinbeck – the new literary generation and the old – never met then or any other time. By 2010 City Lights and the Beat Museum – a well-done retail shrine to the lives and works of Kerouac, Ginsberg and other dead Beats – were the only two reasons left for going to what was once one of the coolest, most cutting edge, most culturally important intersections in America.

## Portrait of an Immortal

The great columnist Herb Caen, who in 1958 coined the word "beatnik" to describe the Beat Generation, also captured a sharp, mid-trip portrait of John Steinbeck. Caen's breezy, literate daily column of insider gossip and smart-alecky opinion about the city he called "Baghdad by the Bay" was a must-read for decades until his death in 1997.

In his Oct. 30 column he detailed the recent afternoon encounter he had with Steinbeck at Enrico's sidewalk cafe, where Caen ate lunch nearly every day. "John Steinbeck, well-nigh immortal writer, was there, looking distinguished, like/as a writer should. Pinstriped suit. Black hat. Silver-topped cane. And a handsome beard." Caen quoted Steinbeck's explanation for the beard: "'Hemingway wears a beard because he has skin cancer. My reason is pure vanity. The cane? I broke my kneecap four times.'"

Steinbeck, pushing away his lunch and ordering a beer, told Caen what he was up to: "'I drove across the country in a campwagon. Alone. My wife met me in Seattle. I've been living in New York – that's not America – and Europe. I hadn't seen my own country in twenty years. I wanted to get to know the people again, hear how they talk and feel. You can't live on memories.' " Steinbeck also told Caen that the American people "'are disturbed, plenty. They feel nobody in Washington has been telling them what's going on. I think Kennedy will win. It's like writing a play – you can't fool people. You can get away with a sensational play, maybe, but not a bad one. Nixon is a bad play, the kind you don't believe.'"

Caen said Steinbeck "lit a cigarette with a lighter strung around his neck on a black cord" and raved about the "magnificent" beauty of the country, especially Montana. Other topics included Steinbeck's upcoming novel about America's lack of morality and a few semi-humorous asides. Charley and Elaine were not mentioned, though they were probably there.

Caen's brief detailed depiction of Steinbeck, like Gentry's longer portrait, is telling. It also almost single-handedly destroys the "Travels With Charley" Myth. The "well-nigh immortal writer" Caen met – dressed flamboyantly for lunch in one of the hottest eateries in town – was not the grizzled romantic road warrior of "Travels With Charley." Nor was he lonely, depressed or sickly. Nor was he roughing it, trying to lay low or searching very hard for America.

# Barnaby Conrad's Joint

During his rest stop in San Francisco, Steinbeck hung around a great deal with his multi-talented friend Barnaby Conrad. Conrad, then 38, was an author, an artist, a musician and an ex-bullfighter, ex-diplomat and ex-secretary to Sinclair Lewis. Conrad met Steinbeck after he chose Conrad's bestselling novel "Matador" as his favorite book of 1952. In 1960 Conrad owned the El Matador, a popular celebrity piano bar in North Beach. The swank hangout was decorated with bullfighting gear, bullfighting photos, bullfighting art and two stuffed bullheads. It was where Sinatra, Judy Garland and the Reagans went when they were in town, where Marilyn Monroe or Lenny Bruce or Duke Ellington or Norman Mailer might drop in. Where Kerouac was comfortable.

El Matador is long gone, but it was just a few doors down on Broadway from Enrico's. Conrad ate lunch at Enrico's with Steinbeck almost every day of his "Travels With Charley" layover. In the spring of 2010, when I began researching Steinbeck's trip, Conrad was one of the first persons I contacted. He was 88 and living in Santa Barbara, California. Steinbeck was "riding high and in wonderful spirits" when they saw each other 50 years earlier, he told me. "He visited me a couple of times in my saloon and took me to see the inside of Rocinante."

One of their adventures together took Conrad and the Steinbecks down the Pacific Coast to Monterey and Carmel. Conrad had been drawn into producing an independent movie based on a Steinbeck short-story called "Flight." According to Steinbeck biographer Jackson Benson, when Steinbeck heard that Conrad was in "deep financial trouble" and having trouble selling "Flight" to distributors, he offered to do a brief "stand-up" introduction for the movie. "Flight" had debuted at the San Francisco Film Festival days before Steinbeck hit town, and had been generally panned.

The scouting trip down the coast took Steinbeck to the city of Monterey, which he had not seen in 24 years. The city was trying to revive Ocean View Avenue and had officially renamed the blighted street of closed sardine factories "Cannery Row" in Steinbeck's honor. When Steinbeck saw what the city had done he was "terribly depressed," Conrad told me. "He hated it," said Conrad, who had told the same story to Steinbeck biographer Benson nearly 30 years earlier.

In his bio, Benson has other details about what happened when Conrad and the Steinbecks got to John's old stamping/writing/drinking grounds. Elaine excitedly pointed out that the movie theater on Cannery Row had been christened "The Steinbeck" and she said she wanted to go inside. But Steinbeck could barely look at it, writes Benson. It wasn't because a naughty Bridget Bardot movie titled "Come Dance With Me" was playing. It was because the theater was branded with his name – one of the early signs that "Steinbeck Country" was in gestation.

Though he had given his permission, Steinbeck hated seeing his name on the marquee, Benson wrote. He knew by then that after he was safely dead his name was going to be used to boost his hometown of Salinas and the city of Monterey. Everything that Steinbeck said happened to Sinclair Lewis in his hometown after his death came true for him, too – by a factor of 1,000. After he died, Steinbeck had a whole country named after him.

Conrad and Steinbeck found a spot to film by the ocean on 17 Mile Drive near Carmel and returned the next day to shoot there. After several takes, the camera-shy Steinbeck was able to deliver the brief introduction to "Flight." It was attached to the movie, but reportedly didn't help it much commercially. A photo of John and Elaine Steinbeck on the location set is in "Looking for Steinbeck's Ghost," a book Jackson Benson wrote about the 13 years of torture he underwent to complete his biography "The True Adventures of John Steinbeck, Writer." The Steinbecks are sitting at the base of a tree eating boxed lunches. Elaine is wearing a headscarf and John is wearing a corduroy sports coat but no tie. Charley and Rocinante were parked elsewhere.

## Peeing in Muir Woods

Based on an another story told in Jackson Benson's biography, at some point during his stay at the St. Francis Hotel Steinbeck drove back across the Golden Gate to Muir Woods, where he said Charley peed on a redwood that "was 50 feet across, 150 feet tall and 2,000 years old." There's a drawn-out scene in "Charley" in which Steinbeck tries to get Charley to pee on a redwood, but the tree is so huge Charley doesn't recognize it as a target. An example of the book's dopey pee humor, it may have been based on the Muir Woods visit.

In any case, since Steinbeck said he went to Muir Woods, it was my job to go there and see how things had changed. Fifty years is a blink of an eye for a redwood, so it was no surprise that Muir Woods was still a cool, quiet, dark, beautiful oasis of old growth Coast Redwoods only 12 miles north of downtown. But a lot of things were different about it in 1960.

It may or may not have been officially called Muir Woods National Monument then, no one could tell me for certain. But the same 500-year-old trees Steinbeck saw were still standing tall. In 1960 there was no visitor center to sell him nature books, organic local salads, coffee and gluten-free pastries. And instead of two miles of boardwalks and paved walkways, he and Charley had only dirt paths to walk on.

Muir Woods was purchased by a private individual more than 100 years ago and then given to the federal government for safekeeping. That was exactly the opposite ownership arrangement my libertarian brethren and I would prefer, but I had to admit that Muir Woods appeared to be well maintained and carefully protected. It was no place for silently communing alone with nature, though. It was a place for weddings and herds of tourists. On a Monday morning at 10, five sightseeing buses and 30 cars had already delivered more than a 100 people through the front gate. Steinbeck wouldn't have liked the Muir Woods I saw – too crowded, too official, too controlled. And Charley would have been displeased to learn Muir Woods, like so much of America in 2010, was no longer a dog-friendly place. Not even on a leash.

## Steinbeck's Libertarian Streak

While I was in San Francisco, back home in Pittsburgh a few regular Tea Party readers of my brother John's hybrid sports & politics blog had an ideological bone to pick with me. They asked why I, a libertarian, was wasting my time writing about a lousy left-wing/commie writer like John Steinbeck.

First of all, as I explained to them in my "Travels Without Charley" road blog, if I only wrote about people whose politics I agreed with even 50 percent of the time, I would have had few people to write about during my journalism career. Second, Steinbeck was not as far left as Hubert Humphrey, George McGovern or Teddy Kennedy. In fact, in some ways – specifically his animosity/bellicosity toward the Soviet Union and communism, his hawkish position on Vietnam and his affection for guns – Steinbeck was far to the right of McGovern and most artists and celebrities of the 1960s.

As a staunch New Dealer, Steinbeck, like most artists of his generation, believed that a bigger, stronger, more pervasive federal government could fix social problems or micromanage the economy without making things worse or diminishing the freedom of citizens. He made constant fun of the John Birch Society's fevered anti-communism, even in the pages of "Charley," which all good 1960 liberals were required to do at least once a year.

But he was no commie and no fool. He knew what was wrong with the Evil Soviet Empire. And when he went behind its fences on cultural exchanges in the 1950s and 1960s, he behaved better than most American writers and celebrities. He didn't kowtow to Soviet officials, but bucked their authority. He was an individual, a free and outspoken American – and he acted like one.

He refused to be a pawn or a fool for Moscow's propaganda purposes and went out of his way to meet and encourage dissident writers. He proved he was no Red in this wise and prescient message he delivered over Radio Free Europe in 1954 to the captive peoples of Eastern Europe, who looked then like they would be imprisoned forever behind the Iron Curtain:

> To my friends,
>
> There was a time when I could visit you and you were free to visit me. My books were in your stores and you were free to write to me on any subject. Now your borders are closed with barbed wire and guarded by armed men and fierce dogs, not to keep me out but to keep you in. And now your minds are also imprisoned. You are told that I am a bad writer but you are not permitted to judge for yourselves. You are told we are bad people but you are forbidden to see and to compare. You are treated like untrustworthy animals, subjected to conditioning as cold and ruthless as though you were rats in a laboratory. You cannot travel, you cannot read freely and you cannot work at the profession of your choice. Your writers are the conditioned servants of a regime. All of this is designed to destroy your ability to think.
>
> I beg you to keep alive the integrity of the individual in his ability to judge and compare and create. May your writers write secretly and hold their writing for the time when this grey anesthetic has passed as pass it must. The free world outside your prison still lives. You will join it again and it will welcome you. Everything around you is cynically designed to destroy you as individuals. You must remember and teach your children that they are precious, not as dull cogs in the wheel of party existence, but as units complete and shining in themselves.

That fine defense of individual rights and freedom, plus his indirect appreciation in "Travels With Charley" of property rights, plus his little anti-government rant at the border crossing at Niagara Falls, prove that Steinbeck was not as left-wing as his friends wished and his enemies thought. For a devout New Dealer, he had a decent libertarian streak.

# 17 – Steinbeck Country, USA

*My departure was flight. But I did do one formal and sentimental thing before I turned my back. I drove up to Fremont's Peak, the highest point for many miles around. I climbed the last spiky rocks to the top. Here among these blackened granite outcrops General Fremont made his stand against a Mexican army, and defeated it. When I was a boy we occasionally found cannon balls and rusted bayonets in the area. This solitary stone peak overlooks the whole of my childhood and youth, the great Salinas Valley stretching south for nearly a hundred miles, the town of Salinas where I was born now spreading like crab grass toward the foothills.*

– "Travels With Charley"

## Steinbeck Timeline

Sunday, Oct. 30 to Nov. 15, 1960 – Monterey Peninsula

*The Steinbecks – John, Elaine and Charley – move 120 miles south to the Monterey Peninsula for a two-week stay with his sister Beth at the Steinbeck family cottage in Pacific Grove. He is interviewed and photographed at the cottage by the Monterey Peninsula Herald. The article, "John Steinbeck Back – But Not to Stay," runs Nov. 4, 1960, and includes a photo of Steinbeck standing in the garden of the cottage with a cigarette in his mouth.*

## Rough Morning in Monterey

City of Monterey. McDonald's. Sonic hell at 6:40 a.m. I was getting off to a bad start for what would be a long Saturday in Steinbeck Country. The Neil Diamond Channel was blasting an acoustical version of "A Song Sung Blue." The place was filling up with a chattering but unintelligible mob of Japanese tourists making a pre-dawn Mac attack.

On my way down U.S. 101 from San Francisco Friday afternoon, I had stopped in San Jose to say hello to some people at San Jose State's Steinbeck Center. I left two things behind in San Jose. I left a note under Professor Susan Shillinglaw's office door, telling her that over the weekend I was going to be in the City of Monterey-Pacific Grove area, where I had been mistakenly told she lived. I'd been gently stalking her for six months by phone and in person at the Steinbeck Fest. I had hoped she'd finally have time to talk to me about what I had been learning about "Travels With Charley" and its problems with reality.

The other thing I left in San Jose was my debit card. I left it sticking out of an ATM on the street corner across from San Jose State's library. No one had used it – though someone had tried. It wasn't really much of a crisis. My bank at home automatically killed my card and I had to switch to my other bank.

When you leave your debit card in an ATM, as I did in San Jose and once in Guatemala City, it can be a real pain. But I can't believe I ever lived or traveled without ATMs, which are one of the great inventions of mankind, a modern miracle of technology and trust. People whine about transaction fees. Young people take them for granted, like cell phones. Not me. I'm old.

In the late 1970s I remember standing in lines 25-people long at a Security Pacific bank on Hollywood Boulevard just to cash a check so I could eat lunch. I remember being in Helena, Montana, in 1980 and trying to cash a check from my bank in L.A. I might as well have been from Mars. I also remember how convenient it was in 2001 to walk up to ATMs on the streets of Lima, insert my magic plastic card from a local bank in Washington, Pa., USA, and get all the *nuevo sols* I needed.

In McDonald's, to a soundtrack of Neil Diamond, I let a middle-aged Japanese guy with a hat step in front of me at the register. I was quickly sorry I had been such a nice guy. He ordered 55 Egg McMuffins and 55 coffees. It turned out he was the driver/tour guide for the column of Japanese tourists that had been pouring out of the bus in the parking lot as I pulled in. I had hustled to the counter to beat the shuffling throng. But without a uniform or clipboard or bullhorn, the driver/guide fooled me into thinking he was just a local guy.

In western Pennsylvania, I would have known better. Pittsburgh is officially the lily-whitest and least ethnically diverse metro area in the country. It's hard to believe, but only 1 percent of the Pittsburgh region's shrinking population is Latino. Asians are 2 percent, and most of them are from India. In Pittsburgh I would have assumed right away that the Japanese guy had to be the tour bus driver. Meanwhile, reflecting California's human rainbow, about 8 percent of Monterey's population is Asian, more than half are Hispanic/Latino and only a third are non-Hispanic white folk. If the average Pittsburgher came across 50 Japanese people in one of their local McDonald's, they'd call the Pentagon. Diversity in German-Irish-Italian Pittsburgh is determined by whether your grandparents were from Croatia or Serbia. Everything turned out OK at the register. I got my coffee in seconds and McDonald's' staff somehow fed everyone. Handling busloads of tourists was something they were used to. About 4 million tourists come to the Monterey Peninsula every year, though most don't sleep in the Salinas Wal-Mart like I did.

The parking lot in Salinas was a whole different Wal-Mart experience. It was small, busy and noisy. Latino kids packed six to a car came and went and came and went until after 11 p.m. I knew Salinas had a deadly gang problem – 3,000 members in 16 youth gangs. But I parked without fear. The local gangsters were too busy gunning each other down over turf and the drug trade to worry about a bald old guy sleeping in a car at Wal-Mart on Friday night. I got 6.7 peaceful hours of sleep. I would need it for my quick tour of Steinbeck Country, much of what I had already seen on my two previous trips.

It was Saturday, Oct. 30. Fifty years earlier, to the day, Steinbeck and his little troupe left the St. Francis Hotel and moved south to the Monterey Peninsula. They briefly visited one of his sisters north of the peninsula in Watsonville, where most of the strawberries the country eats come from. Then he, Elaine and Charley moved in with his sister Beth for two weeks at the modest Steinbeck family cottage on 11th Street in Pacific Grove, a short walk from the black rocks and crashing surf of Monterey Bay.

## When Whistles Blow at Dawn

My first stop was Cannery Row at dawn. Steinbeck said in "Cannery Row" that sunrise there was a magical time. He wasn't fictionalizing. I arrived in time to see the sun come up from behind the low mountains on the other side of cold, choppy, deep green Monterey Bay. It was quiet except for the plump seagulls hanging in the wind above the tourist traps, landscaped plazas, upscale hotels and wide decks standing on piers in the shallows.

As usual, Deborah Hannas was getting Lilly Mae's Cinnamon Rolls ready for the day. Hannas gets to experience dawn on Cannery Row early every morning when she drives down the hill from her house and opens her small shiny shop. Depending on the season and a bunch of unpredictable meteorological things, her dawn could be misty or sunny, rainy or cloudy, pleasant or chilly. The bay could be rough or calm. Sometimes the fog sat gently on the water. Sometimes it flowed ashore like thick soft surf. Whatever kind of dawn greeted her, she agreed with Mr. Steinbeck that it was pretty magical.

I stopped in to say hi to Hannas. I first met her in the spring when I was on my Steinbeck research tour. She's been working on Cannery Row since she was 17 – since 1977. "I know everyone who works on the street," she said, "It's like my own neighborhood. I know a lot of people who worked down here their whole lives, who worked themselves up from busboys to chefs." When I told her I was following Steinbeck's "Travels With Charley" trail around the country, she spoke for all who believe the road to "anywhere but here" is full of steinbeckian romance and adventure. "I want a camper truck. Everyone should have a camper truck. It's the American Dream."

While I was talking to Hannas the previous spring, her old friend Harry Traylor came into Lilly Mae's with his order pad to see if she needed anything. Traylor had sold his wholesale dairy five years before but still supplied fresh milk to a few friends like Hannas. Traylor was 85 with lots of white hair, but he looked youthful and trim in his layered look – long-sleeved shirt, T-shirt and all-weather vest. He migrated to Monterey from Arkansas in 1957. Harry the Milkman remembered precisely what Cannery Row was like in 1960. Dead. He could park on the street on a Saturday night and go to a piano bar or the Steinbeck Theater. Unfortunately, that was it for nightly entertainment – except for the fires. "There was lots of arson at that time," he said. "All the old canneries were being burned down."

Hannas had watched the street's steady resurrection and she knew a bit of its ancient history. Before it was officially renamed Cannery Row in the 1950s, in honor of Steinbeck's 1945 book, it was Ocean View Avenue. During the 1930s a row of canneries built on the water's edge each had its own coded whistle that blew at 1 or 3 or 4 in the morning.

The whistle would alert the cannery's workers that its fishing boats were coming in with bellies full of the sardines that thrived by the billions on Monterey Bay's plankton blooms. The cannery packers were mostly wives of Portuguese and Italian fishermen. They'd hear the whistles and come down off the hill in the dark like extras in a scene from a George Romero zombie movie, clomping in their rubber boots, wearing aprons and hairnets. It must have been a crazy sight.

Like so many of our ancestors, the sardine packers had unbelievably horrible working conditions. They often stood knee-deep for 10 or 12 hours in icy ocean water packing fish into cans on assembly lines. In the late 1930s they were making 58 cents an hour – about minimum wage in today's money. The best thing you can say about those cannery jobs was they were seasonal and were ultimately replaced by machinery or were shipped overseas.

Eighty years later, Hannas was still doing what those poor cannery women did. "Every morning at 5 a.m. my whistle blows," she said cheerfully. But her workday, though long, wasn't a dirty, stinky torture session. And when she got home, she smelled of coffee and cinnamon, not fish guts.

# Confronting Steinbeck's Ghost

Much of the America I had seen so far on the Steinbeck Highway had barely changed in 50 years. But in 2010 Cannery Row was nothing like what Steinbeck saw during his "Charley" trip. It was a hollowed out shipwreck. The lovable lowlifes, rough bars and tender cathouses he knew in the 1930s and immortalized in "Cannery Row" were already long gone by 1960. So was most of the sardine industry – dead from overfishing and natural causes. "The Sardine Capital of the World" no longer employed 5,000 or 10,000 people. Its 19 sardine canneries were closed and already worth nothing but their history.

By 2010 only a few wooden storefronts and a remodeled cannery remained, weathered islands of 1930s character clashing with the glassy modern edifices. The holiest and shabbiest remnant was the brown wood lab where marine biologist Ed Ricketts worked, lived and hosted a party house/ bohemian salon for local artists, musicians and writers like Steinbeck, Henry Miller and the young Joseph Campbell.

Ricketts was Doc in "Cannery Row" and served as a model for characters in other Steinbeck books. He and Steinbeck became great pals and Steinbeck essentially became Ricketts' marine-biology student. The lab, occasionally opened for tours by the Cannery Row Foundation and once a jazz club, had its backdoor to the bay and a walkout basement to the rocks and surf.

Ricketts was more than just a cool guy who listened to Count Basie records and got laid a lot. He was a pioneering intertidal ecologist and amateur philosopher. His holistic and then-innovative ideas about ecology and the interdependence and cooperation of all organisms within a specific habitat were said to have strongly influenced Steinbeck's writing and thinking. Steinbeck was heartbroken when Ricketts was killed in 1948. A bust of Ricketts marks the spot in Monterey where his car was hit by a train. Busts and photos and historical markers haunt the sidewalks, decks and plazas of Cannery Row. But little evidence is left of Steinbeck's real or imaginary street.

Today, as every travel writer and parachuting journalist must mention because it is so obvious, Cannery Row is a PG-rated theme park of its former colorful, sinful self. A street that stunk of dead fish and teemed with cannery workers, fishermen and flies has been spiffed up with wine-tasting rooms and snazzy seaside hotels with names like "Intercontinental: The Clement Monterey.

Over the decades Cannery Row has been reborn, thanks to the midwifery of a collective of entrepreneurs, real estate developers, enlightened government officials and Packard Foundation money. It's become a safe place for wholesome nuclear families from Iowa heading for the Monterey Bay Aquarium or the candy stores and souvenir shops, where Steinbeck's brand name and face are used to sell jewelry, wax museum tickets and refrigerator magnets.

While I watched Cannery Row wake up and ready itself for a busy Saturday, I felt Steinbeck staring at me. Dozens of times. His face and name were everywhere, like a creepy Big Author. Across the street, filling a window at the Cannery Row Trading Company, an oversized black-and-white photo of Steinbeck the Serious Young Writer watched me. If this were not a true story of my trip, I'd write that I finally confronted him. I'd write that I looked deeply into the frozen eyes of his bust on Steinbeck Plaza and spoke directly to his ghost.

*Why so serious, John? Are you thinking about how ironic it is that you no longer recognize the street you made world famous? Are you mad your name is*

*being used to sell everything from jewelry to the entire Monterey Peninsula? Are you pissed at me for laughing out loud at that stunt you tried to pull in North Dakota? Don't you like an ex-newspaper hack coming along after 50 years raising questions and fact-checking your "nonfiction" book?*

Then, employing some of the lowest tricks of creative nonfiction, I'd write that Steinbeck spoke to me telepathically. I'd say that he told me he understood I didn't set out to bring him down or show him up. That he forgave me for my troublemaking. That he was sorry his lies were going to cost me two years of my life. I'd write that he told me it was always good to seek truth for its own sake, even if it disappointed people or made them hate you. Of course Steinbeck did nothing of the kind. As usual, he had nothing to say to me. All I heard was the chattering of seagulls.

He wouldn't be happy that he's been turned into a posthumous marketing tool for "Steinbeck Country." But Steinbeck was no blind romantic or limousine preservationist. He knew restaurants and antique shops or almost anything would be a big improvement over smelly sardine canneries and whorehouses. In "Travels With Charley" he acknowledged that much progress already had occurred across the Monterey Peninsula in the 20 years he hadn't been watching it. He'd grumble and growl, but he'd have to agree that in 2010 Cannery Row – like the rest of the America he toured in 1960 – was a better, safer, cleaner, more prosperous place. And a much nicer place to make your living when your whistle blows at dawn.

# Perfect Pacific Grove

From Cannery Row I drove next door to Pacific Grove to see if anyone was staying at the Steinbeck family's old cottage on 11th Street. America's prime candidate for most perfect community ever was, well, as perfect as ever. Lovely quiet streets lined with million-dollar Victorian homes tilted toward the sea. Its spiffy Victorian-flavored downtown along Lighthouse Avenue purred with the expensive rides of its 15,000 lucky citizens.

Founded by Methodists as a seaside retreat, initially promoted as "a city of homes," dry until 1969, winter headquarters of billions of Monarch butterflies, Pacific Grove is a windier, less nautical West Coast echo of the Village of Sag Harbor. It's just as disproportionately white and rich, but not as self-consciously historical and not as tiny or hard to get to by car.

On PG's main drag I went in to buy a scone and write a blog item at Lighthouse Coffee Company. A steady parade of locals came and went. Mostly middle-age men in blue jeans, they were served their breakfast burritos, lattes and mochas by the sincerely friendly and welcoming owner. She looked like Kim Basinger and seduced every male she knew by first name and every male she didn't know with "dear" or "darling."

Lighthouse Coffee was a neighborhood hangout, with lots of potted plants and tables out front on the wide bricked sidewalk under some small trees. At one table a guy with a latte and hair eight inches too long for his age railed about some public schools being closed for budget reasons in Kansas City or somewhere in Flyover Country.

"Why don't they start educating those kids?" he moaned to his two buddies. "We spend three times as much money on the war in Iraq than on schools." It was the first complaint I had heard on my trip about military spending or the war in Iraq. As a George Washington noninterventionist, I agreed with the guy about Iraq being a terrible waste of blood and treasure. But he had been living too long in his Pacific Grove ivory tower. He had no idea what was going on in the typical city public school system. The last thing they needed was more money. Pittsburgh's city schools – though not as horrible as most urban districts – spent more than $20,000 a kid per year. Half of that, at least, was wasted.

I'd have told the long-haired dude failing urban districts like Pittsburgh's needed to be blown up, i.e., privatized, and turned over to parents, teachers, unions, churches, businesses, neighborhood groups, bridge clubs, the Elks – anyone but the idiots who've been running Big Public Education. Of course, what did I know? He was probably living in a million-dollar dream house by the sea and I was chasing a ghost around the country and sleeping in parking lots.

In between customers I asked the owner of Lighthouse Coffee how Pacific Grove real estate was faring in the "Great Recession." Housing values had crashed more than 50 percent in Montgomery County and were back to pre-bubble 1999 levels. But from all appearances the economic apocalypse had not reached her tony corner of America.

"The real estate market's down a little," she said, "but it's not bad." PG was a town of "money people," she said, and not many houses were on the market or under deep water. A vacant lot with a view of Monterey Bay cost $375,000. She was happy to report that her home, on a double lot, was worth $1 million. The small ex-cottages near Steinbeck's place were going for about $600,000, depending on their condition.

On 11th Street I parked across from the Steinbeck family cottage. Except that it was probably the least renovated and shabbiest structure on the block, it fit in well with its cramped neighborhood of little yellow-and-dark-green-trimmed stucco houses on micro-lots. Two blocks from the surf, with a low gray wood fence at the sidewalk and a dense side garden, it had been remodeled by Steinbeck so it'd have no door to the street. His father, who was neither poor nor un-influential, built the red-and-white cottage early in the 20th century. Steinbeck lived there with his first wife Carol from 1930 to 1936, when he wrote books like "The Red Pony" and "Tortilla Flat" that made him nationally known. Though it was still owned and used by Steinbeck heirs, no one was there when I dropped by to snoop. It was just as well, since all I wanted to do was take photos.

In 1960 the Traveling Steinbecks were at the cottage for only a day or two when the Monterey Peninsula Herald dispatched a writer and photographer to do a story. The resulting feature, which ran in the Nov. 4 paper, was very well written by Mike Thomas and included a photo of Steinbeck standing in the garden with a cigarette in his mouth. Thomas found Steinbeck fixing a wooden front gate, which the author said he had probably built himself 30 years earlier.

John Steinbeck Back—But Not to Stay

Author Visits Old P.G. Home

Describing Steinbeck as a big man with broad features, piercing blue eyes, graying hair and small goatee, Thomas said he was wearing corduroy pants and a shapeless green sweater. His fingers were nicotine stained and he had a Zippo cigarette lighter on a string around his neck. Wife Elaine was there. So was "an aging poodle sitting in a car at the curbside." When Thomas asked if he would ever move back to the Monterey area, Steinbeck said he felt like a stranger on the peninsula and repeated his Thomas Wolfe mantra – "You can't go home again."

## Prices & Politics, 1960-Style

The pages of the Monterey Peninsula Herald that week described life on a simpler, cheaper planet – planet 1960. Display ads read like cruel jokes from a time machine. A Hoover vacuum cleaner cost $80. A wool sweater at the Casual shop in Carmel was $5.77. Three pounds of ground beef cost 99 cents. When you factor for inflation, which you must always do to get an accurate comparison of prices over time, the sweater and the beef were not the deals they seem today. Since the dollar's purchasing power in 1960 was more than seven times what it was in 2010, in current dollars the sweater was almost $42, the meat $7 and the Hoover cost the equivalent of $589.

Meanwhile, a transistorized "microcorder" from Webcor was advertized for $179.95 ($1,326 in 2010 dollars) and weighed 4½ pounds. A ticket to see Mort Sahl at the San Jose Civic Auditorium was $3.75 or $1.80 for the peanut gallery. A new 3-bedroom 3,800 square foot house, built to the buyer's specs, sold for $23,395. A new house one-third that size was $8,695, with 100 percent financing. A classified ad offered a "sharp" used 1959 Ford Fairlane for $1,795. That'd be about $14,000 today, which is not too bad. But it wasn't exactly loaded with options – just a stick shift, AM radio and heater.

On Nov. 1, 1960, the Peninsula Herald's editorial page, which contained the "Dennis the Menace" cartoon strip every day, ran an editorial cartoon depicting JFK and Nixon in a drag race. A letter to the editor defended Truman's use of the atomic bomb on Japan. In sports, the big headline talked about Alvin Dark becoming the new Giants manager.

Going into Election Day, the presidential race was close in both California and the nation, with Kennedy leading Nixon in the Time and Newsweek polls. On Nov. 2, with six days to go, JFK came through San Jose on his way to a fundraiser in San Francisco and Nixon was about to fly into Fresno. The Peninsula Herald put its endorsement of Nixon and Henry Cabot Lodge at the top left of its front page. It ran the same recommendation on Page 1 every day for the next six days.

The plug for "Tricky Dick" may have helped Nixon take Monterey County by a 56-43 majority and narrowly carry the state by 35,000 votes out of 6.5 million cast. But it couldn't sway Steinbeck. On Nov. 8, he cast an absentee vote. Unless he wrote-in the name of his hero Adlai Stevenson, he voted for John F. Kennedy. Two months later he'd attend JFK's inauguration and begin his personal relationship with Kennedy and LBJ. Steinbeck would be pleased to know the voters of Steinbeck Country have done a political 180 in the last half-century. In 2008 they voted 66-33 for President Obama, a nail-biter compared to the 80-20 Obama landslide in San Francisco.

## Purging Steinbeck's Partisanship

Politics is strangely absent from "Travels With Charley." Being a political creature, I noticed that right away when I re-read the book. It made no sense. During a historic, heated election, in a nonfiction book about America written by an openly partisan author, could the names Kennedy and Nixon really each appear just once? I did a quick search on my Kindle. It was true. The names show up on page 177 of the 246-page 1962 Viking Press hardback edition, when Steinbeck arrives in Monterey a few days before Election Day and has a brief, hot, childish argument with his Republican sister.

Part of Steinbeck's original mission had been to take the political pulse of the country. He was quickly disappointed to find how difficult that was. As he wrote in his first draft, he was saddened to learn that the greatest number of Americans he saw "did not have political opinions, or if they did, concealed them whether out of fear or expediency I do not know."

Their silence didn't stop him from lacing his original manuscript with his running commentary on the election, which he obviously followed closely. He was a stanch New Deal Democrat and didn't pretend otherwise. In the first draft of "Charley," he wrote, "It must not be thought that my wife and I are or were nonpartisan observers. We were and are partisan as all get out, confirmed, blown in the glass democrats and make no bones about it." That confession was axed. So was nearly every overt political comment or crack he put in the first draft. For example, all four televised Nixon-Kennedy debates occurred while he was on the road. Based on his letters and the original manuscript, he saw or heard each one in full or in part.

A Stevenson Man until the bitter end, Steinbeck didn't swoon over the prospects of a President John Kennedy. But he loathed Nixon, as the manuscript repeatedly makes clear. At one point, after watching a Nixon-JFK debate on the big TV in his motel room, he criticized Nixon and Herbert Hoover and went on for about 150 words, making fun of their pedestrian Republican reading habits and comparing their low intelligence levels to Kennedy's high one. "Being a democrat," he wrote without capitalizing Democrat, "I wanted Kennedy to win…." That scene was axed.

Also cut was his commentary following the third presidential debate, which he watched in his room at a "pretty auto court" in Livingston, Montana. He sarcastically asked himself if Montanans had any real interest in the major geopolitical issue of that debate – whether the United States should defend the tiny islands of Quemoy and Matsu, which the Red Chinese were shelling and threatening to take from Taiwan.

Other political comments he made in San Francisco, Monterey and Amarillo – some of them refreshingly bipartisan in their cynicism – were chopped out completely. So were two pokes at the John Birch Society, a favorite punching bag. Though it took some of the edge away from an already nearly edgeless book, cutting 99 percent of the presidential politics from "Travels With Charley" was smart and logical editing. First of all, by the time the book would hit bookstores – in late July of 1962 – the 1960 election was ancient history. Who would care by then what Steinbeck thought about the third JFK-Nixon debate?

Plus, his political sniping was petty and one-sided, though that probably bothered no one at Viking Press. It was also boring and at odds with the rest of the book's grouchy but generally likable tone. The trouble was, removing all of the politics left a glaring hole in what was supposed to be a nonfiction account of what was going on in the nation. It also resulted in some sloppy editorial work by Viking. For example, in "Travels With Charley" Steinbeck mentions that the presidential election is occurring and that he cast his absentee vote. Yet he never says anything after that about who won or whether he was pleased by the results.

It was not that way in the original draft. When he was in Amarillo for three or four days getting his cracked camper window replaced, Steinbeck noted in the manuscript that the election was over and Kennedy had narrowly won. He also says he went out into the streets and hotel lobbies to canvass the electorate's views on the results and had a good laugh when a local Republican-demanded recount found more GOP voting irregularities than Democrat ones.

All that information about the election was lopped by editors. Like his wife, who played an even more important part in his actual trip, Steinbeck's politics were purged from his book. In the end it was no great loss, because he had pulled most of his political punches anyway. What he wrote was softball stuff compared to what he expressed in long letters to Adlai Stevenson and his operatives in the run-up to the 1960 Democratic convention in July 1960.

In one letter now among the Stevenson papers kept at Princeton's Seeley G. Mudd Manuscript Library, Steinbeck casually referred to Kennedy as "a bed-hopper." Womanizing was a JFK character flaw the author obviously knew about in the summer of 1960, as did LBJ and J. Edgar Hoover and untold other Beltway media insiders, even if the voting masses didn't. Steinbeck had no interest in throwing his JFK dirt into "Travels With Charley." And though he wasn't shy about making fun of Richard Nixon in the first draft, he wasn't about to share the explosive information he had on the vice-president as early as the spring of 1960.

In a May 24 letter to Stevenson's right-hand operative, Bill Blair Jr., Steinbeck wrote that he knew of a talkative, snobbish "psycho-analyst" in New York who traveled three times a week to Washington to "put Dickie on the couch." Steinbeck said this political bombshell, which could have prevented Nixon from getting the GOP nomination, "should be leaked and if you don't leak it, I will." Steinbeck said it was "pleasant to know that Poor Richard is not happy. But this should be used."

Nixon's secret shrink was Dr. Arnold Hutschnecker. The German-born psychoanalyst had been consulting with the vice president in Washington and in his New York City office since the early 1950s. For years there had been rumors that Nixon was seeing a therapist, but apparently Stevenson's people didn't pass along Steinbeck's tip because JFK's camp didn't find out about Dr. Hutschnecker until the first week of September. The details of Nixon's relationship with the therapist and how the Kennedy campaign learned about it – which took more than 50 years to become public – are the latest evidence of how thoroughly sleazy and vicious the 1960 election was.

Both sides played hard and dirty. In June Nixon's team of tricksters sneaked around in the offices of two Kennedy doctors and found that JFK was gravely ill with Addison's disease. In response, JFK's father Joe asked Frank Sinatra to hire a private detective to look into the old rumors that Nixon was regularly seeing a head doctor. What the detective learned and how he learned it is detailed in David Robb's highly praised 2012 book "The Gumshoe and the Shrink." Though Nixon operatives publicly raised the issue of JFK's potentially fatal illness a few days before Election Day, JFK refused to counterattack by releasing the personal dirt he knew about Nixon.

Too bad Kennedy didn't expose the existence of Dr. Hutschnecker. History would have been changed. It would have blown open a close election, made all that Democrat vote fraud in Chicago and Texas unnecessary and made it virtually impossible for Nixon to become president eight years later. As for poor Steinbeck, he had to endure Nixon's political resurrection and watch him defeat Hubert Humphrey in 1968. Luckily he died that year on Dec. 20, so he never had to witness his hated Tricky Dick being sworn in as president.

## Old Monterey

I went other places on my quickie Steinbeck tour. I didn't need to search downtown Monterey along Alvarado Street for evidence of the bars he regularly drank in. I had already done that in March. Monterey has a fairly healthy downtown, with seven or eight blocks of old stucco buildings with the usual offices, eateries, coffee shops, a cigar store and a Walgreen's. But Steinbeck's favorite bars, including the Keg on Alvarado Street owned by Johnny Garcia, were destroyed with the rest of their vintage block by an urban renewal project of the late 1960s.

Dennis Copeland of the Monterey Library told me Alvarado Street was always the heart of downtown Monterey. The downscale mom & pop grocery stores, restaurants, Army surplus stores and pawnshops that were demolished served the Sicilian fishing community and catered to visiting soldiers and sailors. I loved Copeland. He hated urban renewal and knew how it was used to destroy parts of cities across America. He said old-timers in Monterey still complained about how a lively working-class block was destroyed in the name of progress by city hall and "free" federal money.

As happened in Pittsburgh and later in other cities before and after 1960, the poor part of downtown Monterey was declared a slum so it could be clear-cut and redeveloped by local pols and their favored developers. I don't pretend to know whether Alvarado deserved the wrecking ball, but it ended up with two beastly hotels and a block of sterile storefronts where Johnny Garcia's Keg used to be.

Steinbeck set a lengthy drinking scene in Garcia's place. In the first draft of "Charley," Elaine is sitting at the bar with Steinbeck. But in the published book he sits alone. It was in Garcia's that Steinbeck says he realized how much he and his former pals had changed in the 20 years since they had seen each other. Half of his old pals were dead. He and everyone else had become ghosts to each other. A stranger in his hometown, he writes that Thomas Wolfe was correct when he wrote "You can't go home again." Of course Steinbeck had known for 20 years he could never live on the Monterey Peninsula again. But the theatrical bar scene, real or invented or somewhere in between, was a nice display of his writing talents.

## RIP, Mr. Steinbeck

From Pacific Grove, I pointed my RAV4 due east for the first time since I touched the top of Maine in late September. First stop was Salinas, 15 miles inland. I didn't need to revisit the Steinbeck House or the National Steinbeck Center. But I wanted to pay my respects to my dead road-mate before I made my assault on Fremont Peak.

On state Route 68, as I approached Salinas, I pulled over by an immense strawberry field. For miles I had been watching Fremont Peak's little shark tooth poking into the cloudy sky above the Gabilan Mountains. The peak was not much taller than the others on the jagged gray range, which ran across the horizon and seemed to be propped up by a row of brown and green foothills.

Taking photos of the distant peak with the strawberry field and a dozen Latino farm workers in the foreground made a good photo but it also made the farm workers and their boss nervous. I could see them pointing at me through my zoom lens. Then their pickup truck, hitched to three port-a-potties, started moving directly toward me. Who knows what the poor devils thought I was doing or which government agency I was working for? Immigration? Homeland Security? Border Patrol? I drove off three minutes before the pickup could reach me. The strawberry pickers had no way of knowing I meant them no harm. I didn't care whether they were legal or illegal immigrants as long as they weren't on welfare.

In Salinas at Garden of Memories Memorial Park, hundreds of graves were decorated lavishly with piles of fresh flowers, balloons and flags. It was part of the celebration for *Dia de los Muerto* (Day of the Dead), when Mexicans honor their dead by visiting them and over-decorating their graves. The only other living soul in the cemetery, a young Latino man in a baggy light blue jersey, knelt on the grass by one headstone, head bowed, staring intently into his smart phone.

In the older, grayer part of the cemetery, where there were spiky granite monuments and few fresh flowers, Steinbeck's simple grave was pretty much as I had left it in March. The tiny ceramic poodle guard dog was gone. But several pennies, a marble, a Jesus medal, a crystal miniature Blessed Mother and a few soggy flower parts were scattered on his weathered bronze marker. Set into the concrete next to "John Steinbeck, 1902-1968" was the matching plaque of "Elaine Anderson Steinbeck, 1914-2003." Her marker still had its original copper sheen. His marker and the raised bronze letters of his name had long ago turned a faded gray-blue. With nothing new to say to him, and vice versa, I took a few photos and left him in peace.

# Party on Fremont Peak

Before leaving the Monterey Peninsula and motoring to Texas for a long Thanksgiving holiday, Steinbeck had one last important metaphorical thing to do in "Travels With Charley." He takes Charley to Fremont Peak, the mountaintop he said overlooked "the whole of my childhood and my youth." Looking back in time and space, Steinbeck bids final farewell to the place he no longer belongs to and can never go home to again. He writes it was a "formal and sentimental thing" he had to do before turning his back to his "permanent and changeless past." His brief goodbye to what would soon become "Steinbeck Country" was some of the best writing in "Charley."

Fremont Peak State Park, virtually unknown and off the beaten tourist track, is an incredible place to hike, watch a sunset, camp overnight, gaze at the Milky Way or just be. Just getting there is an adventure. From Steinbeck's grave in Salinas it was a 20-mile trip around the northern end of the Gabilan Mountains, followed by 11 harrowing miles up a twisting narrow road that hangs over steep canyons. Halfway to the peak you expect to see crashed SUVs still burning in the ravines below. From the parking lot it's still a steep walk past a grove of communications towers, then up to a short stone stairway that leads to a jumble of marble rocks that must be scaled mountain-goat style. Needless to say, there's never much of a crowd to greet you on the summit.

During my research tour in March of 2010 I had Fremont Peak to myself for a chilly two-hour sunset. Seven months later, on a partly cloudy Saturday afternoon, I was up there alone again. This time it was warm and the grassy hillsides were brown from the summer sun, not green from winter rains. And this time I was not thinking such fond thoughts about my trying friend John Steinbeck.

By late October of 2010 I knew how much of his "nonfiction" book was faked or dubious. I could no longer assume he actually came up to Fremont Peak in November of 1960. It's a steep hard climb to the summit for a boy and he had a bum knee and a cane. It really didn't matter if Steinbeck mailed it in, because he had been on Fremont Peak so many times he knew its vista by heart. But still, my inner journalist was annoyed at Steinbeck for being so hard to trust.

It was great owning my own mountaintop again, but my solitude was short-lived. I heard voices. Ten people between the ages of 11 and 60-something were working their way up the boulders. Eight of them were part of a picnic outing by an extended Latino family from Salinas.

Being in a crowd on Fremont Peak turned out to be much better than being there alone. On Steinbeck Country's highest point, which is about the size of a tennis court, we had our own spontaneous little photo party. I took a group picture of them, then put my camera around the neck of 11-year-old Marcos Duliba and told him to take a good one of me, which he did. I made a few more friends, though they looked at me funny when I told them I had spent the night before in the Salinas Wal-Mart parking lot.

Two other summiteers, Marty and Sheila Edelen, had arrived on their white and chrome Honda Goldwing motorcycle. Marty was about 65 and Sheila about 54. They had sold their house in Colorado in 2007 and had been living in their RV and traveling the western USA with their bike in tow. They had everything they owned with them on the road, including two dogs, and were having a ball. Like so many other random Americans I had met, including the Latino family from Salinas, the Edelens were happy, prosperous looking and not suffering in the Great Recession. As Sheila said after I photographed them standing proudly behind their gleaming $20,000 motorcycle, "We're living our dream."

I hated leaving the top of Fremont Peak that Saturday afternoon. After two visits, it had become my favorite government mountain. It had no rangers, safety fences or railings. No minimum age requirements. No dumb nanny signs warning you'd die or be arrested if you weren't wearing a helmet and kneepads. Up there you were free and on your own. You were responsible for your own clumsy ass. And it was up to you to get along peacefully with anyone who showed up, without the aid of a cop, a lawyer or a social worker.

If all that freedom and lack of oversight on Fremont Peak sounded like a recipe for lawlessness and personal injury lawsuits, it wasn't. The park spokesperson I called when I got back to Pittsburgh said no one had ever been murdered or even mugged on the peak, and no one had been seriously hurt in a fall. Maybe it was not as dangerous or exciting as I thought, but it was still my favorite mountain.

# 18 – Heading Back East

## Steinbeck Timeline

Tuesday, Nov. 15 to Nov. 18, 1960 – Bound for home

*Steinbeck leaves the Monterey Peninsula on Tuesday, Nov. 15, bound for Amarillo, Texas, which is 1,333 miles away. Elaine flies on ahead. With his boyhood friend and lawyer Toby Street riding with him in Rocinante, Steinbeck goes through Los Banos, Fresno and Bakersfield. He crosses the Mojave Desert and picks up Route 66 at Barstow, California. After four days, Street leaves him in Flagstaff, Arizona.*

## Worshipping Route 66

Like Steinbeck 50 years before, I slipped out the back door of the Monterey Peninsula. East into the dry gut of central California I sped along state routes 156 and 99. They were the same roads Steinbeck took on his way east to a Thanksgiving holiday at a cattle ranch near Amarillo, Texas, only my asphalt – per usual – was smoother, wider and safer. By Saturday night, I had made it past Fresno and Tulare to a $62 motel in Bakersfield. The next morning I breezed south through flat, arid, dead valleys on Route 58. Dodging grassy tan mountains, passing beneath a forest of wind turbines stretched across several ridge tops, I skirted the town of Mojave, slipped by the edge of Edwards Air Force Base and drove through the bleak Mojave Desert to the crossroads town of Barstow.

At Barstow, Steinbeck met U.S. Highway 66, his "Mother Road" from "The Grapes of Wrath," and followed it all the way to Texas. I-40 has replaced, covered or bypassed Route 66, which no longer officially exists. But long, desolate stretches of the historic and culturally powerful road still parallel the interstate. Old Route 66 comes back to life when it becomes the main street of traveler-centric desert towns like Gallup, Winslow, Kingman and Winona. Jazzman Bobby Troup made those dusty places hip & famous forever with the lyrics of his swinging 1946 hit "Route 66," which Nat King Cole sang first and the Rolling Stones, John Mayer and dozens of others have covered.

If any road in America deserved to be worshipped, it was old Route 66. Starting in the 1930s, and until the western interstates were completed in the 1970s, it was the only practical east-west route by car from Chicago to L.A. Route 66 made it possible for migrants of every socioeconomic class to reach for the golden promises of California, not just the desperate "Dust Bowl" migrants of "The Grapes of Wrath."

Long before national chain motels, restaurants and truck stops were invented, the independent motels and mom & pop diners along Route 66 allowed truckers and ordinary tourists to cross a thousand miles of desert in comfort and safety. Like a long, thin travel theme park, the road was lined with wacky restaurants, wild Art-Deco architecture, reptile farms and motel rooms made out of teepees. Neon signs in towns like Grants and Tucumcari lit up the desert sky all night.

I had been on parts of Route 66 a dozen times. The first time was in the summer of 1974, when I was a free but poor divorced bartender/weekly newspaper associate editor in Cincinnati. I was feeling deprived because I'd never been west of Chicago. I had a few hundred bucks to my name and one credit card with a $500 limit, but my younger brother Paul and I decided it was time to tour the Wild West in my tinny 1972 Datsun 510. Paul was 19. I was 26. We did what tens of millions of young Americans with two or four wheels and no serious responsibilities had done before and since. We just went. For a bunch of reasons having to do with a family vacation and returning my kids to my ex-wife in Philadelphia, we started in Canada near Buffalo and drove to Philly. From there it was on to Chicago, Denver, Yellowstone, San Francisco, Yosemite, L.A./Newport Beach, Las Vegas, the Grand Canyon and back to Cincinnati.

We didn't log our mileage, but Google Maps says Paul and I traveled 6,400 miles. It seemed much longer at the time, mainly because Nixon and Congress had imposed their idiotic 55-mph slowdown on the country. Our cross-country drive wasn't very comfortable in a little Japanese bug with no AC, but we thought we were traveling in style because the front seats folded back and we could sleep in the car. We were totally unequipped for life on or off the road. We didn't own a tent or a sleeping bag. We slept in the car a lot. That's also the time I slept on top of the picnic table in Nevada. Our great adventure lasted a month. All we had to guide us, besides the setting sun, was a single Rand McNally road atlas.

We felt like Lewis & Clark every time we turned a bend and didn't care what we ate or where we slept. Of course, we had a blast. We chased the Holy Trinity of the American road – girls, music and beer. We were so happy to be totally free and exploring the West for the first time we didn't notice we were essentially two bums in a car. In San Francisco, where two of my friends from Cincinnati flew out to join us, we sat on a wall in the sun in Ghirardelli Square with our shirts off next to several cold six-packs of Coors. We thought we were in heaven and for an afternoon we were. As Easterners, Paul and I were blown away by the West's open spaces and awesome beauty – at first.

By the time we hit Yosemite National Park, we had overdosed on big sky, natural wonders and official scenic overlooks. We cynically dubbed the waterfall at Yosemite "Ho Hum Falls" and made fun of the camping/hiking ethos, then set out for Los Angeles, a tasteless and ugly place we four spoiled brats agreed would benefit from a 9.0 earthquake. Little did I know that two years later I'd be living in downtown Hollywood and raving about L.A. and its free and open lifestyle.

We finished that 1974 trip the same way Steinbeck finished his 1960 trip – in a non-stop dash for home. We drove to Cincinnati from Las Vegas, with a quick detour to the single most impressive work of Mother Nature on the continent, the Grand Canyon. Four guys packed into a Datsun 510 for almost 30 straight hours is not something I'd ever want to do again. And it was no way to appreciate legendary Route 66, which had not yet been reduced to ruins, relics and memories.

# The French Attack *en masse*

East of Barstow, I came upon the first and only serious traffic accident of my entire trip. Minutes earlier a sleek new silver tractor-trailer had rolled on its side, crushing the nose of its cab and exposing its pristine underside and 18 wheels to the desert blue sky. As a state cop kept the trickle of I-40 traffic moving, the driver, though unhurt, walked down the road with an anguished look on his face and both hands on top of his head. Clear day, good road, no traffic – the poor guy must have fallen asleep or been texting his girlfriend.

Shortly after that rare 30-second burst of interstate excitement, I exited at Newberry Springs to get on a stretch of old Route 66. The sign said I was on the National Trails Highway, which has been Route 66's official name since 1985. When I saw the ruins of a small boarded-up motel, I pulled over and parked, which is always easy to do in the desert. "Free TV" was written on a tall "M-O-T-E-L" sign whose neon hadn't glowed in many years. It would be the first of a hundred dead Eisenhower Era motels, roadside cafes and gas stations I'd pass in the next two days – road kill from when I-40 made Route 66 and its commerce obsolete.

After photographing the motel's sun-baked corpse, I turned around and had the strangest experience of my trip. A gleaming white bus with "Divine Transportation" written on its side had pulled into the parking lot behind me and was disgorging passengers. People in shorts and T-shirts were walking right out into the middle of the highway, where they stood on the yellow centerline in threes and fours and took pictures of each other.

Employing my best journalism skills, and despite the usual language barrier, I quickly learned they were French tourists – cultural pilgrims, really. They had come to stand on old Route 66's pavement and visit the world-famous Bagdad Cafe, which I had never heard of before and hadn't noticed was 100 yards behind me. Fifty-two French people, all from Marseilles, had traveled halfway around the world to come to the Bagdad Café. As apparently every hip French person knows, the little red restaurant with the pointy brown shingled roof is two culturally important things in one: It's a shrine to the memory of Route 66 and it bears the name of an independent West German/American movie comedy that became a cult classic in Western Europe.

I had never seen or even heard of the movie. That was particularly embarrassing, since I was working for the Sunday entertainment section of the L.A. Times in 1987 when “Bagdad Café’ came out. Nominated for an Academy Award, featuring Jack Palance, "Bagdad Cafe" is described by the International Movie Data Base as a film about "A lonely German woman" who "ends up in the most desolated motel on Earth and decides to make it brighter." When I got back to Pittsburgh I watched it. It wasn’t a typical Hollywood hack job, which made sense because it was made by a German, Percy Adlon. It was strange and slow at times, but also funny, sweet and magical. Most Americans would hate it because it involves no car chases or vampires. But it was easy to see why it was so beloved by the nutty French.

The movie was shot on location in Newberry Springs in the Sidewinder Café – what the current Bagdad Café was called in 1987. The original Bagdad Café was actually in the town of Bagdad itself, 50 miles farther east on Obsolete 66. It and the town both turned to dust in the late 1960s after Interstate 40 passed them by. But those trivial realities don't matter to thousands of Western Europeans. They come to the desert by the busload to buy T-shirts, sweatshirts and caps at an oasis of American road culture that's wallpapered to the ceiling with movie posters, banners, flags and thousands of letters and postcards scrawled in a dozen tongues.

## Bagdad Cafe

Andree Pruett and her staff were waiting for the French mob with a lunch of chicken, mashed potatoes and broccoli. Pruett, in her mid-60s, is the owner of the Bagdad Café. She and her late husband Harold moved from California’s biggest desert town – Los Angeles – to one of its tiniest, Newberry Springs. She came to write. He came to raise ostriches. But with no restaurant experience they bought the Sidewinder Café on a whim and a prayer in the mid 1990s, renamed it the Bagdad Cafe and figured out how to attract tourists from around the world. Foreigners were Pruett’s main customers, especially the French.

“They’re wonderful people,” she said, carrying six plates of food into the jammed dining room. “My doors are open because of them. Without the French I’d be almost out of business.” About 75 percent of Bagdad Café’s pilgrims come from France and its former colonies, with 20 percent from the rest of the world and only 5 percent from the United States. The French, Italians and Portuguese flock to the cafe year round. Ten to 15 tour buses arrive each day between March and October, her peak season. Japanese come. Brazilians, also big fans of the “Bagdad Café” movie, usually arrive on motorcycles.

Watching Pruett in action was a seminar in the American work ethic Steinbeck worried was disappearing in 1960. On a lovely Sunday afternoon she was working her tail off, delivering food, running the register, helping people with T-shirt sizes, being pestered by me. She was the boss and she was doing most of the sweating.

Her small place was packed and noisy with the sound of French. Yet she was never rude or brusque to her employees or her customers, whose language was as alien to her as Greek. Pruett wasn't getting rich, which was too bad because she deserved to be. She had built a world-famous small business in the middle of the desert. Literally and literally. How's that for good old entrepreneurship and American knowhow, Mr. Steinbeck?

Pruett was unique, but then again she really wasn't. She was one of more than 8 million American women who owned a small business. Unlike Steinbeck, whose contact with women was limited mostly to irritable waitresses and housewives, on my trip I met dozens of women who owned and operated their own restaurants, coffee shops, motels, bookstores and cinnamon bun shops. Women owned a third of American businesses in 2010, up dramatically since 2000, and their numbers were increasing. They were important job creators and a major source of growth for the economy, but most of them were plain nuts. You had to be nuts to start a small business because running one will drive you crazy.

The French mob belied all of their vicious but largely accurate ethnic stereotypes. They were well-behaved and enthusiastic guests. A mix of old and young, couples and groups, they waited patiently in the café dining room, then wolfed down their meals. If they didn't like American road food, they didn't show it. As the French took turns posing with a genuine "California US Route 66" highway sign and tried on any piece of clothing with a "66" on it, I ate my free lunch with Sonia the Tour Guide.

Sonia was the only French-English-speaking person within 40 miles. She explained that for Europeans the Bagdad Cafe/Route 66/Jack Kerouac/"On the Road"/"Grapes of Wrath"-thing is all part of the American myth. The "Bagdad Café" movie was a huge hit throughout Western Europe. Before her tour group arrived at the cafe, Sonia said, "They had a very special experience viewing the movie and hearing the soundtrack. For them it is part of the American Dream."

Sonia was French Canadian, 30-ish, good-natured and a resident of L.A. She had been to the Bagdad Cafe 40 or 50 times, which must be the world record. The cafe was the first stop on a popular 10-day tour that began in Los Angeles, ended in San Francisco and included the Grand Canyon, Death Valley and Vegas. At the risk of being arrested, Sonia agreed to ethnically profile her clients. "The French were tough but they adapt. The Italians are honeymooners and are always arguing. The Portuguese are very conservative. I prefer the French people," she admitted. "They are more open and flexible."

In the Bagdad Café's parking lot, as the French were reluctantly boarding their bus, Sonia the Tour Guide pointed to the derriere of my red RAV4 and announced something, in French, of course. All I could make out was the word "*journaliste.*" A dozen men and women with cameras crunched down around the back of my car and began taking close-ups.

"What's the big deal?" I asked Sonia. "Did you tell them I was a famous journalist or something?"

"*Pas excitement, mon ami*," she would have said if she thought I understood four words of her native tongue.

It turned out the French are not just crazy about Jerry Lewis, Louis Armstrong and American road culture. They also have a thing about our license plates. In France, Sonia explained, automobile license plates are boring and all look the same – like someone's Social Security number in the USA. To over-bureaucratized French people, America's 50 colorful state license plates were like works of art and they collected photos of them. As Sonia stepped onto her bus, which was bound for the Grand Canyon and then Las Vegas, a fresh load of French tourists pulled into the Bagdad Café's lot. They weren't coming for American road cuisine. They were coming for T-shirts and a chance to worship a part of our rich culture that will never die as long as the French stay French.

# Old 66

East into the flat wide desert I zoomed. In my rearview mirror 20 more people from France were standing in the middle of the road taking pictures of each other. Except for a million scruffy low dirty-green bushes, a string of skeletal telephone poles and a few cinder mountains crawling low on the horizon, nothing but desert lay ahead. There were no cars to meet or pass. There weren't even any old U.S. 66 signs. They had been swiped by souvenir hunters or taken down by the highway department decades ago.

I was officially riding the National Trails Highway, but every four miles or so a fading "Route 66" shield was painted in white on the cracked and rutted asphalt. Not one to miss a photo op or a chance to bend a traffic law in pursuit of journalism, I stopped in the middle of the road and parked. Imitating a French tourist, I used my smart phone to take a portrait of myself standing on a Route 66 logo. With my RAV4 over one shoulder and I-40 and its truck traffic over the other, it turned out to be the signature photo of my trip.

For 28 miles I rode rough old Route 66 as it paralleled I-40. Sometimes I went 75 mph, sometimes 40, when the asphalt was extra bumpy and crumbly. I had never seen a road surface so strangely eroded before – can asphalt rot in the sun? After 30 minutes, and without encountering another car, my joy ride back in time ended at a Dairy Queen/gas station at the I-40 exit for Ludlow, population 23. Ludlow's motor courts, cafes and shade made it a popular rest stop until the late 1960s, when I-40 turned the town into one of Route 66's more photogenic ghosts.

As the sun disappeared I got back on the interstate. Too bad it was getting dark. At Ludlow old Route 66 veered away to the south, curving across the desert floor for 70 miles while I-40 cut straight through the low Bristol Mountains to Arizona. It would have been interesting to track more of the lonely highway that

Steinbeck and the rest of the country had to travel in 1960. Not only that, but Old 66 went past the town of Bagdad – or at least past the empty spot in the desert where it and the real Bagdad Café used to be.

Before I-40 was built 10 miles north of it in 1972, Bagdad was more than an oasis for travelers. The jukebox and dance floor of the Bagdad Café reportedly made the town of 600 the hottest entertainment spot between Barstow and Needles. A lot of cool and tacky things died along old Route 66 because the interstate came and changed everything. But Bagdad – once a prosperous mining and railroad town – didn't even have a ghost. There was no more there there. The town, its buildings, roads, houses and palm trees had literally disappeared. All that was left was a small sign standing by the railroad tracks that read "Bagdad."

I would have liked to have seen that sign for myself, even in the dark, but I was getting itchy. I had turned the far corner on my lap around the USA and I was headed for home. It was Sunday, Oct. 31, 2010. Sag Harbor was 7,265 miles behind me on the Steinbeck Highway. I had seven days, almost 4,000 miles and two more French people to go. I was running two weeks ahead of Steinbeck's pace. His search for the heart and soul of America, such as it was, effectively ended when he hit Seattle. Then he went on his West Coast vacation for a month. Other than driving his truck back to New York, his iconic journey was over by California. So almost was his book.

When he says goodbye to his past from the top of Fremont Peak, it is already Page 184 of a 246-page book. Most of the remaining quarter of "Travels With Charley" is padded with, excuse the French, a lot of finely written bullshit. A lovely but longish description of the desert and its secrets. An encounter with two coyotes he decides not to kill. A dumb conversation with Charley at a dubious campout in a canyon near the Continental Divide. Steinbeck did only two important things between California and New York City, as far as his book was concerned. He celebrated Thanksgiving at a cattle ranch near Amarillo and he went to New Orleans to witness white mothers protesting outside their newly integrated public school. I was going to visit both places and then bolt for home, exactly as he did.

## Steinbeck Timeline

Friday, Nov. 19 to Nov. 20, 1960 – Flagstaff to Amarillo

*Steinbeck writes in "Travels With Charley" that he drove the last 600 miles to Amarillo on Route 66 as fast as he could. Dejected, he admitted to himself that he was "pounding out the miles because I was no longer hearing or seeing. I had passed my limit of taking in or, like a man who goes on stuffing in food after he is filled, I felt helpless to assimilate what was fed in through my eyes." He says he camped alone in a canyon near the Continental Divide east of Gallup, New Mexico. It's possible he spent the night there, but we have only his word for it.*

## Racing to Amarillo

Steinbeck didn't leave his family cottage in Pacific Grove until Nov. 15, 1960. Elaine flew ahead to Texas. His friend Toby Street rode with him in the truck for four days, then bailed at Flagstaff. Street's presence is never mentioned in "Travels With Charley." But in 1975 Street told a San Jose State University Steinbeck scholar that his ride-along in Rocinante was far from romantic: " . . . it wasn't a very good experience because this trailer ... made so much noise. It rumbled so as we went along...."

Just as Steinbeck raced 2,000 miles from Chicago to meet his wife in Seattle, he raced 1,333 miles across the Southwest to rejoin her in Amarillo. Steinbeck – forlorn and tired of looking for America – writes in "Charley" that he camped out overnight by the Continental Divide near Gallup, New Mexico. If he really did, it would have been the first time he slept in his camper in five weeks, when he was in western Montana in mid-October. He then describes in detail the Thanksgiving bash he celebrated with millionaires at a cattle ranch owned by his wife's ex-brother-in-law. I hoped to find that ranch when I got to Amarillo, but first I had to traverse the broad vacant states of Arizona and New Mexico.

At the California line I ignored the night-piercing neon signs advertizing $29.90 motel rooms in Needles, where gas was going for $3.69, exactly a dollar a gallon higher than across the Colorado River in Arizona. I laughed at the $35 motel rooms in Kingman. My goal was the friendly and free Wal-Mart parking lot in Flagstaff, but by 10 I had to give up. East of Seligman I pulled off I-40 at Crookton Road, which was also Historic Route 66. Less than an hour short of Flagstaff, I slept like a baby in my RAV4 in a dusty truck turnaround. It was another anti-Wal-Mart parking lot – pitch black except for the flickering lights of trucks hurtling down I-40 and the gentle glare of a few billion stars.

Sleeping by the side of Route 66 was an American tradition, a lost art. Many a migrant did it on their way to California in the 1930s. So did tourists. An elderly

Pittsburgh businessman I knew told me he drove on U.S. 66 to Los Angeles alone as a high schooler in 1935. He took an Army cot with him. When he was tired he just pulled off, set up the cot next to his car and slept in the desert. A zillion other early road warriors did a variation of that kind of "car camping" before Route 66's commercial amenities caught up with its mostly east-to-west traffic flow. My night by America's most famous road was luxurious by comparison.

## Meteor Crater, Inc.

An hour before sunrise I crept through downtown Williams on old Route 66. With two stop signs, a 15 mph speed limit, vintage storefronts and a dozen mom & pop motels, it was another 1960s time capsule. The sacred Number 66 was stamped on everything and glowed from every retail window. I ate my standard egg breakfast in Flagstaff at dawn. I didn't detour to visit Meteor Crater when I passed its exit 43 miles east on I-40. I had already seen that scary hole in the desert twice. Fifty thousand years old, 4,000 feet wide and nearly 600 feet deep, it's the best natural attraction on Route 66.

Amazingly, the crater is not owned by a state, federal or global government. The Barringer Meteor Crater, its real name, is the private property of the Barringer Crater Company, a family enterprise devoted to preserving the site in its natural state, promoting its scientific study and, in the great American custom, making a buck. Anyone disappointed by the magnificent crater – or not suitably terror-stricken by what a 150-foot space rock going 28,600 miles an hour can do to a flat piece of our puny planet – has been on the road too long.

Central north Arizona is geographically challenged. No wonder Steinbeck had nothing to say about it in "Charley." Eighty-seven miles east of Flagstaff, 98 miles west of Gallup, 5,000 feet above the sea, it was like I had taken a wrong turn and ended up on Mars. At 75 mph I was inching across the world's largest tabletop. Kansas is level, but at least Kansas tilts. North Dakota is big and barren and bad, but at least it had gullies, cows, grass and a third dimension. The brown, endless plateau was so huge its horizons had no mountains. It also had no humans. No water. No soil. No agriculture. No trees. No life. No view. No billboards. Not even a decent stretch of old Route 66 to sell "Welcome to Mars" T-shirts.

Traffic was light, but the number of people on I-40 at any given time still had to be far greater than the local populace. It figured that empty/useless north-central Arizona was Navajo Country. Other than a burning star in a cloud-free sky, there were no natural resources to exploit except petrified wood and rocks, which are the same thing. It was obviously land nobody else wanted to buy or steal, which explains why the poor Navajo nation got stuck with it. I didn't see any sign of Indians – OK, persons of a non-white color who happen to be Native Americans. But I was a believer in justice, or at least irony and revenge. As I left their plateau I wished the Navajo well. I hoped there was 10 centuries worth of oil and natural gas deposits locked into the shale under their property. And that no government agency held the mineral rights.

# Gritty Gallup

My journey through the flat high desert ended at Gallup. I was old enough to remember when I-40 just disappeared outside town and all trucks and travelers were forced to run the gauntlet of cheap motels, bars and eateries on old Route 66. That was 1974. Gallup's main drag didn't have two McDonald's then, but it does now, plus four interstate exits.

Steinbeck and Charley hurried through Gallup and the rest of New Mexico on their way to Amarillo. It probably was about five days before Thanksgiving. In 1960 they wouldn't have seen a McDonald's or half of the familiar places I saw, including Sonic, Papa John's and the ubiquitous Subway. Gallup had 14,000 people then. In 2010 it had about 22,000. The city has sprawled west and east into the desert along four-lane Historic Route 66 – not that that matters much when empty land is as cheap as the dry air. Most of the traffic and trucks stayed on I-40. Yet gritty Gallup's streets and parking lots were surprisingly busy – almost franticly so. Many were locals. But many travelers also were obviously threading through town – a 10-minute ordeal on old Route 66. Or they were shopping at the Indian jewelry and art stores or grabbing meals at Garcia's or El Rancho, indigenous eateries that will never be confused with a national chain.

Lodging-wise, Gallup offered several miles of choices. The El Rancho Hotel & Motel, once a getaway for Hollywood actors and their upscale bunkhouse when shooting Westerns in the area, dates to 1937 but has been restored. Its guests no longer include the Marx Brothers, John Wayne and presidents Eisenhower and Reagan, but the traveling masses. Along with Days Inn and LaQuinta were sketchier independent places like the Thunderbird, a roadside dump whose alphabetically disabled sign could only manage an "M" and half an "O" in "Motel." At $19.95 a night, it still looked overpriced – if it was really open.

I'm sure the city of Gallup, whose population is a third Latino and a third Native American, had good homes and neighborhoods hiding on its side streets. But there were some awfully shifty-looking trailer homes a block behind Historic 66. And on several sprawling empty lots the desert grasses and shrubs were doing a poor job of hiding years of trash and junk.

Nothing rusts or biodegrades in the desert. And nothing old or dead seems to get torn down and taken away, just vandalized or ignored. When I stopped at a graffiti-decorated, fairly new gas-station/Indian Market complex on old Route 66 outside Gallup, it was impossible to tell how long ago it had been abandoned. Its plate glass windows and interior had been smashed and re-smashed and bushes two feet tall were growing from cracks in the parking lot's sandy asphalt. Unless someone burned it to the ground or blew it up, it was another victim of the interstate, slow-cooking in the sun forever.

Gallup had its own prominent Historic 66 eyesores. A few boarded-up gas stations and restaurants. The burned out hulk of a large cheap motel sitting naked in its parking lot. But if you looked beyond the crappy and the new, you could see

Gallup was a living museum, another frozen slice of a travel era everyone imagines was romantic but probably wasn't. Though it would never be called charming, it still had great examples of 1950s/'60s business architecture you'll never see again. It was kind of like what happened in Cuba with 1950s American cars, only in Gallup it was heartless capitalism that had saved the old stuff from destruction, not loving socialism.

Despite the "Historic 66" signs, Gallup was a place a stranger didn't feel like staying in too long. It seemed like it could use a good two-day rain, but that was probably true every day. Yet it deserved some credit and respect. It had adapted pretty well to 50 years of change. It was still clearly making a living by pleasing long-distance travelers, which is nothing to be ashamed of. On the east end of Route 66, I stopped at a jammed McDonald's for a hit of coffee and free Wi-Fi. I was the only adult willing to brave the playroom, where dozens of revved-up kids under four were racing around in circles trying to shout each other to death. I lasted half an hour in McScreamland before I broke and headed for Albuquerque.

In "Travels With Charley," after Steinbeck "rushed through Gallup in the night," he says he camped overnight in a canyon on the Continental Divide. Steinbeck writes about how bummed out he was that night. Rocinante's little kitchen was a mess. For the last several hundred miles he had just put his foot to the floor and deliberately avoided people. He knew his long trip in search of America and its people had not gone well. He knew he hadn't been seeing enough, hearing enough, learning enough. "Why," he asked himself, "had I thought I could learn anything about this land?"

Half an hour east of Gallup, elevation 7,245, I exited I-40 to look at the raggedy and unloved "Official Scenic Historic Marker" for the Continental Divide. It was located near the ruins of what apparently was once the Continental Divide Trading Post. Busy and prosperous when Steinbeck passed by, it had become the overgrown anchor store of another little Route 66 ghost mall. As the sun died in the flaming sky behind me, it lighted up cliffs on I-40 that were redder than it was. Running through big dry empty valley after big dry empty valley, I passed Grants, New Mexico, and saw the best state highway sign of my trip – the philosophically ambiguous, "Gusty Winds May Exist." After it finally got dark, I sailed over the rim of a hill and looked down into a broad valley. Instead of the usual New Mexico nothingness, it was filled with a million lights. It was Albuquerque, a mile-high town of 201,000 in 1960 that had since exploded into a city of 545,000.

## Burned in Albuquerque

I got greedy. Or stupid. And I paid for my mistakes. During my 150-mile desert cruise to Albuquerque, I did a Hotwire search and found a $56 deal for an unnamed four-star hotel in Albuquerque's Old Downtown. I had visions of staying at a Spanish-style Ambassador East or St. Francis Hotel, the wood and marble joints John, Charley and Elaine Steinbeck favored. Instead Hotwire gave me the modern and sterile and cold Hyatt Regency, which I quickly learned specialized in nickel-and-diming its guests into bankruptcy.

After sleeping where I had been sleeping, I hardly qualified as a freelance lodging critic for Lonely Planet. But it seemed like I got burned. My Hotwire bargain price didn't stop at $56. First came $13 worth of surcharges and local hotel taxes. Then there was the $16 overnight parking fee, plus a $4 tip to the attendant for parking my car and listening to me gripe. Hyatt also charged something like $10 to hook up to their house Wi-Fi. I didn't need it because my smart phone had a mobile hot spot, but the charge was particularly galling since every mini-mom & pop place I'd stayed in so far included Wi-Fi for free. "Free Wi-Fi" is the "Free TV" and "Free HBO" of the digital age. Less than $90 for a night at a full-service hotel was still a good deal for any normal adult traveler. But I wasn't normal or adult, plus I was spending my own money not my company's.

Before I went to sleep, I walked two blocks to Central Avenue, which, fortuitously, was old Route 66's route through the city. It bustled by day. But at 9 most of the restaurants had closed and little squads of homeless persons were patrolling the sidewalks. Lucking into the Asian Noodle Bar, I ate a good cheap late-night meal at the counter with one other customer and several waiters. Central Ave had lucked it through the 20$^{th}$ century urban renewal craze largely unscathed. It still had lots of old store fronts, slashes of neon and architectural treasures like the Pueblo Deco-style KiMo Theater, which was scheduled to be demolished but was saved at the last minute and renovated instead.

In the morning I had no interest in "awakening my senses" at the Hyatt with a $12 zucchini and cheese frittata. That breakfast delight and $9.50 worth of seasonal fruits and berries, said the card by my czar-size bed, could be delivered right to my 12th floor room, plus tip. I'd have passed on the cheese frittata if I was Donald Trump's adopted son. Instead, I decided to descend to earth and seek a bagel and coffee in the wide quiet streets of downtown Albuquerque. I was pleasantly surprised to find I didn't have to pay a toll on the elevator.

It was Nov. 2 – Election Day. The historic date the Tea Party was going to seize America from the Democrats and give it back to the Republicans, the party that had taken us to a foolish and tragic war in Iraq, copiloted the economy into a mountainside and squandered federal money it didn't have like a bunch of drunken Democrats.

## Another French Connection

When I left the Hyatt Regency I walked into the first likely storefront I saw – La Quiche Parisienne Bistro. I swear, I didn't notice the French name. To me it looked just like another downtown coffee & bagel shop. But Bruno, the proprietor/baker behind the counter, said there were no bagels for sale – just French pastries and his *quiche du jour*. By the time I was finished eating my tasty quiche Lorraine, Bruno knew I was from Pittsburgh and I knew his wife used to live in Pittsburgh. He went in back to get Sabine Pasco. Not only had Sabine run a French bakery in downtown Pittsburgh in the early 1990s, she used to live only two townships away from me.

Unfortunately, things didn't work out too well for Sabine business-wise in Pittsburgh. It was a town of too many Italian bakeries and few French people. She went bankrupt and moved on to other cities. She was yet another brave/crazy entrepreneurial businesswoman. But she and Bruno were holding their own in "a so-so location," which was haunted by day and ruled by night by a permanent clan of homeless street people.

Sabine and Bruno were the last members of the French race I met on my trip. For some strange reason I had met more French-based people than any other ethnic minority. In 43 days on the Steinbeck Highway, I met exactly 59. I met two French-Canadian vacationers in Maine, a Polish biker from France in Oregon, two French bakers in Albuquerque and 52 French tourists in the Mojave Desert. Plus there was Sonia the French-Canadian Tour Guide and the French Canadian customs officer at Niagara Falls who let me in her country without a passport. Every one of them was so nice I decided to forgive the French nation for its rudeness, cultural chauvinism and Nazi and socialist sympathies. I also decided they were right all along – Jerry Lewis was a genius.

As far as I knew, there were not a lot of French people in my next destination, Texas. I took what used to be Route 66 out of Albuquerque and re-entered the desert. I was sorry I didn't have time to visit my sister Mary, as I had originally planned. Mary lived only about 100 miles straight north of Albuquerque, in the mountains not far from Los Alamos. She became a hippie in the 1960s and pretty much stayed one for the rest of her life. The mother of three daughters, she was a pioneering home-birther and a home-schooler.

With one exception, she was so far off the grid she'd have to be arrested by helicopter. She lived a few miles from the highway at 9,500 feet in a tiny A-frame house made with hay bales. She had a few horses and llamas, but no electricity, no phone, no car, no road. Her water came from a nearby well and she subsisted on a diet of tortillas and beans. Her backyard was a national forest and in winter she needed snowshoes to get to town.

As my brother John once told a Pittsburgh newspaper writer, Mary lived like "it was 1840." That was still true except for two fairly recent additions – a Honda generator and a solar-powered satellite dish for her computer. Mary supported her hermitic, $3,000-a-year lifestyle by making and selling beautiful felt dolls and hats.

At 59, she was perhaps the happiest, most serene, most self-reliant mountain woman who ever grew up in a suburb in the 1960s, wore Villager skirts and went to a Catholic girls high school. It would have been cool to see Mary's new hay house, but I was not interested in any two-day side trips. From Albuquerque I could see the finish line.

# 19 – Greater State of Texas

*I know no place where hospitality is practiced so fervently as in Texas.*
– "Travels With Charley"

## Steinbeck Timeline

Sunday, Nov. 20 to Nov. 29-30, 1960 – Texas

*Steinbeck says in "Charley" he spent "three days of namelessness at a beautiful motor hotel" in the middle of Amarillo while the broken front window of his camper shell was repaired. He says Charley was sick and was left with a kind vet for four days. Elaine rejoined him in her home state of Texas and the pair went to her ex-brother-in-law's cattle ranch in nearby Clarendon, arriving the day before Thanksgiving. Steinbeck doesn't say in the book how long he stays at the ranch and never mentions that afterwards the Steinbecks went 400 miles south to Austin to visit Elaine's sister until the end of the month.*

## Amarillo and the Good Vet

After passing up a dozen cheap, wildly illuminated 1950s motels in Tucumcari, I crossed into Texas on I-40 and pulled in to a mercifully unlighted picnic area where no one in his right mind would have a picnic. A dozen tractor-trailers were parked nose-to-tail. I drove well past them to the edge of a wide empty parking lot and went to sleep quickly.

When I awoke at 5:20 a sliver of moon was slowly climbing over the lights of Vega, Texas. Overnight some unkind trucker in a big rig had parked three feet behind me. His diesel engine was idling noisily. Pulling down the rest of my blackout curtains, all I could see were the sides of monster trucks, all idling noisily/chokingly. I was penned in. I jumped out into the chilly darkness, stepped into my Keens and barely made my escape. It was my closest brush with death on my whole trip, which proves how safe the highways of America are.

By 6:08 or 7:08, depending on whether I wanted to believe my cell phone or my car radio, the eastern horizon was starting to glow. James Carville was crying on CNN News. Overnight America supposedly underwent a historic political change. Republican Tea Partiers had seized the U.S. House and a new Golden Age of limited government, lower taxes and personal freedom was allegedly on the way. It was the usual hype and hysteria. Nothing would be changing on the U.S.S. Big Government except a few deck chairs.

What pleased me most was that Rand Paul, the son of ex-Pittsburgher and libertarian Texas Congressman Ron Paul, was the new U.S. Senator for Kentucky. And poor California. Its people were so desperate. After almost three decades, they had put former Gov. Moonbeam, aka Jerry Brown, back in power. He was going to try to salvage the sorry state he helped wreck 30 years earlier, this time without the help of Linda Ronstadt.

Amarillo – the biggest city of the Dust Bowl with 50,000 citizens in the 1930s and 193,000 now – was rolling out of bed as I joined the morning rush hour. I ate at a Waffle House where the waitress' accent was so strong I could barely understand anything but "Honey." In Amarillo my task was to find what I mistakenly was calling "The Scott Ranch." The ranch was owned by the family of Hollywood actor Zachary Scott, who was Elaine Steinbeck's first husband. Elaine was from Austin. After she divorced Zachary Scott and married Steinbeck, she never burned her bridges to the Scott family, which had a lot of money, cattle and land, which are interchangeable currencies in Texas. Steinbeck's son Thom worked at the cattle ranch as a teenager in the summer of 1960. And Elaine and Steinbeck had been invited there to a millionaires' Thanksgiving "orgy," as he calls it in the book.

They apparently stayed at the ranch for about four days without Charley, who was recuperating from his urinary problems at a veterinarian clinic in Amarillo. Poor Charley. He was in and out of kennels and vet's offices the whole trip. But it was a good thing he went along. He gave Steinbeck somebody to talk to and worry and joke about. And when the editors at Viking expunged his wife's presence from the West Coast part of the original manuscript, Charley saved the day – and ultimately the book. Charley and his personal plumbing issues provided "Charley's" only dramatic thread. He apparently had prostatitis and that chronic medical problem and his bathroom habits were a supposedly humorous running gag in the book. Maybe there was another clever metaphor going on – someday I plan to ask the Steinbeck scholars if Charley's peeing all over America had a double meaning I missed.

If what Steinbeck wrote is to be believed, he took Charley to two veterinarians during the trip. He took a very sick Charley to an uncaring and incompetent Bad Vet in Spokane and to a young and gentle Good Vet in Amarillo. The Spokane vet was a boozy bum. But Steinbeck says in the book that Charley stayed with the good Texas veterinarian for four days and was brought back to health. I meant to try to find that tender animal doctor with "the trained and knowing" hands when I went through Amarillo. But I got so involved in my search for the cattle ranch I completely forgot about the poor dog. After I got home to Pittsburgh I made a few phone calls back to Amarillo, looking for the oldest living vet in town. Hoping the Good Vet was still alive, I talked to several veterinarian offices in Amarillo to see if I could learn anything. My best hope was Dr. Fred Love. He was 74 and had been practicing for 50 years. He'd treated a lot of animals passing through town – including movie stars' pets and circus animals. His name was too perfect to be believed, but Dr. Love was not the Good Vet that Steinbeck took Charley to in 1960.

Dr. Love, along with another old-timer, Dr. Johnny Wise, could not think of any vets of that era who were still alive. Neither could a veteran vet at Dr. Wolf's office. Vets Love, Wise and Wolf? Amarillo's animals were in friendly hands. The vets concurred that there were no old stories in the local veterinarian community about fixing Steinbeck's poodle's plumbing problems. So did the Good Vet of Amarillo really exist? Maybe. But I suspect that like the Bad Vet of Spokane he was just one more character Steinbeck whipped up, or enhanced, to add a little drama to his thin tale.

# In Search of Steinbeck's Ranch

From my corner office at the Waffle House, I called cattle ranch brokers and real estate offices in Amarillo. I called the University of Texas in Austin, where Zachary Scott's papers were stored. I left messages with heirs of Zachary Scott. No one could help me locate the ranch, which I hoped to visit and document with photographs.

I tried all the private-sector angles. I even walked into a real estate office where 12 agents were having a meeting and asked if anyone had heard of "The Scott Ranch." Every single Texan I talked to did their state's friendly reputation proud, but no luck. Someone suggested I call the office of the Potter County Clerks of Courts, which I reluctantly did. I wasn't in the mood to deal with bureaucrats or go deed surfing in a strange county. But by the time I got downtown the good ladies who obviously run Potter County government were already doing the hard work on my behalf.

While one lady was informing me that 640 acres equaled a section and 13 sections was "a small cattle ranch in these parts," another pointed me to a gigantic old framed map of the Amarillo area on which the names of hundreds of property owners were handwritten. (In Texas, even the Panhandle is big.) The map weighed about 150 pounds and was jammed behind some file cabinets. I squeezed in and eyeballed the map for about 10 minutes. Way at the top edge I found a little square of land with "S.L. Scott" written on it. The land Sallie L. Scott deeded to actor

Zachary T. Scott Jr. in 1941 was about 47 miles north, just across the border into Moore County.

Off I went, braving the crosswind and murderous sun. I sailed across an arid, gently rolling short-grass prairie that had more cattle than trees or Republicans – and I couldn't see any cattle. No wonder you had to own 30,000 acres in Texas to make it worth owning land. The only humans I saw along U.S. 87 were a couple of kids hot-rodding a Jeep down the middle of the so-called Canadian River. Near Masterson I turned off U.S. 87 by a garage/office building and drove in on the asphalt road like I owned the place.

After a mile or two I was on a hard dirt road. I passed a few small oil wells and some drilling equipment. A dozen head of Black Angus posed handsomely against the tan grass and blue sky. A couple miles of sandy dirt and low bushes later, I came to a hilltop. I could see for miles in every direction and there was nothing to see. Seven miles from U.S. 87, I came upon a group of buildings with a few big cottonwoods and two pickup trucks. The centerpiece of the compound was a solid one-story white cedar and stone farmhouse. In one of the outbuildings a pack of unseen dogs barked furiously.

I knocked and knocked on the front door. No one was home on the range. The hot wind brushed quietly across the barely green grassland. When the wind paused, the flies appeared. Given Texas' reputation for guns, I didn't dare peek into the house. I took my photos and split. I went into the town of Dumas to the Moore County Clerk of Courts office to look for some historical information about the property. Though they tried, the friendly women there couldn't help me any further. On my way back to Amarillo, I was feeling pretty smart. Once again I had stumbled on to what I was looking for by finding the right people, asking questions and following my nose until I hit something or got shot at. I had discovered Steinbeck's fancy Thanksgiving cattle ranch. Or so I thought.

I drove through downtown Amarillo at evening rush hour and headed south. My plan was to follow, as best as I could, the route Steinbeck and Elaine probably took to Austin, where they visited with her sister until the end of November 1960. My cell phone rang at 70 mph. It was Professor Susan Shillinglaw, the Steinbeck scholar from San Jose State. She was calling to say she was sorry she would be out of town the coming weekend. Huh? I was 1,300 miles east of her and headed in the opposite direction.

It took me a while to realize what was going on. Shillinglaw hadn't found my "Travels Without Charley" business card under her office door until five days after I left it there. She taught classes Tuesday through Thursday. It was Wednesday. Great. My card had been sitting on her office floor in San Jose the whole time I was in Monterey, which somebody at the university had told me was where she lived but wasn't. She actually lived in Los Gatos, 60 miles north of Monterey, so I would have missed her anyway.

It was total confusion, another bungled attempt to have a formal interview with the elusive "Queen of Steinbeck Studies," as I had taken to call her. Shillinglaw knew more about Steinbeck and his life and works than I could learn in another lifetime. I always figured she'd be my literary expert. She'd be the scholar to tell me whether it really mattered if Steinbeck fictionalized and fibbed his way around the USA. But I felt like I was back in high school trying to get her to go to the prom with me. She was always busy, hard to get and rudely or dizzily slow in getting back to me. For months I had been persistent without being pushy. But most of my phone calls and emails to her had gone unanswered or unreturned.

The first time I met her, during my spring research tour of the West Coast, I knocked on her office door on the campus of San Jose State. There was no answer. It turned out she was sleeping in her office. Now there's an unforced metaphor for a book about Steinbeck scholars failing to notice the problems in "Travels With Charley" for 50 years. When she woke up we spoke briefly in her office but she had to leave to teach a class.

It was always something. In August I gently stalked her at the Steinbeck Festival, telling her I wanted to formally interview her when she had time. But she always had something pressing to do during the festival and I was never aggressive enough. Now I had missed Shillinglaw again. I had wanted to tell her what I had learned about Steinbeck's actual trip. Stuff even she didn't know. As with Jay Parini at Middlebury College in Vermont, I wanted to get her reaction to my discoveries for the record. It wasn't meant to happen.

After proudly telling Shillinglaw I'd just found Steinbeck's Thanksgiving cattle ranch, I told her I'd call her after I got back to Pittsburgh. We never spoke again. I called and left messages. We exchanged a few short emails over the next two months. Her student evaluations said she was nice but disorganized, both of which rang true. But she clearly had no interest in talking to me about what I had learned. That night I slept soundly at one of Lubbock's five Wal-Marts. Texas must have 200 of them. It was one more reason to like the well run, fiscally sound state. Steinbeck liked and appreciated Texas, its people and culture. He said it was a state of mind, a mystique bordering on a religion, and he was probably right.

After only one full day in Texas, I had decided Texans were my favorite kind of American. Every one I met had been friendly, helpful and warm. I couldn't have found "the Scott Ranch" without the help of a handful of beautiful Texas gals who worked in the county clerks office of Potter County. Becky, Barb, Judy and their Republican co-workers had no idea I detested George W. Bush, wanted to legalize all drugs and wished I could reduce the size and bite of government by 90 percent, for starters. Even if they knew about my radical politics, I bet they would have searched their land records and their memories just as hard to help me find Steinbeck's cattle ranch. Trouble was, I hadn't actually found it.

## The Real Ranch

I was leaving Lubbock for Austin at dawn on Thursday when I got a call from J.B. Lane, one of the Amarillo people I had left a message with the day before. Lane told me the bad news first. The ranch house I found was the wrong house because I had been on the wrong ranch.

Lane managed L R Hagy Estate, an Amarillo cattle/oil/gas company. Lawrence R. Hagy had been Zachary Scott's brother-in-law and at one time he owned both the wrong ranch I had found and the right ranch I didn't. The place I had seen, what Lane called "the rock house," was the current headquarters of the Hagy Ranch. The other Hagy ranch, the one the Steinbecks visited in the fall of 1960, was 60 miles east of Amarillo in Clarendon, Texas.

Lane, who used to be married to a Hagy, knew the Clarendon ranch intimately. He said it was where the wealthy movers and shakers of Amarillo would regularly go to hunt and fish. "It was a working cattle ranch," he said. "Thom Steinbeck worked at that ranch. Elaine was there that Thanksgiving, too. I've seen pictures." Lane had more bad news. In 2003 L R Hagy Estate sold the ranch to the Crofoot Cattle Company. I thought that was the end of my trail. But Lane gave me the company's phone number and three minutes later I was babbling to Terry Crofoot, trying to explain why some guy from Pittsburgh had called him out of the blue.

Mr. Crofoot was 130 miles away from Lubbock, standing in a pasture. The ranch I was looking for was 156 miles the other way, northeast of Lubbock on the other side of cotton country. I figured I was doomed. Texas was too damn big. Life was too short. No way would I get to visit the ranch. But then that famous Texas hospitality gene must have automatically kicked in. "You'd be welcome to go there," Crofoot said before I even thought of asking. For the next 10 minutes he filled me in on the history of the ranch, going back to Indian days. It had been remodeled since he bought it from L R Hagy Estate, but it was essentially the same place Steinbeck stayed. Next Crofoot recited Google-plus directions to the ranch, down to the big water tower I'd see seven miles from Clarendon. I swear he sounded apologetic when he said his place was just a little under 40,000 acres, which would fit the City of Pittsburgh plus a few suburbs.

The cattle ranch was almost three hours away from where I was in Lubbock. But after 9,000 miles on the Steinbeck Highway, what was a little 156-mile detour? I kicked myself all the way. In my fit of triumph the day before, I had committed the mortal sin of journalism – the sin of presumption. If I had been on the ball, or if I still trusted anything Steinbeck wrote, I would have re-read his description of the place in his book before I declared success. Steinbeck said its one-story brick ranch house "stood in a grove of cottonwoods on a little eminence over a pool made by a dammed-up spring." At the ranch north of Amarillo there was no pond full of trout, no hill and no brick house. Lane's returned phone call had saved me from an embarrassing mistake.

Between Lubbock and Clarendon the first thing I hit was a dusty swath of cotton country. Gigantic fields covered with billions of cotton balls were crawling with insect-like sprinklers half a mile long. Loaves of tightly packed cotton the size of train cars baked in the sun beside the two-lane highway, which was arrow-straight and had little drifts of escaped cotton along its edges. I was flying alone across yet another vast chunk of dry, flat America that had been put to productive and profitable use by invisible men and their magic machines. After a token bump of uninhabited hill country, complete with canyons and curves, the terrain turned into scrubby rolling cattle land. Like so much of the American outback west of Chicago, traffic, houses and people were rare to nonexistent.

In Clarendon the impressive stone entrance to the Bitter Creek Ranch was exactly where Terry Crofoot said it would be on Farm to Market Road 1260. I drove a few minutes across open grassland sprinkled with a few dozen Herefords until I came to a compound in the shade of some old cottonwoods. There were several brick houses, four or five parked cars and pickups, a few horses in a corral, a trout pond, a spacious maintenance garage with its door open and lights on– but no one was home.

Thanks to Terry Crofoot's long-distance trust and hospitality, I was free to roam around the compound with my cameras and notebook like I owned the joint. Though two buildings were new and many upgrades had been made, it was clearly the place Steinbeck described in "Charley."

The main structure, a long one-story redbrick house, had a big screened-in porch overlooking a trout pond surrounded by trees. The great room had a white-brick fireplace and a high white ceiling with heavy beams. Each of the three bedrooms had a Texas-size bed, its own bathroom and a door to the outside. It was like a little motel, only in 1960 the regular guests were members of Texas' richest cattle families. The showroom of heavy wood outdoor furniture on the covered patios was worth more than my house. Yet, notwithstanding the "Dallas" stereotypes, nothing inside or out was ostentatious or in bad taste, just expensive and heavy.

Enjoying the sun and wind and park-like setting, I tried to imagine what it was like to be a vacationing cattle baron. I couldn't. My hat was too small. But I didn't need to imagine anything, since Steinbeck did a thorough job of detailing the cattle-baron lifestyle in "Travels With Charley." When Steinbeck writes about something he really did on his trip, you can usually tell. Instead of inventing pages of wooden dialogue, he delivers detail.

After having the ranch compound and its ghosts to myself for half an hour, I did what I had to do next – set out for New Orleans. As I left a Texas-size pickup truck with a long enclosed trailer came down the driveway. We stopped to talk, window-to-window like we already knew each other. I squinted up at him, established why I was trespassing and waved my Professional Reporter's Notebook around as if it had special powers. He was the 20-something son of Mr. Jones, the ranch manager. Handsome as a movie star, wearing a cowboy hat and work clothes because he needed to, he was like every other Texan I had met – friendly and real.

He thought my crazy Steinbeck story was more interesting than suspicious, probably because Terry Crofoot had tipped off him or his dad that I was coming. Mr. Jones' boy said he had just delivered a few head of cattle to their doom at the meat plant. He, another cowboy and a maintenance man lived full-time at the ranch. It was no surprise and no big deal to him that he slept every night in a bedroom the great John Steinbeck might have used.

## Steinbeck Timeline

Thursday, Dec. 1, 1960 – New Orleans, Upper Ninth Ward

*Steinbeck says in "Charley" he wanted to go to New Orleans to witness the anti-integration protests at a public school. Though he actually left from his wife's sister's place in Austin, which is 500 miles west of New Orleans, in the book he describes picking up Charley at the vet in Amarillo and driving south and east across Texas to New Orleans, a total of 1,000 miles. Hardly sleeping, he says he traveled in the bad ice storm that actually did hit southeast Texas Nov. 29 and 30. He writes that he arrived in "frozen-over" Beaumont, Texas, at midnight and in Houma, Louisiana, at dawn. In New Orleans he says he parked Rocinante and took a cab to William Frantz Elementary in the Upper Ninth Ward.*

# Bound for New Orleans

Again I awoke to the smell of idling trucks. Another sleepover in a Texas picnic area. This time it was on I-20, near Kilgore, east of Dallas and west of Shreveport. The GPS Person, into whose omniscient hands I was fully entrusted, had chosen my route to New Orleans. The day before she had guided me for 597 miles through Texas cotton country to Texas cattle country to Texas oil & gas country. It was the farthest I had driven in a single day.

Now I could smell the finish line. Via New Orleans and the Steinbeck Highway, home was only 1,700 miles away. I hoped to make Pittsburgh by Sunday. I skipped Austin. I didn't need to go there to find Elaine's sister's place. My last major stop, like Steinbeck's, was an elementary school in the soggy Upper Ninth Ward of New Orleans. He went there in early December to see the bigoted white mothers – the so-called "Cheerleaders." Their morning protests against the integration of their neighborhood public school had become a national news story. New Orleans was about 400 miles south and I hoped to reach William Frantz Elementary before dark.

No such luck. As soon as I entered the northwest corner of Louisiana there were serious traffic backups. Slow, thick, stupid traffic for miles along I-49. On I-10 near Baton Rouge was the worst traffic jam of my trip. There obviously were too many bayous and too few roads in the state for all the drivers – and most Louisiana drivers were crazy. George Carlin once observed with his usual keen perception that when you're driving you think the drivers you pass are morons and the drivers who pass you are assholes. The closer I got to downtown New Orleans, the more obvious it became that in Louisiana's case nearly everyone behind a wheel was a moron *and* an asshole. I had never seen so many road jerks in one city in my life. I wasn't a wimpy city driver. I'd had 12 years of training in Los Angeles, where freeways were clogged but fast and drivers were aggressive but good. I also spent half a lifetime in Pittsburgh, where the only thing worse than the drivers was the roads.

At first I thought it was just a few Louisiana hotheads. Then I realized their moronic-aggressive driving style was an ingrained cultural thing – a permanent state of community road rage. The worst ones were young, always white-male and usually driving cheap American muscle cars or pickup trucks plastered with New Orleans Saints decals. When I was going 70 in the fast lane behind a solid line of cars, a Louisiana loser would suddenly appear in my rearview mirror 12 feet from my bumper. Meanwhile, if I left two car lengths of air in front of me another moron/asshole would fly up the slow lane and jam into the space. It wasn't one or two cases of this kind of tailgating or lane-jamming. It was 25 cases in two hours.

The sudden wave of highway hooliganism was a strange development. Not four hours earlier I had told my wife Trudi on the cell phone that I couldn't remember being tailgated once from Maine to Amarillo. I also told her I had not had to flash anyone the finger, which actually wasn't that impressive since most of the time there was no one else on the road with me. Ten thousand consecutive miles of civilized driving behavior ended during three hours on southern

Louisiana's crowded, bumpy, beat-up freeways. Everyone drove aggressively and tailgated at 70 – including Louisiana Highway Patrolmen. I took a fuzzy photo of the tailgating cop car to prove it. It didn't surprise me to find out later that based on 2009 national highway stats, Louisiana was one of the most deadly states I had driven through. Its auto death rate, like Arizona's, was 1.8 per 100 million vehicle miles traveled, compared to the national rate of 1.1.

Montana, Louisiana/Arizona, North Dakota, New Mexico and Texas, in that order, each had fatality rates higher than the national average. The safest state I had crossed (and the safest in the country) was Massachusetts, which makes no sense to anyone who's driven in Boston. Roads in rich Connecticut, where every other family has a chauffer, and Minnesota, where most people drive a John Deere combine to work, were almost as safe as Massachusetts. Montana, with its 2.0 death rate, owed its deadliest ranking to several factors that apparently drive up the number of fatalities per mile in large rural states. Along with the usual reasons, drinking and low seatbelt usage, Montana's nice people kill themselves at a higher rate by wrecking their Ford 150s on remote rural roads, where EMS response times average 80 minutes instead of 15 in cities. Louisiana's cowboys kill themselves in the same ways, plus they're mostly morons and assholes.

# 20 – Hate & Filth in New Orleans

*No newspaper had printed the words these women shouted. It was indicated that they were indelicate, some even said obscene. On television the sound track was made to blur or had crowd noises cut in to cover. But now I heard the words, bestial and filthy and degenerate. In a long and unprotected life I have seen and heard the vomitings of demoniac humans before. Why then did these screams fill me with a shocked and sickened sorrow?*

– "Travels With Charley"

## The White School That Made Black History

It was dark by the time I parked in front of William Frantz Elementary in the Upper Ninth Ward. The stout brick school that made civil rights history in 1960 and drew the attention of America and John Steinbeck was closed, locked and boarded up. The building and its entire block were protected from local vandals and copper thieves by a cyclone fence topped by barbed wire.

Five years after the floods unleashed by Hurricane Katrina had devastated it, the neighborhood on both sides of North Galvez Street looked shabby and unfriendly, at least at night. The street was quiet with no people on the sidewalks and few cars on the move. It was too dark to take decent photos, so I checked into a Holiday Inn across town. The next morning William Frantz Elementary and the small, single-family homes surrounding it looked much better. Despite its broken windows, the building seemed less battered and the neighboring residential streets didn't look so dangerous or blighted. There was a freshly broken beer bottle on the sidewalk – next to the BMW at the curb.

The Upper Ninth Ward is 98 percent black, inordinately poor, troubled by crime, too close to the Mississippi River for comfort and less than a yard above sea level. It was inundated when the city's poorly built levees broke under the strain of Katrina's storm surge. William Frantz Elementary had to be closed and nearly 2,000 homes in the ward were left sitting in polluted seawater up to the tops of their front doors. The post-Katrina population of the Upper Ninth was half what it was in 2000. It was hard to believe, but the Upper Ninth Ward was lucky compared to the Lower Ninth Ward on the other side of the Industrial Canal. The Lower Ninth was virtually swept away when a 900-foot section of the levee holding back the canal collapsed. Half of the 1,577 people in Louisiana who died during or after Katrina lived in the Lower Ninth, where the pre-Katrina population had fallen from 14,000 to 2,842 in 2010.

My best drive-by journalist's guess, after a quick stroll, was that about 80 percent of the tiny homes in the streets around William Frantz Elementary had been fixed, rebuilt or replaced since Katrina. There were vacant homes and at least a dozen vacant lots, including the historic one across the street from the school that used to contain the boyhood home of the Upper Ninth Ward's least-favorite son, Lee Harvey Oswald. The neighborhood was still hurting all over.

The Great Recession's national unemployment rate of 10 percent would have been cause for dancing in the streets. Its jobless rate was pushing 40 percent. There were few iron bars on the windows and front doors, but crime was an issue in a poor and violent city whose drug gangs generated a murder rate nine times higher than New York's. Still, if you didn't count moldy houses sealed with plywood or landscaped with piles of debris left by the flood, the inexpensive new and old homes were well kept.

On Alvar Street, around the corner from the school, a young man armed with a weed whacker and a power mower was attacking a two-foot tangle of weeds and grass choking a partially remodeled vacant house. "It got away from me," he said apologetically. He said things were slowly improving in the Upper Ninth Ward. He was getting the front yard cleaned up because the owner was going to move into the house. "He has to move back because his house keeps getting broken into. He needs to live in it to protect it."

## Steinbeck Goes to School

It was 8:57. Birds were chirping and the ward was still sleeping in the warming sun. Following my neighborhood walking tour, I stood on the sidewalk across the street from the front door of William Frantz Elementary. The small old wood house behind me had electric service but it was boarded up and rotting. Like the school and the other unoccupied homes, its front door still bore the spray-painted code used by the search and rescue teams who went house-to-house after Katrina looking for survivors and human remains.

Fifty years earlier, in late November of 1960, there were no peaceful and quiet mornings on the sidewalks of North Galvez Street. William Frantz Elementary – then an all-white school in a virtually all-white working-class neighborhood – was making national headlines. The city of New Orleans had taken its first token steps to integrate its public schools. The crowded grade school was ground zero in a bitter civil rights battle that segregationists and white parents could never win but were viciously fighting anyway.

On Nov. 14, 1960, the city's color barrier was broken at William Frantz by little Ruby Bridges, the 6-year-old first-grader immortalized in Norman Rockwell's painting "The Problem We All Live With." Three other first-grade girls integrated a second school in the Lower Ninth Ward. When Bridges, escorted by beefy federal deputy marshals, showed up for school in her little white dress and white socks, it was like a bomb went off under Jim Crow's bed. The white teachers immediately quit. White parents pulled their kids out and began mounting large daily protest rallies in front of the building that included racist signs, spitting, slashing tires and throwing rocks. Two days later thousands of white extremists and teen-agers went on a rampage in downtown New Orleans and, as the whole nation watched, a Southern city thought to be (relatively) progressive on matters of race was turned upside down and disgraced.

Steinbeck was following these events from Texas as he prepared to make his dash home to New York. He decided he had to witness the ugly drama playing each morning outside William Frantz Elementary. He was especially interested in the well-publicized "Cheerleaders." He characterized them as "stout middle-aged women," but from the old newspaper photos and newsreels they looked like mostly young, white working-class mothers. The mothers stood behind barricades yelling crude obscenities at Ruby Bridges and the few white parents who braved the boycott by walking their kids into the virtually empty school.

On what was probably Thursday, Dec. 1, 1960, Steinbeck writes that he arrived in New Orleans, parked his truck and took a cab to the school. He says he joined the morning circus at exactly 8:57. That was the time Ruby Bridges arrived each day. The barricaded sidewalks and streets were crowded and angry. Police were there to keep people from being hurt. Local and national media were there in force. Time magazine's Dec. 12, 1960, article, "The Battle of New Orleans," called the scene outside the school "an ecstasy of hatred." White parents and their teen-age kids screamed at anyone going in the school, especially white parents. Time said a Catholic priest who accompanied a local preacher and his child "was met with cries of 'bastard,' 'Communist' and 'nigger lover.'" Homemade signs included "Communists & Jews Behind Race Mixing" and the tellingly misspelled "We want segragation."

Whites in New Orleans lost their fight to preserve their Jim Crow public school system, but they ducked the bullet of integration. They quickly re-segregated their children's educations and themselves. They started their own private schools, sent their kids to Catholic schools or abandoned white city neighborhoods like the Ninth Ward and fled to the suburbs. New Orleans, a city of

630,000 in 1960, was transformed. William Frantz Elementary quickly became an all-black school. Within 10 years, as the city hemorrhaged people, almost three fourths of the students in New Orleans public schools were African American. By 2010, the population – 454,865 before Katrina and 343,829 after – had flipped, switching from 63 percent white in 1960 to 60 percent black. In 2010 the city's integrated public school system was almost as black – more than 90 percent – as its segregated system was white in 1960.

## A Paragraph of Filth

Steinbeck was appalled and disgusted and sickened by the racial hatred he saw and heard that morning. He has no empathy for the white working-class mothers of the Upper Ninth Ward, whose daily lives had been suddenly demolished by moral and legal forces beyond their control. He doesn't hide how much he despised the Cheerleaders for their primitive bigotry. He portrays them as insane, low-class, childlike, egotistical and only interested in their own 15 minutes of local fame.

The Cheerleaders also had very dirty mouths. They specialized in shouting vulgarities that were so foul no news outlet would repeat them. As Steinbeck complained, TV cameras drowned out their voices with crowd noise and the print media hinted only that the words the women howled were "indelicate" or "obscene." But in his book he refused to censor himself. In his best scrawl, he wrote in the first draft that "I don't know how the sick sadness of this morning can be felt without these words. I am going to write down the exact expressions screamed in a banshee voice, a voice in which hysteria was very near the surface. These words will go to the publisher on the manuscript and there is not a chance in the world that my readers will see them. But the texture of the morning can not be expressed without them."

Steinbeck then quoted what he said he heard a "cheerlady" at the barricade shriek at a white man who had dared to bring his child to a school containing a black girl "dressed in shining starchy white, with new white shoes on feet so little they were almost round":

"You mother fucking, nigger sucking, prick licking piece of shit. Why you'd lick a dog's ass if he'd let you. Look at the bastard drag his dirty stinking ass along. You think that's his kid? That's a piece of shit. That's shit leading shit. Know what we ought to do? Strip down them fancy pants and cut off his balls and feed them to the pigs – that is if he's got any balls. How about it friends?"

That paragraph of the filth coming from America's most popular writer would have shocked, outraged or offended the entire country in 1962 – and still could. It also would have seriously diminished book sales, jeopardized "Travels With Charley's" chances to be a choice of the Book of the Month Club and given his PG book a triple-X rating. It was edited out, as Steinbeck and everyone else involved must have always known it had to be. Probably fewer than a dozen eyes ever saw it.

The paragraph was shocking. But there was no way it could have been a verbatim transcription of what any one of the Cheerleaders said. It was too perfect, too scripted, too compact, too masculine, too clunky with that final line "How about it friends?" Given Steinbeck's knack of reshaping the nonfictional world to suit his fictional purposes, it had to be a composite or condensed or embellished version of what he heard. As he wrote earlier in a part of the first draft that also was cut, he believed it was the writer's duty to his readers to straighten out the "chaos" of reality and make it understandable and "reasonably real." In New Orleans he did just that.

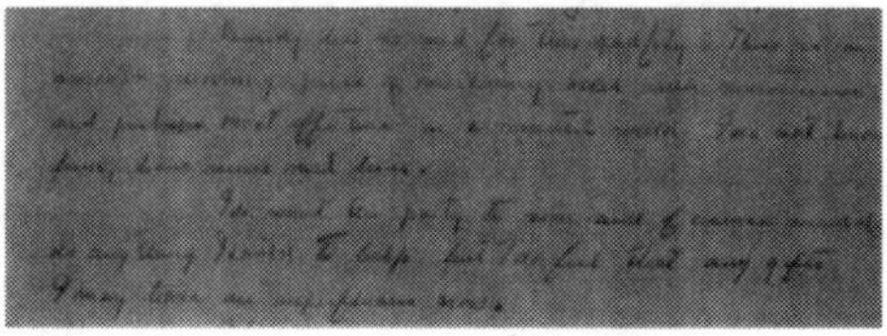

The same X-rated paragraph had been included in the manuscript Steinbeck submitted to Holiday magazine, which serialized a shorter version of "Travels With Charley" in three parts before it was published in book form. In the final installment of what it called "In Quest of America," in February of 1962, Holiday ran Steinbeck's original lead-in to the paragraph of filth and then inserted "{Editors' note: Mr. Steinbeck is right. The Cheerleader's words were a string of unrelieved filth and had to be deleted}."

Steinbeck, who was traveling in Europe with his family, pushed to keep the paragraph in the book. But it never stood a chance of seeing a drop of printer's ink. In the end it apparently was kept out for legal reasons that sound a bit suspicious, as if they were being used as an excuse to overrule or legally bully Steinbeck. In a Jan. 26, 1962 letter to Steinbeck, his editor Pascal Covici said Viking's lawyers feared that some Cheerleaders could say they were identifiable because of Steinbeck's descriptions of them and could sue him. For what? Being made to look like the foul-mouthed bigots they were?

In a letter to his agent Elizabeth Otis a week later, Steinbeck said that the threat of personally losing a lot of money from lawsuits was persuasive. He resented having to be cautious. But he said, "What started out as a simple piece of truth now wears all the clothing of sensationalism and has lost every vestige of its purity. It doesn't feel clean to me any more. The only value of the passage lay in its shock value. Now it has become that book with the dirty words and by a magical turnabout the dirty words are no longer the cheer leaders' but mine."

Steinbeck ultimately rewrote part of the Cheerleaders scene. He still managed to beautifully capture the ugly truths of that morning without using a single dirty word, relying on the reader's imagination to fill in the blanks.

> But now I heard the words, bestial and filthy and degenerate. In a long and unprotected life I have seen and heard the vomitings of demoniac humans before. Why then did these screams fill me with a shocked and sickened sorrow? The words

> written down are dirty, carefully and selectedly filthy. But there was something far worse here than dirt, a kind of frightening witches' Sabbath. Here was no spontaneous cry of anger, of insane rage. Perhaps that is what made me sick with weary nausea. Here was no principle good or bad, no direction. These blowzy women, with their little hats and their clippings, hungered for attention. They wanted to be admired. They simpered in happy, almost innocent triumph when they were applauded. Theirs was the demented cruelty of egocentric children, and somehow this made their insensate beastliness much more heart-breaking. These were not mothers, not even women. They were crazy actors playing to a crazy audience.

Though sanitized, the Cheerleader scenes are generally, and deservedly, thought to be the best in "Travels With Charley." Biographer Jackson Benson said in "The True Adventures of John Steinbeck, Writer" that they were "unforgettable, the dramatic centerpiece of his book, branding on the minds of millions of readers the horror and nausea of the crowd's demented cruelty and the theatrical degeneracy of 'these blowzy women with their little hats and their (newspaper) clippings (who) hungered for attention.'"

Going to New Orleans to see the Cheerleaders in action was the only deliberate act of journalism Steinbeck made on his entire trip, and it paid off. It gave his book of fictional encounters, musings and memories some needed punch and passion and a newsy edge. Not to mention a welcome dose of reality. Being where real people are doing real things always has a way of producing strong writing, whether you're a newspaper reporter covering a house fire or a great novelist covering a race war. Steinbeck's Cheerleaders scenes, unlike any other in the book, prove it. In probably less than an hour, he found a powerful ending for "Charley" without having to rearrange the real world much at all.

## A Rainbow of Fictions

The lineup of Central Casting All-Stars Steinbeck says he met before and after his visit to William Frantz Elementary is another matter. The characters he quotes when he arrives in New Orleans – a parking lot guy and a taxi driver – are no more believable or less wooden than the other fictional people he paraded through his book. They are stereotypical low-class bigots and cretins, human props in a morality play who throw around the n-word, make crude racist jokes and blame the racial unrest in the South on commies or Jews from New York. Like nearly every invented human in the book except the Shakespearean actor, they can't utter a sentence without emitting a "he don't" or a "they wasn't."

Even more improbable are the four stock characters Steinbeck conveniently bumps into as he flees New Orleans. The men – two whites, two blacks – just happen to represent a full spectrum of the Jim Crow South's positions on integration. One white man is an enlightened, tolerant philosopher-type who defies the North's stereotype of the racist Southerner and discusses the nuances of black-white relations with Steinbeck. One is an old black field hand who knows his place, wants to make no trouble and is wary of any white man asking questions. The third is an archetypal white bigot, a poster-cracker for the segregation-forever crowd who gets in an argument with Steinbeck and says he was not "about to allow my kids to go to school with no niggers." The last is a smart, articulate young black college student in Mississippi who is impatient for results and thinks Martin Luther King's methods are too slow.

Knowing Steinbeck's modus operandi, the likelihood that he actually met the four Southerners in 24 hours is somewhere between pretty slim and no way in hell. Even Professor Shillinglaw admitted to Duke University radio documentarian John Biewen they were probably the children of "creative nonfiction" and were used by Steinbeck as fictional devices to present the views of segregation they represented. What's more, Steinbeck has long, complex, conversations or arguments with each of the four men. No one, not even him, could have remembered their words so exactly eight months later without notes.

Nonfiction or fiction, the writing is great, of course. Steinbeck was on the correct side of the integration-segregation argument. And he does a nice job of trying to sort out the rights, wrongs and complicated realities of a moral and political issue that would tear the country apart politically and socially for the next decade and more. He doesn't pretend to have presented a true cross-section of the South in his book. Knowing his own scant experience with black people and racial matters, he humbly comes to no conclusions. His only prediction was that integration was inevitable. It was only the means of achieving it that was going to be in question.

Inventing characters and making up their conversations in a nonfiction book was nothing new or rare or even necessarily wrong. Steinbeck's fictional quartet was harmless and obviously imaginary. It's just too bad that for 50 years scholars didn't notice or care enough to point that out.

## Steinbeck Timeline

Friday, Dec. 2, 1960 – Up the Mississippi

*Steinbeck writes in "Charley" that he left the Upper Ninth Ward, ate a sandwich by the Mississippi River and then stopped at "a pleasant motel." The next day, most likely Dec. 2, he drives north on U.S. Highway 61 along the Mississippi River to Natchez and Vicksburg, then takes U.S. 80 east.*

## Driving for Home

Steinbeck had dreaded seeing the racially torn South and ended up seeing very little of it. His original plan was to swing through the black heart of the Jim Crow South and go up the Atlantic Coast. But he was tired and weary of the road. And he was so rattled by the hatred he witnessed in New Orleans he bolted straight for home. I couldn't blame him for fleeing New Orleans. Spending most of Saturday morning in heavy northbound traffic trying to escape to Mississippi, unkind thoughts filled my head. New Orleans was a city that needed sympathy. It had almost been destroyed, literally, by the incompetence and/or corruption of its government and its own elected political hacks. But of all the places I had been in 30-plus states, it was by far the most annoying and least enjoyable.

I admit I didn't see much of New Orleans and I sure didn't see the fancy parts. I enjoyed my early morning walkabout in the Upper Ninth Ward. But I didn't care how cool the French Quarter was or if Louis Armstrong and jazz were born there. New Orleans was dirty and dank, its roads were horrible and half of it was already below sea level. I didn't want any living thing to get hurt, even male drivers under 25. But if I had looked in my rearview mirror and seen the entire bottom half of Louisiana sinking beneath the sea – from natural causes or from the further ineptitude of the Army Corps of Engineers – I wouldn't have shed a tear.

Following Steinbeck's 1,600-mile route from New Orleans to Manhattan was easy, thanks to a postcard he sent from Mississippi to his agent Elizabeth Otis on Saturday, Dec. 3. "Since I couldn't do everything," he writes from the town of Pelahatchie on U.S. Highway 80, "I went to New Orleans and watched mother love at work." He tells Otis he followed the Mississippi River to Natchez and Vicksburg. Saying he'd have to miss the coastal states and that he'd "be home next week," he ends with, "Darned if I know whether I'm getting anything. At least I'll know what's not so. See you. It's been a long haul. Love John."

Steinbeck was wise. "Knowing what's not so" is as important as knowing what is. That's especially true in a big, diverse, regionalized country that is too often summed up, averaged out or packaged into stereotypes by the national media, experts, politicians and various interest groups with money to be made, laws to get passed or ideological axes to grind.

I followed U.S. 61 through the congested sprawl of Baton Rouge. By the time it reached the Mississippi line, Highway 61 had turned into a beautiful, empty, four-lane parkway that rolled in long waves over the hills and swept through forests and farmland. U.S. 61, aka "The Blues Highway," once connected New Orleans and Duluth and still splits Mississippi Delta blues country. Shadowing the Mississippi River for nearly 1,500 miles, it was a main north-south route before the interstates came and was the star of Bob Dylan's "Highway 61 Revisited." The road may have been widened since 1960, but little else had changed. The surrounding country, of course, had been liberated in the bloody overthrow of Jim Crow.

The scenery was not spectacular, and the Mississippi River was hidden to the west behind the hills. More like a parkway, the road had not been made ugly to interstate engineering standards. There were no guardrails, no overpasses, few signs and no great walls or cliffs of concrete. I saw more hawks than cars and never saw a truck, an exit ramp or a sign of commerce. Not that I had anything against commerce or its signs. Fifty years apart, Steinbeck and I hurried down the main streets of the same few quaint, slavery-era towns and passed by the same plantations with long driveways tunneling through magnolias. I may have been prejudiced because I was going home. But from Natchez all the way to Vicksburg, U.S. 61 was one of the sweetest, smoothest, prettiest roads I'd ever driven.

## Steinbeck Timeline

Saturday, Dec. 3, 1960 – Pelahatchie, Mississippi

*Steinbeck mails two postcards from Pelahatchie, Mississippi, on U.S. Route 80. One is to his agent, Elizabeth Otis, and one is to his editor, Pascal Covici. They're the last reliable evidence of where he was and when. He takes U.S. 80 into Alabama and picks up U.S. Route 11, which runs northeast along the Appalachian Mountains toward New York.*

## Skipping Jim Crow

At Vicksburg I caught I-20 and headed east past Jackson. I took a token spin on old U.S. Highway 80, the parallel pre-interstate road Steinbeck would have used. It was somewhere on U.S. 80 that Steinbeck claimed he picked up the young Negro student hitchhiker "with a sharp face and the look and feel of impatient fierceness" who thought Martin Luther King's peaceful methods were taking too long. U.S. 80 was still basically in the same primitive condition it was before being bypassed in the 1960s by Interstate 20. Like so much of the Old Steinbeck Highway, it was a rural, often shoulder-less, two-lane people-killer strung with a few little towns. I really didn't need to risk my life again on U.S. Highway 80. I had driven it in the spring of 2009, when I was chasing the ghost of a star Pittsburgh Post-Gazette reporter named Ray Sprigle.

Sprigle's daring journalism is forgotten. But in 1948, 13 years before the shocking best-selling book "Black Like Me," he disguised himself as a Negro and spent 30 days traveling around the Jim Crow South in a car. He didn't travel alone or pretend to. He was guided by a black man, John Wesley Dobbs, a prominent 66-year-old civil rights leader from Atlanta and Maynard Jackson's grandfather. Sprigle, who was 61, returned to Pittsburgh and wrote a blistering 21-part newspaper series for the Pittsburgh Post-Gazette. An extended opinion piece, really, it shocked the North, enraged the South and ignited one of the first debates in the national media about ending segregation. Few have heard of Sprigle, but if he had worked for a New York paper, Spencer Tracy would have played him in a movie 60 years ago.

Steinbeck saw little of Mississippi, where King Cotton and the apartheid of Jim Crow were solidly entrenched in power. In 1960, as in 2010, Mississippi was the poorest state in the union. It was doubtless the most racist too. Only 5 percent of blacks dared to register to vote in 1960. About 45 percent of the population was black then, compared to 38 percent in 2010, yet its public schools would be some of the last in the country to be desegregated. At dusk, 26 miles east of Jackson, I stopped on U.S. 80 to get a picture of the yellow brick Pelahatchie post office, where Steinbeck's cards to his agent and editor had been postmarked Dec. 3, 1960.

Then I rejoined I-20 and drove hard to Tuscaloosa, home of the University of Alabama. While the Crimson Tide football faithful were still crying in their beers over their loss to LSU, I was already asleep in the last Wal-Mart parking lot of my travel career. Ten was enough for any grown man. The temperature overnight fell to 37 degrees, coldest since North Dakota, but I had six good hours of sleep and didn't even notice whether the parking lot's lights were on.

## Steinbeck Timeline

Sunday, Dec. 4 to Dec. 6, 1960 – The Home Stretch

*Steinbeck meets U.S. Highway 11 in Alabama and slants through Tennessee and parts of Virginia, West Virginia and Maryland into Pennsylvania at Carlisle. He takes the PA Turnpike to New Jersey and arrives in New York City at the Holland Tunnel. In the book he says he's denied entrance to the tunnel because of the propane tank aboard Rocinante. He takes the Hoboken Ferry, gets lost in evening rush hour in downtown Manhattan and has to ask a cop for directions to his house. In nearly 11 weeks, he had touched 33 states and driven 10,000 miles.*

# You Can Get Home Again

Angling northeast on U.S. Route 11, shadowing the Appalachian Mountains, Steinbeck pushed hard for home. He says he drove in a blur, stopping only to sleep for a few hours at a time. The last town he mentions in the book is Abingdon, Virginia, 650 miles short of New York City. Abingdon is where he says his trip in search of America ended in a kind of road-weary amnesia, but of course it had effectively ended seven weeks earlier in Seattle. No matter. My best guess is that Steinbeck staggered into New York City on about Dec. 5 or 6. He had been gone roughly 75 days. He had racked up about 10,000 noisy, butt-busting miles in his beloved Rocinante, which he quickly sold. He was out of gas physically and psychically. He had gone in search of America and its people and knew he had found neither.

My trip, like Steinbeck's, ended with an almost desperate final push. Sunday was an all-day ordeal from Tuscaloosa, paralleling U.S. 11 on the interstates through Tennessee, Virginia and then north on U.S. 19 and I-79 to my house. The final hours through West Virginia on Sunday night would not end. I blasted my radio and used it as the soundtrack as I videoed the bare black and white highway racing away from me. Thirty minutes from home on I-79 I came around a curve at 65 mph and almost crashed head on into a deer standing on the centerline like a statue. At last, at 1:30 in the morning, at the end of a 19-hour and 809-mile day, I entered my dark house and carefully slipped into bed with a sleeping woman I assumed was my wife.

Except for the furious pace and the low-end lodging arrangements, my trip was remarkably unremarkable. Not counting pit stops in Pittsburgh and San Francisco, I had spent 38 pleasant, sock-free days on the road. The only rain was a two-day deluge in New Hampshire and Vermont. I touched 26 states with my feet or tires and drove 11,276 roundtrip miles – an average of 296 miles a day. I filled every page, front and back, of 10 Professional Reporter's Notebooks. I took 3,100 photos and several hours of HD video. I had joked before I left that to add some thrills to my trip I hoped to be abducted by aliens in Maine. I didn't get so lucky. But I also didn't get shot in the boondocks or mugged in the cities. Of course, I never expected to have any trouble from my fellow countrymen and didn't plan for it. Long after I was home, someone asked what I had taken with me for protection. A handgun? A knife? A baseball bat? Mace?

It was a shocking question. Maybe it was because I had traveled around the USA so much. Maybe it was because as a journalist I was used to being among strangers in strange rural and urban places. Maybe it was because I knew how badly the news media sensationalize and distort reality, exaggerating the level and scope of crime and making an incredibly safe country seem much more dangerous than it really is. Maybe it just was because I'm nuts. But before and during my trip, I never once gave self-defense or my own safety a thought. The only criminal activity I encountered was my own. I broke a lot of traffic rules and slept in places I shouldn't have, though I had just one cheap parking ticket to show for my interstate crime spree.

Meanwhile, my RAV4 performed perfectly, got 24 miles per gallon with a cargo pod on the roof and didn't have a ding on it. I don't know what Steinbeck's luxe quest for America cost him, because he left no records. Maybe the receipts are stashed in the archives at Viking Press/Penguin awaiting some curious retired Steinbeck scholar.

Gas was by far my major expense. At an average of $2.80 a gallon, 469 gallons totaled $1,313. Sleeping in my car and eating only two meals a day kept expenses down. The tab for 38 days of basic American road food was $760. Thanks to Wal-Mart's enlightened sleepover policy, what I thought would be my greatest expense wasn't. Of the 36 nights I needed a place to sleep, I stayed in 16 motels for $936. Of course, to get that number so low meant sleeping in the back of my car 20 times.

So the big three – Gas, Food and Lodging – totaled about $3,000. Throw in another $2,000 for a new smart phone, phone bills, tolls, interest on my credit cards, blackout curtains, road snacks, plus the depreciation of my car, laptop, cameras and me, and you get an IRS-tidy $5,000 – $687 in 1960 Steinbeck dollars. The Pittsburgh Post-Gazette paid me $2,000 for nine Sunday travel articles, which means my adventure with Steinbeck cost about $3,000 net and 43 days of my life. A small price to pay for a once-in-a-lifetime joy ride.

As for my travel-mate Steinbeck, after 11,276 miles I wasn't too fond of him or his overrated book. I had grown from feeling like his pal and defender to resenting him for his audacious trickery and deceit. I had learned to trust virtually nothing he wrote in "Travels With Charley." Yet as I ended my easy road trip I had to give him some major props. The lying bastard blazed the Steinbeck Highway. He did his 10,000 miles. He did them in a truck on roads that were narrower, slower, bumpier, more crowded and infinitely more dangerous and less hospitable to travelers than mine were. And he did it with a talking French dog.

# 21 – America the Mostly Beautiful

*If I found matters to criticize and to deplore, they were tendencies equally present in myself. If I were to prepare one immaculately inspected generality it would be this: For all of our enormous range, for all of our sectionalism, for all of our interwoven breeds drawn from every part of the ethnic world, we are a nation, a new breed. Americans are much more American than they are Northerners, Southerners, Westerners, or Easterners. And descendants of English, Irish, Italian, Jewish, German, Polish are essentially American. This is not patriotic whoop-de-do; it is carefully observed fact. California Chinese, Boston Irish, Wisconsin German, yes, and Alabama Negroes, have more in common than they have apart.*

– "Travels With Charley"

"Big."
"Empty."
"Rich."
"No change since 1960."

Long after the old farms and new forests of New England disappeared in my rearview mirror, I was still scrawling those words in the notebook on my knee. Big, empty, rich and unchanged – a pretty boring scouting report for the America I "discovered" along the Old Steinbeck Highway. You can add a bunch of other boring but fitting words – "beautiful," "safe," "friendly," "clean," and "quiet."

Like Steinbeck, I didn't see the Real America or even a representative cross-section of America, neither of which exists in the real world anyway. The ribbon of the country I cut through was skewed geographically, demographically, socially, politically and economically. Because I went almost exactly where Steinbeck went and stopped where he stopped, I saw a mostly White Anglo Saxon Protestant Republican America, not an Obama one. Mostly rural or open country, it included few impoverished or crime-tortured inner cities and no over-developed/underwater suburbs.

Steinbeck was depressed by the America he found. I "re-discovered" the country I already knew existed from having done 35 years of drive-by journalism. America wasn't perfect and never was. It had the usual ills that make libertarians sick and will never be cured – too many government wars overseas and at home, too many laws, politicians, cops, lawyers, do-gooders and preachers.

Thanks to the bums and crooks in Washington and on Wall Street who co-produced the Great Recession, a larger minority of my fellow Americans than usual was suffering from too much Big Government in their lives. I felt their pain more than most. Little Government was way too big for me.

America the Beautiful was hurting. But it was not dead, dying or decaying. The land I speed-toured in the fall of 2010 was not the broken and doomed one described in the daily headlines of the Drudge Report and the New York Times. There were no signs the country was in danger of becoming a liberal or conservative dystopia. America hadn't been ruined by too many illegal immigrants, too many rich people, too many poor people, too many non-white people, too many imports, too many cars or too many carbon emissions. The U.S. of A., as always, was blessed with a diverse population of productive, wealthy, generous, decent people and a continent of gorgeous natural resources.

Everyday I was surrounded by undeniable evidence of America's underlying health and incredible prosperity. Everywhere I went people were living in good homes, driving new cars and monster pickup trucks and playing with powerboats, motorcycles and snowmobiles. Roads and bridges and parks and main streets were well maintained. Litter and trash were scarce. Specific towns and regions were hurting, and too many people were out of work, but it was still the same country I knew. I didn't seek out poverty or misery or pollution on my journey, and I encountered little of it. The destitute and jobless, not to mention the increasing millions on food stamps, on welfare or buried in debt, were especially hard to spot in a generous country where taking care of the less fortunate is a huge public-private industry – where even the poor have homes, cars, wide-screen TVs and $200 smart phones.

I saw the familiar permanent American eyesores – homeless men sleeping on the sidewalks of downtown San Francisco at noon, the sun-bleached ruins of abandoned gas-stations on Route 66, ratty trailer homes parked in beautiful locations surrounded by decades of family junk. I saw Butte's post-industrial carcass, New Orleans' struggling Upper Ninth Ward and towns that could desperately use a Japanese car plant. But the country as a whole was not crippled or even limping. The Great Recession was nothing like the Great Depression, when unemployment topped at 25 percent in 1933 and was still at 17 percent in 1939 when the build-up to WWII finally turned the economy around.

In the fall of 2010, nine in 10 Americans who said they wanted jobs still had them. The one in 10 who were jobless had 99 weeks of extended unemployment benefits and more than 90 percent of homeowners were still making their mortgage payments. Most of the states I shot through had unemployment and foreclosure rates well below the national averages. I didn't visit the abandoned neighborhoods of poor Detroit – future urban farmland where trees were taking root on the roofs of vacant homes the city didn't have enough money to demolish. I didn't see battered Las Vegas, where 14.5 percent of the people were unemployed and one in nine houses – five times the national average – had received some kind of default notice in 2010. But I spent almost two weeks in the Great Train Wreck State of California, where jobless and foreclosure rates were higher than the national average and municipal bankruptcies loomed.

America from sea to shining sea was noticeably quiet – as if half the population had disappeared. From Maine to Oregon – despite perfect fall weather – public and private golf courses were deserted. Ball fields were vacant. Parks and rest stops and beaches were barely populated. Except for metropolises like Manhattan and San Francisco and college towns like Missoula and Northampton, people in throngs simply did not exist. I went through small towns that looked like they'd been evacuated a year earlier. America's kids apparently were indoors playing videogames or downloading porn, because they sure weren't riding bikes or playing ball in the streets or parks.

Every day I was reminded of a truth the national media never emphasize or even bother to mention. It's so obvious, it's embarrassing to have to write it down: Everyplace I went was unique and different. America is not one big country with its economic or social problems or its ethnic groups – or anything else – distributed evenly from New York to L.A. The "America" the national media talks about all the time does not exist.

There is no "Average America." America is many little "americas," each with their own local or regional realities and problems and strengths and mix of people. It's always been true and always will be. Take race, for example. About 12.6 percent of all Americans are black. Yet there is only one state – Ohio with 12.04 percent – that has a black population near that "average" number. And within Ohio, there are no "average" counties, either. Only seven of 88 counties have black populations of 12.6 percent or more. For 26 counties, the figure is 1 percent or less.

Only 17 states have a black population higher than the national percentage of 12.6 and 33 states – including most of those along the Steinbeck Highway – have 12 percent or less. Of all the states I spent more than 12 hours in, only Louisiana (32 percent), New York (15.1) and Illinois (14.9) had significant black populations. And in New York and Illinois, like Ohio and most states, most black people were concentrated in one or two major cities or counties. Upstate New York was as white as the 1 percent black states – New Hampshire, North Dakota, Maine, Idaho, Vermont and Montana, the whitest of the white.

The Hispanic or Latino population, now 16 percent of Americans, is even more disproportionately distributed/concentrated. More than half live in just three states – California, Texas and Florida. More than three-quarters of America's 50 million Hispanics live in just eight states, and within those states they are concentrated in cities like Chicago and New York. Of the states Steinbeck and I traveled, those with Hispanic populations above 16 percent included California (37 percent), Texas (37 percent), Arizona (30 percent), New York (17 percent) and the highest of all, New Mexico (46 percent).

So forget "Average America." It doesn't exist and never did. And therefore it is literally true that except for a few macro-things like the declining value of the dollar, there is no such thing as "a national problem." All problems, like all politics, are local. Whether it's unemployment or foreclosures, murders or illegal immigrants, traffic fatalities or drug gangs, racism, bad schools, water shortages, droughts or floods, heat waves or cold waves, not every region, state, county, city or town suffers equally or necessarily at all. Even in a Great Recession, many places across the country were never touched by an economic cyclone the national media would have you think had flattened every square mile of America evenly.

There's something else obvious about America that's never pointed out by the media: The states and counties and cities and villages and crossroads are filled with smart, good Americans who can take pretty good care of themselves. They prove it every day. People in Baraboo and Stonington and Amarillo know what's best for them. They'll adjust to whatever changes that come.

Maybe their towns will gradually disappear like Alice or dry up and blow away like Bagdad or suffer a slow de-industrial death like Butte. Maybe their towns will stay frozen in time, like Saltese or Williams, or reinvent themselves as lively tourist traps like Monterey or Livingston. Maybe they'll strike it rich on oil and gas and boom like North Dakota or get the next Subaru plant. Whatever happens in their local worlds, they'll figure it out locally. Usually without any media attention or "help" from Washington, D.C.

As I drove the Steinbeck Highway, it was obvious many important changes had occurred along it since 1960. Industrial Age powerhouses like Rochester, Buffalo and Gary had seen their founding industries and the hordes of humans they employed swept away by technological change and the destructive hurricane of global capitalism. Small towns like Calais, Maine, had lost people and jobs, and vice versa. New Orleans had shrunk by half, and not just because of Katrina. The metro areas of Seattle, San Francisco and Albuquerque had exploded and prospered in the digital age. The populations of the West Coast and the Sunbelt had expanded. The South had shed its shameful system of apartheid and its overt racism, as well as much of its deep-rooted poverty and ignorance. The Northeast had bled people, manufacturing industries and national political power.

Change is inevitable, unpredictable, un-stoppable, disruptive, often cruel to individuals and towns in the short run but steadfastly beneficial to American society in the long run. Nevertheless, it was clear that a great deal of what I saw out my window on the Steinbeck Highway had hardly changed at all since Steinbeck and Charley raced by.

He saw more farmland and fewer forests than I did, especially in the East. But in many places almost nothing was newly built. Many farms and crossroads and small towns and churches were frozen in the same place and time they were eons ago, particularly in the East and Midwest. In Maine the busy fishing village of Stonington was as picturesque as the day Steinbeck left it. He'd recognize the Corn Belt and Redwood Country and the buildings if not the people of the Upper Ninth Ward. And at 70 mph whole states – North Dakota and Montana – would look the same to him except for the cell towers and the McDonald's and Pilot signs staked out at the interstate exits.

## Steinbeck's 'Soft' America

Steinbeck didn't like a lot of things about Eisenhower America and pointed out many of them. Many of his complaints were just the personal opinions of a grumpy old rich fart. He didn't like comic books, rock n' roll, local radio or paperback books. But he also didn't like interstates, standardized motel rooms, plastic, manufactured food and other mundane or magical things that were making life safer, healthier, more convenient and more affordable for the traveling masses.

He also worried about more important issues – suburban sprawl, the polluted rivers and the rings of junked cars and rubbish he saw around cities. He railed against the depravity and hatred of segregation and racism that was practiced publicly without shame or legal consequence by millions of Americans. And he noted that on his long road trip he had not met many "real men" of conviction or found many people with strong opinions about anything except sports. Talk radio and the new digital media would end that shortage of opinions over the next 50 years.

Though it was ultimately cut by editors, in his first draft, when he was in San Francisco, Steinbeck noted that the American people he had talked to about politics weren't specific about their likes and dislikes. They were against things like communism and were in favor of nebulous and subjective abstractions like "the American Way of Life."

"I am interested in the American way of life," he wrote cagily. "Is it the Way described in Harper's Bazaar or Vogue? Is it the way of Playboy or Reader's Digest? Is it one thing or many?" He asked if "The American Way of Life" meant the same to the West Virginia coal miner, the Tammany Hall ward heeler, the

Negro ... in the South or the John Bircher in Santa Barbara." Then he wrote, "The truth is, the American Way of Life is a mystique. To suspect it at all is sacrilege crossed with treason. I found that those who hold the Way most dear, become very uneasy when asked to explain or describe it." That deadly critique of the mindless American flag-waver was cut from the first draft as well.

Though it seems Steinbeck was being tough on his country and his people in "Travels With Charley," he really wasn't. He had pulled most of his punches. In private he was extremely disappointed by the country he had found. He was "angry and demoralized," according to Jay Parini in his "John Steinbeck, a Biography."

Steinbeck thought Americans had become morally, physically and spiritually flabby. They were too content, too comfortable. They had too many things and wanted still more, and they were taking the great country their self-reliant and industrious ancestors had built down the road to national decline.

He spilled his true feelings in an often-quoted July 1961 letter to his editor at Viking Press, Pascal Covici, which he wrote while he was struggling to finish "Travels With Charley" and trying to sum up what he thought ailed America:

> And the little book of ambulatory memoirs staggers along, takes a spurt and lags. It's a formless, shapeless, aimless thing and it is even pointless. For this reason it may be the sharpest realism because what I see around me is aimless and pointless—ant-hill activity. Somewhere there must be design if I can only find it. I'm speaking of this completed Journey now. And outside of its geographical design and its unity of time, it's such a haphazard thing. The mountain has labored and not even a mouse has come forth. Thinking and thinking for a word to describe decay. Not disruption, not explosion but simple rotting. It seemed to carry on with a weary inertia. No one was for anything and nearly everyone was against many things. Negro hating white. White hating negroes. Republicans hating Democrats although there is little difference. In all my travels I saw very little real poverty, I mean the grinding terrifying poorness of the Thirties. That at least was real and tangible. No, it was a sickness, a kind of wasting disease. There were wishes but no wants. And underneath it all the building energy like gasses in a corpse. When that explodes, I tremble to think what will be the result. Over and over I thought we lack the pressures that make men strong and the anguish that makes men great. The pressures are debts, the desires are for more material toys and the anguish is boredom. Through time, the nation has become a discontented land. I've sought for an out on this—saying it is my aging eyes seeing it, my waning energy feeling it, my warped vision that is distorting it, but it is only partly true. The thing I have described is really there. I did not create it. It's very well for me to write jokes and anecdotes but the haunting decay is

> there under it. Well, there was once a man named Isaiah—and what he saw in his time was not unlike what I have seen, but he was shored up by a hard and durable prophecy that nothing could disturb. We have no prophecy now, nor any prophets.

Some paragraph.

Maybe Steinbeck was having a bad day. But those were damning and sweeping conclusions about America, particularly for someone who had seen so little of it on his trip and during the previous 20 years. That same summer of 1961, in a letter to Adlai Stevenson filled with a great deal of geopolitical advice, Steinbeck wrote, "What I saw on my trip did not reassure me. This could be the shortest lived great nation in history. Once the accidents of geography and raw products are withdrawn or equaled, we seem to have no resources, no versatility, and worst of all – no interest." These pessimistic private thoughts were not new. Steinbeck held them long before he started his road trip. "The Winter of Our Discontent," his last novel, was about American immorality as he defined it.

Steinbeck tempered his pessimism about the country before he died. In 1966, when he wrote the text for the photo book "America and Americans," he griped about hippies, lamented the rise of pragmatic and situational morals and complained that gallantry and responsibility had been replaced by a culture of goldbricking, bribery and cheating. But he predicted that in the long run our restless energy would save us from self-destruction and America and its people will "persist and persevere."

It turned out Steinbeck had the future of America dead wrong in 1960-1961. His fear that it was a rotting corpse and that Americans had become too soft and contented to keep their country great and strong was off by about 178 degrees. Fifty years later, despite being stuck in a deep but temporary economic ditch, the country was far wealthier, healthier, smarter and more globally powerful and influential than gloomy Steinbeck could have imagined. Its air, water and landscapes were far less polluted. And, most important, despite the exponential growth of the federal government's size and scope and its meddling reach, America in 2010 was also a much freer place for most of its 310 million citizens.

Libertarians and Democrats and Republicans who seek to protect and maximize individual freedom and still believe the Constitution is a document worth upholding to the letter have good cause to worry and complain. America's bloated welfare/warfare/security state has diminished the civil liberties of every citizen. The federal government's 40-year war on (some) drugs has spawned gangs that kill each other over drug turf at the same time the drug war has filled our prisons with nonviolent offenders who shouldn't be there. But ask women, blacks, Latinos and gays how they're doing today. Their personal and public lives are much freer and richer in opportunity than they were in 1960, when it was illegal for an unmarried woman to buy birth control pills, inter-racial marriages were outlawed in more than a dozen states and just being gay was a crime.

The virulent racism and bigotry being displayed without shame for weeks on the streets of New Orleans in 1960 – which would be repeated across the South and elsewhere during the decade – is extinct in Obama America. Racism has not disappeared. But it is no longer legally, politically, culturally, socially and morally sanctioned in an increasingly colorblind society where 86 percent of people say they approve of marriage between whites and blacks compared to about 5 percent who said they did in 1960. Steinbeck would still find plenty to moan or fret about in today's America. But other improvements he could never have envisioned, but would heartily cheer, include the virtual end of censorship, stronger protections for the accused and the liberalization of divorce laws. I'll bet he'd appreciate GPS and the lower income tax rates on the rich, too.

You don't have to be a hardcore libertarian to know there's plenty of work still to do to free up the personal and economic lives of Americans. But since 1960 the transportation, energy, communications and financial industries have been deregulated and liberated from the worst kinds of government rules that limited choice, protected established businesses from competition and made everything from air travel, electricity and mortgages more expensive for consumers.

Steinbeck might not like it that unions no longer have the power they once did in the private sector, or that sex and violence and stupidity are the rocket fuel of mass culture. He'd probably rail against smart phones and Wal-Mart and Fox News and Facebook. And if he really did learn the lessons of Vietnam before he died, he'd hate the bloody foolish war making of the Bush and Obama administrations. America's not as free as it should be and never will be. But there's no denying that today our society is freer and more open than ever to entrepreneurs, new forms of media, alternative lifestyles and ordinary people who want to school their own kids, medicate their own bodies or simply choose Fed Ex instead of the U.S. Post Office.

## America According to New Yorkers

In 2008, as the American economy plummeted into the Great Recession and Barack Obama was riding the Hope and Change Express to the White House, Bill Barich decided to drive across America. Barich's book about his road trip, "Long Way Home: On the Trail of Steinbeck's America," was inspired by a re-reading – as an adult – of "Travels With Charley."

Barich, a California native in his late 60s, has written for the New Yorker, authored eight books and lived in Ireland for about a decade. He wanted to see if Steinbeck's gloomy prophecy about the decline of America and his concern about the moral flabbiness of its people was finally coming true. He didn't retrace the Steinbeck Highway. For about six weeks he crossed the waist of America from New York City to San Francisco, roughly on U.S. Route 50, which meant he, like Steinbeck and I, saw a whiter, more rural, more Republican small-town America.

Barich thought Steinbeck's private opinion of an America in decay was distorted because he was depressed, in poor health and spent too much time alone on his "Charley" trip, which is a laugh I'll address a few dozen paragraphs from now. But Barich took most of the author's other critiques of 1960 America more seriously. He told the New York Times he thought Steinbeck's "perceptions were right on the money about the death of localism, the growing homogeneity of America, the trashing of the environment. He was prescient about all that."

It's no surprise Barich, an expatriated liberal writer exploring the conservative heart of Red State America, agreed with Steinbeck's socio-political and cultural complaints. For 50 years Barich, Steinbeck and their fellow travelers have set sail into the hinterlands from New York City with the same cargo of elitist clichés about what's wrong with America. Not to stereotype their views too unfairly, but folks like Barich instinctively believe a caricature of Flyover America. They believe the country west of the Hudson and east of the Hollywood sign is overpopulated, over-sprawled, over-malled, devoid of culture, polluted, ruined by national chains and strangled with congested freeways.

Barich made no effort to hide his cultural and political biases. He decried "the pernicious malls and ugly subdivisions" he said were a permanent, unfixable part of America. He also agreed with Steinbeck on some negative points, including that Americans were "frequently lax, soft, and querulous, and they sometimes capitulated to a childish sense of entitlement."

As for Barich's politics, they were as predictable as a New York Times editorial. He made the obligatory complaint about America's "divisive (i.e., conservative) talk-show pundits." He repeated the insulting but common fable that whenever hinterland conservatives criticize Barack Obama or Big Government in Washington they are parroting one of Rush Limbaugh's "latest proclamations that consciously stoke the fear and paranoia of Americans." He also mocked Sarah Palin and the white Middle Americans who came to worship her at a Republican rally in Wilmington, Ohio. "The faces tilted up to her were as vacant as those of stoned kids at a rock concert, absent of any emotion except surrender," Barich wrote. He was not exaggerating about the adoring crowd. But he was being unfair and unbalanced.

I happened to attend a Palin rally in 2008 – her first one – as a journalist. The day after her selection as McCain's VP, on a blisteringly hot August Saturday, she appeared with him at a minor league baseball field 20 minutes from my house south of Pittsburgh. It was like a rock concert – for 10,000 desperately hopeful middle-aged Republicans. Hanging on a cyclone fence taking photos, I got close enough to Palin to see the dark ring of sweat on her collar as she shook hands and hugged babies. The crowd was totally nuts for her, especially the women. No one cared about John McCain or what Palin said in her stump speech, which was word-for-word what she had said on TV the day before. They had clearly come to cheer and hope – and yes, adore.

Barich didn't attend a Barack Obama campaign event on his trip. But every little dig he made about the Palin rally and the Republican crowd's embarrassing enthusiasm for their unprepared heroine also could have been said about the hopers & dreamers packing a typical Obama rally. Not that Barich would have ever considered making fun of Obama's idolaters. Though politically predictable, Barich wasn't a total Steinbeck yes man. He pointed out that the author missed some positives about America – for example, the vast wildernesses that had been saved and "the potential rewards of new technologies." But Barich concurred with many of Steinbeck's complaints about Americans not being able to handle their hard-earned glut of affluence and comfort. Barich characterized his fellow countrymen as “friendly, well-intentioned, good humored, kind, and generous, but also loud, aggressive, clumsy, gullible, and poorly educated.” Naturally, he said he preferred Europe’s older quieter, gentler, more sophisticated – i.e., more socialist – societies, where “pernicious malls” and “divisive” talk shows aren’t so free to disturb the order of things.

That’s fine what Barich thought. He paid his commentator’s dues. He drove the hard miles. So he got to throw his conventional liberal wisdom and biases around in his book. Like Steinbeck’s book and this one, his account of what he saw and thought was purely subjective. It was filtered by his previous experiences, worldview, values and politics and was subject to the randomness and serendipity of the road. All obvious stuff, but it’s rarely noted and always worth repeating in our ruthlessly subjective universe. It’s something Steinbeck pointed out as well in “Travels With Charley.”

Barich was more hopeful about the country’s long-term future than Steinbeck was in 1960. That was a refreshing twist on the usual New York-centric gloom and doom. But you get the sense that Barich’s optimism had more to do with the victory of Barack Obama than what he found on his solo tour of America’s midsection, which he described as “alternately grand and awful, sublime and stomach-turning, both a riddle and a paradox.”

## America Unchained

Like all stereotypes, the Hollywood/Manhattan stereotype of America and its Flyover People is based on reality. But its main ingredient – besides its premise of moral, cultural and intellectual superiority – is exaggeration. Take over-population. Sure, big cities are densely populated. That’s kind of what great, dynamic, productive urban centers are supposed to be. That’s how they generate economic wealth and new ideas.

But anyone who drives 50 miles in any direction in an empty state like Maine or North Dakota – or even in north-central Ohio or Upstate New York – can see America’s problem is not overpopulation. More often it’s under-population. Cities like Butte and Buffalo and Gary have been virtually abandoned. Huge hunks of America on both sides of the Mississippi have never been settled. From Calais to Pelahatchie, I passed down the main streets of comatose small towns whose mayors would have been thrilled to have to deal with the problems of population growth and sprawl.

In a dozen states, I cruised two- and four-lane highways so desolate I could have picnicked on them. If anyone thinks that rural Minnesota, northwestern Montana, the Oregon Coast, the Texas Panhandle or New Orleans’s Upper Ninth Ward have been homogenized, taken over by chains or destroyed by suburban sprawl and too much commercial development, it’s because they haven’t been there.

It's a 50-year-old myth that America has been conquered and homogenized by national chains. It wasn't close to being true in 1960, when Steinbeck was worrying about corner groceries being wiped out by A&P, the largest restaurant chain in the country was Howard Johnson's and Holiday Inn of America was three years old. Today restaurant and motel chains cling to interstate exits, where the heavy traffic is, and they clone themselves in the upscale suburbs. But try to find a Bob Evans, a Holiday Inn Express or a burger joint with a familiar name in a small town or in the sticks. You better like McDonald's or Subway, because in most of the Zip Codes I was in those were your only choices – if you were lucky.

The America I traveled was unchained from sea to sea. I had no problem eating breakfast, sleeping or shopping for road snacks at mom & pop establishments in every state. The motels along the Oregon and Maine coasts are virtually all independents that have been there for decades. Here's a post-trip stat I saw from the American Hotel & Lodging Association that didn't surprise me a bit: Of the country's 52,215 motels and hotels with 15 units or more, 22,200 are independent – i.e., not affiliated with a chain. You can go the length of old Route 66 and never sleep or eat in a chain unless you choose to. Same for U.S. Route 101 in Oregon and Northern California.

Steinbeck, like many others have since, lamented the loss of regional customs. (I don't think he meant the local "customs" of the Jim Crow South or the marital mores of the Jerry Lee Lewis clan.) Pockets of regional culture are not as concentrated and isolated as they once were, which is a blessing for the median national IQ and the English language, but they're not extinct and there are many new pockets.

I didn't go looking for Native Americans, Amish, Iraqis in Detroit, Peruvians in northern New Jersey or the French-Canadians who have colonized the top edge of Maine. But I had no trouble spotting local flavor in Wisconsin's dairy lands, in fishing towns along Oregon's coast, in the redwood-marijuana belt of Northern California, in San Francisco's Chinatown and the cattle country of Texas.

As for the demise of local dialects, it too is exaggerated by those who find such culturally backward things quaint and worth preserving. In Maine, Texas and Louisiana I met white Anglo-Saxon Americans whose accents were so heavy I wasn't always sure they were speaking English. I'll never forget Duke Shepard of Deer Isle, Maine – or his accent.

In the last 10 years, I've had the same experience in the Mississippi Delta, southern West Virginia and the hollers of eastern Kentucky, where I met a proud hillbilly who'd be debunked as a cruel 1930s stereotype if he appeared in a movie. (He kept his ex-wife in a converted chicken coop and had two sons in prison, one for murder.) Pittsburgh's steelmaking jobs may have disappeared but its distinct working-class accent hasn't. Just listen to a C-SPAN call-in show for a random hour and you'll hear hard American accents that half a century of TV have done nothing to soften.

Again, not to generalize, but the New York-Hollywood elites believe in a cultural caricature. They think the average Flyover Person lives in a double-wide or a Plasticville suburb, eats only at McDonald's, votes only Republican, shops only at Wal-Mart and the Dollar Store, hates anyone not whiter than they are, speaks in tongues on Sunday and worships pickup trucks, guns and NASCAR the rest of the week. Those stereotypes are alive and well in Flyover Country. But though I held radical beliefs about government, immigration and drugs that could have gotten me lynched in many places, I never felt like I was in a country I didn't like or didn't belong in. Maybe I didn't go to enough sports bars, churches and political rallies.

Yes, Americans were materialistic as hell. They could afford to be, thanks to the incredible democratization of wealth and luxury that's occurred in the last 50 years. Hundreds of millions of Americans were enjoying the kind of lifestyle that only 1-Per-Centers like Steinbeck could afford in 1960. Steinbeck – and ex-pats like Barich living like lords in Ireland – have a lot of nerve complaining about the greedy materialism of America's commoners when they themselves already have every material goodie they need or want. The hundreds of ordinary Americans I bumped into were real, not made up and not composites. They were unique, hard-working people who were living longer, better, richer lives than Steinbeck could have dreamed. Unlike Steinbeck, who met one unlikable, sour, grammatically challenged person after another (or said he did), I met a procession of happy, friendly saints. I'm not a touchy-feely guy. And I know that as an old white guy by myself I was a threat to no one. But I was treated so well, I fell in love with every other American I met. For five minutes, anyway.

# 22 – The Truths About 'Charley'

*It would be pleasant to be able to say of my travels with Charley, "I went out to find the truth about my country and I found it." And then it would be such a simple matter to set down my findings and lean back comfortably with a fine sense of having discovered truths and taught them to my readers. I wish it were that easy.*

– "Travels With Charley"

## A Good Trip Gone Bad

A stranger passing like a bullet through his own heartland, Steinbeck spent twice as much time relaxing on his 11-week journey than driving. He discovered no new facts or insights about the USA or its citizens, mainly because he did no real journalism and spent relatively little time with ordinary people. Yet he deserved a lot of credit just for taking the road trip. Despite his shaky health and age, not to mention his princely lifestyle and celebrity social circle, he had the balls to roll up his sleeves and take on what was essentially a major journalism project. What other great American writer would have even considered traveling the rough way he did?

Initially, he fully intended to do his trip the right way and the only way it would work – solo and at the grassroots level. His ambitious plan – going alone, taking photos, writing dispatches to newspapers or magazines from the road, going to a different church every Sunday, spending quality time in the Jim Crow South – was basic, sound journalism and a perfect vehicle for his talents. A nonfiction book based on his original plan wouldn't have been as popular with readers or kept its romantic appeal for 50 years, but it would have made a better, more substantive book. It would have slowed him down, forced him to meet hundreds of other real people and given him a chance to discover more of the America he went searching for.

But Steinbeck's great exploration never materialized. He never learned to use a camera, didn't take notes or keep a journal and never wrote a word for publication during his 75 days away from New York. His grand plan was unraveled by the reality of his lifestyle, health and the punishment of the open road. He quickly got lonely and tired and no doubt bored. Ironically, in one sense he may have been lucky he lost heart so early. The daily pressure and logistical nightmares of trying to do real journalism on the back roads of America in 1960 could have killed him. What's more, in the Analog Age it was an unrealistic mission even for a man in good health to circumnavigate America alone.

Transcontinental car travel was still an adventure, not the smooth ride it is today. As Steinbeck learned, just finding a public pay phone so he could call his wife every three days was a major accomplishment.

Before he left Maine he had already realized the obvious – the country was too damn big and diverse to pin down or sum up. No one person, not even a Steinbeck, could discover the real America in 11 weeks or 11 months. Anyway, as he wisely said, there was no single "real" America. As he knew and advised his readers, every traveler must take his own trip and find his own version of America. Trouble was, his was largely a 50 mph blur interrupted by luxurious vacations with his wife. And when his journey ended, he had to sit down and make up a nonfiction book about a real country he never found, never really looked for and didn't really like much.

# The Final Chapter That Wasn't

Six weeks after Steinbeck returned to New York he was invited to JFK's inauguration day festivities in DC. His adventure in Washington, a city paralyzed by a huge snowstorm, was meant to be the final chapter of "Travels With Charley" but was cut from his first draft. Titled "L'Envoi" (*envoi* being the name for concluding remarks to a poem, essay or book), it had nothing to do with his cross-country road trip. It was basically a short piece about him and Elaine enjoying JFK's outdoor swearing-in ceremony despite 22-degree temperatures. It's redundant evidence of how desperate Steinbeck was to pad out his thin material.

While decently written, "*L'Envoi*" added nothing important or exciting. The Steinbecks shared a limo ride to the inauguration ceremony with John's pal and JFK-insider John Kenneth Galbraith and his wife. ABC TV, which was following the Galbraiths around for a broadcast that aired two nights later, had a camera crew crammed into the limo's front seat. Two minutes of the ABC's limo footage, shot by a film crew working for Robert Drew, the great pioneer documentarian, can be seen in Drew's "Adventures on the New Frontier."

The Steinbecks and Galbraiths were a witty and clever bunch. They were impressed by the high ideals and fine phrases of JFK's brilliant speech, which was written by Ted Sorensen and included some of Galbraith's suggestions. Steinbeck joked about the president's proper syntax, noting that no participles were dangled and no infinitives were split. He also quipped to Galbraith that his support for the Kennedy administration would evaporate after 24 hours, which turned out to be a laugh, since he quickly became chummy with Kennedy and even chummier with LBJ. Seeing Steinbeck on film just six weeks after coming home from his "Charley" trip was especially interesting to me – and shocking. He was not yet 59 but looked 75. And he had a very strange, pinched way of speaking. Elaine was seen unflatteringly firing up a cigarette.

Steinbeck stretched hard in "L'Envoi" to connect the inauguration trip to his road journey, which had ended six weeks earlier. Saying his "travels with Charley were a simple, almost humble undertaking" that "piled up a limited heap of information," he writes that "Thinking back, I don't know what, if anything, I learned."

The final lines of the chapter follow a long passage about John and Elaine opting to skip the inauguration ball and watching it on TV in their pajamas:

> And in the morning the snow was past and so was the journey.
>
> And I do know this – the big and mysterious America is bigger than I thought. And more mysterious.

The end. That was it. In three sentences his great road trip was finally finally over.

The "L'Envoi" chapter, kept at the Morgan Library with the rest of his first draft and only made public in 2002, was an extraneous fizzle that didn't work. Perhaps that's why Steinbeck's agent Elizabeth Otis persuaded him not to include it in the final version of the book. As published and read by millions, "Travels With Charley" concludes with Steinbeck road weary, confused and lost in his own backyard in Manhattan. It too was an abrupt, unsatisfying dead end to what started out as a brave quest for America. But at least there was some literary/symbolic/metaphorical meaning hidden in it.

## Making up 'Charley'

Working on and off, Steinbeck took about 10 months to finish "Travels With Charley in Search of America." In the late summer of 1961, virtually without notes and nine months after his trip ended, he was still struggling to complete the last third of the book. In an August 17 letter to his editor Pascal Covici, he wrote, "I'm glad you like the second part of 'Travels.' To me it came very hard. So much confusion in my mind and the distance. I should have finished the whole thing last spring." Though he thought there were "some pretty good essays on various subjects," he was worried that it was "really dragging."

Meanwhile, Steinbeck's friends at Holiday magazine had already begun serializing "Charley" before it was completely written. "In Quest of America," as it was called, was an abridged version of the book. Part 1 had become the travel monthly's cover article for July of 1961. Parts 2 and 3 would run in December 1961 and February 1962. Described as Steinbeck's "firsthand report on the nation," Holiday's series was a big hit with its 500,000 upscale readers.

In early September Steinbeck turned his manuscript over to his publisher, Viking Press. He immediately left for a nine-month tour of Western Europe with his wife Elaine, teen-age sons Thom and John IV and the tutor he hired for them. On Sept. 24, from England, Steinbeck – still shocked by the death of his friend UN Secretary-General Dag Hammarskjold in a plane crash a week earlier – again expressed doubts about "Charley" to Covici. "I imagine you must have read the third part of Charlie (sic) by now. Do you like it at all? I am so confused about this book that I have no ideas about it. It was written under strain and I don't remember it very well. I don't know whether it has any information or not."

Through the winter of 1961-62, the publishing industry worked at its normal tectonic pace to produce Steinbeck's last major work. The editing process at Viking Press removed the Cheerleader's paragraph of filth, 99 percent of Steinbeck's political comments and all presence of Elaine on the West Coast. On Feb. 8, 1962, after Steinbeck had rewritten the Cheerleaders scene, Covici told him in a letter that though he preferred the original version, "the gamble was too great and not worth it."

The edited version still preserved "all the bitterness and disappointment in people... ," wrote Covici, who spent less time editing than holding his friend's hand and patting him on the back. "It is a good book for so many reasons. Almost everything you ever thought, felt, smelled and expressed about people and things in your other books is here succinctly, trenchantly, vividly said, and with humor and infinite pain to yourself."

Despite Covici's high praise, "Charley" was badly flawed – as nonfiction or fiction. But Steinbeck had nothing to worry about. He could have written his grocery list and it would have been a bestseller. A Book of the Month Club choice for August, "Travels With Charley" hit stores on July 27, 1962. It sold like crazy, reaching Number One on the New York Times' nonfiction list on Oct. 21, topping future classics like "Silent Spring" and "The Guns of August."

Steinbeck's only Number One New York Times bestseller, it stayed on the nonfiction lists at the Times and Time magazine for over a year. Viking Press did a smooth job of marketing it as a nonfiction book. The simple half-page ad in the New York Times on July 29, 1962, included a photo of Steinbeck sitting on the ground and facing the camera with Charley. The copy read: "Steinbeck – His enchanted journey across America with an irresistible gentleman poodle is the most warmly personal book he has ever written."

The illustrations by Don Freeman on the front and back covers of the jacket and Freeman's U.S. map showing Steinbeck and Charley's route on the inside covers did their job perfectly. They reinforced the impression that the great author and his faithful dog spent almost three lonely months on the American road, roughing it and camping out like virtual hobos as they slowly studied the soul of a changing nation and its people.

## The Critics Cheer – and Jeer

Steinbeck was never liked by the East Coast literary mafia, which alone is a good reason to friend him. The big critics dismissed him for snobbish intellectual reasons, according to his friendly biographer Jackson Benson: He was from out West. He had a sense of humor. He was too popular, too sentimental, too accessible and insufficiently political (i.e., he didn't keep writing "The Grapes of Wrath" over and over to please lefties like Mary McCarthy at Nation magazine).

Yet when "Travels With Charley" was published, it generally got raves from reviewers in mainstream newspapers and magazines. Most of them embraced/swallowed the romantic man-and-dog-on-the-road storyline. Even critical reviews didn't question the authenticity of Steinbeck's supporting cast of cardboard characters. Harper's, Saturday Review and a few other highbrow places were not particularly impressed by Steinbeck's "predictable" observations. But the New York Times, Newsweek and the Atlantic loved the book.

The Times' reviewer, Eric F. Goldman, lost his grip. The Princeton history professor and world authority on modern American culture blubbered in the Sunday Book Review on July 29 that it was "a pure delight, a pungent potpourri of places and people interspersed with bittersweet essays on everything from the emotional difficulties of growing old to the reasons why giant Sequoias arouse such awe."

Goldman wasn't 100 percent pleased, however. He pointed out, correctly, that the America Steinbeck saw was "hardly coincident" with the real American heartland because he had avoided the most significant new developments of the 1960s – the big cities and the growing suburbs.

But Goldman, like other reviewers, bought completely into the myth of "Travels With Charley." He assumed Steinbeck had exhausted himself on a grueling, undercover, three-month road trip in a truck. He wrote sentences like "To avoid hotel stays and certain recognition he had a manufacturer build for him a cabin body equipped for day-and-night living. He traveled accompanied only by his aged French poodle."

Calling it "affecting and highly entertaining," Newsweek praised Steinbeck for his "quick mind and honest heart" but damned him for "his self-indulgent loathing of every city he drove through." The reviewer in Atlantic's August issue predicted that it was a book "to be read slowly for its savor, and one which, like Thoreau, will be quoted and measured by our own experience."

The Boston Herald enthused that “Travels With Charley” was one of "the best books John Steinbeck has ever written. Perceptive, revealing, and completely delightful." The San Francisco Examiner deemed it "profound, sympathetic, often angry . . . an honest and moving book by one of our great writers." Only Time magazine, whose owner Henry Luce reportedly never forgave Steinbeck for “The Grapes of Wrath's” attacks on capitalism, broke from the slobbering mainstream pack. Time ripped Steinbeck in a two-paragraph review in August 1962:

> TRAVELS WITH CHARLEY, by John Steinbeck (246 pp.; Viking; $4.95). Put a famous author behind the wheel of a three-quarter-ton truck called Rocinante (after Don Quixote's horse), equip him with everything from trenching tools to subzero underwear, send along a pedigreed French poodle named Charley with prostatitis, follow the man and dog on a three-month, 10,000-mile trip through 34 states, and what have you got? One of the dullest travelogues ever to acquire the respectability of a hard cover.
>
> Vagabond Steinbeck's motive for making the long, lonely journey is admirable: ‘To try to rediscover this monster land’ after years of easy living in Manhattan and a country place in Sag Harbor, L.I. He meets some interesting people: migrant Canucks picking potatoes in Maine, an itinerant Shakespearean actor in North Dakota, his own literary ghost back home in California's Monterey Peninsula. But when the trip is done, Steinbeck's attempt at rediscovery reveals nothing more remarkable than a sure gift for the obvious observation.

Tough stuff.

Time’s hatchet job seemed unfair and unnecessarily mean-spirited when I first read it. But given what I’ve learned since, it looks about right. Yet even Time’s hard-hearted reviewer didn’t question the existence of that “interesting” Shakespearean actor from Central Casting.

As "Travels With Charley" rocketed to the top of the nonfiction bestseller list in the fall of 1962, shocking news came from Sweden. Steinbeck, who had been nominated eight times for the Nobel Prize for Literature, had finally won it. The Swedish Academy's choice was influenced in part by "Charley," which the selection committee clearly believed was the true account of Steinbeck's road trip.

Steinbeck's triumph was a surprise that left many literati displeased. A Swedish paper called it one of the Academy's biggest mistakes. The New York Times wondered why the award was given to a has-been whose talent was "limited" and whose best books were "watered down by tenth-rate philosophizing." Fifty years later Steinbeck's award would be further discredited. According to Academy archives opened in 2012 and released in January of 2013, though Steinbeck was as worthy of a Nobel as any American writer who ever wielded a pen, he was a compromise choice. Apparently, the other nominees --

including British writer Robert Graves and Denmark's "Out of Africa" author Karen Blixen -- were considered so weak that Steinbeck took the prize.

Time magazine didn't care what Steinbeck had won. It kicked him and "Charley" around again with a nasty Nov. 2, 1962 article defaming the author and his entire body of work. The magazine sniped that the decision of the Nobel judges "was also reportedly influenced by Steinbeck's latest, bestselling 'Travels with Charley,' which manages to recapture the banality, mawkish sentiment and pseudo philosophy that have marked Steinbeck at his worst."

Academics weren't so rude. But in subsequent years some of their assessments found the book to be too subjective and too personal. Peter Lisca, a godfather of Steinbeck studies, said it represented "all the baggage of the third-rate journalist who sees only the stereotype and the cliché." Lisca apparently never realized, nor suspected, that Steinbeck didn't actually "see" those stereotypes and clichés. He made up most if not all of them. Robert Gottlieb, the book editor and former editor of the New Yorker, saw through the mask when he critiqued "Charley" and Steinbeck's later works of fiction in the New York Review of Books in April of 2008. In "The Rescue of John Steinbeck" Gottlieb wrote that "Steinbeck's heart, as always, is in the right place, but there's something artificial about 'Charley': many of the encounters he reports sound like pure inventions."

To be fair to Steinbeck, he said upfront that his book was never meant to be serious journalism or deep social commentary – and it wasn't. It was nowhere near as deep, wide or historically important as Tocqueville's "Democracy in America." It was not as journalistically meticulous or prolonged or detailed or soul-searching as William Least Heat-Moon's "Blue Highways." In "Travels With Charley" Steinbeck went out of his way, pre-emptively perhaps, to make it clear what his book actually was: the exceedingly subjective account of one man's unique, unrepeatable trip around the USA. It was exactly that. He just didn't bother also to point out that his account was so subjective it was no longer accurate or true.

## 'Charley' Doesn't Go Hollywood

Despite its flaws, "Travels With Charley's" romantic version of searching for America by car has never fallen from the culture's consciousness. Along with Kerouac's "On the Road" – its hipper, edgier, happier and openly fictional older brother – it has become a classic American road book. It gave Charles Kuralt his idea for his popular "On the Road" segments for "The CBS Evening News with Walter Cronkite." But so far, despite a lot of interest, it's never been turned into a dumb sitcom or bad movie.

Not that Hollywood hasn't tried. In 1963 no less than Sam Peckinpah wrote an unintentionally hilarious TV script for Warner Brothers' television division dramatizing "Travels With Charley." Not surprisingly, it included Steinbeck having two knockdown fistfights. Too horrible even for network TV's standards, it was never made.

In the early 1990s, Kevin Costner's production company had an option on "Travels With Charley" with plans to shoot an eight-part miniseries. It died a deserved death. Knowing Hollywood, it wasn't because Costner's project was an incredibly stupid idea. It was probably because they couldn't get Sam Peckinpah to direct. Finally, somewhere in a file cabinet at HBO sits a less-tortured screenplay of "Travels With Charley." Written in the early 2000s by Steinbeck's son Thom, it's not likely to include any fistfights but it apparently was written as if the book was true.

Unfortunately, in 1968, shortly before John Steinbeck died, "Travels With Charley" did travel to TV Land. Producer Lee Mendelson of "Peanuts" fame turned it into an hour-long "documentary" for NBC. Narrated by Steinbeck's buddy Hank Fonda, who played an unseen but amply quoted Steinbeck, it was watched by tens of millions of Americans.

An early example of the "docudrama" genre at its worst, it was presented by Mendelson as the true story of Steinbeck's lonely journey. Skipping the southern leg of Steinbeck's trip, Mendelson sent out a Rocinante-lookalike to retrace the "Charley" route from Sag Harbor to the top of Fremont Peak. The dumbest mistake Mendelson made was hiring 15 actors to look into the camera and pretend to be the characters Steinbeck pretended he had met on his trip. Many of the performances are painful, but arguably the worst fictional character was our friend the mythical itinerant Shakespearean actor of Alice, North Dakota.

To heap hokum on top of hokum, Mendelson threw in a few silly cartoon segments and a hideous Rod McCuen song, "Me & Charley," which was sung over and over by Glen Yarbrough whenever Charley streaked across the grassy fields of America. Mendelson paid $1,000 to rent a stand-in for the dead poodle, who, in a rare and merciful concession to reality, wasn't made to talk. The show's last stop was high atop Fremont Peak, where Fonda delivered Steinbeck's great lines from the book as the camera swept up the spectacular view. The program ended with Fonda standing next to Rocinante, as Charley sat in the cab.

Fonda explains that Steinbeck's trip didn't end on Fremont Peak, but continued on through the South where he saw the agony of school integration in New Orleans and talked with Negroes and whites about the violent changes that were occurring. After Fonda mistakenly says the 11-week trip was "over four months long," he asks what it was that Steinbeck had learned about America. In a tight close-up, the man who played Tom Joad in the movie of "The Grapes of Wrath" reads two spliced-together passages from "Travels With Charley":

"It would be pleasant to be able to say of my travels with Charley, "I went out to find the truth about my country and I found it." And then it would be such a simple matter to set down my findings and lean back comfortably with a fine sense of having discovered truths and taught them to my readers. I wish it were that easy .... What I have set down here is true until someone else passes that way and rearranges the world in his own style."

Fonda then looks into the camera and says, "John Steinbeck saw it one way. Charley saw it another way. And now it's your turn if you so choose to pass that way and rearrange the world as you see it. Goodnight." Millions of viewers had no reason to doubt that they had just watched the true story of Steinbeck's journey, which, if Mendelson and NBC were to be believed, was a lonely "four-month" ride around America with a dog in a truck.

Shortly before Steinbeck's death in late 1968, Mendelson screened his awful rendition of "Travels With Charley" for Steinbeck and Elaine in New York City. "Steinbeck was crying when the lights came on," Mendelson remembered in a 2003 interview. "I didn't know if he was crying because he hated it, but he turned to me and said, 'That's just the way the trip was.'" Poor Steinbeck. He was probably crying from guilt.

# 23 – Debunking ‘Charley’

*Thom and I are convinced that he never talked to any of those people in Travels with Charley. He just sat in his camper and wrote all that shit. He was too shy. He was really frightened of people who saw through him. He couldn't have handled that amount of interaction. So, the book is actually a great novel.*

– John Steinbeck’s late son, John IV, from “The Other Side of Eden: Life With John Steinbeck”

## Steinbeck’s Un-lonely Trip

John Steinbeck hid many large and small creative fictions among the facts of "Travels With Charley." Only his ghost knows where all of them are buried. In 2010, from coast to coast in libraries and on the highway, I discovered a few of his biggest whoppers. It wasn’t because I was some kind of a literary Woodward or Bernstein. Any decent journalist or skeptical scholar could have done what I did. All the important incriminating evidence had been sitting in plain view in the Steinbeck biographies and archives. In the last 35 years any high school kid with a library card could have proved “Travels With Charley” was a literary fraud.

I knew from Steinbeck’s letters or other sources that a few people he met were real. He saw the Cheerleaders in action that morning in New Orleans. He met the young girl who sat on the floor at the Texas cattle ranch cleaning her .22 rifle. He met Eleanor Brace and her cat George on Deer Isle, Maine. But the reality of everyone else – from the submariner on the ferry to Connecticut and the New York cop in Manhattan to the vets in Spokane and Amarillo and the Canucks in Maine – is as suspect as the most implausible character in a lousy TV docudrama.

My rough guess is 90 percent of the humans in “Travels With Charley” were made up in whole or in part. It’s easy to spot some of the fakes – the actor in North Dakota, the quartet of civil rights characters in New Orleans, the father & son at the dumpy motel in Idaho, the mobile-home owners – because he makes up long chunks of dialogue for them. I doubt it, but it’s possible his heroic rescue of his sailboat during Hurricane Donna, his troubles at the U.S.-Canada border and his adventures with the gas-station man in Oregon were real or at least honestly based on fact. Likewise for the little party he threw in his camper for the Canucks. Likewise for the “Lonesome Harry” character at the Ambassador East Hotel and nearly every other major or minor scene he spins.

Until I stumbled onto the truth and spoiled everyone’s fun, the “Travels With Charley” Myth had fooled a lot of smart people. For 50 years it got a pass from scholars. It’s not, but it should be especially embarrassing to the Steinbeck Studies establishment that it never exposed the book for masquerading as nonfiction. On every other page it screams "I'm a work of fiction." I don't pretend to have read every back issue of the Steinbeck Review to see if anyone heard those cries of fiction from "Charley's" pages. But scholars who liked Steinbeck apparently were too busy looking for deeper meaning in the conversations of a French poodle or trying to prove Steinbeck was a great writer or a prescient environmentalist. If they had been more critical, more skeptical, more scholarly, they might have saved me a lot of work.

## A victim of the 'Charley' Myth

One journalist who quickly saw through a large part of the "Travels With Charley" Myth in recent years was the aforementioned Bill Barich, the author of "Long Way Home." In a 2010 interview with the Los Angeles Times, Barich hit the bull's-eye when he said, "I'm fairly certain that he made up most of the book." Reading the book again as an adult, Barich had no trouble recognizing fictional characters when he met a coast-to-coast parade of them. Any veteran reporter/writer like Barich who's worked on the road alone for weeks at a time knows how improbable/unbelievable it was that Steinbeck – a shy man, not an aggressive journalist – could have run into all those perfect people/characters he packed into his book.

But Barich was another unwitting victim of the "Travels With Charley" Myth. He told the L.A. Times he thought the source of Steinbeck's gloominess about America and its future was because he spent too much time sitting alone in his camper with only a dog and a cache of booze. Barich was totally wrong, but he had a good excuse. He was working under the mistaken assumption that the book was an accurate account of Steinbeck's travels. He believed Steinbeck spent most of his time alone, camping out and poking across the hinterland, too shy to interact with his fellow Americans and depressed by thoughts of his looming mortality.

Steinbeck being alone all the time is the most laughable part of the "Charley" Myth. A complete day-by-day accounting of where he was on his entire trip is not possible, but enough is known to discredit the idea. A more honest title for the book would have been "Travels With Elaine." Based on basic TV-detective logic and clues I found in his book, his road letters, Jackson Benson's biography and several newspaper articles, Steinbeck traveled with and slept with his beloved wife on about 43 days of his 75-day trip. They stayed together in hotels, motels, resorts, family homes, Adlai Stevenson's house and a fancy Texas cattle ranch.

The handful of times when Steinbeck did sleep in Rocinante, it was usually near other people. He slept in the camper for two nights on a dairy farm near his son's Massachusetts school and two nights at Eleanor Brace's house on Deer Isle, Maine. He slept in it at two busy truck stops in the Midwest and at trailer courts in New Hampshire, Upstate New York and Montana. That's nine more un-lonely nights, for a total of 52.

In "Charley" or in his road letters, Steinbeck said he stayed by himself at 10 motels. Don't forget, he also had another passenger he forgot to mention in the book. His boyhood pal Toby Street joined him aboard Rocinante for four days from Monterey to Flagstaff, Arizona. That adds up to roughly 66 of 75 nights when Steinbeck was definitely not parked alone in the starry outback, drunk and feeling blue.

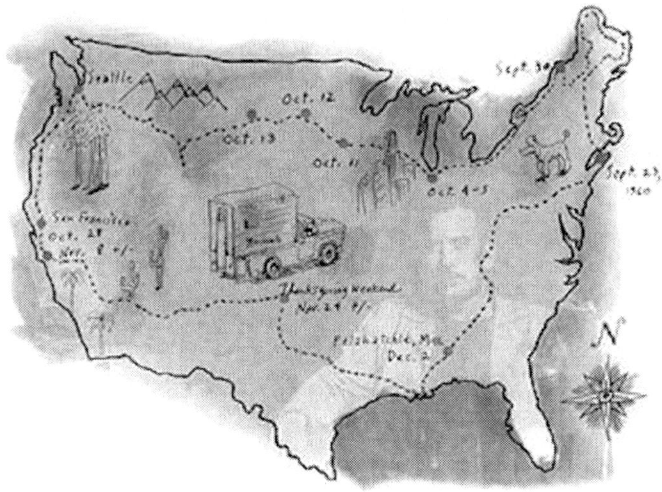


Stacy Innerst

The idea that Steinbeck was depressed during his trip is impossible to prove or disprove. But when he was on the road, he exhibited no signs of being bummed out or sick. His published letters to Elaine are playful and filled with humor, not misery. And based on Jackson Benson's biography and columnist Herb Caen's description of Steinbeck dolled up and hanging out at Enrico's Café, he seemed to have had a pretty good time in San Francisco. Kind of a quiet grump in his natural state, Steinbeck had a suitcase full of legitimate reasons to be glum. His poor health. His troubled kids. The realization that he wasn't getting much material or discovering great truths about the "decaying" country he loved. But no way was he depressed on his trip because he was spending too much time drinking alone. Steinbeck did a lot of drinking in the fall of 1960, but hardly ever by himself.

The real question should be, "Was Steinbeck ever alone?" He spent probably 250 hours by himself in his truck, but it was when he was driving his 10,000 miles of two-lane highway. He traveled solo for a week or more at a stretch when he was slogging through New England to Chicago and then again when he was speed balling from Chicago to Seattle. He was alone, but it wasn't like he was at sea. He was on busy highways and passing in and out of cities and towns. Averaging more than 300 miles a day, he was constantly stopping for gas, stopping to talk to locals in coffee shops and bars, stopping at motels, stopping at post offices, stopping to buy hats and guns, stopping to see the Custer Monument and Yellowstone Park. He may not have met the "great" characters he put in his book, but he bumped into dozens of ordinary Americans every day.

Of his estimated 75 nights away from New York, about nine are unaccounted for. Three or four of them occurred on his final non-stop marathon from New Orleans to New York City. Four other mystery nights were spent in Maine on the coast near Calais, in northern Ohio or Indiana on the way to Chicago, in eastern Washington on the way to Seattle and on Route 66 on the way to Amarillo. It's possible Steinbeck stopped and did a leisurely and lonely campout on one or several of those mystery nights. It's just highly unlikely, or he would have written about it. Plus, since he was usually hurrying to rejoin his wife, he probably either made motel stops or no stops at all. So how often did Steinbeck live up to the "Travels With Charley" Myth and actually sleep in his camper under the stars in the middle of the American nowhere? Not very often – if ever.

He wrote in the book that he did it five times. But the overnight campout on a farm in the mountains of New Hampshire and the two in the wilds of North Dakota were pure inventions. He also wrote that he camped on a farm near a private lake between Toledo and Chicago and in a canyon in New Mexico along Route 66 by the Continental Divide. Maybe he did. But both times he was hustling to meet his wife and all we have is his word for it.

That leaves one desolate, forlorn "camping" scene described in "Charley." It's the one in the deep, motel-less backwoods of Maine's interior, when he parked by the roadside near a concrete bridge with the rain drumming on his metal roof. Unless he lied to his wife, that night really happened. In a letter to Elaine dated Thursday, Sept. 29, 1960, Steinbeck wrote, "night caught us and rain so we are bedded down behind a bridge and it is still raining." Though it was only six days after leaving Sag Harbor, he told her he was "terrible lonesome tonight." If he was drunk, depressed and worrying about his rotting country, he didn't mention it.

## A Distorted 'Vision of America'

The young, the gullible and the romantic read "Travels With Charley" and believe it's true, usually because they're young, gullible and romantic. But it was not true. It was not reality. It was not how a 10,000-mile road trip works in the real world – Steinbeck's world or anyone else's. It was not about real people or real events. It was not nonfiction. Not good journalism, not incisive commentary. Not even a good novel.

The "vision of America" Steinbeck presents in his book is invariably praised by his fans and defenders. But it was not a prescient look at America's future or even a useful snapshot of America in 1960. Steinbeck missed too much of the country, as he realized. He avoided the dirty overcrowded cities. He never mentions the word "suburbs," which were exploding into the countryside from Long Island to Marin County and providing affordable new homes with backyards for millions of young middle-class families. He spent barely 24 hours in the Jim

Crow South. He worried about the disappearance of localism and regional dialects, yet went to only a few of the places they thrived then and now.

Steinbeck was badly out of touch with America and its people and changing culture and it showed. He was a decade late in "discovering" the mobile home culture. He goes on at length about trailer homes, which he called "new things under the sun" but which were already home to about 4 million Americans. He insisted he wasn't against change. Yet he didn't like most of what was still new in 1960 – the interstates, affordable motels, rock n' roll, TV, mass produced products, even cellophane and sanitary wrap.

His political soul mates today venerate him for being ahead-of-the-curve on important issues like the environment, integration and sprawl. Voicing his concerns about pollution and racism are held up by his defenders/protectors in academe as "the greater truths" he told with his fictions. In the upside-down world of higher education, these alleged "greater truths" are supposed to excuse or justify the myriad liberties he took with facts in a professed nonfiction book. But what Steinbeck "discovered" in 1960 about the ills of the country is vastly over-rated. His brief warnings about pollution and sprawl didn't come from any real reporting or thorough observation or study. They weren't groundbreaking or prophetic. They were opinions you'd find in 1960 in the New Yorker magazine.

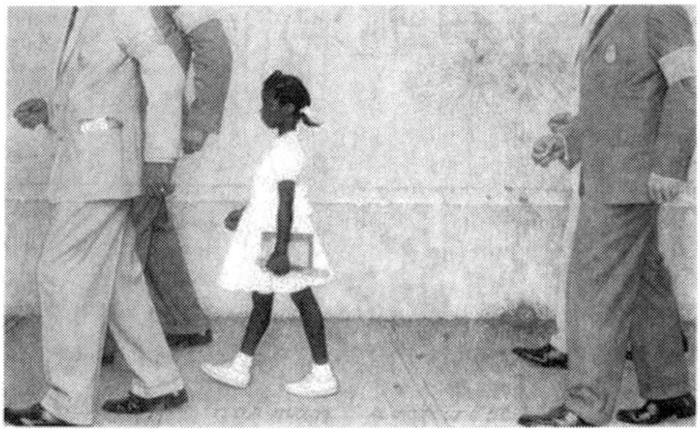

His disgust for segregation and legalized racism was genuine and obviously admirable. But his moral outrage wasn't unique or pioneering or particularly brave, since he lived in Manhattan and on the far end of lily-white Long Island, not in racist hotspots like Jackson or Birmingham. Meanwhile, Steinbeck's fans don't seem to notice how politically incorrect he was in "Travels With Charley" by today's liberal standards. He was a gun nut and a hunting nut who considered coyotes vermin to be exterminated. He smoked and drank to excess. More than a few commentators at Amazon.com and elsewhere have accused Steinbeck of misogyny. With one or two exceptions women are portrayed as miserable, unattractive, fat or stupid. The white mothers in New Orleans were not only shown to be vulgar racists, they were described as "stout" and trashy looking.

Steinbeck also could be two-faced about what he thought of the common folk. In one of his dialogues in the book he describes the residents of a trailer home as "good, thoughtful, intelligent people." But in a letter from the road to

Elaine he said what he really thought. After eating dinner in a mobile home on his way out of New England he derided their disposable plywood and aluminum "homes" and their lifestyle. "These are Martians," he wrote. "I wanted to ask them to take me to their leader. They have no humor, no past, and their future is new models" of trailer homes.

Lastly, Steinbeck's environmental sainthood was not earned. He's been given a posthumous green card for hyperbolizing in "Travels With Charley" that "all" cities were ringed with rubbish and junked cars (then the best source of affordable used car parts). He has also won points for mourning the pollution of the country's air and waterways by the chemical, metal and atomic wastes of industry. But some of the things he wrote would get him in serious trouble with today's religious environmentalists.

For example, when he was rhapsodizing about the redwoods Steinbeck told a story about the time a "newcomer" to Monterey bought a local grove of the trees and cut them down for lumber. He said the man was widely and forever hated for the sacrilege he had committed. But Steinbeck also pointed out that as the property owner, the man had every right to slaughter his trees and turn them into a chain of Curly Redwood Motels if he wanted. Steinbeck's automatic defense of an individual's right to do what he wants with his own property is endearing to strict constitutionalists, but today it would get him kicked out of the Sierra Club. And though few of his fans seem to notice, his concern for what industrial man was doing to the environment apparently didn't affect his own behavior. He thought it was pretty neat that he could use disposable aluminum cookware to fry a fish on his boat, and then, as he said, "throw the pan overboard."

# 24 – The Media & Me

*What can I say about journalism? It has the greatest virtue and the greatest evil. It is the first thing the dictator controls. It is the mother of literature and the perpetrator of crap. In many cases it is the only history we have and yet it is the tool of the worst men. But over a long period of time and because it is the product of so many men, it is perhaps the purest thing we have. Honesty has a way of creeping in even when it was not intended.*

– John Steinbeck, in a letter to John P. McKnight of the U.S. Information Service in Rome, circa 1956

## First, the Washington Post

I thought the hardest part of my long ride with John Steinbeck was over when my wheels stopped turning. All I had to do next, I figured, was write a big piece for the Pittsburgh Post-Gazette summing up all the juicy "Charley" stuff I had learned, plus add my impressions of 11,276 miles of America. Then it wouldn't be long before I'd be written up in the mighty New York Times, get signed by a Madison Avenue literary agent and land a six-figure publishing deal. Michael Keaton would play me in the movie.

But getting the attention of the New York Times book team was not easy. It took five months, a lot of help, some lucky timing and a well-placed friend inside America's Paper of Record. Meanwhile, I hadn't been hiding anything important about "Travels With Charley" except the exact wording of his paragraph of filth. As I traveled, everything I had found out on and off the road was posted for the whole world to enjoy on my Post-Gazette blog "Travels Without Charley." Trouble was, fewer than 3,000 people had been enjoying it. And no one in the national media or the world of Steinbeck studies seemed to notice or care about my discoveries.

One person in the important mainstream media was following my road blog, however. It was Rachel Dry, the cheerful Washington Post staffer who ambushed me in Chicago in the lobby of the Ambassador East Hotel. On Nov. 12, 2010, a week after I got back to Pittsburgh, she whipped up a fine travel feature about how she had fulfilled her dream to retrace part of Steinbeck's "Charley" trip from Vermont to North Dakota. "Following Steinbeck to Fargo" appeared in the Post and was spread around the USA via the paper's wire service. When it appeared in the Bismarck Tribune the inoffensive piece somehow managed to really tick off college professor Clay Jenkinson, a North Dakota cultural commentator and nationally renowned Thomas Jefferson scholar and historical impersonator.

Jenkinson was offended by what he deemed Dry's casual, sacrilegious disregard for what he called the "True Steinbeck Spirit." He wrote a stern column for the Bismarck Tribune on Nov. 21 bearing the headline "Post reporter followed the itinerary but she missed the journey."

Professor Jenkinson, the avowed "road trip purist," summed up the prevailing cultural myths about "Travels With Charley" in a single embarrassing paragraph:

> If you want to invoke the great Steinbeck, several essential criteria must be observed. First, you have to make the whole journey – New York to Maine, Seattle, southern California (sic), Texas, New Orleans, New York. 10,000 miles. You cannot ditch the rental car in Fargo and fly home. Second, you have to sleep and cook in a camper. You get none of the "on the road" effect in hotels. There has to be a droll, slightly vulnerable, "roughing it" feel to the accommodations. Third, you cannot take your mother. I love my mother dearly and have traveled the West extensively with her. She's a great companion. But she's no Charlie (sic). You cannot be Steinbeck unless you are essentially alone with your thoughts and your observations in the heart of America. If Steinbeck had taken another human being, including his wife Elaine, he could not have written an American classic.

Just about everything Jenkinson assumed was true about Steinbeck's trip was false. After Google alerted me to his pompous column, I fired off an email to Bismarck Tribune editor Ken Rogers. I offered to write a freelance column pointing out the professor's errors. I hoped to make $50. That's a pathetic figure, but it's the standard insult paid to freelancers by all but the biggest newspapers. Rogers took the cheap way out. He turned my hasty email to him into a Dec. 4 letter to the editor. It shamed Jenkinson for his delusions and broke the news to the lonely people of central North Dakota that Steinbeck never camped overnight on their soil and that his classic American road book was "somewhere between a fiction and a fraud."

## Dropping the F-word

My first major debunking of "Travels With Charley" in print came just a day later in a full-page article in the Pittsburgh Post-Gazette's Sunday opinion section. When I wrote "Sorry, Charley" for the P-G I hadn't dared to use the loaded word "fraud" to describe the book. But John Allison, the editor who wrote the headlines, neatly summed up my adventures with Steinbeck and deftly dropped the f-word into the subhead. Atop my article Allison wrote: "After crisscrossing America in the tracks of John Steinbeck's 'Travels With Charley,' Bill Steigerwald came to a conclusion: The esteemed work is something of a fraud." I loved the restrained yet unlawful sound of "something of a fraud" and have used it ever since.

Unfortunately, I made a foolish mistake at the end of my Post-Gazette article. Though I had caught Steinbeck red-handed in his fictions & lies, I wussed out and let him off the hook. “So what if he did a lot of fictionalizing?” I asked, unconsciously impersonating an English professor with an advanced degree:

> “Travels With Charley” has always been classified as a work of nonfiction, but no one ever claimed it was a “Frontline” documentary. Does it really matter if Steinbeck made up a lot of stuff he didn't do on his trip or left out a lot of stuff he did do? Should we care that “Charley” could never be certified as “nonfiction” today…?
>
> All nonfiction is part fiction, and vice versa. It's not like Steinbeck wrote a phony Holocaust memoir that sullies the memories and souls of millions of victims.... It doesn't matter if it's not the true or full or honest story of Steinbeck's quixotic road trip. It was never meant to be. It's a metaphor, a work of art, not a AAA travelogue.

At that time I was satisfied merely exposing his trickery and deceit. I had been a literary detective. I didn’t feel qualified to be the prosecutor or the judge. That was a job for people with PhDs in literature. “My work is done,” I wrote. “I'll let the scholars sort out whether Steinbeck's ghost deserves to be hauled on to Oprah's stage to defend himself for his 50-year-old crimes against nonfiction.” Boy, was I naïve. I actually thought Steinbeck scholars would be disappointed to learn that a great American author had been caught in a major lie. They weren’t. I thought they’d care. They didn’t. I thought they’d thank me for my hard work, or maybe give me an honorary degree in something. Hah.

In a few weeks I returned to my senses. I clearly wasn’t thinking straight when I wrote that it didn’t really matter what Steinbeck and Viking Press had done to twist and hide the truth. Of course it mattered. I was a journalist. Finding out the truth about “Travels With Charley” – or anything else – did matter to me. It had been my career to seek truth and report facts. Truth – big or small – should always matter to any honest journalist, no matter what their politics or biases were.

Speaking of which, the only national journalist to show an early interest in my findings was Bob Garfield, the host of NPR’s “On the Media.” Garfield’s show, which I listened to regularly, is devoted to explaining "how the media 'sausage' is made" and criticizing the news media from a liberal point-of-view. Our political biases were more contradictory than congruent. But in the eternal war between fiction and fact in nonfiction, Garfield was my first ally. He has a bias for nonfiction that is true – albeit with a liberal spin.

About a week before Christmas I got a call from “On the Media” producer P.J. Vogt. We talked for an hour, then Garfield called a few days later and interviewed me on tape for almost another hour. On Christmas weekend 200 NPR stations around the USA carried 5 minutes and 27 seconds of my rant about John Steinbeck and his book of fibs. Unlike a certain NPR Saturday morning show starring Scott Simon that shall remain nameless, the “On the Media” gang did a great job all around. I managed to sound credible and almost sane and the links to my web site functioned.

Immediately after my appearance "On the Media" presented an interview with Lawrence Weschler, a professor at New York University. Weschler was billed as a master of "narrative nonfiction," which is a slippery form of writing similar to creative nonfiction that employs fictional techniques to tell true stories. Think composite characters and telescoped time and blurred and stretched facts. Think lots of subjectivity and inventing and shaping and spinning of reality by the writer. Think TV docudrama tricks done in print. Weschler didn't critique me by name for too strenuously or too literally fact-checking Steinbeck's non-nonfiction. But he told Garfield and his radio audience that readers are expected to be "adults." When they read nonfiction they should be able to see when the writer's flights of fiction take off – or land, or circle, or crash.

To Garfield and other old-fashioned journalists who prefer their nonfiction to stick to facts, Weschler proclaimed in mock disbelief, "This was news to you that a novelist was making stuff up in 'Travels With Charley'? Come on! And he wasn't exactly making stuff up. He was telling it in a certain kind of register. It was a different sort of activity than daily journalism and needs to be read that way." Weschler was smart, persuasive, funny. He made good points about the importance of maintaining high standards of fairness, accuracy and "creating something that is true to life." He acknowledged the obvious but seldom uttered dirty truth that Steinbeck knew from experience – all journalism and nonfiction is by its nature unavoidably subjective and selective.

But Weschler put too much trust in writers to always do the right thing. Plus he expected readers to have the sophisticated radar gear they needed to detect "flights of fiction" in nonfiction like the ones Greg Mortenson took his trusting readers on in "Three Cups of Tea." And he had some scary ideas about how much fictionalizing and reality fudging a journalist can do without being arrested for fraud. Speaking of which, Steinbeck proved at an early age that he was too creative to be a totally trustworthy journalist, if there is such a thing.

In 1926, at 24, he worked for the New York American, a Hearst paper. Not surprisingly, he had trouble being an objective observer/reporter. Jay Parini says in his biography that when Steinbeck was sent into the streets of New York to look for stories his reporting style "was much too florid – full of metaphors and images – to satisfy his editors." He was assigned to cover federal court, a beat that could quickly squeeze the life and color and style out of any cub reporter's prose. But apparently Young Steinbeck was unable to adhere to the strict, dry and often arbitrary rules of city-desk journalism. He was ultimately fired from the American – which, if you know anything about the way newspapers can ruin creative writers, was not necessarily a bad sign. He was already better at re-arranging reality than dryly recording it.

It's not that Steinbeck didn't appreciate journalists, but he knew their limitations. He writes in "Travels With Charley" that he "always admired those reporters who can descend on an area, talk to key people, ask key questions, take samplings of opinions, and then set down an orderly report very like a road map. I envy this technique and at the same time do not trust it as a mirror of reality. I feel that there are too many realities. What I set down here is true until someone else passes that way and rearranges the world in his own style."

Steinbeck does a good job of explaining this general theory of subjectivity in "Travels With Charley." He tells a story about the time he was flying out of Prague and met the great journalist Joseph Alsop. They both had been in the city the previous week. But as Steinbeck noted, Alsop had been talking to officials and ambassadors while he had been roving "about with actors, gypsies, vagabonds." On the flight home, Steinbeck writes, Alsop told him about Prague, "and his Prague had no relation to the city I had seen and heard. It just wasn't the same place, and yet each of us was honest, neither one a liar, both pretty good observers by any standard, and we brought home two cities, two truths. For this reason I cannot commend this account as an America that you will find."

In the subjective universe we all live in, facts are often arguable and unknowable. They are distorted and abused and invented all the time. But facts and truth also really do exist and they are worth honestly pursing. Fact and fiction are not interchangeable or equals – and should never be. Readers shouldn't have to guess or deduce whether what a writer of nonfiction writes is really real or fake or somewhere in between. Whether it's Greg Mortenson or John Steinbeck.

# The Road to the New York Times

In mid-January of 2011 I got my big break. It happened in the beautiful heart of California's "Steinbeck Country" when the Monterey County Weekly put a Steinbeck story on its cover that included me in a supporting role as the mini-bad guy. The alternative paper's article, "Travels With Steinbeck," was hooked around the 2008 cross-country trip made by Bill Barich for his Steinbeck-inspired on-the-road book, "Long Way Home." Written by Paul Wilner, the article focused mostly on Barich's opinions about the travels, writings and dispirited psyche of local hero John Steinbeck.

Eventually, Wilner brought me on stage for a stoning by the elusive Professor Susan Shillinglaw. He wrote that my "mini-jihad" had uncovered what I believed "were major falsehoods" in "Travels With Charley." Then he said there were questions from Professor Shillinglaw about the documentation for my "'scoop.'"

> "None of the photos [in his blog] seem to be documented, which is peculiar for someone who prides himself as a stickler for accuracy," says Susan Shillinglaw, scholar in residence at the National Steinbeck Center in Salinas and director of the Center for Steinbeck Studies at San Jose State University.
>
> "He missed the forest for the trees – it's like that 'controversy' over whether George Orwell really shot an elephant. Yes, it's nonfiction, but [Steinbeck] really did take the trip! He doesn't say he spent every night in the trailer.

> "What's more important are how he addresses issues like the race issue," the attempted integration of a New Orleans school which took place despite racist heckling from a group of white mothers who called themselves the Cheerleaders. He spent a lot of time with his publisher about the importance of using the language of the Cheerleaders, not watering it down. "They took out one or two words but for the most part retained it, which was courageous at the time. That's far more important than where he slept," Shillinglaw adds.

When I whined to the Monterey County Weekly's editors, they kindly gave me a chance to response to Shillinglaw and bitch-slap Wilner for being a shoddy journalist.

The paper ran my edited letter on Jan. 27, 2011:

> Travels with Steigerwald
>
> It was an honor to be included in your Steinbeck cover story this week.... I only wish your editors had asked writer Paul Wilner to give me a quick call before he let Steinbeck scholar Susan Shillinglaw discredit me as a journalist....
>
> I also would have asked Wilner to be a teeny bit skeptical about the dismissive reaction of a Steinbeck scholar when she is faced with evidence that much of what Americans have thought about the truth and accuracy of Steinbeck's iconic "nonfiction" book has been a myth bordering on fraud.
>
> Shillinglaw pooh-poohs what I did with my research, which shows in numbing detail that Steinbeck's actual trip is not accurately or honestly represented in "Charley."
>
> She also makes silly/fallacious points to try to make me seem like I cared more about where Steinbeck slept than what he wrote about the issue of racism.
>
> I understand Steinbeck is your local hero. And Shillinglaw, whom I've met and exchanged emails with, is your local Steinbeck expert. But you unfairly let her do a disservice to me and my hard, honest work.
>
> Bill Steigerwald | Pittsburgh

****

For eight months Shillinglaw had been a pain. She couldn't have been less helpful or more evasive. Now she was trying to discredit the messenger, me. She had absolutely no idea what she was talking about when she told the Monterey paper that only one or two words of the Cheerleaders' filthy language was taken out of the first draft. She had never read the first draft. The real total of deleted words was 77.

Shillinglaw was understandably unhappy to learn about the discrepancies between Steinbeck's book and his real trip. It kind of made her and the whole West Coast Steinbeck Studies Industrial Complex look bad when an ex-newspaperman from Pittsburgh proved "Charley" was "something of a fraud" by using information that had been gathering dust in the Steinbeck books and archives for 35 years. Ironically, Shillinglaw's public attack on my credibility was Heaven-sent. It would turn out to be just the element of controversy I'd need to get my Steinbeck findings discussed in the hallowed pages of the New York Times.

## Attack of the Steinbeck Scholars

My national breakthrough began with the magazine Reason. I had done half a dozen articles for the libertarian monthly over the years and knew the editors but never thought to pitch my Steinbeck story to them. The magazine of "Free Markets & Free Minds" focused on politics and economics and modern culture, not exposes about famous dead authors. But one day out of the blue Reason called and said it wanted to reprint my Post-Gazette article and pay me $500. That sounded like a lot of free money to me and in April of 2011 Reason ran "Sorry, Charley: Was John Steinbeck's 'Travels With Charley' a fraud?" A longer version of my Post-Gazette piece, it repeated my charges of literary fraud and dishonesty to a small national audience.

I used the Reason article to try to get Atlantic Monthly, Slate and the New York Times and L.A. Times book sections interested in what I had discovered, but had no luck and no responses from their editors or book bloggers. It seemed nobody left in journalism knew how to return a phone call or reply to an email.

Things were looking bleak when a chance email exchange with some fellow libertarians resulted in a New York Times staffer showing my Reason piece to a Times arts & entertainment editor. In less than a week, out came "A Reality Check for Steinbeck and Charley." Written by Charles McGrath, it "broke" my 50-year-old Steinbeck "scoop" in the Book section of the New York Times on April 3, 2011 – five months after it was in the Pittsburgh Post-Gazette. Interviewing me, author Bill Barich and professors Shillinglaw and Jay Parini, Mr. McGrath played it fair and balanced.

But the clout and credibility of the Times was tilted to my side. My favorite paragraph from McGrath's piece:

> "This is just grunt journalism," Mr. Steigerwald said of his research methods. "Anyone with a library card and a skeptical gene in his body could do what I did." He added that he was a little surprised that his findings hadn't made more of a ripple among Steinbeck scholars: " 'Travels With Charley' for 50 years has been touted, venerated, reviewed, mythologized as a true story, a nonfiction account of John Steinbeck's journey of discovery, driving slowly across America, camping out under

the stars alone. Other than the fact that none of that is true, what can I tell you?" He added, "If scholars aren't concerned about this, what are they scholaring about?"

Professor Shillinglaw pooh-poohed my charges in the Times article, demonstrating she still had no idea how little the book resembled the actual trip or the extent to which it was fictionalized or edited to mislead readers. "Any writer has the right to shape materials, and undoubtedly Steinbeck left things out," she said. "That doesn't make the book a lie."

As for the authenticity of the cast of unbelievable characters in "Travels With Charley," said Shillinglaw, tightening the noose around her neck, "Whether or not Steinbeck met that actor where he says he did, he could have met such a figure at some point in his life. And perhaps he enhanced some of the anecdotes with the waitress. Does it really matter that much?"

What Shillinglaw said about the veracity or believability of "Travels With Charley" echoed what she had said nearly a year earlier in an interview with Duke University radio documentarian John Biewen. Biewen, who had gone to six locations Steinbeck stopped on his journey for his NPR series "Travels with Mike," asked Shillinglaw if she agreed with him that some of the book's characters were, um, a little too good to be true.

Biewen specifically questioned the reality of the actor in Alice, North Dakota, where he had visited and taken suspicious note of the desolation. Shillinglaw agreed with him that the Shakespearean actor "does seem too much of an unusual character," but she suggested it was common to meet unusual people on the road. She described "Travels With Charley" as "an honest book," a model of participatory journalism that reflected Steinbeck's curious, engaged personality. Shillinglaw admitted it was unlikely Steinbeck actually met the full spectrum of civil rights characters he said he did in New Orleans. But she excused these rearrangements of reality as harmless acts of "creative nonfiction," something she said he also did in his World War II journalism.

Professor Parini was just as forgiving and equally uninformed. In 1995, when he wrote an authorized bio of Steinbeck, Parini spent a lot of time with his widow Elaine. He admitted to the Times that he was surprised to learn from my discoveries that Elaine was with her husband for more than half of his trip. Elaine had misled him, Parini said.

Parini wasn't the only one Elaine misinformed about the extent of her presence on her husband's trip. In "Steinbeck: A Life in Letters," a massive collection of 850 letters she and Robert Wallsten edited and published in 1975, she protected the myth that Steinbeck was alone most of the time. After running most of the letters Steinbeck wrote to her as he traveled from Chicago to Montana, this editor's note appears in the book of letters: "Because Elaine Steinbeck joined him for a few days at a time along the way, the letters to her stopped. After coming down the West Coast he crossed the country through Texas and Louisiana and returned to New York."

Let's see: "Elaine Steinbeck joined him for a few days at a time," did she? It was actually 28 straight days, from Seattle to Monterey, and then another 10 or so in Texas. Elaine had to know that the "a few days at a time" line was not true. She also had to know she had been cut out of the first draft of "Travels With Charley." She was covering for her hubby. It might be of interest to scholars to see what she deleted from those road letters before she published them.

Being misled by Elaine and learning what I had proved about Steinbeck's trip didn't change Parini's mind. According to McGrath, when Parini was asked about the book's accuracy he said, "I have always assumed that to some degree it's a work of fiction. Steinbeck was a fiction writer, and here he's shaping events, massaging them. He probably wasn't using a tape recorder. But I still feel there's an authenticity there."

Talking about my discoveries, Parini asked himself: "Does this shake my faith in the book? Quite the opposite. I would say hooray for Steinbeck. If you want to get at the spirit of something, sometimes it's important to use the techniques of a fiction writer. Why has this book stayed in the American imagination, unlike, for example, Michael Harrington's 'The Other America,' which came out at the same time?"

In other words, in the world of Steinbeck scholarship, two of the top people knew all along that "Travels With Charley" was fictionalized but didn't want to spoil anyone's fun by saying it publicly. Or they didn't care how much Steinbeck made up in a nonfiction book because he still captured the authentic spirit of the country – or at least the spirit of the country the professors agreed with. This "So-what?" response to news that Steinbeck had been caught lying didn't go over too well with the truth-tellers at the New York Times editorial page.

On April 9, 2011 the editorial "The Truth About Charley" began with "Bill Steigerwald has made an intriguing, if disheartening, discovery that seems to have eluded admirers and scholars of John Steinbeck for decades. Steinbeck's 'Travels With Charley in Search of America' is shot through with dubious anecdotes and impossible encounters." The Times' editorial ended with a paragraph on the importance of telling the truth in a nonfiction book, a principle people unburdened by Ph. Ds in literature tend to know intuitively:

> It is irritating that some Steinbeck scholars seem not to care. "Does it really matter that much?" one of them asked a Times reporter. Steinbeck insisted his book was reality-based. He aimed to "tell the small diagnostic truths which are the foundations of the larger truth." Books labeled "nonfiction" should not break faith with readers. Not now, and not in 1962, the year "Travels With Charley" came out and Steinbeck won the Nobel Prize for literature.

Professor Shillinglaw sent a letter responding to the Times' editorial. They didn't print it, but she allowed it to be run in the Steinbeck Gazette, a small Internet newsletter for Steinbeck collectors and experts. Here is what she wrote:

> The title of Sunday's editorial, "The Truth about Charley," suggests a certainty that Steinbeck himself lacked. He knew that truth was a slippery notion, that any supposed truth was "warped" by human consciousness. As he noted in Sea of Cortez (1941), "Let us ... not be betrayed by this myth of permanent objective reality. If it exists at all, it is only available in pickled tatters or in distorted flashes."
>
> Neither Sea of Cortez nor Travels With Charley is "true" in the sense that the Times editorial and journalist Bill Steigerwald demand. Journalists and scholars have long recognized the fictive quality of Charley, something that Orville Prescott's 1962 review for the Times makes clear: "Relaxed, informal and chatty, [Steinbeck] indulges in whopping exaggerations, tells tall stories, sketches odd characters he met and tosses off a series of capsule essays on scores of subjects."
>
> Henry David Thoreau, living by Walden Pond, entertained visitors more often than he reports in his account of that year, fails to mention the tasty pies he consumed. Does knowing those "facts" undercut the power of Walden? Does being told that Steinbeck spent nights in "deluxe hotels" or met his wife more often than he admits "break the faith of readers," as the Times editorial asserts? True, Steigerwald's accusations dip into the current debate about the ethical boundaries of creative non-fiction, and that is a critical discussion for any newspaper to consider. The simplistic and reactionary tone of the Times editorial on Steinbeck's "truth" is not, however, the thoughtful response one might expect from this paper.
>
> As he pulled his truck out of Sag Harbor, Steinbeck himself was simply "In Search of America," the subtitle of this

admittedly highly personal, idiosyncratic, funny and playful narrative. His America. Not a "true" account, simply his own.
Susan Shillinglaw

My 93-year-old mother, who dropped out of the University of Pittsburgh in the early 1940s after three years as an English major on a journalism track, had a different reaction to the Times' editorial than Shillinglaw. In an email to me she wrote:

"That's great. The tone of the editorial seems to reflect your attitude and it agrees with your assessment. It really is disillusioning when the contents of the book prove to be so at odds with reality. Especially when the readers of the book have been gullible enough to believe it is truth, not fiction. And it is important enough for the Times to editorialize.

"Good job. Love, Mom."

# The Steinbeckies React

It was a bizarre thrill to find myself praised by the editorial page of a paper I had spent half my career criticizing for its liberal politics and slanted news coverage, but I was grateful. Being covered by the New York Times and then receiving the imprimatur of its editorial page instantly validated my findings as being newsworthy and credible. It also did wonders for my global obscurity. The Times' feature article by Charles McGrath was reprinted, rewritten or used as fodder by columnists in papers from Brisbane to Toledo to Budapest. I was interviewed by CBC Radio's evening program "As It Happens," which was heard across Canada. And my findings were praised, damned and ridiculed throughout the blogosphere for about 15 minutes.

Academic types who believe fact/fiction/truth/myth are impossible to ascertain, or are interchangeable, or don't matter, thought I had wasted my time proving the obvious or the inconsequential. Likewise for folks whose politics were in synch with the "greater truths" Steinbeck allegedly told. Reaction was generally supportive from my fellow journalists. In California, the editor of the Daily Pilot newspaper, John Canalis, wrote how disappointed he was to learn that one of his favorite books was not nonfiction, but fiction, and that one of his favorite authors was, well, somewhere between a serial exaggerator and a liar.

Canalis' column, appearing in a chain of local papers in California, caught the ire of Gail Steinbeck, wife of Steinbeck's son Thom. She lives in Santa Barbara and protects her husband's time like he's a movie star. Before and during my trip I had called and emailed her, hoping to arrange an interview with Thom either in person or over the phone, but she never allowed it to happen.

Gail was cool when I first contacted her before I went on my road trip, but later she warmed up. During my layover in San Francisco she sent me two friendly emails, which she signed off by telling me my perspective and blog articles were "always interesting." Six months later, however, she was obviously sick and tired of my international fame as a professional "Travels With Charley" debunker. Here's her letter in response to John Canalis' column, which appeared in the Daily Pilot and a few other California papers:

> Mailbag:
>
> Steinbeck's daughter-in-law says 'Travels' is true
>
> April 29, 2011
>
> Any educated scholar who has studied that journey knows that Bill Steigerwald simply hasn't enough facts to "debunk" that journey ("Sorry, Charley, Was Steinbeck's 'Travels with Charley' a fraud?" Reason magazine, April 2011).
>
> For some reason the press continues to give this guy way too much ink. As far as I'm concerned, and I know mountains about that journey, the author of that Reason article is just another individual who wants to build a career on rumor and innuendo. Please let his absurd story go away.
>
> If you were at all moved by "Travels With Charley," and have done as much research over the years as I have, and if you really even care, you should speak with Dr. Susan Shillinglaw, scholar in residence at The National Steinbeck Center, to get the true facts of the journey. After all, she has read all of the letters, while Steigerwald claims to have read the rather limited collection of letters at the Mercantile Library.
>
> When we saw this guy's first article, we thought, "Well it's just another one trying to follow the journey and sell a book." That's something we deal with all the time and frankly, there is some wonderful work out there by others inspired by the original journey, e.g.: "Travels with Max," by Gregory Ziegler. But this fellow decided it was his duty as a "journalist" to invalidate the entire work, "Travels With Charley" and John Steinbeck, as an aside. It's one thing to do the proper research and quite another

to simply look for a point of view that will "stir the pot," as it were.

Normally, the Steinbeck family would step back and let the story run its course, but Steigerwald has managed to keep the story running ad nauseam. To tell you the truth, I would never have jumped into the fray, but he is so ill-informed and has managed to reach such a wide audience, that it has become a little creepy. He is misleading the public and the problem is that he is incorrect in the majority of his assumptions.

My husband, Thomas Steinbeck, author of "Down to a Soundless Sea" and "In the Shadow of the Cypress," wrote a screenplay for HBO based upon "Travels with Charley" and the research we did for that project was voluminous. Thom was also a teenager at the time of the journey and he agrees that while his stepmother was on board for short segments of the trip, she would never have agreed to make that sort of a trip in a camper. She was used to a rather different sort of travel and lifestyle.

Basically, the Reason story is bogus. There are some wonderful scholars out there who are more capable of giving you the facts than I am, or certainly more so than he. As I mentioned earlier, Dr. Susan Shillinglaw has read every letter and article ever written on the subject, while Thomas and I have been busy with our own life journey. Sadly, Steigerwald missed the entire purpose of the journey and of course the spirit of a nation to which John Steinbeck was bidding adieu.

I only wrote to you because it made me sad to think that you were being duped.

Gail Steinbeck, Santa Barbara

Editor's note: The author is the daughter-in-law of John Steinbeck. She wrote to Daily Pilot Editor John Canalis in response to his column about the controversy surrounding "Travels with Charley."

It was one of the many great pleasures of my adventures in Steinbeck World to respond to Gail Steinbeck's silly rant, which proved how little she and her husband knew about John Steinbeck's trip. Here is my response, as printed in the Daily Pilot:

## Community commentary: 'Travels Without Charley' takes another turn

May 03, 2011 | By Bill Steigerwald

Gail Steinbeck's Mailbag entry is full of too many mistakes, wild assumptions and misrepresentations about me, my motives and my research/reporting habits to address all of them here.

But before she decided to accuse me of being a lousy journalist and some creepy sort of publicity hound who set out to debunk "Travels with Charley" to make a name for myself, she should have done a little more research. Here's what I wrote in my Reason article:

"My initial motives for digging into Travels With Charley were totally innocent. I simply wanted to go exactly where Steinbeck went in 1960, to see what he saw on the Steinbeck Highway, and then to write a book about the way America has and has not changed in the last 50 years"....

I've consistently said the same thing on my Post-Gazette web site TravelsWithoutCharley2010.com and when I was interviewed by the national news media outfits she thinks I control (NPR, the CBC in Canada, the New York Times): I never set out to debunk Steinbeck, his trip or his book.

The truth is, I started doing research/reporting and merely followed the facts (which have been gathering dust in the Steinbeck archives for 35 years). Any "educated scholar" with a skeptical gene in her body could have found out what I did.

And I don't know where Steinbeck got the idea that all I did was read a few letters at "the Mercantile Library" — whatever that is (there is a library by that name in Cincinnati, but I've never been there). I think she meant the Morgan Library, which is in New York City, and which is where I went last summer to read the original handwritten manuscript of "Charley."

The specifics of my library research are scattered on my web site, but here they are in one place:

In addition to the Morgan, I went to Stanford's Green Library twice, San Jose State's Steinbeck Center twice, the National Steinbeck Center, the Mudd Library at Princeton, the Monterey Public Library, the San Francisco Public Library, the Carnegie Library in Pittsburgh. Plus, I've gotten help from librarians in Austin, Butte, St. Johnsbury, Vt., Amarillo, Seattle and elsewhere.

My several attempts to interview Gail's husband Thom Steinbeck never succeeded. But I've interviewed dozens of people, including Steinbeck biographer Jackson Benson and authors Curt Gentry and Barnaby Conrad, who interviewed or socialized with John and Elaine Steinbeck in San Francisco in 1960 during the "Charley" trip. Also, last fall I retraced most of John Steinbeck's route around America, racking up 11,276 miles in 43 days.

Contrary to what Steinbeck assumes, I've read all the letters John Steinbeck wrote from the road that are in libraries or books. And while Steinbeck scholar Professor Susan Shillinglaw of San Jose State has read them all as well, I believe she has yet to do what I did – trek to Manhattan to compare the original handwritten manuscript of "Charley" with the final version.

If Shillinglaw had done that, she'd have seen a handful of scenes cut from the first draft in which Steinbeck describes leisurely traveling from Seattle down the Pacific Coast with Elaine – in the pickup truck/camper – to downtown San Francisco, where they "camped out" at the St. Francis Hotel for about five days.

Last fall, Gail Steinbeck apparently followed my road trip by reading the daily road blogs I posted to TravelsWithoutCharley2010.com. (She sent me two friendly and complimentary emails and said she found my articles interesting.)

Seven months later she dismisses me as "this guy." And she accuses me — without offering any proof of her own to the contrary — of "misleading the public" and of "being incorrect in the majority" of my "assumptions" about the reality of her father-in-law's iconic road trip; trouble is, they're not assumptions, they are facts.

Readers who want to judge for themselves which of us really knows what we are talking about are invited to read my web site, "Travels Without Charley."

# Paul Theroux Joins the Fun

My book and movie deals were slow in coming. But it was amazing to see how quickly and widely my discovery of Steinbeck's untruthfulness spread and was accepted, at least among journalists. Wikipedia's entry for "Travels With Charley" added my findings about the book's untruthfulness. And when travel writer and novelist Paul Theroux read my charges against Steinbeck in the New York Times he believed them immediately.

Theroux, the patron guru of travel journalism, had suspected that Steinbeck's actual trip and how he described it in "Travels With Charley" were not, shall we say, congruent. He wanted to include what I had learned in "The Tao of Travel: Enlightenments from Lives on the Road," his 2011 collection of insights and observations about travel, travel writers and the lies travel writers tell. But it was already at the printer. In an email to me, Theroux wrote, "I compared his published letters with his travels and saw great discrepancies. These facts have been public for years, but no one cared to mention them. …I didn't see the piece (in the Times) until my book was in the press, and couldn't quote it (though I wanted to). I disagree with his biographer {Parini} and the Steinbeck scholar {Shillinglaw}. He falsified his trip. I am delighted that you went deep into this."

The kind support of Theroux made my summer of 2011. He has almost always traveled light and alone and is not one to excuse the fictions, falsities or "concealments" of nonfiction travel writers, especially famous ones who pretended they traveled solo. Speaking at the Hay Literary Festival in Britain, he used my findings to blast Steinbeck for playing fast and loose with the truth. If they're lying about that, he asked, what else are they fabricating and concealing in their books?

Good point, Paul, old buddy. And then he said to a Brit writer:

"I think a lot of travel writers make it up. Travel books are a lot of fun but are maybe not the complete truth of what happened. I did travel alone, and it is hard to travel alone. When I was alone, I got shot at; people were angry, they threatened me and there was no one there. I didn't have any backup. Certainly the more travel literature I read, the more I realized a lot of it is invented."

## Good Dutchmen

One travel journalist who doesn't make things up is Geert Mak, a celebrated Dutch newspaperman, author and historian. I didn't know Mak existed until late August of 2012 when I received an email from a guy in Holland telling me he had seen my name in Mak's new book about America, which was based on Mak's road trip retracing Steinbeck's "Charley" route.

Mak and his wife left Steinbeck's Sag Harbor house the same morning I did, on Sept. 23, 2010, but since they didn't travel at Steinbeck Speed they quickly fell behind my pace. His handsome, footnoted, nearly 600-page book was primarily devoted to inspecting and critiquing the politics and culture of the United States from a European point of view. That of course means Steinbeck, Bill Barich and the entire staff of New Yorker magazine would agree with most of Mak's opinions, but not me.

Unfortunately, I honestly can't say for certain what Mak said was right or wrong about America because 99.2 percent of "*Reizen zonder John: Op zoek naar Amerika*" was written in Dutch. I do know that throughout "Traveling Without John in Search of America" he sprinkled 10 references to me and my discoveries about the fraudulent nature of "Charley." He even published Steinbeck's paragraph of filth, in raw English. He was the first to put the paragraph in print, but I gave it its world debut on the Reason magazine Web site in July 2012.

The emailer who tipped me off about Mak's book, Kees van de Bovenkamp, kindly offered to translate the paragraphs in which I was mentioned. Mak, who first heard about me, my road blog and my discoveries while in Lancaster, New Hampshire, wrote many nice things about my "tenacious" and "skilled" drive-by journalism. He agreed with my findings and drew conclusions of his own about the impossibility of Steinbeck doing some of the things he said he did in the book.

Mak and I soon were exchanging emails. We found we had some things in common, including, thank God, English. We are both career journalists and virtually the same age. Though Mak is obviously far more successful and better educated than I am, and though our politics are a North Atlantic apart, we are kind of like journalistic brothers separated at birth. We both had the same idea about using Steinbeck's trip as a way to document half a century of change in America. And in 1999, he did something that sounds like something I would have done – if I had his brains and fame.

As a way of telling the tragic history of Europe in the 20th century and trying to discover whether Europe really deserved to be defined as a union, Mak spent the entire year of 1999 driving around the continent. From Paris to Vienna to Chernobyl, he filed a front-page dispatch each day for the Dutch national daily paper, *NRC Handelsblad.* Later Mak turned this newsprint version of a road blog into "In Europe: Travels Through the Twentieth Century." A nicely written history book/ travelogue/memoir, the 900-page epic was a critical and commercial success and was translated into English and a dozen other foreign tongues.

Mak couldn't have been nicer to me. He sent me a copy of "*Reizen zonder John,*" "so you can at least see how your name is printed with honor in this small, windy European country." He was a bigger fan of Steinbeck's work than I was. And he was simpatico with his New Deal politics, which as a Ron Paul libertarian I sure wasn't. But Mak and I were on the same page when it came to the untruthfulness of "Charley."

As he wrote to me, "although we are in politics very different – I am a typical latte-drinking Citroën-driving half-socialist European journalist and historian – I agree totally with your final conclusions: that 'Travels with Charley' is more fiction than nonfiction and that Steinbeck's son, John Steinbeck IV – who was often around when Steinbeck wrote the book – was right when he made the remark that his father 'just sat down in his camper' and made up most of the stories he wrote."

Unless Mak's book is translated into English, I'll never fully know what he thought about the America he saw in 2010. Mak didn't trash America in his book, but he apparently found a lot not to like. Based on a long interview with him I read online (awkwardly translated from Dutch by Google's computers), it was the standard New York/Euro critique: the USA was politically polarized (i.e. too many non liberals), neglecting its public infrastructure, losing its middle class, losing its small towns, too cocky about its greatness and held back by a conservative ideology that considers taxes a form of legal theft. Etc. Etc.

In one of his emails to me Mak said his book was more balanced and his conclusions about America were not as pessimistic as they appeared in the interview. He wrote: "We in Europe have always idealized the American way of life, and that is one of the reasons, I think, that I was sometimes shocked by what I saw on the road." He added that "the USA has still an enormous amount of resources and possibilities; it has a flexible, rather young and hard working population, but somehow the political system is blocked and more and more corrupted, and that worries me."

It's hard to argue with that assessment. But it was clear Mak and I had plenty of room for disagreement. Someday, we've promised each other, we'll meet in Holland over a Heineken and have a friendly debate about the totally different Americas we found along the same stretch of Steinbeck Highway.

# 25 – The Truth Gets Told

*I am, as ever, fascinated by people who write about trips they did not take, or ones who falsify their trips – and Steinbeck's is a lulu.*

– Email from Paul Theroux, author of "The Tao of Travel"

–

## Triumph of the Greater Truth

Despite a lot of media publicity and the support of the New York Times editorial page, my charges that the book was "something of a fraud" had no immediate effect on the Penguin Group, Viking Press' corporate parent since 1975. Penguin didn't challenge my charges. And its marketing people continued to describe its various editions of "Travels With Charley" as though it was a true and honest account.

In October of 2012 the company's web site was still describing "Charley" as "a picaresque tale," with "picaresque" perhaps being a subtle attempt to intimate that it might be a little less than realistic or factual. Penguin called the book a chronicle of his road trip that "is animated by Steinbeck's attention to the specific details of the natural world and his sense of how the lives of people are intimately connected to the rhythms of nature – to weather, geography, the cycle of the seasons. His keen ear for the transactions among people is evident, too, as he records the interests and obsessions that preoccupy the Americans he encounters along the way."

In an email to its publicity department, I asked if the Penguin Group had "an official response to my discovery that 'Charley,' though marketed and reviewed and taught as a nonfiction account of Steinbeck's 1960 trip, is heavily fictionalized?" (I didn't ask how he could have had such a "keen ear" for the preoccupations of Americans when most of the book's Americans were fictions.) The company's spokesperson in New York said it had no comment. Penguin's PR department, which for obvious reasons was not interested in helping me find more smoking guns, also told me that the company did not have Viking Press' old "Travels With Charley" files "on site" and that they were probably with Steinbeck's estate. Perhaps future scholars will want to dig them out and study them for further evidence, but it no longer matters.

On Oct. 2, 2012, Penguin confessed – grudgingly, secretly, and as quietly as possible. The company finally admitted the truth about "Travels With Charley" when it published a $16 Penguin Classics Deluxe Edition to mark the book's 50th birthday and to co-celebrate the 50th anniversary of Steinbeck's Nobel Prize.

The official synopsis on Penguin.com still gave no warning "Charley" was not meant to be a work of nonfiction. But the lengthy introduction of the book, first written in 1997 for a paperback edition by Middlebury College English professor, author and Steinbeck biographer Jay Parini, had been surgically edited in several places to tip off readers that what they were about to read was not to be taken literally. In his original 1997 intro, Parini had pointed out Steinbeck's heavy use of fictional elements, especially dialogue. But otherwise he had treated "Charley" the same way he had done in his 1995 Steinbeck biography – as if it was essentially a true account of the author's trip and an authentic snapshot of 1960 America. Into the introduction to the special 2012 edition, however, Parini – at the behest of Penguin – had inserted a few new sentences and several parenthetical disclaimers:

> Indeed, it would be a mistake to take this travelogue too literally, as Steinbeck was at heart a novelist, and he added countless touches – changing the sequence of events, elaborating on scenes, inventing dialogue – that one associates more with fiction than nonfiction. (A mild controversy erupted, in the spring of 2011, when a former reporter for the Pittsburgh Post-Gazette did some fact-checking and noticed that Steinbeck's itinerary didn't exactly fit that described in the book, and that some of the people he supposedly interviewed, such as an actor at a campsite in North Dakota, never existed.)
>
> It should be kept in mind, when reading this travelogue, that Steinbeck took liberties with the facts, inventing freely when it served his purposes, using everything in the arsenal of the novelist to make this book a readable, vivid narrative. The book remains 'true' in the way all good novels or narratives are true. That is, it provides an aesthetic vision of America at a certain time. The evocation of its people and places stay forever in the mind, and Steinbeck's understanding of his country at this tipping point in its history was nothing short of extraordinary. It reflects his decades of observation and the years spent in honing his craft.

Though Professor Parini was still using academic "logic" to defend Steinbeck's travel fantasy as quote-unquote "true," I was naturally very pleased to see Penguin had decided to tell the truth about "Charley" – after half a century. But I was amazed – and disappointed – that though Parini obviously had relied on my discoveries, he never credited me by name.

"The mild controversy" Parini mentioned was my expose – certified as credible by the New York Times – that "Charley" was a literary fraud. And the controversy erupted not because of "some fact-checking" at the local library but because of some exhaustive journalism. I was also annoyed to see that in the new edition's existing list of further readings Parini had not inserted my Post-Gazette writings or Reason magazine article. He had inserted the article Charles McGrath *wrote about me* and my conclusions for the Times.

What chicken crap. I sent a snippy email of complaint to Parini, sarcastically thanking him for using my hard-won discoveries to cover his rear end while not seeing fit to mention my name. Impugning his scholarship, I said it was especially "laughable" to see McGrath and the New York Times in the list of further readings when it took the Times five months to get around to covering what I had published in the Pittsburgh Post-Gazette. Barely exaggerating, I also told Parini that despite his "vague disclaimers and caveats" he still wildly understated the level of fiction in "Charley." I told him he came nowhere close to addressing the level of fraud and dishonesty that went into the writing, editing and marketing of Steinbeck's multi-flawed "nonfiction" book.

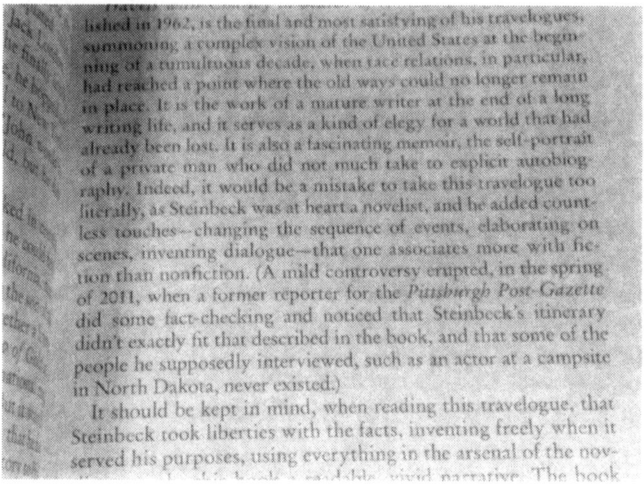
lished in 1962, is the final and most satisfying of his travelogues, summoning a complex vision of the United States at the beginning of a tumultuous decade, when race relations, in particular, had reached a point where the old ways could no longer remain in place. It is the work of a mature writer at the end of a long writing life, and it serves as a kind of elegy for a world that had already been lost. It is also a fascinating memoir, the self-portrait of a private man who did not much take to explicit autobiography. Indeed, it would be a mistake to take this travelogue too literally, as Steinbeck was at heart a novelist, and he added countless touches—changing the sequence of events, elaborating on scenes, inventing dialogue—that one associates more with fiction than nonfiction. (A mild controversy erupted, in the spring of 2011, when a former reporter for the *Pittsburgh Post-Gazette* did some fact-checking and noticed that Steinbeck's itinerary didn't exactly fit that described in the book, and that some of the people he supposedly interviewed, such as an actor at a campsite in North Dakota, never existed.)

It should be kept in mind, when reading this travelogue, that Steinbeck took liberties with the facts, inventing freely when it served his purposes, using everything in the arsenal of the nov-

Ignoring my serial insults, Parini took the classy road. In an email he said he had always seen "Charley" as a work of fiction. It had never worried him that Steinbeck "rearranged some of the events or stayed at a fancy hotel or created dialogue." Then he apologized profusely, graciously, abjectly, acknowledging my hard work and admitting he should have credited me.

Oddly, he wrote, "I am startled in fact that I didn't credit you. Again, apologies." I forgave him, though I really don't know why. Two years of journalism grunt work discovering, digging up, proving and then publicizing a major literary cover-up – and that's all I got from a top Steinbeck scholar? I didn't expect a book deal or a thank-you note from the CEO of Penguin. But no credit? Was it Penguin's editorial sloppiness or spite?

In the long run, it didn't matter. Truth was its own reward, right? At least Wikipedia, the New York Times and my mom will always know who uncovered "Charleygate" and blew the whistle on Steinbeck and his accomplices. And at least the story of my travels with Steinbeck had a happy ending. Truth had triumphed. No one who buys a new copy of "Travels With Charley" will ever be fooled again.

# Trip's End

Trips often take unexpected twists and turns. Steinbeck knew this to be true. As he wrote, every trip is unique and subjective – just like the individuals that take them and write about them. Every journey has its own personality, magic, logic, motives, politics, beginning and end. Steinbeck also famously said in "Travels With Charley" that no matter how well you plan, "You don't take a trip; a trip takes you."

I grew to really hate that quote. But now I know exactly what he meant. I spent almost three years with John Steinbeck's ghost, on the road and off. I'm not complaining. It was a priceless adventure made possible only because I was a journalist. It couldn't have gone better, unless I had met Steinbeck's ghost on Fremont Peak or been abducted by aliens. My solo dash around my homeland was as I expected it to be – easy, safe and fun. It took me to scores of little Americas I'd never have visited otherwise. It introduced me to hundreds of decent people who reaffirmed my faith in the country to survive the never-ending train of abuses the Washington-Wall Street Axis of Evil throws at it.

Journalistically, I struck gold. I had set out with the modest goal of comparing the America I found in 2010 with the America he found in 1960. But I got unbelievably lucky. By the time I was done, I had uncovered the myths and lies of "Travels With Charley," embarrassed the country's top Steinbeck scholars for failing to notice or expose his deceit and earned a pat on the back for truth finding from the New York Times. I didn't learn a blessed thing about myself on my ride with Steinbeck. It was several decades too late for that. But I learned a ton about how a great American writer thought and wrote and lived. I grew to like him in many ways. But I also saw the ethical corners he and his accomplices at Viking were willing to cut to make up a book and pretend it was true.

For half a century "Travels With Charley" was marketed, reviewed and taught as a work of nonfiction. It wasn't. People say "So what? There are no victims." What Steinbeck did obviously was not as serious or calculatedly self-serving as Greg Mortenson, who used "Three Cups of Tea" to raise tens of millions of dollars. But sorry. There were many victims of Steinbeck's deceit. Two and half generations of trusting readers of all ages were duped – including smart people like Susan Shillinglaw, Jay Parini, Ted Conover and Bill Barich. And Viking Press made tens of millions of dollars selling a "true" book by one of the world's best writers under false pretenses. I'd call that consumer fraud. No famous writer could get away with that today. No one would even try.

Early on, it became clear my discoveries were going to disappoint a lot of "Charley" fans. "Leave 'Charley' alone, you old crank," they said in emails or on their blogs. "You're ruining everyone's fun. 'Charley' is a wonderful book about wanderlust and hitting the road to find your country or yourself. So what if it's not the true story of Steinbeck's road trip? It's a metaphor, a work of art, not a Lonely Planet travelogue. Who except for a cynical old newspaper hack like you cares where he slept or if he made up a few characters and stuck them in his little travel book? Who does it hurt? No harm, no fraud."

To tell the truth, I didn't feel their pain. In any case, I had zero interest in apologizing for what I had done. I had never intended to unmask Steinbeck as a serial fabricator or wreck the romance for readers who love "Travels With Charley." I thought and acted like a journalist. I merely followed the facts where they led me – and learned that Steinbeck, his wife, his agent, his editors and his publishing company Viking pulled a fast one on American readers in 1962. It wasn't Steinbeck's fault entirely. In the first draft of the book there's clear evidence he initially was more honest about his real trip. It was the sly editing at Viking that disguised its true nature and created the "Travels With Charley" Myth. Now it's up to scholars to decide whether Steinbeck's trashing of the truth in "Charley" constitutes a serious literary crime that diminishes the credibility of his other nonfiction.

A lot of people still don't want to hear that "Charley" was a literary fraud – and a multi-flawed book. But it is everything the critics and reviewers said in 1962 and more. Timeless in many ways, dated in others, it's entertaining in spots, excruciatingly dopey in others. One friendly responder to my revelations called the book "disheveled," a perfect description. It's suspiciously short, ends with a clunk and leaves gaping geographical and chronological holes in his trip, yet at the same time it's stuffed with blatant filler and things Steinbeck clearly made up.

Despite its literary shortcomings and Steinbeck's lapses in the truth & honesty department, the book flashes with his great prose and wise humor. It's not a confessional, but it exposes some of his personality, which until 1962 he had hidden with his career-long aversion to publicity and interviews. Absent the edits made to its first draft, "Charley" also would have revealed his partisan political opinions and his and his wife's upscale lifestyle.

Thanks to Steinbeck's superb writing skills, Viking's devious editing and marketing, the gullibility of the age and the subsequent lack of scrutiny by scholars, Steinbeck was able to turn a failed journey into an American road classic. "Travels With Charley" remains an iconic travel book. It will be sold and read all over the world for a long time. Everyone interested in its author, literature or America should read it once – but critically, skeptically, with an adult eye. And as John Steinbeck's last major work of fiction.

###

# Bill Steigerwald bio

I was an editor and writer/reporter/columnist for the Los Angeles Times in the 1980s, the Post-Gazette in the 1990s and the Pittsburgh Tribune-Review in the 2000s. My interviews and libertarian op-ed columns were nationally syndicated for about five years at CagleCartoons.com, and I worked briefly for CBS-TV in Hollywood in the late 1970s. My freelance articles, interviews and commentaries have appeared in many of the major newspapers in the USA and in magazines like Reason, Penthouse and Family Circle. I retired from the daily newspaper business in March 2009.

I welcome all praise, criticism, quibbles and corrections at my web site "The Truth About 'Travels With Charley' " (TruthAboutCharley.com).

# Many, many thanks

Thanks to the hundreds of people I met or called or emailed in the last 2.5 years who were so kind to me and helped me write this book. Special thanks to my good friend Bob Hoover for his unflagging encouragement and advice about the slow, frustrating world of books and publishing. Thanks to the editors at the Pittsburgh Post-Gazette and Reason magazine who helped me break the bad news to the literary world about "Charley." Thanks to NPR and especially "On the Media" for discovering me early and to the New York Times for discovering me later but giving me and my journalism eternal credibility. Thanks to my agent Peter Rubie. Thanks to authors Curt Gentry, Paul Theroux, Geert Mak and Nancy Steinbeck – and especially to "The Bookman" Jim Dourgarian and humor columnist/author Tom Purcell – for their help, praise and/or moral support. Thanks to all the people I forgot to thank – like Herb Behrens of the National Steinbeck Center. And may God bless all the wonderful librarians in public and university libraries from New Hampshire to Butte to Stanford.

## Chronology of articles & media coverage

NPR, "Weekend Edition Saturday," Oct. 2, 2010: Scott Simon interviews me in Vermont while I'm making my trip.

Pittsburgh Post-Gazette, Dec. 5, 2010: "Sorry, Charley" Though "Travels With Charley" has been marketed, reviewed and taught as a work of nonfiction for half a century, I charge that it is mostly fiction and a dishonest account of his actual journey.

NPR media watchdog show "On the Media" with Bob Garfield, Dec. 24, 2010: The first national media coverage of my literary "scoop."

Monterey County Weekly, Jan. 20, 2011: In "Travels With Steinbeck" Steinbeck scholar Susan Shillinglaw discredits my journalism and pooh-poohs my findings when interviewed for a feature story on Bill Barich's Steinbeck-inspired 2010 book, "Long Way Home: On the Trail of Steinbeck's America."

Reason magazine, April, 2011: "Sorry, Charley: Was John Steinbeck's 'Travels With Charley' a Fraud?" A longer, stronger indictment of Steinbeck's literary fraud.

New York Times editorial, April 10, 2011: In "The Truth About Charley" the Paper of Record's editorial page credits me with having made an "intriguing" and "disheartening" discovery about the high level of untruth and dishonesty in "Charley" and expresses irritation Steinbeck scholars were so blasé about my findings.

Washington Post, April, 2011: In "Steinbeck's true enough 'Travels With Charley'" Post editorial page staffer Rachel Dry describes her own Steinbeck road trip, her encounter with me in Chicago and why she thinks Steinbeck's fictions and lies don't matter.

Daily Pilot, April 16, 2011: Editor John Canalis explains why he was disappointed by my discoveries about his literary hero's fictions and fibs. Gail Steinbeck, the wife of Steinbeck's son Thom, said Canalis had been duped by me and questioned the depth of my research and my motives in "Steinbeck's daughter-in-law says 'Travels' is true," a letter to the editor that ran April 28, 2011.

Wikipedia: Its "Travels With Charley" entry added information about my questioning of the book's veracity in 2011. (In 2013 it included a portion of the disclaimer Penguin Group had Professor Jay Parini add to the introduction of the 50th anniversary edition of Charley.)

Reason magazine, July 25, 2012: "Whitewashing John Steinbeck: Why partisan politics and virulent racism were cut from the celebrated 'non-fiction' road book Travels With Charley" Steinbeck's "Paragraph of Filth," which was edited out of his first draft in 1961 because it was too vulgar to publish then or now, is seen by the public for the first time.

*Reizen zonder John: Op zoek naar Amerika* ("Traveling Without John: In Search of America"), August, 2012: In his 573-page book famed Dutch journalist and author Geert Mak recounts his 2010 retracing of Steinbeck's "Charley" trip, publicizes my discoveries about Steinbeck's fictions and lies and praises my dogged journalism (in Dutch).

Pittsburgh Post-Gazette, Oct. 14, 2012: "'Travels With Charley': Now officially mostly fiction" My article points out that because of my discoveries Penguin Group had quietly inserted disclaimers into the introduction of their latest edition of "Charley," making it clear the book was so fictionalized it should not be believed as the true story of Steinbeck's trip.

CPSIA information can be obtained at www.ICGtesting.com
Printed in the USA
LVOW10s2133260115

424472LV00005B/407/P

9 781481 078764